AGE DISCRIMINATION IN EMPLOYMENT: CROSS CULTURAL COMPARISON AND MANAGEMENT STRATEGIES

Perspectives of Aging in Afghanistan, Turkey, Jamaica, the United States, and Japan

Bahaudin G. Mujtaba
Frank J. Cavico

BookSurge Publishing – An Amazon.com Company

Bahaudin G. Mujtaba and Frank J. Cavico, 2006. Age Discrimination in Employment.

Produced by:
      Dr. Bahaudin G. Mujtaba & Dr. Frank J. Cavico
      Nova Southeastern University
      H. Wayne Huizenga School of Business and Entrepreneurship
      3301 College Avenue
      Fort Lauderdale FL 33314-7796
      Phone: (954) 262-5000 Or (800) 672-7223 / (800) 338-4723
      Email: mujtaba@nova.edu, bahaudin66@cs.com
      NSU's Website: www.nova.edu

Key Words: Culture, Age, Age Discrimination, Philosophy of Aging, Discrimination, Ethics, Expatriate Training, Afghanistan, Turkey, The United States, Turkey, Japan, Employment Practices, Attracting and Hiring Older Workers, and Workforce Generations.

Cover Design: By Cagri Tanyar, Nova Southeastern University

ISBN: 1-4196-1587-4

BookSurge Publishing
Website: booksurgepublishing.com and www.BookSurge.com
Phone: (866) 308-6235 or: (843) 579-0000

Manufactured in the United States of America

BookSurge Publishing – An Amazon.com Company, USA
www.booksurgepublishing.com
www.BookSurge.com

Dedication

This book is dedicated to those who strive and push for a just society while knowing that perfect justice will not come until the world hereafter!

Preface

Age discrimination has many causes and one of them seems to be cultural conditioning based on stereotyping of older workers. The word stereotype comes from two Greek words: *stereo* meaning "solid," and *typos* meaning "a model." Initially the term was used to refer to metal plates that were used for printing pages of the same writing or diagrams. When applied to people, it symbolizes rigid, repetitive, and formalized behavior. Schneider (2004) states that "Stereotypes have been accused of being bad because they are created or at least supported by cultures that are prejudiced and discriminatory." Of course, the impact is that in adopting and using stereotypes, people can let their cultures do their thinking for them instead of using factual information or evidence to be their guide. Schneider (2004) asks the question of whether stereotypes regarding age and other such characteristics are cultural products. The answer, according to Schneider and many other experts, is yes. Schneider (2004) goes on to say that cultures provide many "accurate generalizations and some really faulty ones as well." Stereotypes become bad, ugly, and ineffective when people use them to discriminate against a person or groups of individuals without considering the current facts or evidence. The word discrimination takes its root from the Latin word *discrimino*, which means "to divide or separate" into a division or category. While discrimination has it positive meanings, in most cases it is used to refer to making judgment about an individual's or people's behaviors solely based on their unique characteristics based on stereotypes or generalizations. Such is the case about age discrimination, which negatively impacts many "older workers" in the twenty first century's work environment.

Through personal observations and conscious thinking about employment practices, one can tell that it is not unusual to quickly find several headlines each week about employment discrimination cases through various genres and media outlets. Jeffrey M. Bernbach (1996), in a book entitled "*Job Discrimination: How to Fight, How to Win,*" states that "Job-related bias, unfortunately, is big news…and big business." Bernbach mentions the case of a secretary, suing a large law firm, who was awarded $7.1 million for sexual harassment; a pilot that blew the whistle on Tail-hook received an undisclosed settlement from the navy and received $6.7 million in a sexual harassment case against a hotel chain; a salesperson who won $8.4 million from his employer for age discrimination; and, a woman that was awarded her job back along with $100,000 because she was fired for being "too fat." Of course, there are many other such cases currently that are keeping lawyers, law firms, and the court system busy as they attempt to bring about fair employment practices.

Gregory (2001) states that "Discrimination against middle-aged and older workers has long been a common practice of American business firms. Nearly all middle-aged and older workers, at some time during their work careers, will suffer the consequences of an age-biased employment-related action." Gregory (2001) continues to state that while the law prohibits age discrimination in the American workplace, workers over the age of 40 are "nevertheless subjected to adverse employment decisions motivated by false, stereotypical notions concerning the physical and mental abilities of older workers." As such, older workers in the American workplace are often encouraged into premature retirements, denied developmental opportunities that can lead to promotions, denied deserved transfers or job promotions, terminated for causes that have little to nothing with their performance, and are excluded from long-term decision-making due to biases and assumptions. Gregory (2001) pointed out that "I can still state, without fear of contradiction, that age discrimination continues to be a common practice in the American business firms." Gregory ends with an optimistic view by stating that "isolated instance of enlightened thinking on the subject of age discrimination might very well be a harbinger of fairer days for older workers in the future. Gregory (2001) concluded by saying that "America will be an even better country once age discrimination in the workplace is eliminated." We also hope that the elimination of age discrimination in the workplace comes faster; and, of course, you (the reader) can be a huge factor in this process by doing your part to become aware of such biases and not letting inaccurate stereotypes and myths about older workers negatively impact your hiring decisions.

Furthermore, managers and leaders should take the time to think about their lives, their attitudes toward others and, most importantly, to determine how they want to live their lives, and how they want to be remembered by their family members, friends, and colleagues. In other words, take the time to determine your life's purpose which is really the secret to the "fountain of youth," and that can be the beginning of your journey to living purposefully. According to Sophia Loren, the actress, "There is a fountain of youth: it is your mind, your talents, the creativity you bring to your life and the lives of the people you love. When you learn to tap this source, you will have truly defeated age."

The purpose of this book, therefore, is to examine the important and challenging subject of age discrimination in employment in a variety of contexts – legal, cultural, ethical, and practical across five different countries: the United States, Jamaica, Turkey, Japan, and Afghanistan. A cross cultural comparison is provided whereby the laws, moral beliefs, social norms, and employment practices of these countries are compared and contrasted. An additional cross cultural comparison regarding age and value difference between Japan and the United States is provided. The objectives of the authors are to determine the laws prohibiting age discrimination in employment, ascertain the moral standards regarding age discrimination, and to discuss current employment practices regarding older workers. An important goal of the authors is to provide appropriate recommendations to employers to help them deal with the challenge of attracting, developing, and retaining older workers in the workforce in a value-maximizing manner for all the organization's stakeholders.

TABLE OF CONTENTS

Acknowledgements

Since there are many individuals that have contributed to this volume, *first,* we would like to especially thank our students and workshop participants, especially the following colleagues, for their formal and informal contributions to the content of this book:

- Adam Kinney, Nova Southeastern University
- Cagri Tanyar, Nova Southeastern University
- Carrol Pickersgill, Nova Southeastern University
- Courtney Smith, Nova Southeastern University
- Cuneyt Oskal, Nova Southeastern University
- Donovan A. McFarlane, City College of Fort Lauderdale
- Edward F. Murphy Jr., Embry Riddle Aeronautical University
- Harriette Carlton, Nova Southeastern University
- John D. Gordon, NASA Ames Research Center
- Mele K. Akuna, University of Phoenix- Hawaii
- Pamela Blount, University of Phoenix-Tampa
- Rose Marie Edwards, University of West Indies
- Stephanie Ferrari, Nova Southeastern University
- Thomas L. Anderson, Napa Flight Training Center
- Trevor Pendleton, Nova Southeastern University
- William Richardson, University of Phoenix-Tampa

In particular, the authors want to note that the technological component of the survey was developed, organized and made ready for global distribution by Cuneyt Oskal and Trevor Pendleton. The authors wish to express their gratitude for this contribution. Special thanks go to Cheryl Clayton, Estuardo Jo, Shruti Salghur, and Sylvia Lanski of Nova Southeastern University for assistance in the preparation of this book. At BookSurge, thanks go to George (Hugh) Henry, Emily Zeleski, the editors, and the visual artists for making this book a reality.

Second, we would like to thank all those "younger" and "older" professionals and family members who have helped us both personally and professionally get to this point.

Third, we thank you for reading this material and we trust you will find this book interesting and beneficial. You can always contact us at work: (954) 262-5000. Thank you!

Bahaudin and Frank

Besides being a culturally conditioned response, age discrimination is learned in the workplace, and is unethical. It can, and should, be unlearned.

CHAPTER 1

CULTURE AND DISCRIMINATION

*R*esearch shows that the number of individuals aged 40 and above in the United States, and certain other developed nations is growing at a much faster rate than the overall population (Schramm, 2005). Schramm states that "This trend has a tremendous impact on the ratio of retirees to workers, which is estimated to reach one retiree per every four workers by 2050." Consequently, the decrease in labor pool in proportion to the number of retirees will have a huge impact on retirement, the experience level of the workforce, training and development strategies, and the recruitment efforts of most large, global organizations. While many countries will soon be dealing with the challenges of an aging workforce, the United States, Japan, and many of the European countries are already dealing with the effects of an aging population. Jennifer Schramm (2005) states that "Eventually, even countries that currently enjoy relatively large populations of young workers are likely to face this trend because even in these countries—usually developing nations—women are having fewer children and life expectancy rates are increasing." Schramm also states that the growing "older worker" population means a "major increase in government spending and budget outlays." As a result of this aging workforce, human resource professionals are strategizing to make sure they have the experienced workers needed to be successful in the competitive global environment of twenty-first century. Some of the actions the human resource professionals are taking in response to the aging workforce, according to Schramm (2005), are:

1. More investments in training and development to boost employee skill levels.
2. Succession planning and development.
3. Training line managers to recognize and respond to generational differences.
4. Brining retirees back into the workforce.
5. Offering customized benefits packages to employees.
6. Conducting studies to determine projected demographic makeup of organization's workforce.
7. Conducting studies to determine projected retirement rates in the organization.
8. Changing employment practices to address the issue of discrimination against individuals with disabilities.
9. Offering employment options designed to attract and retain semi-retired workers.

10. Offering employment options designed to attract and retain Generation X and Y workers.
11. Changing employment practices to address the issue of age discrimination.
12. Changing health and safety policies to reflect the aging of the workforce. And,
13. Using retirees as mentors.

Of course, the actions taken by human resource professionals to retain a competent and experienced workforce might be inclusive of many more strategies that are not listed above. However, the above list does provide a comprehensive category of "best practices" that can assist employers in the retention of an experienced workforce. While the above list mentions generational differences and discrimination based on disability and age, it does not mention cultural differences which are also an important reality of today's workforce.

Cultural differences such as languages spoken, clothing designs and music played are often apparent among people living in different cities, countries or continents. On the other side, certain cultural differences such as beliefs and values are not always apparent at the surface level but they are practiced among different human groups. People's view regarding aging and older workers is one of such cultural differences that lie beneath the surface but experienced in the day-to-day activities. Employers in the United States are dealing with such views regarding age as well as the challenges and opportunities that come with it. As matter of fact, the average age of the American workforce is higher than previous years and the workers now are much more diverse. In the next forty years, the percentage of Caucasian (white non-Hispanic) workers in the United States is expected to see at least a twenty five percent reduction, while the percentage of Asian and Hispanic workers is likely to rise. Due to generational differences, some occupations and industries in the United States are likely to see fewer numbers of experienced and skilled individuals in the labor pool. Due to globalization and limited resources, some organizations have fewer numbers of managers and hierarchal levels in their organizational charts. So, there are many changes that employers have to tackle in the coming decades and they are dealing with a much more diverse workforce. Some of the differences in the workforce stem from cultural backgrounds, while others come from generational upbringing. There are more individuals who retire earlier than previous generations in order to have more time for some of their favorite activities and dreams. The American workforce is now seeing a larger percentage of baby boomers retiring which means that organizations are dealing with a shortage of experienced labor pool. The second decade of this new century and millennium is going to see more American workers (baby boomers) retire as they reach the traditional retirement age of 65 years. As such, employers will have fewer choices of candidates seeking jobs to as they recruit, attract, and hire qualified individuals for various positions. Thus, employers will have to employee various means of competing to acquire a larger percentage of this limited resource, skilled workers; and many of the experienced workers fall in the category of older workers. As such, the recruitment, attraction, development, and retention of older workers become critical for competing in the new economy which promises fast and rapid changes. Employee retention programs for experienced workers will not only work for gaining older workers, but it will also increase the likelihood of getting more applicants from all generations of available labor pool. However, in an effort to attract, hire, and retain older workers many organizations in the United States face the challenge of cultural or generational biases and stereotypes the negatively impact experienced workers. Therefore, it is important to understand culture, cultural views related to age, stereotypes, biases, and the impact of culture on people's behavior in the workplace.

Culture is a way of life; and culture conditions people's behavior toward specific norms, customs, and societal expectations. One function of culture, therefore, is to regularize behavior within the society. As such, by understanding the culture, one can predict the individual's behavior living within that culture toward dilemmas, employment practices, and day-to-day activities. Every individual comes from a society that conditions the person to respond to challenges based on the specific values and morals of his or her upbringing. People of some cultures value experience and age, while at other times and locations people are conditioned in stereotypes and myths. Such stereotypes and conditioning, unfortunately, accompany individuals in the workplace, thus leading to prejudice and discrimination of various forms, including age. It should be noted, however, that while years of conditioning can be a very strong influence on a person's behavior, each person can think for him- or herself, and thus make decisions according to the situational factors surrounding the dilemma. This result is especially true in the workplace, as managers and professionals are expected to treat each other with respect and dignity, as well as according to industry practices. Therefore, it is extremely important for professionals, managers, and leaders to have a clear understanding of culture, discrimination, stereotypes, laws, and industry practices in order to make ethical and moral decisions. With a strong moral foundation, every worker and manager can become a transformational leader by thinking critically and helping others to reflect upon the facts before making important decisions that impact their future and the future of current and prospective employees. Denis Waitley, speaker and author, once said: "Don't dwell on what went wrong. Instead, focus on what to do next. Spend your energies on moving forward toward finding the answer." This book is about reviewing the past, understanding the current policies and circumstances, and moving forward by planning for the future to minimize or eliminate age-related biases in the workplace.

Stereotypes and Age Discrimination

The word stereotype comes from two Greek words: *stereo* meaning "solid," and *typos* meaning "a model." Initially the term was used to refer to metal plates that were used for printing pages of the same writing or diagrams. When applied to people, according to experts, it symbolized rigid, repetitive, and formalized behavior. Schneider (2004) states that, "Stereotypes have been accused of being bad because they are created or at least supported by cultures that are prejudiced and discriminatory. There is something to be said for this argument." Of course, the impact is that in adopting and using stereotypes, people can let their cultures do their thinking for them instead of using factual information or evidence be their guide. Schneider (2004) as the question of whether stereotypes regarding age and other such characteristics are cultural products? The answer, according to

Schneider and many other experts, is yes. Schneider (2004) goes on to say that cultures provide many "accurate generalizations and some really faulty ones as well." Stereotypes become bad, ugly and ineffective when people use them to discriminate against a person or groups of individuals without considering the current facts or evidence. The word discrimination takes it root from the Latin word *discrimino*, which means "to divide or separate" into a division or category. While discrimination has it positive meanings, in most cases it is used to refer to making judgment about and individual's or people's behaviors solely based on their unique characteristics based on stereotypes or generalizations. Such is the case about age discrimination which negatively impacts many "older workers" in the twenty first century's work environment.

Through personal observations and conscious thinking about employment practices, one can tell that it is not unusual to quickly find several headlines each week about employment discrimination cases through various genres and media outlets. Jeffrey M. Bernbach (1996), in this book entitled "*Job Discrimination: How to Fight, How to Win*" stated that "Job-related bias, unfortunately, is big news…and big business." Bernbach mentions that case of a secretary suing a large law firm who was awarded $7.1 million for sexual harassment; a pilot that blew the whistle on Tail-hook received an undisclosed settlement from the navy and received $6.7 million in a sexual harassment case against a hotel chain; a salesperson who won $8.4 million from his employer for age discrimination; a woman that was awarded her job back along with $100,000 because she was fired for being "too fat"; and, of course, there are many other such cases currently that are keeping lawyers, law firms, and the court system busy as they attempt to bring about fair employment practices.

The United States' Supreme Court recently ruled in a 5-3 vote that older workers can win age discrimination claims in court without having to prove intentional discrimination. The court said that employers who adopt policies that disproportionately affect older workers (those over the age of 40) can be sued. Age discrimination laws and issues are targeted toward protecting quadragenarian, someone between 40 and 49 years of age, quinquagenarian, and other older workers. Naturally, these laws impact not just American businesses, but also foreign businesses operating in the United States.

In an age increasingly dominated by the globalization of business, unique opportunities exist for international entrepreneurial endeavors and business expansion by organizations in the United States as well as foreign businesses. As trade and commerce thereby become truly global, businesses outside the United States increasingly will view the United States as a key market, and thus seek access to a very large market composed of "first world" consumers. These foreign firms may already be exporting goods to the United States, and they also may be contemplating setting up direct operations in the United States, such as branch offices, distributorships, joint ventures, as well as using agents. Perhaps a foreign firm also will be contemplating establishing manufacturing and service operations within the United States. However, foreign firms that attempt to enter the U.S. market, particularly by forming small U.S. business enterprises, must be keenly aware of the scope and detail of U.S. law – statutory and regulatory – federal and state – that governs labor and employment relations in the U.S. Many of these foreign firms, especially small and legally unsophisticated ones, may not possess the knowledge of the scope or the specific detail to U.S. government regulation of business law. These foreign firms, moreover, may not possess the resources to secure legal counsel so as to be advised of the U.S. legal requirements; and furthermore, even if educated as to the requirements of U.S. law, these firms may not possess the necessary resources to be or to remain in compliance. Consequently, the willingness of these foreign firms to invest in, and then to remain in, the U.S. may be impeded by U.S. legal requirements as well as the concomitant need to comply with powerful regulatory agencies, such as the Equal Employment Opportunity Commission (EEOC). As one commentator noted, "The United States has a reputation abroad for supercharged mass litigation, while of limited benefit to some consumers in deterring dangerous conduct and compensating for injury, is detrimental to commercial and financial institutions and the development of new technology" (Weinstein, 2002). Moreover, "the threat of prosecution in United States courts for civil rights violations and other torts throughout the world is substantial" (Weinstein, 2002). Consequently, in order to maximize profitability, foreign firms must try to control employment costs in the United States, but in order to do so, the foreign firms surely will confront a wide variety of regulatory law; and compliance with that law will surely increase the costs of doing business in the United States. The U.S. business climate, therefore, may be perceived as too anti-business or non-competitive due to the legal environment; and thus certain foreign investors may conclude that it is not worth the time, effort, and money to embark on U.S. entrepreneurial ventures. At the very least, the foreign investor must be aware of the legal environment, especially the laws pertaining to labor and employment. In addition, the prudent foreign businessperson who seeks to invest in the U.S. and commence a business therein must be aware of U.S. ethical and cultural norms, which may be markedly different from those in the foreign business person's home country.

While the entire range and application of U.S. business regulation law, even "limited" to labor and employment law, is beyond the scope of this book, one important objective of this study is to address one key aspect of U.S. Civil Rights law – age discrimination – from U.S. legal, ethical, and cultural perspectives, as well as from selected international perspectives.

The proliferation of business opportunities overseas also poses serious problems for U.S. business people. When U.S. business managers assume international responsibilities, they frequently will encounter new and difficult legal challenges. The law, of course, plays a central role in planning and conducting business operations and in making business decisions. It is therefore important for the U.S. business manager to understand the legal ramifications of doing business abroad, especially the foreign laws relating to labor and employment issues. The manager of the U.S. multinational firm must be concerned not only with the law of his or her home country, but also the law of host country where it is doing business. Consequently, there is an increased potential for legal risks and legal sanctions for contravening the laws of different national systems, particularly relating to labor and employment activities. A principal employment law discrimination issue for U.S. companies, therefore, is whether any host country laws are applicable to their foreign operations.

To truly complicate matters for the manager of the U.S. multinational firm, there also arises the distinct possibility that the laws of the U.S. will conflict with the laws of the host country. In particular, the extraterritorial effect of U.S. law regulating business emerges as a significant and troublesome legal issue. Extraterritoriality is the exercise of jurisdiction by the United States over activities and practices outside the national borders of the United States. Extraterritoriality in employment refers to the legal effect of U.S. employment laws overseas, particularly the Civil Rights Act. The extraterritorial effect of U.S. discrimination law raises difficult and contentious questions – not only legally but also practically – regarding the appropriate reach of U.S. law, especially in a rapidly changing world, and one increasingly dominated economically, socially, and politically by the United States. Accordingly, in the legal section to this book, not only U.S. age discrimination law, but also the law of selected other countries will be examined. In addition, the law pertaining to the extraterritorial effect of U.S. civil rights law, particularly age discrimination laws, on the U.S. multinational firm operating in the U.S. as well as in foreign countries, will be examined.

The manager of the U.S. multinational firm, moreover, not only must be concerned with the laws regulating his or her business, but also with ethics, and especially with the ethical norms of the U.S. and the host country. The U.S. multinational business manager, therefore, must be sensitive to not only the legal ramifications of business decision-making, but also the moral consequences. One purpose of this study, therefore, is to present traditional ethical schools of moral philosophy in a practical international business context. Accordingly, in the ethical section to this book, two traditional, secular, ethical theories – ethical relativism and Kantian ethics – are examined in depth in the context of age discrimination in employment. Ethical egoism also is examined and then applied to the age discrimination in employment issue in the recommendations section to the book. Ethically, the practice of employment discrimination overseas will be explored first and in depth pursuant to the doctrine of ethical relativism. A determination will be made regarding the moral norms of selected countries concerning age discrimination in employment. Next, as a balance to and "check" against ethical relativism, the ethics of the German philosopher, Immanuel Kant, will be explicated and applied to the topic. The ethical theory of ethical egoism also will be addressed. The ethics discussed herein thus will provide a foundation for the business person to more intelligently and skillfully apply ethical theories and engage in ethical reasoning so as to arrive at moral solutions to problems in the international business arena.

Finally, appropriate practical recommendations regarding employment issues will be offered based on the legal, ethical, and cultural analysis conducted herein. Ethical egoism is underscored as a viable philosophical and practical approach for employers to deal with such complex and difficult international business issues, such as age discrimination in employment.

Appearance Based Discrimination

There are many forms of discrimination, including gender, body size, race, age, appearance, and many other dimensions of diversity. Appearance is a very widespread form of discrimination that impacts people of all backgrounds. Employers and customers in the business world regularly make decisions based on appearance. Yet, there is no law explicitly prohibiting the use of appearance as a consideration for hiring or other employment decisions. Nevertheless, appearance issues increasingly are arising in the context of conventional employment discrimination law cases.

Employers realize that an employee with a professional, clean, and neat appearance may make the difference in making a big sale or securing an important deal. Employers understand that persons who do not look like they can take care of themselves will not elicit confidence that they can take care of a client's or customer's business. Consequently, employers frequently attempt to control appearance in the workplace. For example, employers will institute dress codes, appearance guidelines, and grooming policies in order to ensure a minimum appearance level. Employees often have challenged these policies with many Fortune 100 organizations.

Accordingly, courts in the U.S. have been asked to become considerably more involved in appearance-based questions. Although there is no law that prohibits discrimination based on personal appearance, appearance-based discrimination arises pursuant to several discrimination laws, especially the Civil Rights Act and the Americans with Disabilities Act. The legal theory is for the employee to connect his or her appearance case, based on unprotected physical characteristics, to a protected category, such as age, race, national origin, sex, religion, or disability. Thus, by utilizing an expansive legal approach, the employee attempts to get his or her appearance-based claim to a court and before a judge and jury as a traditional civil rights discrimination case. The results, however, at best, have been mixed for employees.

Dress codes, grooming requirements, or other appearance-based employment policies generally are permitted under discrimination laws so long as they are enforced in a fair and even-handed manner. These policies, in order to be legal, must not have a disparate impact on any particular protected class, either on its face or in its application. Yet, some variations in requirements may be permissible. For example, in one case, a male employee was discharged for wearing an earring to work in violation of the employer's dress code. The federal district court rejected the employee's discrimination claim. The court explained that minor differences in appearance regulations that reflect "customary modes of grooming" do not constitute sex discrimination within the meaning of Title VII of the Civil Rights Act. In the court's view, so long as both men and women were held to similar standards of professionalism, gender-based differences in standards were not discriminatory, presuming they complied with traditional or customary practices. In another case, two men were fired when they wore ponytails after the effective date of a revise grooming policy that required hair to be clean, neatly combed, and arranged in a traditional style, and for men, no longer than mid-collar in the back. The terminated male employees asserted that because their former employer applied its hair length and style rules differently for men and women, they were discriminated against on the basis of their sex. The court, the New Jersey appeals court, relying on federal precedent, determined that hair length policies generally do not constitute sex discrimination under Title VII of the Civil Rights Act. In yet another case, this one by female Department of Corrections officers, who filed a class action in federal court contending that the DOC's dress code policy of requiring men and women officers to wear trousers violated their 1st Amendment rights under the Constitution. In particular, the women claimed that their religious beliefs prohibited them from wearing pants. The court decision, affirmed by the U.S. court of appeals, rejected the women's claims, citing emergency and safety reasons for a rule prohibiting skirts, and also noting that the DOC should be given great latitude in determining the dress code for its correctional employees.

Similarly to the sex discrimination cases, the U.S. courts have held that grooming and dress code policies must also be fair and even-handed in their treatment and enforcement between majority and minority races. In one case, an African-American woman brought a racial discrimination case against her employer because it required her to seek prior approval of hairstyles she planned to wear at work. The policy also required hairstyles to be neat and well-groomed. When she wore a "finger wave" style, the employer revised its policy to prohibit "eye-catching" styles. The federal court allowed the woman's discrimination to proceed, on race discrimination grounds, because of evidence that Caucasian women were not subject to the prior approval or "eye-catching" requirements. In another appearance-race case, an African-American woman wanted to display her heritage through her choice of clothing by wearing African-styled attire and also by wearing her hair in dreadlocks and braids. The woman, however, was terminated; but she was replaced by another African-American woman. The terminated employee contended that because of her choice of clothing and hairstyle, she represented a subset of African-Americans whose claim of race discrimination could not be defeated by the hiring of another minority woman whose appearance was more typical of corporate America. The federal district court, however, refused to find that her claim was actionable, and stated that she had failed to provide sufficient evidence for a court to infer discrimination.

Even when employers do not have an established dress code or grooming policy, employers can still be subject to appearance-based lawsuits. In one case, a female employee wore skirts and blouses that, in the employer's opinion, were too tight, short, shear, and revealing. The employee was repeatedly counseled, especially by the firm's chief financial officer, a male, as to the inappropriateness of her clothing. The employee eventually was fired, and her appearance was a contributing factor in the termination decision. The employee sued for sex discrimination, but the federal appeals court upheld her discharge. The appeals court emphasized that there was no evidence that the chief financial officer had never sexually harassed the employee. Moreover, the court underscored that in addition to the CFO, two female supervisors had informally counseled the employee as to the inappropriateness and unprofessional nature of her attire, thus indicating that she had not been singled out by the CFO. In another case, an employee was fired for failing to cover a racially offensive tattoo on his arm. The employee was a member of the Klu Klux Klan, and the tattoo showed a hooded figure and a burning cross. The employee sued, contending religious discrimination, but lost. The court pointed out that even if the employee could show a sincere religious belief, it nonetheless would be an undue hardship for the employer to have an employee in the workplace with a racially offensive tattoo.

The U.S. cases indicate that the courts are reluctant to accept appearance as a legitimate basis for discrimination claims. However, if an employee can successfully tie appearance to a protected class, such as being an older worker, and there is evidence that the protected class is treated differently from the majority, such claims may be successful. Although employers are prohibited from unevenly enforcing their dress codes or grooming policies, such policies may reflect differences that are considered reflections of customary appearance standards.

Another issue that generates lawsuits in the U.S. is that of an employee's weight. Such cases often are tied to appearance or grooming standards, and thus can be the basis of a sex discrimination case, but weight cases can also be framed as a disability discrimination claim. An important initial point to underscore is that weight is not a protected class under Title VII of the Civil Rights Act, and thus discrimination based on weight alone is not illegal.

To succeed in cases alleging sex discrimination based on weight, there must be evidence that the employer treated men and women differently based on their weight. In one case, a federal district court case, a woman who weighed 270 pounds was repeatedly passed over for an outside sales position. She sued when she learned that a "thin and cute" female with less experience had been promoted to an outside sales position. The basis of her suit was that the employer applied weight standards to women but not to men. The employer admitted that she was denied the promotion because of her weight, but denied any gender discrimination in violation of the Civil Rights Act. The court agreed with the employer, particularly because the employee could not identify one overweight male outside sales person.

In another case, the federal appeals court found United Airlines weight policy to be discriminatory on its face. Although both men and women were subject to weight restrictions, the court found that the airlines was imposing more burdensome weight restrictions on women by requiring female flight attendants to meet maximums for a medium-framed person, while men were allowed to reach maximums for larger-framed persons.

The majority of weight-based discrimination claims in the U.S. arise as ADA claims. Accordingly, the employee must show that he or she has a substantially limiting impairment that limits one or more of major life activities. The EEOC guidelines, however, state that the definition of impairment does not include physical characteristics, including height, weight, and muscle tone, that are in the "normal" range and are not the result of any physiological disorder. Moreover, the EEOC guidelines explicitly provide that obesity, except in rare circumstances, is not considered a disabling impairment. Consequently, unless an employee's weight problem is so serious as to rise to the level of a "morbid" obesity that is caused by a physiological condition, the employee will not be able to use the ADA's protections as the basis of a lawsuit. The ADA, as one court emphasized, was designed to protect people who are truly have a disability, and should not be used as a "catch-all" lawsuit for discrimination based on size, weight, and appearance. Employers, therefore, can make decisions based on an employee's weight; but the employer must be very careful to treat all employees in a fair and even-handed manner; and must ensure that weight, and not race, sex, religion, or disability, is the actual consideration.

Based on the foregoing legal considerations, employers in the U.S. can take precautions to prevent appearance-based lawsuits. If an employer does promulgate appearance and grooming standards as well as a dress code, the employer must make sure that discriminatory standards are not built into the policies. Most importantly, men and women, as well as the young and old, must be treated comparably. The exact requirements may be different, but they must be similar and fair. Any differences in the standards between men and women, as well as the young an old, however, must reflect what is considered customary in society.

The development and implementation of rational, fair, and objective policies and standards, and consistency in the treatment of employees, especially between men and women, are the employer's "best practices" to ensure a successful defense to an appearance-based discrimination lawsuit in the U.S. court.

Culture and Discrimination

Hodgetts and Luthans (2003), in the textbook entitled *International Management: Culture, Strategy, and Behavior* defined international management as "the process of applying management concepts and techniques in a multinational environment" (p. 5). They further said that "culture is acquired knowledge that people use to interpret experience and generate social behavior." Of course, this acquired knowledge forms people's values, creates their attitudes, and influences their behavior in a predictable pattern (Hodgetts & Luthans, 2003, p. 108). Hofstede (1980) defined culture as the collective programming of the mind, through locally held value systems, which distinguishes one group of people from another. Today's managers, with diverse value systems, are global managers as they mostly manage people of diverse beliefs in an international environment. As such, understanding culture plays such a critical role in international management. For an organization to operate in several countries with different cultures, such as Jamaica, Turkey, Afghanistan, and the United States of America, it is important for the management team to understand the culture of these countries in order to efficiently and effectively operate interdependently among them. The norms and practices of one culture may not be the norms and practices of another. This book examines one of the cultural challenges in international management, age discrimination, as well as suggests recommendations to assist managers toward a more efficient and effective operation both in small and multinational corporations. A starting place is to understand cultures as a way of better management practices in the international work environment.

Hall and Hall in 1987 stated that each culture operates according to its own internal dynamic, its own principles, and its own laws, written and unwritten. However, there are some common threads that run through all cultures. *Culture* can be likened to a giant, extraordinary complex, subtle computer. Its programs guide the actions and responses of human beings in every walk of life. This process requires attention to everything people do to survive, advance in the world, and gain satisfaction from life. Furthermore, cultural programs will not work if crucial steps are omitted, which happens when people unconsciously apply their own rules to another system (Hall & Hall, 1987). Culture and cultural conditioning of people can affect technology transfer, managerial attitudes, managerial ideology, and even business-government relations. Furthermore, and perhaps most important, "culture affects how people think and behave" (Hodgetts & Luthans, 2003, p. 109). An example of observing the differences in cultures is when researchers and managers compare the "Priorities of Cultural Values." Time and time again, it has been shown that there are difference in priorities of cultural values between the United States, Japan, and Arab Countries (Elashmawi & Harris, 1996, p. 63). For example while Americans often rank freedom as their first value, Japanese tend to choose belongingness and Arabs choose family security first. Of course, similar differences exist between the culture of Jamaica, Turkey, Afghanistan, and the United States of America which can impact employment practices among them.

From the comparison of cultural values by Elashmawi and Harris (1996), one can observe that freedom and independence are the two main priorities in the American culture; while in Japan it is belonging and group harmony; and in Arab countries it is family security and harmony. In the United States, the Constitution stands for freedom and independence while in Arab countries, it is taught that family is the most important aspect of life. While "Age" or seniority was ranked as forth by the Japanese and Arab respondents, it did not even make the top ten List in the United States. Of course, such values and orientations toward age come from society; and society conditions human behavior which might lead to discriminatory decisions. Another behavior "driver" is the common misconception that older workers are not interested in technology. Becker (2000) stated that "The technological innovations, demographic movements, political events, and economic forces have changed over time and are continuing to change human behavior in the future." As a matter-of-fact, one can say that "In today's increasingly competitive and demanding international free market economy, managers can't succeed solely on their domestic cultural understanding skills alone" (Becker, 2000, p. 1). It is very important for managers to understand the protocols of business operation in each particular culture / country, before making hiring, developing, and promotional decisions.

Harris, Moran, and Moran (2004) provided ten basic categories that are important for understanding culture and these categories can be useful when studying another culture. The ten categories offered Harris, Moran, and Moran include (2004, p. 5):
1. Sense of Self and Space
2. Communication and Language
3. Dress and Appearance
4. Food and Feeding Habits
5. Time and Time Consciousness
6. Relationships
7. Values and Norms
8. Beliefs and Attitudes
9. Mental Process and Learning

10. Work Habits and Practices

While the focus of this book is on "Work Habits and Practices" relating to age discrimination and effectively managing this process, one cannot escape a discussion of the other categories as they impact how people make decisions and why they behave the way they do. As such, it is appropriate to begin with a discussion of culture and what discrimination means to workers of an organization. Culture, as stated before, and in its simplest form, is a way of life. For example, Afghans, and most Muslims, often greet each other by saying "*Assalam-u-alaikum,*" which basically means "peace be upon you." In this respect, Afghan greeting is very similar to other practices or ways of life. For example, in the tribes of northern Natal in South Africa, they greet each other by saying "*Sawa bona,*" which means 'I see you,' and the other person would reply by saying "*Sikhona*" meaning "I am here." The concept is that by acknowledging that you are seeing the person, you bring him or her into existence. In Afghanistan, the proper reply for "*Assalam-u-alaikum,*" would be "*Wa`-alai-kum-Assalam*" which means "and peace be unto you." Afghans use this greeting because Afghanistan is an Islamic country and Islam is about the universal unity of every human being on earth. As such, managers in Afghanistan are not allowed to discriminate based on race, culture, ethnicity, country of origin, or any other societal factors which one cannot change (when it is not a job requirement). In this case, Islam is a way of life as it has imposed a complete ethical code that expects honest, fair, generous, and respectful conduct and behavior from its members in all situations (Mujtaba, 2005). This code also prohibits waste, adultery, gambling, usury, alcoholic beverages, and eating certain meats (such as pork). Each and every Afghan is responsible for his or her actions to a higher power, and culturally are conditioned to behave according to the societal norms. Similarly, Afghans are conditioned to see age and experience according to the local cultural expectations.

While culture can condition individuals both positively and negatively, at times the conditioning can be stereotypical and lead to illegal or unethical discrimination. The word discrimination is synonymous with bias, making a distinction, taste, favoritism, bigotry, inequality, injustice, prejudice, unfairness, and intolerance. While many of these synonyms are negative, it is important to note that not all forms of discrimination are illegal or unethical. In society, a man may choose to discriminate against women who do not have a high school education when he decides to marry a woman; thus he may marry someone who has a college degree, while not even considering those who have not acquired this status. Similarly, a female might choose to marry a male who earns a comfortable salary and one who owns a house; as such, she may not even consider those who are unemployed, employed in low paying jobs, or those who have chosen to spend their money in other means versus owning a house. These forms of discrimination are based on personal values and preferences. However, such personal values and preferences do not always apply in the workplace when one is deciding who to hire, since hiring practices are based on one's ability to perform the job. Professionally, managers and leaders discriminate based on organizational values, educational qualifications related to the job, level of experience, and many others when looking for potential candidates in the workplace. However, these decisions do not always negatively impact others based on their age, gender, or race when practiced as intended by the organizational values and job qualifications. Yet, societal stereotypes and myths do lead some individuals to discriminate against others based on their gender, race, age or other such non-job related variables that are not necessarily indicative of a potential candidate's level of performance. These forms of discrimination are illegal in many nations and, certainly, highly unethical. Another important point is to understand that cultures do not discriminate, but people do in terms of their thoughts, words, actions, and behaviors. While cultures cannot be changed easily, people's thoughts, words, actions, and behaviors can be changed; and this change takes place best when it is intrinsically initiated through knowledge, education, awareness, critical thinking, and self reflection.

Overall, each person is likely to achieve fairness in hiring, development, and promotion of individuals as per his or her own efforts, education, self reflections, behaviors, and ability to effectively work with others. George Adams, philosopher, is reported to have said "There is no such thing as a 'self-made' man. We are made up of thousands of others. Everyone who has ever done a kind deed for us, or spoken one word of encouragement to us, has entered into the make-up of our character and of our thoughts, as well as our success."

Self-reflection about national and international issues is critical for personal growth and development as a global leader. Hopefully, all scholars of management, human resources management and global leadership do this often, and accordingly evaluate their actions and progress on a daily, weekly, monthly, and yearly basis. Of-course, one way to answer the question of why study age discrimination issues or global human resources management is to say that continuously getting more education in today's complex world allows for better leadership and upward mobility which can provide for a greater financial reward in today's changing environment. While these are good goals, often times they are not the primary motivators for making the decision to such challenging endeavors. The opportunity to learn and grow personally tends to be the deciding factor for many individuals who choose to continue learning. As has been said many times, global knowledge can open many avenues and prevent many embarrassments. Phillips (1999-2000) said, "...the opportunity to learn, enhance one's ability as a self-learner and explore the fascinating explosion of information is one that highly qualified students should not miss." Therefore, it is the vast amount of knowledge to be acquired in this world that continues to provide motivation and excitement for many people.

Today's world is an ever-changing place, providing avenues of learning at a pace that most people cannot keep up. These changes can only occur as a result of continued learning. It is the need to question that drives change. It is always easy to do it the way that it has always been done, but if one never looks past the obvious then how do we know what lies beyond. To truly learn, one must open his/her mind and try to put away preconceived notions. People must become and be critical thinkers in order to continuously learn and grow in understanding national and international human resource practices. The goal of a formal education program is to increase one's knowledge and insight. It allows people to increase their understanding of business management by expanding on subjects that were studied during the completion of a previous degree. A formal program allows one to take real life experiences and learn from them. The people participating in a formal program each bring a different background to the group, which allows for new perceptions to be shared and new interactions to occur.   Such a program provides a support group to "bounce" ideas off of each other and gather encouragement from diverse perspectives.

With the current economic conditions, international firms are looking to fill vacant positions with people that have global experience and cultural sensitivity with regard to gender, age, local norms, and other issues related to hiring practices. They are looking for the candidate that has the "edge," the ability to understand and manage the business in a fair manner. Formal and informal education, especially in the area of international business and human resources, provides the framework for these qualities. For those already with a company, senior management often sends the message that a degree is needed to move up the corporate "ladder." While promotion is a good reason to obtain a global awareness, sensitivity and education, the desire to accomplish one's tasks as a manager in a fair, just, ethical, and moral manner must come from a personal place – the inner-self. The opportunity for personal and professional growth should be a secondary accomplishment, not the primary.

Understanding cultural differences is a necessity for the growth and success of doing business with others throughout the world and serving each market in an effective and efficient manner. International expansions have been on the rise in the past few decades; and they present managers with new challenges on how to deal with the differences in culture. One of the benefits that such expansions offer is the access to new markets for economies of scale. With globalization of markets, competition and organizations, individuals increasingly interact, manage, negotiate, and compromise with people from a variety of cultures. Over a quarter of century ago, Hofstede (1980, 2001) identified five dimensions of cultural values: Power Distance (PD), Uncertainty Avoidance (UA), Masculinity / Femininity (Mas), Collectivism/Individuality (COLL), and Long Term-Short term Orientation (LTO) that characterize cultural differences among diverse countries or cultures. According to Hofstede (1993), a country's position, on these five dimensions, allows predictions on the way societies operate, including the management principles that are applied.

Other researchers developed theories to explain the extent to which one culture can affect others as people migrate and interact in the global marketplace (Dastoor, Roofe, & Mujtaba, 2005), including convergence, divergence and crossvergence (CDC). *Convergence* describes the merging of different cultures due to the influence of globalization and other factors that bring them into close contact with one another. *Divergence* is the extent to which distinctiveness is exhibited by a specific culture despite interaction with other cultures. Finally, *crossvergence* is the development of a new culture with its own characteristics that result from cultures interacting with each other over time (Dastoor *et al*, 2005).

Many economies are shaping their management practices to model those of the United States (U.S.) and may, ultimately, transform their national cultures as well. According to some experts and writers, the export of U.S. management theories and practices through universities and management development workshops in other countries assumes that other countries are eager to become Americanized, that is, to converge with the culture of the US. Other researchers, however, think that there is a general lack of success in countries adopting the so-called western management practices to develop their economy (Hofstede, 1993; Dastoor *et al*, 2005).

Many third world countries, including Jamaica, Turkey, and Afghanistan, have adopted Western management practices to achieve economic stability. Many foreign nationals work in the U.S. and many students study there as well. The diversity of the cultures within the U.S. presents opportunities and challenges as foreign students and workers are exposed to the U.S. culture for a prolonged period of time. According to Dastoor, Roofe, and Mujtaba (2005), "when they return to their home country they sometimes discover that they no longer fit into the culture, and many end up returning to the US on a permanent basis."

Immigration has become one avenue for many individuals from some Third World countries, including Jamaica and Afghanistan, as the relative prosperity in the United States and other western countries becomes more attractive. People are drawn by the free way of living and independence of the courts, the social security system, developed schools and education systems, as well as the thriving "gray" market or "shadow" economy (Dougherty, 2004; Dastoor *et al*, 2005). Irrespective of their education, immigrants and undocumented residents find employment in low-paid jobs that are unattractive for the local population. Such jobs might be in agriculture, catering, and housework as well as in the building sector, mostly so-called 3-D jobs, "3-D" referring to the fact that these jobs are often dirty, dangerous, and difficult (Dastoor *et al*, 2005). This situation is, however, better for many of the immigrants than the conditions in the developing countries.

Cultural Differences in Time Orientation

A manager once made a comment that based on his personal experience, older Japanese workers are not as concerned about efficiency and tend to work at a very slow pace. This manager had worked with several Japanese who were considered to be "older workers", meaning they were at least 40 years of age or older. Based on limited observations with a few Japanese managers, he concluded that older Japanese workers are not concerned about efficiency (getting things done fast) and they work at a slow pace, focusing on one task at a time. First of all, while his observations may very well have been true, he didn't realize that one cannot generalize limited observations to a large group of people. Second, this manager did not realize that while the American culture conditions people to focus on *efficiency*, perhaps doing many things at one time and/or doing them fast, other cultures tend to condition people to focus on *effectiveness*, doing the right things right. While many American firms spend very little time in the planning stage of projects, compared to some Japanese firms, American workers tend to end up spending much more time in the rework and fixing of problem process. Perhaps the Japanese culture conditions employees to start with a slow pace at first in order to produce quality products, so there is less rework and fixing of quality-related problems. This might be the result of such conditioning that has made Japanese automotive industry stay focused on producing fuel-economy quality cars that have captured a huge market share in the United States at a cost to its American competitors. General Motor Corporation, an American firm, recently announced that they will be laying off about 25,000 workers between 2005 and 2008, while their Japanese competitors announced that they raise the prices of their cars in the United States to help American firms. Perhaps such examples show that the Japanese, despite their slow pace, are very concerned about efficiency and long-term success.

Managers and professional workers need to understand that each culture has its own pace and paradigm, with regard to how fast or how slow things should get done. While some cultures are urgency-driven, others have a more balanced approach to tasks since they put relationships first. In the context of manufacturing work environment, the balanced approach means spending more time on the planning stage so there is less rework, and spending time to get things done right the first time instead of experimenting until one gets it right. Understanding such differences about cultures and time orientations can help managers avoid stereotyping and lead people according to their local norms and customs. Some of the earliest researchers on culture and time are Hall and Hall. As such, the following paragraphs and concepts regarding time are comprehensively illustrated in the work of Edward T. Hall and Mildred Reed Hall, especially in their 1987 textbook, titled *"Understanding Cultural Differences"* (Hall and Hall, 1987).

Hall and Hall (1987) stated that each culture operates according to its own internal dynamic, its own principles, and its own laws, written and unwritten. Even time and space are unique to each culture. There are, however, some common threads that run through all cultures. *Culture* can be compared to a giant, extraordinary complex, subtle computer. Its programs guide the actions and responses of human beings in every walk of life. This process requires attention to everything people do to survive, advance in the world, and gain satisfaction from life. Furthermore, cultural programs will not work if crucial steps are omitted, which happens when people unconsciously apply their own rules to another system. According to Hall and Hall, *cultural communications* are deeper and more complex than spoken or written messages. Effective cross-cultural communication has more to do with releasing the right responses than with sending the "right" messages. *Context* is the information that surrounds an event; it is directly associated with the meaning of that event. The elements that combine to produce a given meaning—events and context—are in different proportions depending on the culture. A *high context* (HC) communication or message is one in which most of the information is already in the person, while very little is explicit. A *low context* (LC) communication is just the opposite; i.e., the mass of the information is vested in the explicit code. For example, twins who have grown up together can and do communicate more economically (high context format) than two lawyers in a courtroom during a trial (low context format), a mathematician programming a computer, two politicians drafting legislation, two administrators writing a regulation.

Most Japanese, Arabs, and Mediterranean peoples that have extensive information networks among family, friends, colleagues, and clients, and are involved in close personal relationships, tend to be high-context in their interactions. As a result, for most normal transactions in daily life they do not require, nor do they expect, much in-depth, background information (such much information already exists or is common knowledge among them). Hall and Hall state that life on earth evolved in response to the cycles of day and night and the flow of the tides. As humans evolved, a multiplicity of internal biological clocks also developed. These biological clocks now regulate most of the physiological functions of our bodies. Therefore, it is not surprising that human concepts of time grew out of the natural rhythms associated with daily, monthly, and annual cycles. From the beginning humans have been tied to growing seasons and were dependent on the forces and rhythms of nature.

Hall and Hall explain that there are other time systems in the world, but two are most important to international workers and managers. *Monochronic time* means paying attention to and doing only one thing at a time. *Polychronic time* means being involved with many things at once. Like oil and water, the two systems and cultures do not mix. In monochronic cultures, time is experienced and used in a linear way—comparable to a road extending from the past into the future. Monochronic time is perceived as being almost *tangible:* people talk about it as though it were money, as something that can be "spent," "saved," "wasted," and "lost." It is also used as a classification system for ordering life and setting priorities: "I don't have time to see him." Because monochronic time concentrates on one thing at a time, people who are governed by it don't like to be interrupted. Monochronic time seals people off from one another and, as a result, intensify some relationships while shortchanging others. Time becomes a room which some people are allowed to enter, while others are excluded. Monochronic time dominates most business in the United States. Other Western cultures—Switzerland, Germany, and Scandinavia in particular—are dominated by the "iron hand" of monochronic time as well. German and Swiss cultures represent classic examples of monochronic time.

Polychronic time is characterized by the simultaneous occurrence of many things and by a great involvement with people. There is more emphasis on completing human transactions than on holding to schedules. Proper understanding of the difference between the monochronic and polychronic time systems will be helpful in dealing with the time-flexible Mediterranean peoples. In monochronic time cultures, the emphasis is on the compartmentalization of functions and people. In polychromic Mediterranean cultures, business offices often have large reception areas where people can wait. Polychronic people feel that private space disrupts the flow of information by shutting people off from one another. In polychronic systems, appointments mean very little and may be shifted around even at the last minute to accommodate someone more important in an individual's hierarchy of family, friends, or associates.   Some polychronic people (such as Latin Americans and Arabs) give precedence to their large circle of family members over any business obligation. Polychronic people live in a sea of information. It is important to know which segments of the time frame are emphasized. Cultures in countries such as Iran, India, and those of the Far East are past-oriented to the present and short-term future; still others, such as those of Latin American, are both past-and present-oriented. In Germany, where historical background is very important, every talk, book, or articles begins with background information giving an historical perspective. This fact irritates many foreigners who keep wondering, "Why don't they get on with it? After all, I am educated. Don't the Germans know that?" The Japanese and the French also are steeped in history, but because they are high-context cultures, historical facts are alluded to obliquely.

As surely as each culture has its spoken language, each has its own *language of time*; accordingly, to function effectively in France, Germany, and the United States, it is essential to acquaint oneself with the local language of time. When one takes his or her own time system for granted and projects it onto other cultures, one fails to read the hidden messages in the foreign time system and thereby denies oneself vital feedback. For Americans, the use of appointment-schedule time reveals how people feel about each other, how significant their business is, and where they rank in the status system. In France almost everything is polychronic whereas in Germany monochronic promptness is even more important than it is in the United States. Rhythm is an intangible but important aspect of time. Because nature's cycles are rhythmic, it is understandable that rhythm and tempo are distinguishing features of any culture. Rhythm ties the people of a culture together and can also alienate them from members of other cultures. In some cultures, people move very slowly; in others, they move rapidly. When people from two such different cultures meet, they are apt to have difficulty relating because they are not "in sync." This is important because synchrony—the subtle ability to move together—is vital to all collaborative efforts, be they conferring, administering, working together on machines, or buying and selling. People who move at a fast tempo are often perceived as "tail-gating," those who move more slowly; and tailgating doesn't contribute to harmonious interaction—nor does forcing fast-paced people to move too slowly. Americans complain that the Germans take forever to reach decisions.

To conduct business in an orderly manner in other countries, it is essential to know how much or how little lead time is required for each activity; how far ahead to request an appointment or schedule meetings and vacations, and how much time to allow for the preparation of a major report. In both the United States and Germany, schedules are sacred; in France, scheduling frequently cannot be initiated until meetings are held with concerned members of the organization to permit essential discussions. This system works well in France, but there are complications whenever overseas partners or participants are involved since they have often scheduled their own activities up to two years in advance. *Lead time* varies from culture to culture and is itself a communication as well as an element in organization. For instance, in France, if the relationship is important, desks will be cleared when that person arrives, whether there has been any advance notice or not.

Another instance of time as communication is the practice of setting a date to end something. For example, Americans often schedule how long they will stay in a foreign country for a series of meetings, thus creating the psychological pressure of having to arrive at a decision by a certain date. This is a mistake. The Japanese and, to a lesser degree, the French are very aware of the American pressure of being "under the gun" and will use it to their advantage during negotiations. Choosing the correct timing of an important event is crucial. In general in northern European cultures and in the United States, anything that occurs outside of business hours, very early in the morning, or late at night suggests an emergency. In France, there are times when nothing is expected to happen, such as national holidays and during the month of August, when everything shuts down for vacations. Culturally patterned systems are sufficiently complex so that it is wise to seek the advice of local experts. In the U.S., the short business lunch is common, and the business dinner rarer; this is not so in France, where the function of the business lunch and dinner is to create the proper atmosphere and get acquainted. The way in which time is treated by American and German managers signals attitude, evaluation of priorities, mood, and status. Since time is highly valued in both Germany and the United States, the messages of time carry more weight than they do in polychronic countries. Waiting time, for example, carries strong messages which work on that part of the brain that mobilizes the emotions (the limbic systems). In the U.S., only those people with very high status can keep others waiting and get away with it. In monochronic cultures such as those in the U.S. and Germany, keeping others waiting can be a deliberate "putdown" or a signal that the individual is very disorganized and can't keep to a schedule. In polychronic cultures, such as those of France or Hispanic countries, no such message is intended. Clearly, interactions between monochronic and polychronic people can be stressful unless both parties know and can decode the meanings behind each other's language of time. The language of time is much more stable and resistant to change than other cultural systems. Speed of messages, context, space, time, information flow, action chains, and interfacing are all involved in the creation of both national and corporate character. In organizations, everything management does, communicates; when viewed in the cultural context, all acts, all events, all material things have meaning.

The majority of Americans living in the United States are monochronic with regard to their time orientation, especially in business and entrepreneurship endeavors. Accordingly, for many Americans time is scheduled and compartmentalized so that they can concentrate on one thing at a time. Schedules are sacred and time commitments are taken very seriously. There are polychronic Americans, usually from families with origins in Latin American, the Mediterranean countries, or the Middle East. They handle time differently and are neither prompt nor necessarily scrupulous in observing deadlines. In their business and professional lives, however, most Americans adhere to the monochronic norms of Anglo-Saxon culture. American time and consciousness are fixed in the present. Most Americans don't want to wait; they want results now. They move at a rapid pace; everything about their business lives is hurried. Wanting quick answers and quick solutions, they are not used to waiting long periods of time for decisions and become anxious when decisions are not made promptly. This attitude puts them at a disadvantage in dealing with people such as the Germans, the Japanese, and Latin Americans, all of whom, for different reasons, take more time to reach decisions. When Americans talk about the "long term," they usually mean no more than two or three years. Perhaps, this impatience in time orientation is what is causing the growing cases of age discrimination as well. Or, at least, one can conclude that perhaps there is a relationship between a culture's time orientation and how people respond to older workers. Most American businesspeople tend to think in short-term intervals and this also means getting quick results without employees having to ask too many questions. Of course, older workers are experienced; and they tend to ask questions and challenge a manager's decisions.

Global Thinking and Learning

Managers, particularly top leaders and all human resources managers, need to concern themselves with more than just profits or "making the bottom-line numbers" at the end of each week, month, or year. They need to concern themselves with the well-being of their people. Carol Hymowitz, in her Wall Street Journal on March 8 (2005, p. B1) titled *"When Meeting Targets Becomes the Strategy, CEO Is on Wrong Path"* stated that when companies become fixated on hitting quarterly or daily targets, oftentimes they don't produce sustainable profit growth. She quoted organizational psychologist Richard Hagberg who said "It's hard to capture employees' hearts, and best efforts, with numbers alone." In a recent study of 31 corporations, Hagberg's staff found that the highest returns were achieved at companies whose CEOs set challenging financial goals but also articulated a purpose beyond profit making, such as creating a great product, and convinced employees their work mattered. Similarly, Susan Annunzio, CEO of the Hudson Highland Center for High Performance in Chicago, found that the biggest impediment to high performance–defined by her as making money for the company and developing new products, services and markets – is short-term focus. She and her staff in 2003 researched 3,000 managers and knowledge workers at global companies, such as Microsoft, Intel, and J.P. Morgan Chase. About 10% of the respondents said they worked in high-performing groups, and 38% said they worked in "nonperforming groups." Yet almost one-third of the non-performers said their businesses used to be high performing. Annunzio and her staff asked what had happened, and the respondents had said "top management raised our targets, cut our budgets and staff, and we couldn't sustain results."

Global managers need to concern themselves with the "people" side of the business. Global managers need to be concerned with culture shock-both upon arrival and departure, issues to be considered when relocating to another country, family issues, health care issues, education of children and family members, taxes, living quarters, salary, cost of living equity, transportation, local laws, etc. Besides culture, a country's political and economical consideration further complicates the equation for international human resources managers. An example of such complexity in the global management arena is the situation with the culture of Russians. Russia has been and is a market with huge opportunities for businesses, but most of its institutions are still in infant stage, giving rise to economic instability and limited market conditions. Its high unemployment and lower GDP per capita also seem a constraint for a constant consumer purchase power. The Russian culture is evolving, helped by a group of young Russian professionals that are becoming more individualist. For any enterprise endeavor is advisable to have a good national partner, to plan taking into account some of the business infrastructure limitations, and conceive the enterprise with goals beyond only the shareholders as, in many cases, happens in the US. Cross-cultural training is a mandatory activity for all employees involved in international business. For expatriates, it is also critical to train the immediate family members and relatives. Otherwise, failure could come not only from the economic activities, but also from political, marketing, interpersonal, and cultural differences.

With the convergence of a global workplace, there is a need to ensure that people are not discriminated against nationally as well as internationally. So, to ensure continuity throughout the company, everyone should be required to attend sensitivity training. Sensitivity training involves understanding different cultures and how people of different cultures act in various situations.

Diversity in the workplace is becoming more and more common in today's society. Especially in the United States where more and more businesses are becoming global, the diverse workplace is becoming more apparent. Moreover, most firms are becoming a "melting pot" of different cultures and ethnic backgrounds. This global diversity and the increase in import penetration in the United States are forcing more and more companies to create a diverse workplace and to have diversity training to promote a wide range of different cultures, but without the participants being afraid of expressing one's view or losing business unnecessarily. Accordingly, companies will continue to conduct cultural awareness training that will create awareness of the different cultures and the diverse generations of workers, and how appreciating these differences are an asset to the overall success of the company in the long-term. Greater awareness of diversity and cultural differences should provide time for personal reflection on how age is an important dimension of today's diverse workforce, and how aging is a normal part of human growth and development. An Indian writer by the name of J. Krishnamurti said that "In oneself lies the whole world, and if you know how to look and learn, then the door is there and the key is in your hand. Nobody on earth can give you either that key or the door to open, except yourself." Living with honor and integrity often requires learning, patience, and standing for what is right, which are all virtuous endeavors. However, living with honor, by being honest and standing up for what is right, is the only way that one can remain truly happy in the long term and become successful in the business of life. After all, as Khushal Khan Khatak once said "Without honor and glory-What is this life's story," which relates to a leader's character and integrity. Character and integrity mean living what one preaches, and not cheating others or oneself in this life. The poem entitled *"The Man in the Glass,"* written by Dr. Dale Wimbrow, emphasizes that living with integrity requires personal reflection and looking at the mirror every day, while communicating with oneself by asking and honesty answering the questions: Am I doing what is right? Did I do what is right? Am I doing all that I can do for me, my family, my community, and this society?

The Man in the Glass- by Dale Wimbrow

When you get what you want in your struggle for self
      And the world makes you king for a day,
Just go to a mirror and look at yourself
      And see what THAT man has to say.

For it isn't your father or mother or wife
      Whose judgment upon you must pass;
The fellow whose verdict counts most in your life
      Is the one staring back from the glass.

Some people may think you a straight-shootin' chum
      And call you a wonderful guy,
But the man in the glass says you're only a bum
      If you can't look him straight in the eye.

He's the fellow to please, never mind all the rest,
      For he's with you clear up to the end.
And you've passed your most dangerous, difficult test
      If the man in the glass is your friend.

You may fool the whole world down the pathway of life
      And get pats on your back as you pass,
But your final reward will be heartaches and tears
      If you've cheated the man in the glass.

CHAPTER 2

DIVERSITY AND AGING CHALLENGES

*N*aturally and spiritually, all human beings are a child at heart. Some people associate aging with wisdom and spirituality, while others relate aging to deterioration of physical and mental capacities. Of course, there is probably some truth to both views related to aging by some or many individuals. However, it must be noted that a twenty-five-year old person might be much more spiritually mature than a sixty year-old man or woman. Similarly, a sixty year-old man or woman can be physically stronger than many twenty five year olds. So, aging can not be a predictor of each unique individual's level of knowledge, maturity, or capacity to perform at certain standards. Therefore, philosophically, age should not be a factor in employment practices. However, realistically and practically speaking, age has become a major aspect of employment decisions in many modernized and developed countries.

Age discrimination in the American workplace impacts people of all sizes, races, colors, religions, and ethnicities. Such forms of discrimination, which can be highly unethical, are causing many managers anxiety, and are driving many of them to court. One of the greatest fears of company officials and individual managers is the likelihood of either being sued for something they have done intentionally or unintentionally, or for something they should have considered doing but did not. It is no secret that age-related lawsuits are proliferating; and more recently age related claims have been on the rise due to layoffs, which even though may nit target older workers, nonetheless may have an impermissible disparate impact o them. Juries often side with aggrieved employees, even if the evidence is flimsy. Because of these trends, companies and their managers are realizing the need to protect themselves by periodically reviewing workforce diversity and examining for latent signs of discrimination (Administration on Aging, 2001). The focus of such discussions on discrimination based on age is to create awareness and to reduce the negative impact of stereotypes associated regarding "older workers." It is imperative that older workers are kept in the workforce as long as possible, as there will be a shortage of skilled labor as early as 2007 and 2008, if older workers continue to retire early (Harvey & Allard, 2002).

According to Secretary of Labor Elaine L. Chao, "Nowhere is the case stronger for tapping the strengths of older workers than with employers facing the skills gap. Everywhere I go, employers tell me they are having difficulty finding workers with the right skill sets for the jobs they have to offer." Of course, this shortage of experienced labor presents a great opportunity for focusing on the recruitment, development, and retention of older workers at an age where an unprecedented number of Americans are approaching retirement in today's workforce.

Workforce Diversity and Expectations

Today's population is more diverse than ever before and the workforce population has been changing rapidly along with it. Being an effective manager and educator in a diverse environment requires expecting the same standards from all employees regardless of their race, gender, age, language, and general background. Managers should not evaluate workers differently because of their age, gender, nationality, or language, since such differences have a negative consequence as a result of self-fulfilling prophecy.

One of the needed skills for all managers is to acknowledge differences and actively incorporate each worker's experiences into the work environment and decision-making process. Recognizing and understanding these differences are neither easy, nor automatic since they require conscious focus and a good level of comfort on the part of the manager with cultural and generational diversity issues. In order for managers and workers to be successful, they need to become culturally competent. *"Cultural competency"* for all practical purposes refers to the continuous learning process that enables one to function effectively in the context of cultural differences in the workforce.

Culturally competent managers should be aware of and eliminate the presence of a "hostile learning environment" in their organization. A *"hostile learning environment"* can be described as a situation where inappropriate remarks related to age, gender, sexual orientation, etc. consistently take place, and this situation is not corrected by managers and leaders. This is a situation where insensitive and inappropriate remarks should be addressed publicly by the managers so everyone in the department understands the ground rules and the fact that inappropriate/insensitive comments are not appreciated nor tolerated. Today, we have a very diverse workforce population in terms of their background, abilities, age, language, body size, geographic location, culture, desires, learning styles, cultural conditioning, etc. Diversity describes the many unique characteristics and qualities that make a person (or student in this case) similar to or different from others. Some of these characteristics might be apparent such as skin color, hair color, body size, and general appearance. Yet other characteristics such as age, ethnicity, disability, religion, financial status, values, cultural background and many others may not be apparent based on first impressions. It is imperative that one does not judge workers based on assumptions, and accordingly must treat everyone fairly and equitably.

Diversity also encompasses the multitude of experiences, aptitudes and attitudes available in today's workforce. Diversity initiatives encourage leaders and managers to empower their associates as well as to tap into their wealth of differences in order to achieve synergistic results. In return, these associates will be ready to satisfy, excite, and delight their diverse customers and achieve organizational effectiveness by delivering superior customer value as a result of diversity initiatives modeled by the leaders. Robert Reich,

Secretary of Labor during Clinton's Administration, said, "No longer are Americans rising and falling together as if in one large national boat. We are, increasingly, in different smaller boats." So, our classroom associates, customers, organizations, and societies will become progressively more diverse and managers need to tolerate differences, respect them, understand their nature, and educate all workers about them so they can successfully work with their diverse colleagues and customers. Eventually, this may lead to each worker's personal and professional success; and they can be as successful as they so desire to be. What is success and who defines it? According to Sophocles, "success is dependent on effort" and not necessarily physical characteristics or limitations. According to Brian Tracy, Author and Speaker, "One of the most important rules for success is this: Every great success is the result of hundreds and thousands of small efforts and accomplishments that no one ever sees or appreciates." At his primary school, Malcolm X (African American leader) was told by one of his (white) teachers that he should not dream of becoming a lawyer since he could not be very successful in that job and should pursue something that requires the use of his hands. Unfortunately, due to strong biases and stereotypes, such incompetency may still exist in the society and managers need to do everything possible to ensure it does not happen in work environments. Ralph Waldo Emerson said, "What is success? To laugh often and much; to win the respect of intelligent people and the affection of children; to earn the appreciation of honest critics and endure the betrayal of false friends; to appreciate beauty; to find the best in others; to leave the world a bit better, whether by a healthy child, a garden patch, or a redeemed social condition; to know even one life has breathed easier because you have lived." Simply put, success can be "practicing what you preach," progressively realizing predetermined goals/ideals, and doing one's best to make worthwhile contributions to society.

Research has shown that homogeneous teams are neither as creative nor as productive as heterogeneous teams when dealing with or solving complex problems. Diverse teams can achieve synergistic results if they appreciate, understand and value their differences effectively. *Synergy* is where the whole is greater than the sum of its parts. Ultimately, synergy is the performance gains that result when individuals, teams and departments coordinate their actions toward the same goals. Synergistic teams, colleagues, peers and departments tend to function more cooperatively and productively than if they were operating in isolation. Synergy happens when two or more individuals working together produce more than their combined efforts individually. For example, a team of four workers should produce a final project (product) that is much better than the combined results of each of their work that is produced individually. Diversity awareness can help teams function harmoniously in the context of cultural differences, and also produces synergistic results. On the other hand, lack of diversity awareness and lack of respect for diversity can lead to negative synergy. Negative synergy is when two or more people working together produce less than what they could produce individually. According Stephen R. Covey, author of *"The Seven Habits of Highly Effective People,"* negative synergy takes place when people do not respect and appreciate each other's differences.

Stereotyping, prejudice, or biases about aging and other diversity characteristics impact the society in many ways. One way is that human beings, as individuals, may not treat some people very well because of societal conditioning and autobiographical perceptions. Many people experience unpleasant and unjust incidents daily solely due to some readily apparent physical characteristics. These incidents are referred to as daily indignities. Educators must make sure that such unpleasant and unjust incidents do not exist in their classrooms or work environments.

Understanding diversity and effectively managing it is imperative in today's rapidly changing global environment of our work force. It has been said that about two thirds of the world's immigration is coming into the United States of America, which also brings much global competition for the skills of associates. Immigration trends have greatly shifted during the past one hundred years. In the early 1900's, the majority of immigrants were from Europe; today, the majority of immigrants come from Central and Latin America, Asia, Africa, and the Middle East. Today, approximately one out of three American workers are African-American, Hispanic, or Asian; 6 out of 7 working age women are at work, and 1 out of 10 workers has some form of legally recognized disability. There are over 50 different forms of legally recognized disabilities and many of them are not apparent to the naked eye. English is expected to be a second language for the majority of Californians as well as those living in Miami, Florida.

In the mid 1980's, the Department of Labor commissioned the Hudson Institute to conduct a study on the demographic, sociological, economic, and political trends in America from post-World War II to the year 2000. The results, published in 1987 in a document titled "Work Force 2000: Work and Workers for the 21st Century," indicated the following trends:

- The pool of younger workers is decreasing and the average age of workers is rising.
- More women are visible on the job and overall minorities comprise 1/3 of new workers. More immigrants are in the workforce and this trend is likely to continue.
- Service and information jobs are increasing and higher skill levels are required to compete effectively in today's global world of business.

As one can see, the challenge for businesses will be immense. Educational institutions, governments, corporations, managers, and communities are now recognizing the necessity of valuing diversity to remain competitive in today's complex global world of business. Since the current workforce is indeed demographically diverse, leadership and management techniques of inclusion are imperative. Creating an inclusive environment (and eliminating the exclusive world of bias and stereotypes) is necessary for an effective work environment. Managers must create an inclusive work environment for people of all ages and differences.

Keep Them Talking and Laughing

Workers, as they get older, tend to have better interpersonal and reflective skills. This is why older workers and senior citizens tend to be better speakers, better listeners, and better overall communicators. As a matter of fact, many older individuals enjoy talking with and listening to others. For example, NPR's Susan Stamberg did an interview with a former interpreter to see why she is at the center of so many conversations. According to Susan Stamberg (2005), Miss Lilly is a senior citizen who thinks seniors have much to offer the world based on their years of experience, interpersonal relationships skills, and very effective listening abilities. As such, Miss Lilly's goal is to get strangers to talk with one another whenever she can. If there is to be designated smoking areas throughout airports and other public areas, then why not have designated "talking areas" where people can just talk with each other? Miss Lilly has the advantage of speaking at least four languages based on the needs of others as she speaks English, German, Dutch, and her native Hungarian. She can also converse in Spanish.

Miss Lilly is in France which is said to be a nation of talkers. According to Stamberg (2005), in Paris intense one-on-one conversations take place everywhere, all the time. To a foreign ear it sounds like pigeons cooing. In the Luxembourg Gardens, the most beautiful park in Paris, a small white-haired woman sits in the sun inviting conversation. She holds a sign in her lap that reads "Hello! Let's talk." Miss Lilly wants people to talk to each other. She suggests that people avoid conversations related to religion and politics since these two subjects are the cause of much war, animosity, and hatred in the society. Perhaps, she is saying that senior citizens and older workers tend to be great listeners and, overall, good communicators. As such, it is best that they use such capabilities and speak with others who need to just talk. Of course, corporate managers can create an infrastructure for their older workers to have time for idle conversations which can serve as networking opportunities and better interpersonal relationships among all workers. Certain, there are productivity benefits to the organization when workers speak openly and have strong bonds with each other. As a matter-of-fact, many "older individuals" now continue to work for its fun, write interesting books, get involved in their favorite hobbies, and stand up for good causes in the society way after their retirement age.

At the ripe age of 88 years, Phyllis Diller recently published a memoir and appeared in the film *The Aristocrats*. According to Simon (2005), a new documentary focuses on her last stand-up act. Even at this age, retirement hasn't dulled Diller's sharp wit as she continues to make people laugh and enjoy life's wonderful insights. According to Phyllis Diller and many other comedians, you know you are old when:

1. You bend down to tie your shoe laces and you wonder "what else can I do while I am down here."
2. Your walker has its own airbag.
3. They discontinue your blood type.
4. Someone compliments you on your shoes and you are barefoot.
5. Your favorite drink is prune juice.

Cultural Challenges Associated with Aging

Cultural and generational differences convey themselves in various forms. For example, in the Afghan culture people respect and cherish age and older individuals. Accordingly, older worker and older members of the community often serve as coaches, mentors, and advisors in settling disputes and guiding major decisions. Many Afghans tend to view the progression of life as a continuum of beginning, growth, and ending with the latter part being the most valuable due to the impact of accumulated experience. Perhaps, this mentality comes from the spiritual lessons of continuous development each day as many Afghans believe that "if today one is not better than yesterday then a whole day has been wasted." The accumulated lessons of many days and years can not be gained through quick or unrealistic expectations. As such, age has its value and there is no effective substitute for life's learning experiences. However, despite the fact that aging is inevitable, the old age is not necessarily something that many American people look forward to as they grow up. Another way to look at it is how people view the ending of movies. In the Afghan culture, it is not rude to tell others what happened in a movie that they just saw, while in the United States discussing the end of a movie is not recommended unless both parties have seen the movie. Perhaps people in Afghanistan see movies for enjoying the process of reflecting on what leads to the ending while Americans may have a tendency to see movies with the expectation of a surprise ending. Whatever the case or differences with regard to the old age, education and training are not always good substitutes for years of personal experience and intrinsic reflections.

The Society for Human Resource Management (SHRM, 2002) stated that the education system in the United States has failed to deliver graduates who are perceived to be qualified to successfully enter and meet the demands of today's labor market. Consequently, more and more organizations are trying to retain, recruit and hire senior citizens because of their skill and accumulated knowledge. Many of the best firms in the world are in search of wisdom, the type of wisdom that comes with age and experience that makes their first successful. Plato, philosopher, said that "It gives me great pleasure to converse with the aged. They have been over the road that all of us must travel and know where it is rough and difficult and where it is level and easy." The demand for the aged and wise with corporate, management and leadership experience should be on the rise. While there seems to be a global decrease in the labor supply, there is a rise in demand for experienced workers. Jamrog and McCann (2003) mentioned that about 43% of the civilian labor force will be eligible for retirement within the next ten years (by 2013). Therefore, there will be a shortage of talented and skilled professionals that accompany top leadership.

It is evident that the pace of change in today's post-industrial organizational environments is increasing. These changes are dynamic and evolutionary, yet not always predictable. Such evolutionary and dynamic changes can include or be caused by the increase in mergers, downsizing, flattening of organizational structures, increased globalization of businesses, increased complexities dealing with cultural and gender differences, increased aging or longevity of the population, and an increase in the number of employees working past the retirement age. These changes have created added responsibilities for managers who now have significantly more diverse generation of employees with varied cultural backgrounds. While managers attempt to juggle an overwhelming number of changes, priorities, and demands on their time, developmental activities for the aging workforce often have fallen to the bottom of the priority list, even though developing these experienced employees has been found to be a key factor in maintaining an organization's strategic advantage, and thus are critical to developing a learning organization.

The United States of American (USA) has a diverse population of nearly 300 million diverse individuals. A culture's perspective on aging in the USA can be seen from their comedy. The comedian George Carlin, uses aging in his appearances and states:

> If you're less than 10 years old, you're so excited about aging that you think in fractions. "How old are you?" "I'm four and a half!" You're never thirty-six and a half. You're four and a half, going on five! That's the key. You get into your teens, now they can't hold you back. You jump to the next number, or even a few ahead. "How old are you?" "I'm gonna be 16!" You could be 13, but hey, you're gonna be 16! And then the greatest day of your life . . . you become 21. Even the words sound like a ceremony . . . YOU BECOME 21. . . YESSSS!!! But then you turn 30. Oooohh, what happened there? Makes you sound like bad milk. He TURNED, we had to throw him out. There's no fun now, you're just a sour-dumpling. What's wrong? What's changed? You BECOME 21, you TURN 30, then you're PUSHING 40. Whoa! Put on the brakes, it's all slipping away. Before you know it, you REACH 50 . . . and your dreams are gone. But wait!!! You MAKE it to 60. You didn't think you would! So you BECOME 21, TURN 30, PUSH 40, REACH 50 and MAKE it to 60. You've built up so much speed that you HIT 70! After that it's a day-by-day thing; you HIT Wednesday! You get into your 80s and every day is a complete cycle; you HIT lunch; you TURN 4:30; you REACH bedtime. And it doesn't end there. Into the 90s, you start going backwards; "I was JUST 92." Then a strange thing happens. If you make it over 100, you become a little kid again. "I'm 100 and a half!" May you all make it to a healthy 100 and a half!!

Such views, expressed by the American comedians, associated with aging are common in the United States. They are representative of how the American society feels about aging and as such youthfulness is valued, and "older age" is not. These mindsets are causing an increasing number of the aging baby boomers to constantly search for the "fountain of youth" when in reality there is no such panacea. Nonetheless, such societal views tend to impact the workplace since senior executives and managers that make hiring decisions do come from the society, and they do not always check such mindsets and stereotypes associated with aging at the door. This societal conditioning is like personal traveling luggage that accompanies a person from one airport to another airport, and from one hotel to another, and finally back home. Unlike one's luggage, stereotypes and biases do not become lost, at least not automatically. They must be consciously replaced by appropriate new "luggage" or new "paradigms and mindsets."

The American culture seems to be obsessed with youth (Kelly, 2003), as can be seen from the increasing number of cosmetic surgeries while members of media are fully capitalizing on such obsessions in their ads and selling efforts. Such youth-mindedness is also accompanied by a negative perception of aging in the society, which is inclusive of the workplace. While many of the Asian cultures value and respect older individuals (both in their personal and professional lives), Americans view aging from a negative perspective as if it was a bad thing. These negative perceptions tend to convey the message that older workers are not able to keep up with new technology or new ways of doing things because they are not open minded. Besides the perception of not being open-minded, older workers in the American society are seen as: "deadwood, incompetent, closed minded, un-trainable, and less productive" (Kelly, 2003). Of-course, these are stereotypes and myths that are not factual; and individuals disproving these myths are ubiquitous in today's workplace. Nonetheless, such views tend to put older individuals at a huge disadvantage as they attempt to compete in the job market with their younger counterparts. On the other hand, young Americans tend to have this "unearned privilege" or "unearned advantage" that comes to them at a cost to "older workers."

Unearned Advantages and Cultural Ally

With regard to "unearned advantage," young people are also affected in ways that are very subtle. The term often used to refer to this concept is *"unearned privilege." Unearned privileges* are advantages given to some individuals and withheld from others, without regard to their efforts or abilities, because of their perceived difference. Every individual falls into a group/club based on his or her age, gender, body size, skin color, culture, ethnicity, race and other characteristics. If one's group has large numbers or power and prestige, one fits right in the middle of the curve, right in the "norm." Those people in the norm have some privileges that those outside the norm do not have. In real life terms, they get a little boost, a leg up, a "bennie," or a little extra. This does *not* mean that life is handed to them on a silver platter and they do not work hard. Despite the fact that they work hard for what they get, in addition to that, they may still get a little boost. The paradox is that they do not even know it. When told of it, they might even disbelieve it. When one is in the "norm" one thinks that is the way it is *for everybody*. It is not! There is the old Afghan parable about the king and his son, which illustrates this point. The king and his six year-old son were watching the poor people of the country pass through their castle and yell bad things about the king because of the inflation and hunger. The son asked, "Dad, why are they on strike and yelling such bad things about you?" The king replied, "they are hungry and need bread so they can eat and survive." The son replied by confirming his understanding and making a suggestion to solve the problem by saying "well, if they are hungry and don't have any bread, why don't they just eat cake and cookies?" While eating cake and cookies was the norm for the king's son it is a colossal luxury for a person who cannot even afford to buy a piece of dry bread so that s/he can survive another day. The moral of this story is that when you are in the "norm" you think that is the way it is *for everybody*. However, in reality it may not be so regardless of how much one may want things to be that way.

The existence of unearned privilege for younger workers can lead to increased tension, stress, and frustration because it usually comes at a cost to someone else which in this case is older workers. Sometimes, the society automatically affords you an unearned privilege because you fall in the norm (for a specific characteristic such as age, gender or body size) and sometimes you may have to work harder because the society is not structured toward your needs. Let us focus on something other than age to demonstrate unearned privilege. For example, society structures everything for right-handed persons, which means that left-handed individuals have to function in a right-handed world. The school desks, manufacturing machines, scissors, doorknobs, golf clubs, and other necessities of life are usually built for right-handed individuals. Many people can think of their own characteristics that have earned certain privileges without any effort or work on their part. For example, being a male can have certain advantages as well as certain disadvantages. Also, being "short" or "vertically challenged" can have many advantages, and at other times many disadvantages. In the case of age in the American society, it is an advantage until one gets to be an "older worker." During the young age, people enjoy "unearned advantages / privilege" and tend to lose them as they become older. Unearned privilege is a subject that requires deep and introspective thought but one can conclude that those who have unearned privileges are seldom aware that they have it. Those who do not have the privilege are very much aware that they do not have it. Unearned privileges are very subtle in society and such advantages can create tension, stress, and frustration in diverse environments. When people are aware of such advantages, they can personally assist in making sure another person is not impacted negatively in their department. So, refuse accepting privileges that you have done nothing to earn (that is if one is ever offered a job simply because ones is young when a more deserving person who happens to be an "older worker" did not get it because of his/her age) and become a "cultural" ally for those who are not in the norm. Sometimes when one thinks about the magnitude of the challenges that exist in the society, one may feel that he or she cannot make a difference. However, educated and trained individuals can make a difference by becoming cultural allies when they see instances of unfair employment practices in the workplace. Companies should expect their managers to be allies in the workplace in order to eliminate age discrimination. As you become more culturally competent with regard to age discrimination, you will find more and more opportunities to be a cultural ally. *Cultural ally* refers to those individuals who intervene or interrupt in order to stop mistreatment or injustice from occurring to other individuals. Such mistreatments can be as subtle as age discrimination toward "older workers" that cannot be seen but is very widespread in the American workplace. So, one solution for eliminating age discrimination is for everyone to personally become a cultural ally, which will eventually replace the stereotypes with the truth about "older workers."

It may not always be obvious to some people how important older workers are to the economy and businesses; yet older workers contribute immensely to the success of not only the United States, but to other countries of the world. In a national survey, older workers were found to possess the following qualities: functioning well in crisis; possessing basic skills in writing, reading, and arithmetic; loyal; solid performers; and good interpersonal skills (Harvey & Allard, 2002). Older workers have various talents that are vital to many businesses in the world today, and those skills are not just restricted to multinational or huge corporations only, but they also apply to smaller and specialized organizations. For example, a company by the name of Vita Needle, in Needham, Massachusetts, manufactures stainless steel tubing and needles have a reputation of employing mainly older workers, with an average age of 35. This company hires older workers because utilizing older workers is part of their core competency. There are certain qualities that the older workers possess that fit into the goals and policies of the company. When the President of the company, Fred Hartman, was interviewed by Tom Brokaw, NBC Nightly New, he said that the primary reason he continuously recruits older workers was because the assembly of their metal components was done by hand, and older employees were "extremely conscientious employees: loyal, dedicated, aware of quality requirements, and very reliable" (Harvey & Allard, 2002). Another example of a company that has benefited immensely from managing older employees is the Aerospace Corporation in El Segundo, California. They have a "Retirement Transition Program" which makes available to its highly skilled employees four different options namely, pre-retirement leaves of absence, part-time status working towards retirement, post retirement employment based on consultancy, and post retirement in the form casual employment.

Daily Indignities in the Workplace

Thinking back to your life experiences you will recall that we all, at some point in time, have undergone experiences when we were treated differently because of our physical differences and other such characteristics. While we all have experienced unfair treatment at one time or another, we will see how some individuals in society may be exposed to this type of treatment on a more consistent basis. In fact, some individuals may experience such unfair treatment on a daily basis. This unfair treatment is called *daily indignities*- negative things that individuals do or say to or about one another on a continuous basis, because of their biases and perceived differences. This is one definition of "daily indignities" that one of the authors has used in diversity workshops for managers and executives. Also, the National Multi-Cultural Institute (NMCI), a Washington-based non-profit institution, has used similar definitions to begin discussions on subtle and blatant forms of discrimination in society.

These daily indignities are demonstrated in many different forms and age discrimination is one of them. Several documentaries have been created that show these various forms of daily indignities or discrimination. These documentaries depict various forms of discrimination in actual work and daily life situations. Typically, two people, called "testers" are used. The testers are equal in all characteristics except the chosen discriminatory one, like age, appearance, skin color or gender. Usually the testers are sent to a location to check on public response to a diversity characteristic in real life settings such as applying for a job, buying a car or making a major purchase, using the services of an employment agency, renting an apartment, and shopping in a store. An example of such a documentary that focuses on age discrimination is titled "*Age and Attitude*" which was aired several times to national and international audiences at ABC's "Prime Time" in the 1990s.

The *Age and Attitude* documentary focused on discrimination based on age and attitude. In this documentary, a single male tester assumes two identities. He is "made up" to be a 27-year old candidate (named Joseph) and a 53-year old candidate (named Michael) seeking employment. Michael, the older tester, possesses slightly better job qualifications than Joseph. They enter into identical employment opportunity situations with the following results. The 27-year old tester consistently received various employment offers even though the 53 year old tester possessed better qualifications. In one instance, the older tester is told during the interview, "this is a young boy's game!" When the employers were confronted and asked to explain these results, they could not offer any logical explanation as to why the younger tester was consistently offered the employment opportunity over the older tester. Some of these decisions may be attributed to the myth that older workers are more sickly, not as committed, and will not stay with the company as long. Once again, facts prove these myths are all false! Based on the authors' combined forty years of corporate and management experience throughout Afghanistan, Jamaica, Turkey, and the United States of America, associates over the age of 40 tend to be much more experienced and often times more dependable than younger associates who are in their early twenties. They also tend to be mature, more customer savvy, loyal, honest, quality focused, relationship oriented, and skilled in positive interpersonal communication.

Data shows that age discrimination is such an integral part of American society that it is even more difficult to detect than either racial or gender discrimination. It is also a fact that older workers (over 40) usually require 64% more time to obtain employment than their younger counterparts. It should also be mentioned that discrimination did not occur every time in this *Age and Attitude* documentary, some of the discrimination might have been unintentional, and it is possible that some of the discrimination that occurred was not because of the particular characteristic being tested. Nonetheless, such forms of age discrimination are prevalent in the United States and possibly widespread in the workplace. A pattern of such discrimination could cost the company major losses in lawsuits.

Cultural Values, Morals, and Decision-Making

Personal, organizational, and cultural values can be subconscious and can effect decisions. Values have an impact on one's everyday life, and they shape as well as define one's character.

Living by a personal code of ethics helps managers and leaders remain consistent when defining themselves and shaping the perception of others. The result of a decision often times characterizes the process in which people follow when making decisions. By analyzing the decision-making process, it will help improve the practice of applying one's values in every decision. Understanding the reasons behind our decisions requires thoughtful consideration of the action one takes. Personal, organizational, or cultural values are the foundation on which decisions are made in the day-to-day operations.

If personal values are a definition of who ones is and what one does, then ensuring one's actions are ethical is crucial to social development. Personal values are not always perceptible, so one can judge the effect one has on a situation by examining one's actions. Personal values can be as simple as being nice to people or multifaceted as handing down a clean environment to the children. Regardless of the degree to which one's values are defined, developing the framework of one's moral fiber should be the true objective in decision-making.

Michael Maccoby (2005), in his article titled "*Creating Moral Organizations*," raises the argument that "organizations cannot be moral; only people can be moral" (p. 59). Do organizations have the responsibility to put forth a set of values that encompass their ethics and morals then ensuring the values are upheld? By encouraging executives and managers to make decisions based on personal ethics and morals, organizational values can be carried out at all levels. Furthermore, the article titled "*Survey Shows Need for More Ethics Awareness*," by Curtis C. Verschoor (2004), states that "Compliance means nothing without a culture of integrity" (p. 15). Verschoor continues by stating that the company's responsibility, when defining its organizational values, is to characterize its true beliefs and expect employees to lead by example. Encouraging employees to lead provides them with a sense of unity and gives them the empowerment to suitably represent the organization.

American business culture typically views the global business arena as the marketplace where competition is encouraged. Although the American culture always has had an international flavor, many individuals living in the United States understand very little about the cultural values outside of their comfort zone (Cant, 2004). More than ever, boundaries in which global businesses were once limited, are now open, making it more important than ever for people to embrace their cultural values. Seeking to understand one's values provides opportunities to reflect on who one is, and gives one reason to explore the values of other cultures. However, there is a sense of individualism that exists in the American business culture and acts as a barrier to higher learning (Barnett, Weathersby, and Aram, 1995). This individualistic approach can adversely affect the decisions one makes when representing oneself in the global environment. Therefore, understanding values, specifically cultural values, will provide one with the tools to make good choices when representing oneself outside of the culture.

The values in which one lives by influence one's everyday decisions; thus having a solid understanding of one's values is essential in not only making good choices but also influencing the decisions others make. For example, according to one colleague's business trip to Bangalore, India (late 2004 and early 2005) to conduct training of a new staff, a personnel conflict materialized where intervention was required. The conflict developed between an American business manager who worked for the firm's most important business partner, and their Indian technical support outsource vendor. Upon arriving, members of the Indian outsource vendor greeted them with open arms and treated them extremely well. The vendor was a very large company, much larger than their company, and the level of respect in which they showed was very impressive. A couple of days into the month long trip, the manager, who worked for their business partner, was becoming noticeably agitated by inconveniences outside of the work environment. Things such as the food choices, transportation challenges, solicitors, and communication barriers seemed to set him off on rants. This seemed quite odd because everyone else was having a wonderful time, and these inconveniences were a minor price to pay for such a great experience. Unfortunately, after a few days of this type of behavior, his attitude began to spill over into the workplace. This behavior caused tension between everyone involved in the project, including their hosts who seemed to sense the negative posture and withdrew some of their generosity. With the tension rising and the project at risk of falling behind schedule, the decision was made to counsel the business manager on the effects of his behavior. The complicated aspect of this dilemma was trying to rectify the situation without offending their most important client. Although the company's organizational values are not formalized, there is a clear understanding that maintaining the well being of business partner is a top priority. However, this colleague's personal and cultural values of treating all people with respect and total equality are values that follow him into any situation. Therefore, weighing the company objective against doing the right thing was obviously going to be a challenge. The first step in educating the business manager was to point out all of the wonderful things that India had to offer. Continuing to iterate that one of the core values of the Indian culture is being a great host, pointing out that their friends had gone to great lengths to ensure that all of their needs are taken care of, and by complaining they will most likely offend their Indian host. They also found out that one of the Indian executives had an MBA from the top business school in the U.S., and was once a professional golfer on the Nike tour. Moreover, the technical support agents that they were there to train all had advanced engineering degrees. The goal was to educate him on the culture and to make him realize his misunderstandings of a developing country, all the while assuring him that the people they are working with have similar goals and aspirations as my colleague's organization. Later that evening there was a noticeable change in his tone of voice, evolving from a condescending tone to one that showed more respect. Not surprisingly, soon after, some of the issues that were bogging them down went away, putting the project back on track.

The types of decisions made along the way will most likely determine the level of success a business or an individual achieves. "An executive is a person who always decides; sometimes he decides correctly, but he always decides" John H. Patterson (Moncur, 1994-2004). Making decisions is a way of life but in order to make good decisions one must have a firm understanding of the effects that morals, ethics, and values have on the outcomes.

Today, the United States is made up of such a diverse population of people with different ethnic backgrounds, from different parts of the world, and with different cultural values. So, how does one define cultural values in today's society? "Cultural values can be viewed as a desirable or preferred way of acting or knowing something that has been reinforced by the social structure and, ultimately, governs one's actions or decisions (Leininger, 1985, p. 209-212). These values can be reflected in a person's cultural perception of time, personal space, communication style, role of gender and family, as well as in their practices regarding such aspects of daily living as diet, modesty, self-care, and "hot" versus "cold" remedies. However, "a person's country and culture of origin and his or her current country of residence can complicate differences that seemingly reflect prevailing cultural norms" (Laukaran & Winikoff, 1986, p.121-128). The diversity of the people in the world today has changed the way one views and understands what cultural values are all about.

Based on personal visits to Honolulu by the authors, and according to a colleague from Hawaii (Personal Communication with Mele K. Akuna, March 2005), the Hawaiian cultural values seem to embrace the importance of family, and the land. Respect for family and land seem to be the most important values that continue to be practiced today by many families in Hawaii. Mele Akuna went on to say that many businesses in Hawaii are beginning to understand the importance of Hawaiian cultural values, and are incorporating these values into the way they conduct business as well as the way they treat their employees. Hawaii has its own culture that makes operating different to do "business as usual" for mainland and foreign companies. Businesses have survived on their long standing relationships with their customers, and continue to survive on loyalty. Unfortunately, new businesses have attempted to open up shop in Hawaii, but failed. Their failure was not because their product was not attractive to the people who live here but the fact that they did not recognize the need to respect the cultural values of the people. Hawaii may seem like islands made up of a small population of people; however, the communities are very close-knit. Many people base their decisions on what the family has been doing for the past many years, or by word of mouth. People in Hawaii respect each other to the point that they do not always look into matters themselves, but they trust the word of their family and neighbors. Even with the opening of superstores like Wal-Mart and Costco so many "Mom and Pop" stores remain in business because of their loyal customers and personal relationships. Overall, to be a successful manager working for a business in Hawaii, cultural values need to be understood and practiced. Hawaii is such a diverse state that successful managers need to have a good understanding of who their employees are, where their values are formed, and how diverse are their ethnic backgrounds. Management must also take into consideration the family lifestyle in Hawaii, and how they decide to do business there will determine how successful the business will be in the long-term.

In addition to cultural values, personal ethics also plays an important role in being a successful manager. How does one define personal ethics? "*Personal ethics* have been defined as principles of good behavior, a moral code of conduct or a system to decide between competing options. But simply stated, *personal ethics* are nothing more than the rules we impose on ourselves that govern our daily actions" (David, 2003, p. 230). So, how do personal ethics and cultural values impact management's decision-making process in Hawaii? Well, just like the importance of cultural values and the impact it has on business, personal ethics is just as important. Like most small cities, the lifestyle of people living in Hawaii is so close-knit that news of someone or a company that does not conduct business in an ethical manner will travel quickly. It would not take the nightly television newscast to spread the news to the people of Hawaii. Therefore, as a manager, proper training in ethical conduct is a must. Hawaii is such a small place, and as a respected business person, proper ethical conduct is necessary in order to continue to do business. Friedman (1970) states that the sole moral responsibility of a business is to maximize profits, while respecting the laws and ethical rules of the society in which it is located.

The success of a business is a reflection of management of the business and their cultural, personal and organizational values. "A culture evolves on its own and reflects the goals and values of an organization." In turn, "the organization's ethical decisions can have a strong impact on the organization's culture and this gives top management a degree of control on the composition of the corporate culture" (Reidenbach and Robin, 1989). As a manager in today's world, profits play a very important role in the success of a business; however, it can all be for nothing if people within the business are not practicing good ethical conduct, have respect for the place where their business is conducted, and respect for the people who help make the business a success. Continuous training in ethical practices and cultural and organizational values will keep employees honest, and they consequently will value the company's goals as if it were their own.

Cultural values, which include freedom, prosperity, and security, are the bases for the specific norms that tell people what is appropriate in various situations (Schwartz, 1999). Cultural values are shared in societal institutions such as family, political systems, religious references, and education or economic institutions. Therefore, their goals or ways of operations represent the values they believe in. The leaders of these institutions, for example, parents, teachers, a CEO of a corporation, or a president of a country can draw on them to select socially appropriate behaviors. These behaviors are committed to the societal members through everyday exposure to family rules, regulations from the workplace, or laws (Schwartz, 1999). Societal members adapt to the functions of the institutions they spend their time with (Schwartz, 1999). In sum, a culture exists where a group of people share a set of belief, norms and customs (Singhapakdi, Marta, Rawwas, & Ahmed, 1999). There are no national boundaries for a culture to exist; however, for nations that have been established for some time, the sharing of culture is substantial (Hofstede, Neuijen, Ohayv, & Sander, 1990).

In a capitalist society, individual ambitions and success are highly valued; the structures of the economic and legal systems are competitive. In contrast, the social culture tends to be in more cooperative economic and legal systems (Schwartz, 1999). A study was done to compare consumers from Malaysia and the USA in terms of their corporate marketing ethics; and the result reveals some significant differences between the two countries. Malaysians specifically and people in the developing nations in general tend to have lower ethical perceptions than the people from the United States or the industrialized countries (Hofstede, Neuijen, Ohayv & Sander, 1990). Another research was conducted on how business ethics is perceived across cultures among college students in different countries. The study confirms that cultural differences do exist and they effect how people perceive ethical business differently (Ahmed, Chung & Eichenseher, 2003). At the time of the study, Malaysia's economy had boomed along with its competition; therefore, the pressure was on for many Malaysian managers. Some believed it is acceptable to conduct business unethically. Similarly, the U.S. corporate executives continue to struggle with the unrealistic earning expectations (Tinkler, 2004). Could this type of pressure on management be the cause of the latest round of scandals, such as Enron, Worldcom, and others?

Individual values are the products of shared cultures and unique personal experiences. For most individuals, family is the first institution in which values are instilled in children through their parents. Family is where the first and the most fundamental training on ethics is acquired. Religious institutions are another avenue where values and beliefs are taught. Children are raised not to lie, not to cheat, be responsible for their actions, treat people as they want to be treated, etc. As such, most individuals seem to know the difference between right and wrong. Studies have shown that people who commit unethical acts know they are doing something wrong (Tinkler, 2004).

The most basic moral values are learned when one is a child, and as children entering adulthood, more values are acquired at different institutions. When adults enter the workforce, there are rules of conduct imposed by companies and organizations that employees must follow. These professional values can be defined as "values relating to one's professional conduct that are commonly shared by the member of a particular profession" (Singhapadki, & Vitell 1993b, p. 528). These organizational values are communicated through written codes of ethics, formal and informal trainings. While there are no "right" or "wrong" values, there are values that are better aligned with the organization's culture and codes of ethics (see Pohlman and Gardiner's book entitled *Value Driven Management*, 2000). Corporate values must be explicit, and they are applied to everyone in the organization including top management (Patten, 2004). Everyone must see that top managers are responsible for their ethical behavior and employees need to be rewarded for ethical behavior and face consequences for unethical behavior (Patten, 2004).

In recent years, many corporate scandals have come to light. Ethics has become so important and often emphasized in the society that it has become an academic topic. The cultural values, the workforce and personal standards are interrelated; individuals exposed to these values will need to form their own rules of conduct. Life presents people with many choices, and choices will be made based on personal rules of conduct; it thus is best to choose not the most convenient way to conduct business or personal affairs, but one that is aligned with one's overall life goals.

Asian culture is one of the many cultures in the United States and it is different from the American culture in many ways. For example, Asian children are taught that it is impolite to talk back to elderly but in American culture it is a way for children to express themselves. People, who are exposed to both cultures, sometimes find it difficult to balance and/or determine which culture to adopt; especially for the younger generation. Religion also plays a strong role in shaping up a person to act right toward another individual and have respect for Superior Powers. Again, while people know the difference between right and wrong, factors such as emotion, time constraints, and social pressure will become the major factors in their personal as well as professional lives. In challenging times, one needs to step back when faced with difficult decisions and find a balance where one would feel comfortable and happy while respecting everyone else's cultural norms.

CHAPTER 3

CULTURAL AND LEGAL PRACTICES OF AGE IN EMPLOYMENT

*I*n the global business environment of the 21st century, effective management of personnel enhances internal business relationships, perceived career success, organizational commitment, overall job performance, and the reduction of turnover.

The United States surely possesses the most extensive and comprehensive body of laws against discrimination of all types in employment. Other countries, however, perhaps because they are composed of more homogeneous peoples, may not have felt the need to develop anti-discrimination legal schemes. Yet, in certain other countries, the laws actually may require discrimination based on religion or national origin, if certain characteristics are synonymous with a particular religion, especially an official "state religion," or a dominant ethnic group which controls a country. The global business person must take into account all such laws that govern the employment relationship. This understanding must encompass not only the laws of his or her own country, but also the overseas application of his or her country's laws, as well as the laws of the host country.

United States Law

The United States certainly has a very well developed corpus of law governing the employer-employee relationship in the United States, most notably the Civil Rights Act, which among other provisions prohibits discrimination in employment based on certain protected categories. For years, however, there has been significant disagreement in the governmental, legal, and academic communities regarding whether U.S. employment discrimination laws apply abroad; and if so, which laws, and how so. These questions certainly are more than "academic" for U.S. business managers operating in an increasingly competitive global economy. For example, how can a U.S. firm conduct business in a country that may legally require discrimination in employment against women or people of a certain religion or national origin, if the U.S. firm is under legal enjoinment pursuant to U.S. civil rights laws to treat all its employees equally and thereby not to discriminate?

The United States today is only one of a small number of countries that afford comprehensive legal protection against discrimination in employment. Title VII of the Civil

Rights Act of 1964 prohibits discrimination in employment on the basis of race, color, religion, sex, and national origin (Thomson West, 2005b, section 2000e). The Age Discrimination in Employment Act of 1967 added age as a protected category (Thomson West, 2005a, sections 621-634). The Americans with Disabilities Act enacted in 1990 extended these protections to employees with disabilities (Thomson West, 2005b, s. 12101b). There are significant sanctions that confront the foreign as well as the U.S. firm that intentionally violates U.S. anti-discrimination laws, including the payment of monetary damages, the reinstatement of the adversely affected employee, and the payment of attorney's fees and costs. These legal protections safeguard the employees of covered U.S. firms in the U.S. as well as the employees of foreign multinational firms in the U.S. The crucial questions, of course, are whether these important U.S. legal protections extend overseas to safeguard U.S. citizens working abroad for U.S. firms as well as the foreign employees of the U.S. firms in the host country.

The Age Discrimination in Employment Act (ADEA)

The Age Discrimination in Employment Act of 1967 is a federal law which prohibits an employer from failing or refusing to hire a protected individual, or discharging an employee within the protected age category, or otherwise discriminating against such individuals, because of their age regarding compensation and the other terms and conditions of employment (Thomson West, 2005, s. 623). The ADEA covers hiring, termination, compensation, as well as other terms and conditions of employment. The term "employee" is defined very broadly under the statute and extends protection to public as well as private sector employees; however, the employees in order to be protected must be at least 40 years of age. There is no upper level age limit to the statute's coverage. The ADEA defines "employer" as a "person" involved in an industry affecting commerce with twenty or more employees for each working day in each of twenty or more calendar weeks in the current or a preceding calendar year. A "person" is defined as one or more individuals, a partnership, an association, a corporation, or a labor organization, among other entities and relationships.

The purposes of the statute were to promote the employment of older persons predicated on their capabilities and not their age, to prohibit arbitrary age discrimination in employment, as well as to assist employers and employees to find approaches to solve problems stemming from the impact of age on employment. The ADEA is enforced by the Equal Employment Opportunity Commission (EEOC). The EEOC is permitted to bring a lawsuit on behalf of an aggrieved employee, or the aggrieved employee may bring a suit himself or herself for legal or equitable relief. In either case, the ADEA provides the right to a jury trial.

It is important to note that the ADEA does not bar the termination of older employees; rather, the Act only bars discrimination against them. Accordingly, an employer can defend an ADEA lawsuit by establishing that an employment decision was based on reasonable and legitimate non-discriminatory reasons other than age, such as poor performance. Moreover, despite the connection between age and high salary, the ADEA does not automatically prohibit the discharge of a highly paid employee solely based on financial considerations (*Bay v. Times Mirror Magazines, Inc.,* 1991). Employers thus are allowed to save money by eliminating highly paid positions; however, each employment decision must be handled on an individualized, reasonable, and fair basis, and consequently any "blanket" rules that would adversely affect older employees could trigger an ADEA lawsuit. Finally, an employer may involuntarily retire an employee who is at least 65 years old and who has been employed during a two year period in a legitimate executive or high level policy-making position, and who is immediately entitled to an enumerated employer-financed pension. Consequently, one commentator has noted that U.S. firms, pursuant to the influence of U.S. Civil Rights laws, are moving in the European direction of an expectation of lump sum buyouts for older workers when their jobs end, typically called "early retirement buyouts" (Olson, 1999).

The employer can also defend an ADEA lawsuit by interposing the bona fide occupational qualification doctrine (BFOQ). Pursuant to the BFOQ doctrine, the employer will be obligated to show that the challenged age criteria is reasonably related to the essential operation of the employer's business, and that there is a factual basis for believing that only employees of a certain age would be able to do the particular job safely or effectively. Examples would include airline pilots, police, firefighters, and bus drivers, as well as others for whom certain physical requirements are a necessity for efficient job performance (*Orzel v. City of Wauwatosa Fire Department*, 1983).

In 2005, the U.S. Supreme Court enunciated a major decision regarding age discrimination in employment in the case of *Smith v. City of Jackson, Mississippi* (2005). The decision significantly expands the protection afforded older workers pursuant to the Age Discrimination and Employment Act. The decision thus allows protected workers, over the age of 40 to institute age discrimination lawsuits even evidence is lacking that their employers never purposefully intended to discriminate against the workers on the basis of age. As a result, the decision substantially lessens the legal burden for employees covered by the statute by allowing aggrieved employees to contend in court that a presumably neutral employment practice nonetheless had an adverse or disparate or disproportionately harmful impact on them. However, the Court allowed the employer to defend such an age discrimination case by interposing that the employer had a legitimate, reasonable, and job-related explanation for the "neutral" employment policy. The Supreme Court case initially was brought by older police officers in Jackson, Mississippi, who argued that a pay-for-performance plan instituted by the city granted substantially larger raises to employees with five or fewer years of tenure, which policy, the officers contended, favored their younger colleagues. The lower courts had dismissed the lawsuit, ruling that these types of claims were barred by the statute. The U.S. Supreme Court, however, in a 5-3 decision, ruled that the officers were entitled to pursue the age discrimination lawsuit against the city. Justice John Paul Stevens, writing for the majority, stated that the Age Discrimination in Employment Act of 1967 was meant to allow the same type of "disparate impact" legal challenges for older workers that minorities and women can assert pursuant to the Civil Rights Act. Yet Justice Stevens also noted in the decision that the same law does allow employers the legal right to at times treat older workers differently. It is important to note that pursuant to the Civil Rights Act, employers can successfully defend a disparate impact case only by showing the "business necessity" for a neutral but harmful employment policy, which is a much more difficult test to meet than the "reasonable" explanation standard of the ADEA.

The U.S. Supreme Court's age discrimination decision emerges as a significant victory for older workers covered by the ADEA. Such protected workers now do not have to have direct or "smoking gun" evidence of intentional age discrimination in order to file a civil rights lawsuit; rather, all that is required is evidence of disproportionate harmful impact stemming from a neutral age employment policy. Employers, whether U.S. employers or foreign employers doing business in the United States, now must be much more conscious of the consequences of their employment policies on older workers, particularly regarding the criteria used to determine hiring, termination, especially layoffs, as well as pay scales and retirement plan changes. Employers also must be prepared to provide and explain the "reasonable" factors other than age that would justify the employment policy causing the disparate harmful impact on older protected workers.

The Extraterritorial Effect of U.S. Employment Discrimination Law

Another important employment discrimination issue concerns the rights of workers who are employed by a U.S. employer or by a foreign employer in a workplace in a foreign country. The difficult issue is whether the extensive U.S. legal protections afforded to employees in the U.S. carry overseas. This legal question typically is regarded as an issue of the "extraterritoriality" of U.S. law.

The early, leading Supreme Court case ruling on the extraterritoriality of U.S. law was not an employment discrimination case, but rather dealt with federal anti-trust law. In *American Banana Company v. United Fruit Company* (1909), although both parties to the dispute were U.S. citizens, the alleged violation of the Sherman Anti-Trust Act occurred in Panama. The Court unanimously ruled at the time that the Sherman Act did not apply to acts occurring beyond the borders of the U.S. Moreover, a majority of the court expressed reservations concerning even extending a statute extraterritorially. Another concern, raised by Justice Holmes writing for the majority, was that extending a statute extraterritorially would contravene the fundamental sovereignty principle of international law. American Banana Company consequently set forth the general rule governing extraterritorial jurisdiction; that is, a very strong presumption exists against the extraterritorial application of U.S. law. This presumption, furthermore, can be overcome only in exceptional instances.

The leading employment discrimination extraterritoriality case was the Supreme Court's 1991 decision in *EEOC v. Arabian American Oil Company* (*EEOC v. Arabian American Oil Company*, 1991). In the so-termed *Aramco* case, the Supreme Court was called upon to decide whether Congress intended to apply Title VII of the Civil Rights Act of 1964 to United States citizens working for U.S. companies in foreign countries. The Supreme Court, in a 6-3 decision, which affirmed the lower court's decision, ruled that Title VII did not reflect the requisite clear expression of U.S. Congressional intent to overcome the presumption against extraterritoriality of statutes. Consequently, the Court held that the protections of Title VII did not extend to a U.S. citizen working for a U.S. company overseas. The Court compared Title VII of the Civil Rights Act to the Age Discrimination in Employment Act (ADEA), which as will be seen, was amended in 1984 by Congress so as to add provisions that specifically addressed conflicts with foreign laws, thereby revealing Congress' extraterritorial intent, which was "ambiguous" in the language of Title VII. The judicial limitation thereby expressed on the extraterritorial scope of federal law, absent a clearly stated statutory intention to the contrary, underscores the deference the courts give to sovereignty concepts and international law comity concerns that might be contravened if U.S. courts attempted to extend too broadly and intrusively U.S. law, especially labor and employment laws, to other nations. As the Court noted in *Aramco,* it is a "longstanding principle of American law that 'legislation of Congress, unless a contrary intent appears, is meant to apply only within the territorial jurisdiction of the United States,'" (*EEOC v. Arabian American Oil Company*, 1991) (quoting *Foley Bros. Inc. v. Filardo*, 1949).

Very soon after the Supreme Court had ruled in the *Aramco* case, Congress attempted to overrule the decision by at least partially extending U.S. employment discrimination law overseas. Accordingly, the Civil Rights Act of 1991 (Title VII of the Civil Rights Act of 1964, as amended by the Civil Rights Act of 1991, (Thomson West, 2005, section 2000) was promulgated to protect certain employees of U.S. firms overseas. Congress thereby expressly amended and enlarged the scope of Title VII (as well as the Americans with Disabilities Act) to provide a clear indication of Congress' extraterritorial intent to reach U.S. business firms that operate outside the U.S. as well as those under the "control" of a U.S. entity.

The 1991 amendments to the Civil Rights Act expanded the definition of the key term "employee" to include any U.S. citizen employed by a U.S. company in a foreign country or foreign company that is controlled by a U.S. firm. Foreign employees working within the U.S. are protected, whether working for U.S. or foreign multinational firms, as are U.S. citizen employees, of course. However, and most significantly, outside the U.S., only U.S. citizens working for U.S. firms or firms controlled by U.S. firms are protected, since foreign employees were expressly excluded from protection when employed in a foreign country, even by a U.S. firm. Therefore, Section 109 of the Civil Rights Act of 1991 amended both Title VII and the ADA to extend certain extraterritorial protection to employees.

When the U.S. Congress has legislated with an explicit intent to have extraterritorial impact for U.S. law, the courts will recognize that intent. However, if there is a "gray" area, the courts can determine the legal result by judicial interpretation. Yet, even where there has been an express Congressional intention to have extraterritorial effect, the courts can interpret the law in a manner that allows defenses and qualifications. Accordingly, the courts developed three main defenses to allegations of employment discrimination overseas. These defenses are as follows: 1) Was the discriminatory employment decision made by a foreign person not "controlled" by a U.S. employer? 2) Does either Title VII of the Civil Rights Act or the ADEA conflict with the host country's laws, so that the U.S. employer confronts "foreign compulsion"? That is, would compliance with U.S. law violate the host country's laws? 3) Does the performance of the job reasonably necessitate a particular characteristic, such as age, gender, or religion, thereby permitting the employer to interpose the standard "bona fide occupational qualification" (BFOQ) defense to employment discrimination? Since the 1991 amendments to the Civil Rights Act have made Title VII and the ADEA co-extensive in their extraterritorial protection, the courts have interpreted these seminal employment protection statutes with reference to one another. These post-amendment cases provide guidance generally on the nature of extraterritoriality, and specifically when extraterritoriality will be applied in a particular case.

An essential extraterritoriality legal issue is whether the foreign company is sufficiently controlled by a U.S. "parent" company, so as to be subject to U.S. anti-discrimination employment statutes. Determining exactly, however, the nationality of a business' controlling person or entity is a difficult undertaking. The ADEA initially declares that when an employer "controls" a corporation whose place of incorporation is a foreign country, any prohibited employment practices engaged in by such a corporation shall be presumed to be engaged in by the employer. The ADEA also holds that the protections of the Act shall not apply to the foreign operations of an employer that is a foreign "person" not controlled by a U.S. employer. The Act, finally, articulates four factors to determine the crucial corporation "control" test: (1) the interrelationship of operations; (2) the existence of common management; (3) the centralized control of labor relations; and (4) the common ownership or financial control of the employer and the corporation.

The application of the "control" test, therefore, is critical to determining whether these seminal employment anti-discrimination statutes will be enforceable against a foreign subsidiary of a U.S. "parent" corporation. If the foreign firm is not controlled by a U.S. company, then U.S. citizens employed overseas by the foreign company will not be protected by U.S. anti-discrimination laws; and these employees rather will have to seek redress pursuant to the labor and employment laws of the nation where the foreign firm was incorporated or does business. Therefore, a foreign firm as well as its putative U.S. "parent" must consider whether, applying the four "control" criteria, it is sufficiently controlled by a U.S. multinational corporation (*See, e.g., Denty v. SmithKline Beecham,* (*Denty v. SmithKline Beecham,* 1997), where the federal district court rejected the EEOC's view of nationality, and thereby prevented a U.S. citizen from instituting a lawsuit against a firm with very substantial U.S. operation).

The ADEA also has an explicit "foreign compulsion" defense which allows U.S. firms the legal "license" to discriminate in employment when the enforcement of U.S. discrimination laws would result in a violation of foreign law (Thomson West, 2005a, 623(f)(1)). This defense, typically called the "foreign laws" defense, means that a U.S. employer will not be liable if compliance with Title VII would cause the U.S. firm to violate the laws of the country where the workplace is located (*ALPA v. TACA,* 1985). An example of this "compulsion" defense is provided by the EEOC in its Enforcement Guidance, which states that an employer will have a "foreign laws" defense "for requiring helicopter pilots if employed in Saudi Arabia to convert to Moslem religion where Saudi Arabian law provided for beheading of non-Moslems who entered holy area" (EEOC Compliance Manual, 1993). The degree of flexibility provided by this defense is well illustrated by the federal appeals case of *Mahoney v. RFE/RL, Inc.* (*Mahoney v. RFE/RL,* 1995), where the court ruled that when U.S. law would cause a U.S. firm to violate a foreign collective bargaining agreement, which technically is not even a law, the foreign compulsion defense nonetheless applies. It is important to emphasize that the U.S. federal court rejected the EEOC's view of the matter. The decision is noteworthy because in many countries the demarcation between legalistic law and social customs and practices is not as distinct as it is in the U.S.

The aforementioned bona fide occupational qualification defense (BFOQ) explicitly arises from Title VII of the Civil Rights Act. The BFOQ defense has been deemed by the courts to have extraterritorial application too. Thus, pursuant to the BFOQ doctrine, an employer may engage in discrimination if certain characteristics are reasonably necessary to the normal operations of the particular business or enterprise. For example, in *Kern v. Dynalectron Corporation* (*Kern v. Dynalectron Corporation*, 1984) the court held that conversion to Islam was a BFOQ for a pilot flying helicopters to Mecca since non-Moslems flying into Mecca would be, if caught, be beheaded.

The Age Discrimination in Employment Act first was amended by Congress in 1984 to make it applicable extraterritorially. The term "employee" was amended to include any individual who is a citizen of the U.S. employed by a U.S. employer or its subsidiary in a workplace in a foreign country. Unless a person is a U.S. citizen, he or she is not included in the definition of the term "employee" if he or she works overseas. That is, nothing in the ADEA, or the amendments thereto, or the courts' interpretations thereof, regulate age discrimination by U.S. firms against foreign nationals in foreign countries in a foreign workplace. The ADEA also has been interpreted by the courts not to cover foreign nationals when they apply in foreign countries for jobs in the United States (*Reyes-Ganoan v. North Carolina Growers Association*, 2001).

The Age Discrimination in Employment Act also protects U.S. citizens working overseas for a U.S. controlled foreign employer (*Morelli v. Cedel*, 1998). The ADEA provides that the prohibitions of the Act shall not apply where the employer is a foreign person not controlled by an U.S. employer; *Morelli v. Cedel*, 1998). "At a minimum," declared one court, "...the ADEA does not apply to the foreign operations of foreign employers – unless there is an American employer behind the scenes" (*Morelli v. Cedel*, 1998). The ADEA, therefore, does not apply to a foreign corporation operating outside the U.S. even when the foreign firm employs U.S. citizens unless a U.S. company controls the foreign corporation. Regarding the important "control" issue, the aforementioned four critical factors are specified in the Act; and thus are used by the courts in ADEA cases to determine control: 1) interrelation of operations; 2) common management; 3) centralized control of labor relations; and 4) common ownership or financial control of the employer and the corporation. The purpose of the statutory "control" element, according to one court, is to protect the principle of sovereignty; that is, "no nation has the right to impose its labor standards on another country". The Act, however, does protect employees working in the U.S. for a domestic branch of a foreign company (*Morelli v. Cedel*, 1998).

An exception to extraterritoriality also exists if the application of the Age Discrimination in Employment Act would violate the law of the other country where the workplace is located. This principle, termed the "foreign laws" or "foreign compulsion" defense, means that a U.S. employer will not be legally liable if compliance with the ADEA would cause the employer to violate the laws of the nation where the workplace is located.

In one aforementioned ADEA case, the U.S. Court of Appeals for the District of Columbia ruled that where the U.S. law would cause a U.S. company to violate a foreign collective bargaining agreement, which technically could be argued as not equating to a "law," the foreign compulsion defense applied (*Mahroney v. RFEIRL,* 1995).

Summary

Legal complexity naturally results from the globalization of business – in the employment field and otherwise. Foreign firms consequently must be keenly aware of U.S. law; and also U.S. firms must be aware of not only foreign law, but also the extraterritoriality of U.S. laws. A "simple" solution to the extraterritoriality problem examined herein might be to apply U.S. employment discrimination laws to any company incorporated in the U.S., regardless of where its employment operations take place. Yet, this "answer" is not feasible due to the very strong presumption in U.S. law against the extraterritorial application of U.S. law, which typically is predicated on concerns about sovereignty, comity, and jurisdiction. This presumption is overcome only in exceptional instances.

U.S. anti-discrimination employment laws clearly protect U.S. citizens working for U.S. employers, no matter where the workplace is located. The Civil Rights Act, the ADA, and the ADEA now have been amended to include protection for U.S. employees working overseas for U.S. firms. Thus Title VII, the ADA, and the ADEA currently are coextensive in their extraterritorial effect. These Acts accordingly have a very broad extraterritorial reach, encompassing not only U.S. firms doing business in the U.S. and overseas, but also U.S. controlled firms. A crucial issue, therefore, for a foreign firm to ascertain is whether it is sufficiently controlled by a U.S. firm. Yet it is essential to emphasize that the courts consistently have held that only U.S. citizens are protected; and thus only a U.S. citizen may properly institute a discrimination lawsuit under Title VII of the Civil Rights Act and the ADEA based on employment decisions made at a foreign workplace by a U.S. employer or by a foreign employer controlled by a U.S. multi-national firm. Therefore, resident aliens and foreign nationals working overseas for U.S. companies are excluded from the protections of the Civil Rights Act as well as the the ADEA.

Legally, and most significantly, the distinct possibility exists of different global business practices and employment standards, as well as different degrees of legal protection, for U.S. employees and non-U.S. employees working for the same international business firm and in the same workplace. Failure to be cognizant of U.S. employment discrimination law, including its extra-territorial aspects, as well as the labor law of the host country, will result in increased exposure to legal liability for the multinational firm. Consequently, the manager of the multinational firm must ensure to the extent possible that the firm complies with both U.S. anti-discrimination employment law as well as the employment law of the host country.

Perspectives of Aging in Jamaica

Jamaica is one of the many islands of the Caribbean with strong historical and cultural ties to both West Africa and Great Britain. The population, almost three million, is a diverse blend of many different races with the majority being of African descent. Over the centuries, there has been a variety of marriages of both different races and cultures, inevitably resulting in a fair tolerance of diversity. However, there are issues of discrimination arising out of what has been loosely called the *"classis model"* or more formally, *"class discrimination."* This, of course, is a legacy of the Island's history of slavery and colonialism, where the slave owners and colonizers were the "haves" and the working class members were the "have-nots." During slavery, and later colonization, Jamaicans were identified not only based on skin color, but also based on wealth and status.

The advent of the information age, aided by the Worldwide Web and Cable Television, has exposed Jamaicans to various other cultures. One could assume that with the majority of Jamaicans being of African descent, as well as the British influence on their culture, Jamaicans would have very distinct ideas on social issues such as age discrimination. And, ostensibly they do, but in reality Jamaicans seem to take their cues from the outside world - the "first world." In this regard, no single culture has impacted the Jamaican people as much as that of North America. Jamaican attitudes tend to mirror American norms, beliefs, and values more as the years progress.

As has been the case in North America, there has been a trend towards age discrimination in Jamaica. While there are no specific laws governing this issue locally, and accordingly, very little public reflection on the matter, an informal review of several typical Jamaican companies reveals that persons between the ages of forty five (45) and sixty five (65) are more likely to be "downsized" or laid off, and less likely to be hired. There is also a noticeable trend towards encouraging early retirement. As a matter-of-fact, a colleague at NSU stated that, during early 2003, her brother was forced into early retirement from his long-term employment in Jamaica because he was 55 years of age and he was boldly told it was because of his age.

Over the past decade many Jamaican organizations have engaged in some form of restructuring, leading to changes in their workforce. Quite often, restructuring that involves automation or reengineering results in redundancies of supposedly "less qualified persons" and the recruitment of more *"technologically savvy"* personnel. These new recruits somehow mostly seem to fall within the ambit of the age group defined as *"Generation X"*, and more recently, *"Generation Y."*

In discussions with various local (Jamaican) managers involved in the recruitment process revealed an interesting trend (Mujtaba, Hinds, and Oskal, 2004). While most managers are willing to admit to a preference for hiring from the Generation X pool of knowledge workers, hardly any is willing to call that preference "age discrimination." When prodded for a classification of this type of behavior, managers cite other factors as their motivation. One manager indicated that he assesses recruits for *"a bias towards particular mindsets."* He indicated that it has been his experience that job seekers from the Baby Boomer Generation are more likely to suffer from *paradigm paralysis* and are less likely to be open to new perspectives, especially from younger colleagues. Accordingly, he said, he would be willing to admit to *mindset* discrimination, not age discrimination (Mujtaba et al., 2004).

Another factor cited was the knowledge level of the younger workforce compared with that of the older generation. Although the older recruits inevitably have more experience, this is not always a requirement for the job (Mujtaba et al., 2004). Recruitment Managers indicate that they would prefer to hire younger, "brighter" workers who are open-minded and trainable, than older workers who are *"set in their ways."* It is believed that the younger generations are more teachable because they pursue higher levels of academic learning, which better prepares them for experiential learning. Supposedly, they are also more in tune with and open to new technologies compared to their counterparts. Conversely, Jamaica being a third-world country with only one major university during the 1960s to 1980s, only a small percentage of the local Baby Boomers were afforded tertiary level education. Therefore, they have less appreciation of the need for continuous learning, a feature of the new "learning organization."

Managers also cited a third "honorable and justified" reason for their preference of younger workers: this being the *"economic reality of diminishing returns."* It is believed that older workers cost more to maintain and are less energetic than younger workers (Mujtaba et al., 2004). One Manager actually cited his views based on *"personal experience"* that *"a person's performance tends to peak after a number of years (roughly eight years) and after that the rule of diminishing returns sets in."* The authors consider these views expressed in support of this preference for a younger workforce to be very disturbing, especially in light of the fact that many of these views are not supported by factual research, but merely on perception. It is also disturbing that Managers do not see their behavior as being discriminatory.

Jamaica, like many other third world countries, is just beginning to view human resources management as a multi-dimensional field and, as such, many sensitive issues, including age discrimination, are not routinely addressed (Mujtaba et al., 2004). However, as a member of The International Labour Organization (ILO), and also based on Jamaican's habit of mirroring American norms, Jamaicans will no doubt become sensitized to, and take appropriate actions against, such issues as age discrimination in the workplace in the foreseeable future.

Despite the fact that age discrimination in employment is legal in Jamaica, it is practiced by employers. For example, in that nation's leading newspaper appeared an ad by a employment staffing company requesting candidates for certain business and management positions, and specifying among other requirements that the applicants "Must be between the ages of 26-40 years" (The Sunday Gleaner, 2005, p. 16). Such an ad in the U.S. would subject the employer and the recruiting company to a Civil Rights age discrimination lawsuit, at least by the candidates who met the requirements and who were over forty years of age. The ADEA specifically makes it illegal for an employer or an employment agency to print or publish any employment ad that indicates any preference, limitation, or specification based on age.

During the 1990s, "the Jamaican economy performed poorly as shown by the macroeconomic indicators" as stated by Dastoor, Roofe, and Mujtaba (2005). There were high levels of unemployment and negative, or very low, economic growth rates (Downes, 2003). The government, along with other major political leaders, agreed to the gradual liberalization of the economy and to implement a system similar to that in the US. Problems during this period led the Jamaican government to use economic liberalization to try to achieve low inflation, but the huge debt burden caused the exchange rate to depreciate and interest rate to continue to rise. This resulted in increased imports and decreased exports (Dastoor, Roofe, & Mujtaba, 2005).

Jamaica's pursuit of the policy of neoliberalism in the 1980s under Prime Minister Edward Seaga followed a period of democratic socialism that left a battered economy (Dastoor, Roofe & Mujtaba, 2005). Dastoor, Roofe, and Mujtaba (2005) stated that "This policy called for a coalition between the state and the private sector. This was successful in some sectors but the general picture of the Jamaican economy still looked grim" (Henke, 1999). Liberalization is a move in which the state opens up a predominantly free economy and relinquishes control over key industries. This U.S. style economy was adopted to encourage prosperity through a low inflation model, following the continued deterioration of the economy and the inability of the government to stabilize the economy (Dastoor, Roofe & Mujtaba, 2005). There is no current consensus on the extent to which Jamaicans and Americans are the same or different in terms of cultural value orientation. Some research indicates there are no differences (Cavico & Mujtaba, 2004) while others, for example Hofstede (2001), report there are differences. According to Cavico and Mujtaba Jamaican students tend to be very competitive and often attempt to earn the highest score within their teams and classes. This is, perhaps, partly a consequence of the rigid British orientation. Cavico and Mujtaba report that Jamaicans are similar to Americans in terms of Machiavellian thinking. Machiavelli's name is often used in business and leadership literature to symbolize a sinister "real-world," "moral jungle" view. Cavico and Mujtaba's results, based on Jamaican and American students' Mach V Attitude Inventory scores, showed that there is no difference between the two groups (t=0.0929, p=0.9264). Even though the students were raised in two different cultures (countries), there are no significant differences between Jamaicans and Americans (Mujtaba & Hinds, 2004). It appears that both the Jamaican and American cultures encourage similar attitudes with regard to management styles and strategies in the corporate environment to get ahead and secure resources for one's personal or professional objectives. A large percentage of men (approximately 54%) were "high Machs" compared to only 28% of women who scored high in this study. Therefore, Cavico and Mujtaba's research indicates that Jamaicans and Americans have similar views and attitudes toward the Machiavellian style of management (Dastoor, Roofe & Mujtaba, 2005; Mujtaba, Hinds & Oskal, 2004).

With respect to national culture, Hofstede (1980) initially identified four cultural dimensions to explain work-related cultural differences among societies. Later Hofstede (1993) added another dimension to individualism, masculinity, power distance and uncertainty avoidance, when he put forward the long-term/short-term orientation dimension. *Collectivism* (COLL) characterizes a culture in which people from birth onwards are integrated into strong, cohesive in-groups that, throughout their life, protect them in exchange for unquestioning loyalty (Hofstede, 2001). Collectivist cultures value group loyalty over efficiency.

Individualism (IND) denotes a cultural value that stands for a society in which the ties between individuals are loose, and "everyone is expected to look after himself or herself and his or her immediate family (Hofstede, 1997, p. 51). Dastoor et al's (2005) research followed Hofstede in viewing collectivism and individualism as end points of a single dimension. The average world score on IND is 43 and US has the highest score (99). Jamaica's lower than average score shows that the members of the society are far more concerned about the welfare of the other members of the society than are those in the US culture ((Dastoor, Roofe & Mujtaba, 2005).

Femininity (sex roles) describes a society in which social gender roles overlap (Dastoor, Roofe & Mujtaba, 2005). Both men and women are supposed to be modest and concerned with the quality of life (Hofstede, 2001). There is no strict distinction between the work roles of men and women. *Masculinity* (MAS) describes a society in which gender roles are clearly distinct: Men must be assertive, tough and focused on material success; women are supposed to be modest, tender and concerned with the quality of life (Hofstede). Masculinity versus femininity differentiates countries that value economic growth and the acquisition of material goods over social and sometimes family relationships (Dastoor *et al*, 2005).

Paternalism (PAT) describes managers who take a personal interest in the private lives of workers (Dorfman & Howell, 1988) and who assume the role of parents because they consider it an obligation to support and protect their subordinates (Redding, Norman & Schlander, 1994). A Western perspective of PAT appears in Dworkin's (2002) description: the interference by an individual or a state in one's life justified by a claim that the person will be better off or protected from harm (Dastoor *et al*, 2005).

Power Distance (PD) denotes "the extent to which the less powerful members of institutions and organizations within a country expect and accept that power is distributed unequally" (Hofstede, 1997, p. 28). When PD is high, hierarchical differences are respected and organizations are highly centralized. Where it is relatively low, decentralization is popular and subordinates expect to be consulted. Hofstede calculated the world average score for PD as 55. The score for both the US and Jamaica (40) is lower than the world average and indicates that there is moderate equality between the various levels within the society including families and government. This, Hofstede (2003) states, makes for a more stable cultural environment (Dastoor *et al*, 2005).

Uncertainty Avoidance (UA) is "the extent to which members of a culture feel threatened by uncertain or unknown situations" (Hofstede 1990, p. 113). Low UA describes a culture that is tolerant of ambiguity and futures unknowns. High UA fosters career stability, formal rules and long job tenure and views innovation and change as potentially dangerous. The U.S. score of 46 is below the world average of 64; Jamaica's very low UA score points to a society that is open to taking risks and willing to undertake changes and innovations. This may relate to long periods of political and economic instability in Jamaica. The higher US score indicates less tolerance of risk and shows a preference for more defined set of rules and regulation governing its citizens (Dastoor *et al*, 2005).

Soeters and Recht (2001) posit that education prepares people for future roles in society and serves to create commitment to the implementation of societal values. The American classroom is multinational, and one role of teaching in this atmosphere is to bridge differences in values and reduce prejudices and stereotypes (Hambrick, Davidson, Snell & Snow 1998). Although Hofstede (1993) stated that one's basic value orientation is not easy to change, there is no evidence that after a prolonged exposure to the American culture, the value system of the Jamaican student would not be affected.

Examining the value orientation of Jamaicans and assessing their willingness to adapt to the American culture, is a way to test divergence, convergence, and crossvergence theories. Convergence speaks to the merging of different cultures by such factors as technology, globalization, economic growth and industrialization (Connor et al., 1993). Divergence, on the other hand, is a state in which there is a marked strength exhibited by individual cultures despite globalization. Crossvergence occurs as cultures are exposed to each other and new cultural characteristics are formed that are distinct from other cultures (Holt, Ralston & Terpstra 1994). Some research supports the three.

Dastoor *et al's* (2005) empirical study compared value orientation for adult learners of two nationalities (Jamaican and US) and also Jamaican students in the US. Results indicated that there was only one significant difference among 10 possibilities: Uncertainty avoidance (UA). Jamaican students in the United States (U.S.) were higher on UA than U.S. students. Dastoor *et al*, further concluded that the theory of divergence can explain the finding that Jamaican students in Jamaica and in the U.S. are significantly different on Uncertainty Avoidance (UA) than United States (U.S.) students because Jamaican students in the US maintain their distinctiveness (on UA) despite their interaction with the US culture. The findings of no differences on the other four dimensions lends support to Convergence theory which proposes that different cultures become similar due to the influence of globalization and other processes that bring cultures into close contact with others.

Over the last five centuries, there has been some convergence and crossvergence within the U.S. As immigrants come to the U.S. from a greater diversity of cultures than previously (for example, more Afghan and Turkish immigrants), and as globalization and the internet continue to bring more nations together to interact in the marketplace, we may expect to see more changes (Dastoor *et al*, 2005). Awareness of possible societal transformations can assist workers, managers and leaders to empower themselves and others to contribute the demands and challenges of globalization in the twenty first century work environment.

In earlier years many older workers seemed to have been less aware of the increasing trend towards the recruitment of a younger work force by some Jamaican companies. Many were in denial and some assumed that those from their age group who were being "sent home" prematurely were either poor performers or, were having difficulty adapting to changes. As these Baby Boomers become more aware of their vulnerability to a similar fate, based mainly on their age, many have become more thoughtful of this phenomenon and some are very outspoken on the issue. One bank manager who believes he can see his early departure from his lifetime career looming just around the proverbial corner (in this case the corner may be a matter of months at worst or one to two years at best) was quite passionate in expressing his views on the issue. In a discussion about the issue he said, "I believe that organizations that are embracing this trend are making a big mistake. Take for example the West Indies Cricket Team; they are currently suffering from a lack of experience on the team (Personal communication with Rosemarie Edwards, August 2005). The managers and selectors threw out all the experience without any clear vision for succession planning or continuity through knowledge management. Of course, the fresh ideas and energies that the younger workforce brings to the table are good for growth and innovation. However, companies need to employ a blended approach in order to maintain balance, as a failure to manage the transition from one generation to the next will result in failure for the organization." He also noted that while North America, which had been among the trendsetters in this age discrimination phenomenon has changed its approach, Jamaican Companies continue the practice.

Another manager in the same organization had even more thought provoking views on the issue. He believes that many of the aging workforce members do not even realize that they are "aging" because they still feel so relevant, energetic, and enthusiastic. They know they have much to offer and so they often do not realize that management feels otherwise. This older Generation Xer feels that the plight of the Baby Boomers will soon be impacting his own generation and this he believes, is creating an unsustainable trend. He suggests that organizations should make themselves aware of those aging workers that have retooled and seek to leverage *their* fresh ideas and invaluable experience. Younger workers often have very innovative ideas but they lack the benefit of past experiences and the wisdom of age. This can lead to costly mistakes for the organization. "As a matter of fact", he said, "organizations will eventually realize that this practice is costing them more than just good experience, it will eventually impact the bottom line negatively". He posits the view that having a larger workforce of younger employees, especially at higher levels where labor is more costly, is not financially prudent. "Younger persons," he explains, "require more time off during their child bearing years (Jamaican women are entitled to three months paid maternity leave for up to three children); demand more expensive benefits, such as housing subsidies and educational assistance; and, are more likely to move on to another organization, which will increase recruitment and training costs."

The other major factor cited by the persons interviewed is the psychological impact of being delineated by age. Often such persons respond to this phenomenon as a type of prejudice that alienates them from their younger counterparts. There is a perception of superiority assumed by the younger recruits who feel that they are replacing others by virtue of the ineptitude of those being replaced. This breeds disrespect towards the older workers still on the job and negatively impacts morale and team spirit. As a result, older workers sometimes become unwilling to share their wisdom and experience and younger workers form cliques. The younger workers also develop a mentality of wanting to amass as much as they can in the shortest possible time because they are mindful that the same fate may one day reach them. This sometimes results in the worst kind of individualistic and Machiavellian behaviors.

Dorothy Leonard, co-author of *Deep Smarts: How to Cultivate and Transfer Enduring Business Wisdom* had this to say in a recent article: "...people with deep smarts can be indispensable. Why? Because their particular brand of expertise is based on long, hard-won experience." Leonard further stated that, "... deep smarts are experienced based and often context specific, they can't be produced overnight or readily imported into an organization". The focus of this and other literature on the value of experience has been impacting new approaches to the retention of a more experienced workforce. Even so, many organizations are slow to adapt to changes in their environment and so, many are still practicing age discrimination; some without even realizing that they are doing it.

Perspectives of Aging in Turkey

Turkey is a Middle Eastern country with a population of about 70 million people. About 90% of the total population consists of moderate Muslims, mostly struggling to become economically stable society with the morals that comes from a religious, but still laicized background. It has been a secular country since 1923, in which the founder of Turkish republic called Ataturk established the democratic and secular Turkey. About half of the population is in the range of 20-40 years of age. As such, Turkey may be the one of the largest countries that has a high percentage of young population in the Middle East, maybe in Europe as well. Nevertheless, the government has not devised a feasible long-term strategy to benefit from this generation or fact. There are two kinds of corporations and businesses in Turkey: private companies that belong to the individuals and families; and government-owned and government-managed companies.

The difference in performances of those two sectors is quite remarkable. Because of the fact that the private sector is purely profit-oriented, the private sector tends to be more open to new ideas from the young/dynamic employees. Eventually, this openness to new ideas and innovation makes the private sector more competitive and up-to-date. The reason for the Turkish government to be involved with business life was mainly because of the fact that when Turkish Republic was established almost 80 years ago, after the collapse of the biggest empire in the history called the Ottoman Empire, almost none of the Turkish people and Turkish families were financially able to invest or establish any corporation. That is why the new government of the new-born Turkish Republic decided to be the frontier of a new industry for almost 80 years ago. Ataturk's original idea was to establish corporations that are necessary for survival in the industries that play an important role in country's future; then, to sell them out to the interested individuals and families that want to run them. Since then, it has been a continuous project for the government to leave the management of government-owned incorporations to the private sector. Presently, the Turkish government mainly runs the corporations that deal with water management, power plants management, heavy metal industry (steel, etc.), and so on. The challenge for an older employee in the private sector is more difficult than that of the government-owned ones'. Moreover, the perception on the private sector is that the government-owned companies suffer from the lack of dynamism and innovation.

The common view of the Turkish culture is that the older a person is, the more maturely he or she will react to crisis, not only in the businesses, but also in one's personal life. Moreover, there are plenty of common sayings that emphasize the importance of being older and experienced. For example; one's words do not count, unless one is able to grow facial hair (the sign of getting old).

In comparison to the Western countries, despite the fact that the percentage of young generation is higher in Turkey, the average ages of employees in the corporations tend to range close to 40's. In other words, they are still remarkably higher in Turkey than that of other countries in Europe, and the young generation still suffers from not being able to find enough opportunities to start their professional business life.

In terms of job security, Turkey is a country in which mostly the experience of an employee that comes with age is superior to the advantage of youth. The common perception is that, unless the company is going bankrupt or one commits a shameful crime, most companies tend to keep the employees until they retire. In government-owned sector, one has the opportunity to continue working even after the retirement age. On the negative side, so much security for an employee sometimes causes lack of motivation for productivity and a decrease in performance that usually lead to loss of profit.

In Turkey, almost all of government-owned companies suffer from the fact that there are too many employees working for a few available positions. This eventually affects the overall performance, and causes Turkish government plenty of problems like the millions of dollars in deficit. In addition, most of the young generation, who are getting ready to start building their professional careers, end up losing hope in finding a decent position to start with, after spending remarkable amount of time searching for a job. Because of the security of the existing jobs for current employees, mostly the older employees, the younger ones do not tend to have enough opportunity to prove themselves as young and dynamic members of the workforce. Even if they do get an opportunity to start working, they usually find themselves in the middle of conflicts or disputes with older and more experienced employees in order to apply their "young" and fresh ideas to their organizations. This fact is also considered to be one of the reasons for the migration of young Turkish workforce to other countries such as the United States, Canada, Australia, and Europe where the youth seem to be more appreciated. Research conducted by different universities in Turkey, such as the Middle Eastern Technical University, shows that the young workforce want to explore the possibilities in other countries that prefer employing young individuals.

As implied above, sometimes a country's cultural preferences and conditioning for older workers can cause difficulty for the younger generation. The young generation in Turkey is trying to find alternative solutions to the existing challenge (age discrimination toward younger employees) so they can become a dominant force into the business world and in the government sector. Unfortunately, because of the fact that brining a lawsuit is almost impossible against the Turkish government and its integrated system in professional business life, the young generation continues exploring possible solutions to be able to step into the professional business life by traveling to other countries. Turkey is now seeking to join the European Community and when and if Turkey becomes a member, it will have to adjust its laws accordingly.

European Community

The European Community's Social Charter sets forth twelve fundamental employment law rights, to wit: free movement, fair pay, improved working conditions, social protection, collective bargaining, vocational training, worker consultation and participation in management, health and safety protection in the workplace, protection of children and adolescents, protection of the aged, and protection of those with disabilities (Dowling, 1996). However, as noted by one legal commentator: "The Social Charter and the social documents it spawned are virtually silent on the employment doctrine which worries U.S. most: anti-discrimination law. With the conspicuous exception of sex discrimination, the European social agenda omits anti-discrimination protections for racial minorities, religions, and, notwithstanding the Charter rights protection for the aged and handicapped, these groups as well" (Dowling, 1996, p. 77.). The European Union, however, has issued a Directive to its members, called the Equal Treatment in Employment Directive, which seeks to address age discrimination in employment; but one commentator has criticized the Directive as a "minimalist approach" and "defective" because it only covers access to employment and does not cover training, education, and health care issues (Sargeant, 2004). Yet another commentator related that instead of proposing a ban on age discrimination, certain European Community legislators have proposed that employees should possess a presumptive right to be free of age discrimination, but also that employees should be afforded the freedom contractually to relinquish voluntarily that right (Sunstein, 2002).

Perspectives of Aging in Afghanistan

The word "*Afghan*" represents all people born in Afghanistan, descendants of Afghans, and those who were official citizens of the country, as agreed upon by the ten-day deliberation of *Loya Jirgah*, the General Assembly, in the 1964 constitution. Symbolically, the term Afghan stands for love, courage, devotion, dignity, commitment, loyalty, and the desire to make sacrifices for one's country and people. It further symbolizes loyalty to local norms, patriotism, and dedication to the Afghan customs. Afghans are known to be people of honor, great hospitality, and are committed to being masters of their own destiny. Many Afghans are also known for their stubbornness and loyalty to the traditional norms of behaviors transferred on from one generation to the next via actions, words and cultural infrastructures. Such stubbornness and royalty, beneficial or costly to one's well-being, comes from centuries, generational, and many years of being conditioned to the local values of the Afghan culture.

Afghanistan is about the size of the state of Texas in United States, and with an approximate population of 28,000,000 people. There are people of different ethnic backgrounds in Afghanistan and some of the common ethnic are Pushtuns, Tajiks, Baluchis, Nuristanis, Uzbeks, Khirghiz, Hazaras, and Turkmans. Pushtuns and Tajiks make up the largest groups of Afghans and majority of the rules have been set by them or their ancestors which may amount to unearned privileges for those who of these majority backgrounds. There are more than twenty different languages being spoken in Afghanistan, with the main ones being Persian (Dari or Farsi) spoken by at least 60% of Afghans and Pushtu spoken by about 38% of Afghans. Afghanistan also has about 2.5 million Kuchis (nomads) who travel, sometimes thousands of miles, to different parts of the country as the seasons change. Historically, the nomads used to bring and pass information from one place to another; however, with the advent of technology their information transfer role has diminished. The dominant religion is Islam, practiced by about 99% of the population, with the other one percent making up the minority religions such as Hinduism, Christianity, and Judaism. As such, over many centuries, Afghans have integrated Islam into their way of life both at home and in the workplace. Spiritual beliefs have also been integrated into their politics, thereby leading to strong nationalism. As a matter-of-fact, Afghanistan's flag has three distinct colors of black, red, and green. *Black* color represents the occupation of foreigners, the *Red* portion represents the blood of freedom fighters, and the *Green* part represents freedom and Islam. Therefore, their perceptions of age and aging are heavily influenced by their spiritual beliefs and nationalistic ideals which are passed on from the older generation to the younger ones in the community.

While age discrimination toward older workers currently does not seem to be a huge challenge in Afghanistan as they can use all the work experience that they can get, Afghans have their share of other ethnic and war animosities which they must overcome. Those who are familiar with the Afghan history know group conflict has existed in Afghanistan for many centuries, and the ethnic animosities are deep rooted.

An Afghan-American physician and author, name Khaled Hosseini, recently published his best selling novel entitled "*The Kite Runner*" in 2003, which explains some of the cultural challenges facing Afghans. According to a book reviewer named Mir Hekmatullah Sadat (2004), *The Kite Runner* presents a glimpse of sociopolitical climate in Afghanistan and the Afghan community in California. The book offers a fictional portrait of events challenged by tribalism and religious conservatism and aggravated by foreign interferences but overcome through the humanism and bravery. Sadat states that first Khaled Hosseini "engages in nostalgic childhood recreation of a lost Afghanistan during the last days of the monarchy of Zahir Shah and the regime that overthrew him. Second, the book explores emigration during the Soviet occupation of Afghanistan and the tragedies thereafter, along with the challenges facing the expatriate Afghan community. Third, the book explores the Taliban's ruling of Afghanistan. Throughout the book, Hosseini confronts many prejudgments indoctrinated in some Afghans groups and families. As a microcosm of Afghan society, he tells the fictional tale of people growing up under the same roof but treated tremendously differently. The novel is about two friends who symbolize opposite ends of a sociopolitical hierarchy. Amir is Pashtun, Sunni, wealthy, and literate; whereas his servant's son, Hassan, is Hazara, Shia, poor, and illiterate. They both have lost their mothers and shared the same wet nurse. Amir wishes he could trade families for a moment of compassion that Hassan receives from his father. Amir realizes that in the long run he is better off because he is Pashtun and not a Hazara in such a discriminating society. Historically, Hazaras of Afghanistan have been one of the most oppressed ethnicity groups.

Sadat (2004) explains that the Afghan history is not that simple but a complex jigsaw of interrelated equations as there has been people of many backgrounds and ethnicities in this land. Sometimes ethnic and linguistic ties outweigh every other variable, and then at other times regional ties prove to be stronger than ethnic ties. Hosseini's novel and writing "slices through skin and flesh to expose the socio-political and economic skeleton, which has beleaguered a nation-state formation in Afghanistan" (Sadat, 2004). So, *The Kite Runner* is a good reading for understanding some of the cultural complexities plaguing the Afghan community as the Afghan people attempt to secure and rebuild a functioning government and legal system.

Summary

This chapter has provided a brief background on some of the legal and cultural expectations surrounding employment practices in the United States, which has the most complex and detailed legal system. Besides providing a brief country background, the chapter also presented the cultural norms and expectations of individuals in Jamaica, Turkey, and Afghanistan. There are both extensive as well as explicit policies and rules regarding employment practices related to older workers and aging in the United States of America. However, there seems to be very little legal policies regarding older workers and aging in the countries of Jamaica, Turkey and Afghanistan where cultural practices are guiding many employment decisions in the workplace and also, surprisingly, in the European Community.

CHAPTER 4

ETHICAL ANALYSIS OF AGE DISCRIMINATION

*I*n addition to ascertaining the legal aspects of doing business internationally, the moral implications of doing business must be examined. Since most international business decisions have both legal and moral implications, the prudent manager of a multinational firm must be sensitive to the ethical implications of decision-making, and be prepared to confront ethics in a philosophical as well as practical sense. Foreign business people must be aware of U.S. moral norms, particularly as they apply to employment. Moreover, U.S. business people must be able to address the differences between U.S. employment moral standards and the standards of the host country where one's firm is doing business.

The legal "answer" to this issue is clear, at least initially, to the U.S. business person. That is, when the business activity of the firm takes place within the host country, the U.S. multinational firm need only comply with the legal precepts of the host county; if any exists, presuming, of course, there is no extraterritorial application of the U.S. multinational firm's home country law. The ethical "answer" to this question is much more perplexing, indeed. What if the host country has standards that are different, and arguably "lower," than those of the United States? How should the ethical U.S. multinational firm proceed? One, perhaps too simple, ethical solution is for the U.S. firm merely to comply with the moral standards of the host country. Yet what if compliance with these standards results in harm to the host country's society or to the firm's own employees?

Ethical Relativism

The multinational business enterprise clearly will be confronted with different ethical beliefs and moral standards in the various countries and societies in which it does business. Moreover, there may be a conflict between the moral norms of the U.S. compared to the moral norms of the home or host country. How should the multinational firm proceed? Should it merely adopt the conventional moral practices of the host country? That is, "When in Rome, do as the Romans"? Or rather should the firm apply the, perhaps "higher," moral standards of the U.S. to its operations in the host country? The existence of different, societal-based, ethical beliefs and moral standards perforce evokes the ethical theory of ethical relativism.

Basic Tenets

Are there objective, universal, moral rules, upon which one can construct an absolute moral system? Are there moral rules applicable to all peoples, in all societies, and at all times? An ethical relativist firmly denies the existence of any universal truth in morality. There are no universal standards by which to judge an action's morality; morality is merely relative to, and only holds for, a particular society at a particular time. Morality is a societal-based phenomenon. Morality is nothing more than the morality of a certain group, people, or society at a certain time. What a society believes is right is in fact right for that society. The moral beliefs of a society determine what is right within that society; if the prevailing moral view says an action is "right," the action is right. Society consequently is the source of all morality (Cavico & Mujtaba, 2005).

In China, for example, reverence and respect for the aged have long been enshrined as moral norms. As a matter of fact, the Chinese moral precept of filial piety recently has been "translated" into a Chinese legal precept. The newspaper, *The Herald*, of Miami, Florida, reported that there is now a law in China that requires Chinese people to provide for the care and well-being of their elderly parents, including, the paper noted, "comforting them and catering to their special needs" (Johnson, 2005, p. 17a). Respect for a person's family elders, especially one's parents, is ingrained in the Chinese tradition, culture, ethics, and values; and now this societal norm has been promulgated as an enforceable law. It is interesting to note that the Chinese law, called "Protecting the Rights and Interests of the Elderly," maintains that support for the elderly "shall be provided for mainly by their families," thereby shifting responsibility away from the government. The *Herald* also noted that the law requires spouses to "assist in meeting the obligation" for their in-laws. The law does not state the level of assistance grown children must give to their parents; but the law does allow parents to sue their children in court for a lack of support. Yet, the *Herald* also quoted a Chinese lawyer, who stated that such lawsuits "never happen"; rather, the situation usually is reconciled, thereby underscoring other important Chinese societal norms – avoidance of conflict and "loss of face," as well as cooperation, mediation, compromise, and peaceful resolution.

Different societies, of course, have different conceptions of right and wrong. What one society thinks is right, another society may conceive as wrong. The same act, in fact, may be morally right for one society and morally wrong for another. Since according to ethical relativism there are no moral standards that are universally true for all peoples, in all societies, and at all times, and since there is no way of objectively showing that one set of beliefs is to be preferred, the only way to determine an action's morality is to ascertain what the people in a particular society believe is morally right or wrong (Cavico and Mujtaba, 2005). So, if a society believes that discrimination in employment based on religion, national origin, or gender is morally appropriate, or even required, then such discrimination *is* moral, at least for that society. Of course, the following countries are part of this society analysis, and thus, as the research results for this book will show, have their own distinct cultural perspectives and policies:

◊   Afghanistan – Age Discrimination Moral Norms

◊   Turkey – Age Discrimination Moral Norms
◊   United States – Age Discrimination Moral Norms
◊   Jamaica – Age Discrimination Moral Norms

Effect on Business People

Because different societies have different customs and beliefs, the relativism of morality is an important issue that the manager of a multinational business firm inevitably will encounter. Many employment issues, such as discrimination and sexual harassment, raise significant trans-societal and cultural concerns. U.S. and foreign opinions as to the morality of these practices might differ sharply, for example, as to what constitutes sexual harassment. An ethical relativist simply would advise the business manager who operates in different countries, and who thus confronts societies with different moral beliefs, simply to follow the moral standards prevalent in whatever society he or she finds himself or herself. Following the host country's morality is certainly a convenient approach to take; yet the doctrine of ethical relativism probably has persuaded more people, particularly business people, to be skeptical about ethics than any other line of thought.

Justification

There is some rational justification for respecting some set of conventional moral beliefs. Some moral prescriptions are necessary in the area of social as well as employment relationships; and people are, and should be, inclined to respect those prescriptions which have in fact survived and which have a history of respect. It is, moreover, well and proper to know something of the customs of other peoples, so as to more rationally judge one's own customs and to avoid thinking that everything contrary to one's own beliefs and conventions is wrong. Ethical relativism can appeal to tolerance of every kind of society; it militates against being "judgmental" toward other groups of persons. It also is advantageous, for eminently practical reasons, for the manager of a multinational firm to be cognizant of the culture and mores of the societies where the firm conducts its business operations.

Problems with Ethical Relativism

Defining "society." A fully realized and individualized society is at best a rare phenomenon. Even within relatively simple societies there are diverse cultures, subcultures, social classes, and kinship and work groups. These fragments constantly confront one another and interact; and in so doing exchange and modify conventions and beliefs. A united and distinct group, which one reasonably could term a society, might even tolerate a great diversity of practices and beliefs. Regardless of how small and socially homogeneous the group, there still will be some divergence in moral opinion. In large, complex, heterogeneous, social systems, the "society" will contain a myriad of smaller "sub-societies" that co-exist, yet that reflect different standards and attitudes. Definite moral beliefs also can be ascribed to many of these "sub-societies." An individual, moreover, can simultaneously belong to distinct sub-societies, cultures, and groups, all with different moral norms and beliefs (Cavico and Mujtaba, 2005).

Regarding the societal view of age in the U.S., the Supreme Court of the United States in an age discrimination lawsuit related that "one commonplace conception of American society in recent decades is its character as a 'youth culture,' and in a world where younger is better, talk about discrimination because of age is naturally understood to refer to discrimination against the older" (*General Dynamics Land Systems, Inc. v. Cline*, 2004).

In a heterogeneous world, filled with heterogeneous societies, the presence of so much diversity offers a serious challenge to the ethical relativist. What constitutes a society for the purposes of ethical relativism? What are the boundaries of a society; how does one determine where one society ends and another begins; whose beliefs and practices form the core of values for the society; and what exactly are these beliefs and practices? Particularly in an age of multinational business firms and the increasing "globalization" of economic activity, the doctrine of ethical relativism raises many serious questions. In the context of employment discrimination overseas, for example, certainly a U.S. firm and its personnel, due to a very strong U.S. societal belief in individual human rights in employment and otherwise, will have difficulty in doing business in a society that straightforwardly upholds discrimination as the moral norm against women, older people, and minority groups in employment.

Comparative moral judgments. One obvious drawback to ethical relativism is that no comparative moral judgments are possible. Since there are no external, universal, objective, moral standards, there is no impartial way of evaluating and deciding among different practices and beliefs. One cannot say that any practice or belief is better or worse from a moral perspective than any other. No matter how seemingly reprehensible or praiseworthy a society's practices and beliefs, nothing correctly can be adjudged wrong or right because comparative judgments require absolute moral standards, which the ethical relativist denies (Cavico and Mujtaba, 2005). There may be some absolute "moralists" who argue that U.S. law, especially anti-discrimination law, should be even more extensively and forcefully applied abroad. Yet some foreign societies, particularly those dominated by a particular religion, may be offended morally by such U.S "cultural imperialism"; and thus may reject U.S. criticism of their practices, and may resent any attempt to expand U.S. influence overseas. The attempt to "export" U.S. moral norms may result in international and political difficulties for U.S. firms as well as the U.S. itself. An ethical relativist, of course, would neither condemn nor praise any employment practice, but merely adopt to the relevant society's moral norms.

Societal agreement. The norms in one society very well may differ from the norms in effect in another society. What is right and what is wrong will not always be the same in different societies; but under ethical relativism, what is right for a society is right for that society. As a consequence of taking this ethical relativistic perspective, two bizarre and contradictory results ensue: agreement on morals is, in principle, impossible; and no societal disagreements are possible (Cavico and Mujtaba, 2005). Since each society has its own true "right" view, no two societies, in principle, can disagree as to the morality of an action, such as discrimination in employment.

Criticizing a society. If one is an ethical relativist, it makes no sense, and it would in fact be wrong, to criticize the practice and beliefs of other societies, as long as they adhere to their own standards. One can no longer say that the customs or beliefs of other societies are morally inferior to one's own. One's own society has no special status, it is merely one among many.

There is certainly no place for moral reformers. One must cease condemnation of other different societies, regardless of how "atrocious" their practices are. It would be arrogant to evaluate the practices of a society and attempt to persuade the other society to change its view. Rather, one should adopt an attitude of tolerance. All one can, and should, do is report what a society believes about an action, and conform accordingly (Cavico and Mujtaba, 2005). Thus, if discrimination in employment based on race, religion, gender, or national origin is morally acceptable in the host country, then all the ethically relativistic firm has to do is conform to the prevailing discriminatory norms in its employment practices.

If one accepts ethical relativism, it is also wrong, and makes no sense, to criticize the practices and beliefs of one's own society. If right or wrong is relative to a society, it must be relative to one's own society too. Consequently, one's own established standards are correct and any attempt to reform them must be taken as "mistaken". Since right or wrong is determined by the standards of a society, one cannot propose changes for the "better" because there is no way to judge the reforms as better (Cavico and Mujtaba, 2005). Thus, the U.S. firm wanting to impose the presumably "higher" moral standards of its home country to its employment practices overseas might be accused of being overly righteous and perhaps even condemned as a "cultural imperialist".

Yet people do recognize that moral standards of their own society, as well as other societies, are wrong; and this judgment implies that the moral standards that a society accepts are not the exclusive criteria of right and wrong. (Cavico and Mujtaba, 2005). The idea, for example, that the practice of slavery cannot be evaluated ethically across societies, cultures, and times by a common moral standard appears not only mistaken but also quite ridiculous. Similarly, the idea that because certain discriminatory employment practices are morally accepted in certain societies does not make them immune to "higher" and more absolute ethical judgment.

Illogical approach. Common sense informs one that conventions and beliefs do differ among societies, cultures, groups, and times. Yet, the culturally relativistic fact that societies have different beliefs, including moral beliefs, does not logically mean that all societal-based moral beliefs are equally acceptable and right (Cavico and Mujtaba, 2005). The ethical relativist's approach is a flawed one. He or she argues from the fact of societal diversity to a conclusion about the lack of any universal, objective, and true morality. The approach is not logically sound because the conclusion does not follow from the premise. Even if the premise is true, the conclusion may be false. To say that morality derives from societal norms and beliefs is not to say that whatever is customary is right and true. One cannot infer logically from the fact of societal diversity that there is no way, and can never be any way, to establish one view as absolutely correct. One should not be tempted to conclude from the fact of diversity that there are not any true moral standards to resolve differences in beliefs. When two societies have different moral beliefs, for example, regarding discrimination in employment, all that logically should follow is that one of them probably is wrong.

Universal moral standards. The fact that there are differences in moral positions among societies does not mean that there are no universal moral standards and rules. There are reasons to think that all societies actually do share the same basic moral norms. The underlying similarities of human beings the world over, the actual, well-established, normal habits of people, revealed in their conduct and language, and the similar conditions necessary for survival and advancement, are all evidence of common human needs, dispositions, and aspirations. Human beings share a belief in fundamental human rights that apply to all people, in all places, and at all times. People, moreover, speak out whenever and wherever universal human rights are denied or violated (Cavico and Mujtaba, 2005).

There are moral standards that clearly are universal and that have been, and are, esteemed by the peoples of every society. There is agreement, commonalty, and invariability concerning a core of moral rules that forms a part of the ethical system of all societies. Standards, for example, which treat murder, stealing, lying, treachery, cruelty, uncontrolled aggressiveness, discrimination, self-indulgence, selfishness, and laziness as immoral vices are universally held. Standards that treat equality, fairness, honesty, integrity, promise-keeping, faithfulness, loyalty, kindness, self-control, and industry as moral virtues are accepted by all societies. These standards are constant and universal and do not depend on societal variation (Cavico and Mujtaba, p. 2005). It makes no sense to say that a rule against causing unnecessary suffering, or a rule respecting property rights, or a rule against discrimination in employment, may be held for one group of people and not for another. These universal norms recognize that people are social beings, that cooperation is necessary for survival, and that people need moral rules and prohibitions to lead a common life.

These moral norms are the minimally necessary pre-conditions for any society to exist at all. There are certain basic moral rules that must be followed in each society if a society is to survive and its members are to interact with each other effectively. Norms, for example, against killing or injuring the members of the society, taking their property, and using language untruthfully when communicating with them, form part of this moral minimum. If these norms are not complied with, if there is not some protection for persons, property, representations, and promises, then the social system will not survive and there will not be any society at all. One cannot avoid these minimal moral obligations, not to murder, steal, and lie, without removing oneself from society altogether (Cavico and Mujtaba, p. 2005). The same arguments can be asserted to support a universal moral norm against discrimination in employment.

Societal moral norms, despite surface differences, do tend to converge on a common core; and thus may not be so diverse as the ethical relativists contend. One accordingly can recognize "different" moralities as being one universal morality through their common, invariable, and constant core.

Factual v. moral disagreement. Are moral disagreements among societies really disagreements about facts? That is, are disagreements based not on differing moral beliefs, but on nothing more than the attempt to apply universally recognized moral rules to specific factual situations? The apparent diversity of beliefs among societies may be only apparent. Societies do agree on certain fundamental moral standards. Different views on specific moral issues may not reflect deep differences in fundamental moral beliefs, but instead are reflections of differing factual circumstances and different experiences among people (Cavico and Mujtaba, 2005). One commentator accordingly has suggested that "tackling age discrimination is not just about removing measures that treat one age group less favorably than another. Not all differences between the young and the old are as a result of age. There is, for example, the idea of 'cohort phenomena....' These are the result of different experiences of people born at different times. Older people may, for example, have grown up in a very different cultural and educational system than young people and may have been taught how to learn in a different way. Failing to appreciate this may place older people at a disadvantage in training, as the approach used now will be the one which young people are more accustomed to. Perhaps, therefore, in order to remove any discriminatory treatment of older people in training there is a need to consider culturally appropriate techniques" (Sargeant, 2004).

Universal moral rules v. universal practice. Although people from different societies actually may not agree on all moral norms, this automatically does not mean that there are not ultimate, fundamental, moral norms which everyone ought to believe. Fundamental moral rules are universal, but they may be not universally practiced. Members of one society, for example, will agree that they should not kill, steal, lie to, and discriminate against, one another, but they may think it permissible to inflict these actions on members of other societies. Morality, therefore, is not relative; it simply is not practiced universally (Cavico and Mujtaba, 2005).

One important example of universal moral norms is the United Nation's *Universal Declaration of Human Rights*, adopted by the General Assembly of the United Nations on December 10, 1948. In the context herein of employment discrimination, the Declaration states that "everyone is entitled to certain rights and freedoms, without distinction of any kind, such as race, color, sex, language, religion, political or other opinion, national or social origin, property, birth, or other status" (United Nations,1948, Art.2).This fundamental non-discrimination principle applies to the specific rights enumerated in the Declaration. For example, Article 23 states that "everyone has a right to work, to just and favorable working conditions, to a just remuneration ensuring for himself and his family an existence worthy of human dignity." Such rights are posited by the United Nations as "Universal," though in practice they may not yet be universally adhered to. The ethical firm, therefore, may have to apply higher, and more stringent, universal ethical principles in order to be a truly moral firm with respect to its overseas employment practices.

Experience. People's own experiences contradict ethical relativism. People do make comparative moral judgments; and people do marshal ethical arguments in support of their moral criticisms. There are conflicts in societal conceptions of morality and people do make moral judgments (Cavico and Mujtaba, 2005). The global business context, a practice in one's home country, such as employment discrimination based on race, national origin, religion, or gender, very well could be deemed an immoral practice, yet that very same practice could be construed as quite proper in the host country. How does the global business firm contend with such a conflict in societal moral norms? The answer is not to retreat to the too simple and easy confines of ethical relativism. Rather, trans-societal and trans-national moral judgments can be, are, and should be made. If ethical relativism is true, such judgments, criticism, and arguments are doomed to failure. Moral reformers, moreover, certainly would have no place in an ethically relativistic universe. For a U.S. multinational firm, for example, it would be problematic, to say the least, to engage in employment practices such as discrimination based on race, religion, gender, or national origin, because the vast majority of U.S. citizens, including the firm's own employees, would find such practices morally odious, and would vociferously condemn them as such. In the new global marketplace, moreover, the standards for appropriate conduct, both legally and morally, have been evolving so rapidly and extensively that they have blurred the concepts of nationality, society, and citizenship, which historically have been determined by applicable national law and distinct societal moral norms.

The fact that moral judgments are made, however, does not imply that there is a single and complete ethical theory to answer satisfactorily all moral issues, and that it is always easy to ascertain what is right and wrong. Ethical analysis does mean that societal rules, actions, and beliefs can be determined to be right or wrong based on reasoning from ethical principles. Ethical principles do allow one to dismiss certain societal "moral" rules as inadequate. One pernicious consequence of ethical relativism, with its emphasis on culture, custom, and convention, is to "short-circuit" the ideal of the universal-absolute-good out of human consciousness (Cavico and Mujtaba, 2005). The challenge for the multinational firm, rather, is to establish consistent ethical methods to rationally raise, discuss, and resolve moral issues, to classify actions as right and wrong, and to make the classification universal and operational.

Summary to Ethical Relativism

Moral beliefs may be in part the internalized reflection of the views of one's society, transmitted by one's parents and other societal influences. The resulting moral norms can be prescribed, explained, and reinforced by the society's customs and conventions. The norms, in addition, can function as instruments for maintaining social cohesion and stability. Following the customs of one's society, therefore, does provide an explanation for performing an action. The international business person, moreover, is well-advised to be keenly aware of the moral norms where he or she is contemplating doing business.

Adherence to social convention, however, does not provide a complete justification for engaging in an activity. Acceptance of societal norms generally is not the product of logical ethical reasoning. Moral norms need further justification. Rational arguments are necessary to establish what a societal practice ought to be; and to determine whether a person should be guided by an essentially non-reasoned conformity to societal convention. A too ready disposition to conform to the practices of a society may not in fact be a virtue, but rather a weakness and vice.

Fundamental moral rules are not relative. Not every moral rule varies from society to society. Societies may differ in some moral beliefs, but there is agreement on fundamental rules. It is a mistake, therefore, to overestimate the amount of differences among societies; and certainly to construct an ethical theory based on these differences. Several societies have believed in the morality of the practice of slavery throughout history; yet slavery was morally wrong then, as well as now, despite societal norms. The same absolute arguments can be made against discrimination, discrimination in employment, and age discrimination in employment.

Kantian Ethics

The Kantian approach to ethics, in contrast to ethical relativism, views morality from the perspective of universal rights and duties, thereby superseding any viewpoint of morality based on societal norms (Cavico and Mujtaba, 2005). Kant's Categorical Imperative, therefore, clearly will demand that the international firm do more than merely comply with the host country's moral norms or even legal regulations regarding discrimination in employment. The Categorical Imperative will demand that the moral person, regardless of the law and any prevailing ethically relativistic or cultural norms regarding discrimination against certain types of persons or people with certain characteristics, treat human beings as worthwhile and valuable "ends" deserving of dignity and respect, and never treat them as mere "means" or things or instruments and never subject them to disrespectful or demeaning behavior (Cavico and Mujtaba, 2005). In the context of the age discrimination, Kantian ethics would demand that one treat an older person, or for that matter a younger person, not solely on his or her age, but whether the person possesses the capability to do the particular job.

Kantian ethics is fundamentally based on rationality; that is, the clear-thinking, objective, and intelligent person will be able to reason to the moral answer to the problem (Cavico and Mujtaba, 2005) The rational person surely would realize that discrimination based on age or other, especially immutable characteristics, such as race, color, national origin, and gender, may be the consequence of incorrect and impermissible stereotyping and prejudice, both individual and societal. The rational person certainly would want to be considered for a job or a promotion based on his or her ability, not age; and thus the rational person will reason that other people similarly situated want to be judged for what they can do, and not who they are or how old (or young) they are, and regardless of any contravening laws (or absence of laws), or ethical or societal norms. Accordingly, the rational person will reason to the logical ethical conclusion that it is immoral to discriminate against people based on their age.

Summary

The moral assessment of a business situation is naturally made more difficult by the presence of different national, societal, and cultural perspectives as to what it means to be moral. Ethical relativism, of course, is an ethical theory that gives precedence to these societal cultural beliefs in determining moral conduct. Ultimately, however, the international business person morally may be required to act not only above and beyond the law, but also above and beyond relativism in ethics; and thus may be required to apply universal ethical principles and moral standards to employment practices wherever and whenever business is conducted. Just as the law differs from one country to another country, so does the definition of moral behavior and the delineation of appropriate cultural norms. The law, of course, can be viewed as a foundational "value" prescribing one's behavior; yet ethical codes, moral rules, and cultural norms may impel one to exceed the "moral minimum" required by the law. The United States possesses a highly developed legal system proscribing discrimination based on race, religion, national origin, gender, and age. Other nations, however, do not possess such comprehensive legal prohibitions. When an American manager or employee is called upon to evaluate the propriety of an action, such as employment discrimination, one must consider not only the whole legal context, including U.S. employment discrimination law as well as the host country's law, but also the ethical, moral, and cultural context. Because the laws of the host country are frequently different from those encountered in the U.S., managers must review them carefully, not only for legalistic reasons, but also for the ethical attitudes the laws may reflect. A nation's laws historically have been shaped in part by its social traditions and conventions and beliefs, including its moral standards and mores.

Recommendations

United States multinational business firms, as well as foreign firms operating in the U.S., first obviously must be aware of U.S. civil rights law when conducting business in the United States. These firms also must be keenly aware of the important and far-reaching legal extraterritorial rule that a U.S. company that employs U.S. citizens anywhere in the world generally will be subject to a civil rights lawsuit if these employees are discriminated against based on the protected categories. These employees, moreover, can maintain a lawsuit in the U.S. for discriminatory employment conduct that occurs overseas. The BFOQ doctrine, although theoretically a defense, may not work in practice as a viable strategic approach for U.S. operations or U.S. employers operating abroad. Ascertaining ahead of time what is "reasonably necessary" for "normal operations" of the business is at best a difficult challenge. Perhaps the BFOQ doctrine could be useful as a tactical defensive tool to the firm when it is attempting to defend itself after the fact; but the doctrine is simply too nebulous, and its use too hazardous, to be useful in international business employment determinations.

Any multinational company, cognizant of the law and ethics, and acting pursuant to the principles of ethical egoism, will adopt a code of ethics and engage in proactive self-education and regulation to ensure that it is acting in a lawful and moral manner when it comes to its employment practices. The corporate code of ethics naturally must stress respect for and adherence to the law, not only the home country's law, but also the host country's law as well. Moreover, the code must state that the traditions, customs, norms, and beliefs of the countries in which the firm operates will be valued and followed too. However, the code also must clearly state that, even if legal, customary, and accepted locally, the firm will not engage in any practice or commit any act that is in contravention of universal ethical principles and moral norms, particularly the human rights to dignity, respect, and fairness for the firm's own employees. The code, therefore, must strike a balance between the laws, values, beliefs, and practices of the home country and those of the host country. Nevertheless, the scales must be tipped in favor of the universal ethical principles and moral norms embodied in the firm's code of ethics. The higher, universal, moral "law" thus must guide the multinational firm and govern its employees in its international dealings, employment or otherwise.

In addition to national legal systems and societal and cultural moral norms, each organization has its own unique culture, which includes its values, traditions, customs, and beliefs, including its organizational ethics. Anyone within an organization making decisions or taking actions must understand the organizational context within which they must be made (Pohlman and Gardiner, 2000). To truly complicate matters, in an international context, when a multinational firm has divisions, offices, or operations in different countries, each likely has its own culture. A multinational business firm that intends to establish global employment practices must comprehend, therefore, the true meaning of the culture of the firm as one that encompasses the culture of the firm's particular foreign offices as well as the laws and ethical norms that govern the practices of these offices.

United States' firms, as well as U.S.-based ones, influenced by the U.S. legal system as well as cultural and ethical beliefs, should have certain cultural conceptions regarding discrimination in employment. These firms very well may have global operations and thus should be considered as global firms. Key legal, philosophical, and practical questions thereby arise: Should the policies against discrimination and harassment that have been adopted and implemented in the firm's U.S. divisions and offices be imposed on the firm's foreign offices? Can and should the U.S. firm's corporate culture of non-discrimination be transposed overseas? What will be the anticipated reaction of the U.S. firm's foreign offices when these issues are even raised? Will the foreign executives object to U.S. legal and cultural "imperialism"? Will they deride the proposed overseas policy against sexual discrimination and harassment? Clearly, the multinational firm that is solely focused on the value of maximizing short-term profit, and is swayed by narrowly legalistic and conveniently relativistic notions of what is "proper," will not be establishing a corporate culture that is conducive to long-term success and value-maximization for the firm and all its stakeholders.

The corporation entity, of course, is an artificial legal "person," functioning through its essential human components, principally the employees. Yet, the paramount object of the corporation is to maximize profit for the owners, the shareholders. Thus, a corporation, especially in the international context, may subordinate the interests of its employees to those of the shareholders. Of course, many countries have enacted laws to protect workers from discriminatory and abusive practices. Government regulation, however, varies widely, ranging from the extensive German safeguards for employees, to virtually non-existent or non-enforceable "laws" in many developing nations. Yet, in some many instances, U.S. law will be more protective of employees, for example, with regard to mandatory retirement or benefit plans that cannot discriminate against women workers. Thus, should a U.S. firm formulate its policies only for U.S. employees overseas or should it apply its policies equally to its U.S. workers and foreign workers? Even in the absence of law, or the presence of conflict in laws, the prudent and ethically egoistic firm must balance the values of these two important stakeholder groups and must strive for "win-win" mutually rewarding, long-term, value-maximizing solutions (Pohlman and Gardiner, 2000).

Clearly, foreign executives and foreign employees of a U.S. firm may have some different views on discrimination in employment. Perhaps it is a common practice in the host country society to see an employment candidate's marital status or religion on a job application. Since the laws and cultural beliefs may be quite different from the U.S., the U.S. firm's foreign employees may have different understandings as to how business is to be conducted, legally as well as ethically. There may be very little law in the host country, let alone guidance and training, on employment discrimination and sexual harassment issues. Values and beliefs can differ among employees, especially between the managers from the home country and the employees of the host country. Accordingly, the prudent and ethically egoistic international firm will seek to ascertain these values, and then attempt to accommodate and balance them, in order to avoid any cross cultural misunderstandings and friction, so as to ensure an amicable and smoothly functioning workplace (Pohlman and Gardiner, 2000).

Attention also must be given to the values of the organization's distributors and suppliers in order to maximize the organization's value over time. (Pohlman and Gardiner, 2000) Treating distributors and suppliers fairly, creating "partnerships" with suppliers, and acting on their other values will lead to greater value over time, for the suppliers and also the organization. Distributors and suppliers may possess certain attitudes and beliefs, especially regarding discriminatory practices, based on their unique political, cultural, religious, economic, and legal backgrounds. These attitudes and beliefs can affect the way a firm does business in a foreign country. In a global context, multinational firms should seek distributors and suppliers with similar organizational values, especially such core values as fairness in employment practices and respect for employees. Establishing and preserving this network of mutually valuable relationships will be critical to the firm that seeks to maximize value in the long-term. A multinational company ascertaining and weighing the consequences of its employment practices, particularly regarding discrimination, must take into account the values of its suppliers, and the impact its decisions will have on the values of the suppliers and the relationships that the firm has with its suppliers.

When a multinational firm establishes very close working relationships with its suppliers, the firm must be cognizant that if it is deemed to "control" a foreign supplier, U.S. civil rights law will apply to U.S. citizens employed by the supplier. In this era of companies hiring outside foreign firms, not only to supply goods in the traditional sense, but also to handle major responsibilities for product design to technical support to employee benefits, the U.S. firm must be cognizant that its control of these foreign functions may be deemed to be legal "control" for extraterritorial legal purposes.

Clearly understanding what customers and consumers value, for example, quality of product and service and reliability, and satisfying customer value are critical to the success of any business. In order to serve customers, the values of the customers and the employees of the organization serving them must be congruent (Pohlman and Gardiner, 2000). Customers today are more concerned with the employment practices of U.S. firms overseas, especially regarding employment conditions and practices. If a U.S. multinational firm, for example, develops a negative image regarding its employment activities overseas, it may become vulnerable to profit loss due to decreased sales, even consumer boycotts, as customers will not want to patronize a firm that contravenes the cherished U.S. values of equality and non-discrimination. Customers rather will purchase products and services from firms that have a deserved reputation for respecting workers' rights and treating employees in a fair and equitable manner. Thus, from the very practical perspective of corporate profits, possessing a "good," credible reputation for acting legally and morally in the global marketplace will emerge as a critical component to business success for the multinational firm.

Understanding what government legal systems, especially regulatory agencies, value, such as authority, rules, and compliance, can be very important in making decisions and taking actions within an organization. (Pohlman and Gardiner, 2000) In the context of international business, especially when dealing with the issue of employment discrimination, the business manager of the multinational firm, for example, must be cognizant of not only U.S. law, and its extraterritorial effect, but also the host country's law.

Any international enterprise, whether controlled by investors in the U.S. or from some other country, relies on employees to function. Consequently, the business is influenced by the host country's employment and other laws in addition to the laws of the United States. The United States, of course, almost surely has the most comprehensive corpus of law prohibiting discrimination in employment. Since most other countries were created as the geographic physical and legal embodiment of homogeneous ethnic groups, they have felt relatively little pressure to promulgate legal anti-discrimination systems. Since in many nations the vast majority of the people residing therein are ethnically homogeneous, there has not arisen a need to protect against national origin discrimination, in employment or otherwise. Accordingly, the U.S. business manager doing business internationally seldom has confronted any legal compulsion to avoid ethnic discrimination. However, foreign laws may emerge as a very serious constraint when the laws of the host country require discrimination based on ethnicity, gender, or religion, particularly since these foreign laws may conflict with U.S. civil rights law. Consequently, the principal employment discrimination issue for the U.S. international business person is whether the Civil Rights Act, the ADEA, and other anti-discrimination statutes apply to the firm's foreign business operations. As each nation can regulate the affairs of multi-national firms within its borders, the prudent firm will be cognizant of all the relevant laws, and the potential for conflict, so as to avoid legal gridlock.

Labor organizations, moreover, have increasingly become active opponents of allegedly unfair labor practices by firms, and not only domestically but also overseas; and these labor groups will identity, target, protest, and urge the boycott of such "exploitative" companies. The threat of such retaliatory actions should provide a very practical and "valuable" incentive for global companies to act in a legal and moral manner.

Today, illegal and immoral business practices have become more readily apparent in the increasingly transparent global business arena. Thus, the prudent and ethically egoistic firm will be aware that other parties, in addition to the firm's core stakeholders and government, will be monitoring the firm's business practices. The media, for example, is a significant third party that the multinational firm must factor into its decision-making analysis. The media in reporting and publicizing a firm's perceived role as a violator of human rights for employees can add tremendous pressure to a firm's corporate image, which naturally can adversely affect the firm's reputation and its sales. Private consumer and labor groups are addition third parties that will be examining the company's practices, and publicizing any perceived unethical conduct towards employees, especially regarding discrimination in employment. The prudent and ethically egoistic multinational company, cognizant of its public relations, surely will recognize the media's and other private groups' influence and their potential financial impact on the firm.

In addition, understanding one's competitor's values will lead one to a better understanding of one's competitors; and thus will help one's own organization formulate its strategy. (Pohlman and Gardiner, 2000) The world of international business is one characterized by risk, encompassing, of course, legal risk. How well a firm manages such risk will determine how well a firm does in relationship to its competitors. For example, understanding the laws and ethical norms of the U.S., as well as the laws of the host country, especially any differences from U.S. laws, will help the U.S. multinational firm to achieve and maintain a competitive advantage.

The law and legal system provide the basis for government regulation of international business. The law thereby directly affects the environment in which an international business firm's strategies are developed and its strategies are made operational. Changes in the law, particularly regarding such emotional topics as discrimination in employment, will impact the multinational firm's strategic planning and decision-making. An astute firm that seeks to sustain a competitive advantage will be attuned to such legal changes. The firm that wishes to compete successfully in the global marketplace thus must be cognizant of the law, especially the potential impact of U.S. discrimination law on the workplace, including the extraterritorial effect of U.S. law on their overseas employees.

Yet, admittedly, there is a concern that the legal and moral multinational firm will act in a legal and moral manner with regard to its overseas operations, but its "Machiavellian" competitors will not, thus placing the "good" firm in a "bad" competitive position compared to its competitors who do not "play by the rules." However, this disadvantageous viewpoint is a short-sighted and erroneous approach. Ethical egoism requires that a firm take a long-term perspective. Thus, obeying the law and adhering to high ethical principles, even if "costly" in the short-term, will afford the prudent firm an advantageous position and a sustainable competitive advantage in the long-term.

The owners, the shareholders in a corporate context, finally, have a set of values. They value, for example, a return on assets and equity, sustained growth, a profitable investment, and prestige of the firm. Of course, when a firm is properly balanced and is working well, the values of the owners, the values of the other "stakeholder" groups, and the values of legality and morality will be in harmony (Pohlman and Gardiner, 2000).

Nevertheless, the multinational firm's shareholders may be aware of the firm's activities overseas, and may be concerned with the firm's image as a perceived violator of workers' rights to impartial and fair treatment. Shareholders consequently may criticize the firm and thus put further pressures on the firm to change its practices to conform to the values of equality and non-discrimination. Current shareholders also may threaten to disinvest. Furthermore, potential shareholders as well as other sources of capital also may adversely affect the firm by not making investment decisions. The prudent and ethically egoistic multinational firm, therefore, will practice non-discrimination in its employment practices.

Conclusion

The globalization of business clearly presents both unparalleled opportunities, but also potential problems and dangerous risks for multinational business firms. As the world economies apparently are beginning to blend into a truly global economy, U.S as well as foreign firms, even small ones, are beginning to explore business opportunities overseas. This globalization, though arguably beneficial in the long-term for global society and peoples as a whole, has produced nonetheless in the short term certain legal, ethical, and cultural clashes.

The ever-increasing integration of the world's economy in recent years has generated a growing demand for international business managers to assure that their firms are in compliance with the various nations' laws, especially employment laws, when business operations take place across borders. As more business firms enter the global marketplace in a material manner, these firms must consider when and to what extent the employment law of the U.S. applies to their overseas workforce. Business decisions now involve not only the analysis of U.S. law and its extraterritorial effect, but also the law of the host country. The result is that multiple levels of at times conflicting legal analyses must be performed.

CHAPTER 5

CULTURAL PERCEPTIONS AND EMPLOYMENT PRACTICES

*E*ffective leadership in employment practices and decision-making is an essential element of business in the twenty-first century's global environment. International business practices vary from country to country; therefore global leaders should be aware of the culture and social standards of foreign nations where they operate. Global leaders and managers should be prepared to make decisions that are effective and aligned with both local and international norms and policies. These leaders need to ensure processes throughout the global organization are accurate, and all the subsidiaries are treated fairly and as an equal to the parent company. Before international managers and leaders of multinational corporations are asked to make global employment decisions, they should be given factual information, training, and awareness about the local laws, norms, perceptions, and expectations of people in each country in order to make fair hiring and retention decisions. This chapter provides the survey purpose, methodology, results of the qualitative research, and the actual comments about age discrimination practices provided by respondents from the countries of Afghanistan, Turkey, Jamaica, and the United States. These comments represent the qualitative aspect of what people think with regard to age in their cultures and how they perceive age discrimination practices in their workplace.

Purpose of Study and Methodology

There seems to be cultural convergence in many human resources practices among various countries as a result of technological advancements and commonalities. However, often times, employee hiring and retention practices are heavily influenced by cultural norms and mores and international managers should be aware of different practices at various localities. The purpose of this qualitative study has been to ascertain the cultural views of aging and employment practices regarding older workers from the people of the United States of America, Jamaica, Turkey, and Afghanistan. The research question herein is: "*Is age viewed differently among the people of Afghanistan, Turkey, Jamaica, and the United States of America?*" The authors propose that there are some cultural differences in how people view age in each country surveyed; and such cultural views regarding older workers do impact employment practices and hiring decisions. Gathering data can provide a clearer understanding of differences from the view of people in these presumably four different cultures. This factual information can be used by global employees, managers, and human resource professionals working in multinational corporations as they design procedures and policies for attracting, hiring, developing, promoting, and retaining an experienced workforce within each country. The four countries chosen for this study were selected because the authors had access to workers, managers, and professional organizations in them that would cooperate in the information gathering and research process. Furthermore, these are cultures that the authors have the most experience with as they have lived in them, worked in them or with people from them, and have completed studies about them in previous projects. It is expected that such studies will be duplicated in other countries to further provide factual and practical information that can be used by global managers and multinational corporations as they design and practice fair employment policies.

Several years ago, the authors set out to have discussions with employees, managers and researchers from various countries around the world regarding age and older workers. As a result, in early 2005, it was decided that a structured qualitative survey could be used to formally gather information on how the people of Afghanistan, Jamaica, Turkey, and the United States view age as per their cultural conditioning and the current employment practices related to older workers in their country. A simple and straight-forward survey was designed so it could be distributed to a "convenient" sample of individuals from each country that can speak, read and understand English. As such, the survey questions were worded so the survey could be easily understood by individuals whose first language is something other than English. Initially, in a pilot study, the surveys were handed out face-to-face to a sample of about 30 diverse individuals in Fort Lauderdale to see how they interpreted each question on the survey. As a result, a few of the questions were separated into several questions and some words were changed to further clarify what was being asked. This process led to the final version of the survey (see "Age and Cultural Values Questionnaire" in the Appendices) which was used for this study.

The individuals who received the surveys were colleagues, friends, professional educators, trainers, staff, students, government employees, contractors, or simply members of various newsgroups that facilitate or distribute up-to-date information to subscribers. Participants were provided sufficient information about the study and its purpose on a cover letter within the electronic communication (email). To minimize confusion and simplify the data gathering process, separate links for surveys in each country were created and sent to the people of those countries. The directions provided each person a link for the survey. On the average, the survey took about ten minutes to complete. The response rate could not be determined mathematically since the number of subscribers to some of the newsgroups was not known to the researchers. However, a response rate of 20% is estimated as per the known number of colleagues and possible number of subscribers to various newsgroups that may have received the survey information. Participants in each country were given a period of three weeks to asynchronously complete the survey as per their availability, and they were encouraged to respond within the allotted time since it would only take about ten minutes. However, participants were able to complete the survey even months after the allotted time since the survey was available to them. During a given month, only individuals from one country were sent the survey for completion. During a four-month period, the surveys were sent to people of four different countries and the responses were received electronically within this four-month period (February to May 2005). Surveys were sent first to Afghans, then to Jamaicans, Turkish, and finally to Americans in the United States. The survey was first distributed electronically through the internet to a group of professional Afghans living in Afghanistan, the United States, and many other countries throughout the Middle East, Europe, and Asia in the early months of 2005. The participants were encouraged to complete the survey within a three-week period. A month later, the survey directions and link were sent to people in Jamaica and they too were asked to respond within a three-week period. In the following two months, similar procedures were followed with Turkish and American populations. The demographics of respondent populations and their views on age related questions from the questionnaire are shared in the next section.

Survey Results and Implications

As discussed before, there was an estimated 20% response rate (a total of 206 individuals) to the survey from the countries of Afghanistan, Jamaica, Turkey, and the United States. Parts of this research were originally published in the January issue of Journal of Applied Management and Entrepreneurship (Mujtaba, et al., 2006). As can be seen from Table 1 and Figure 1, there were 57 respondents from Afghanistan, 42 from Jamaica, 36 from Turkey, and 71 respondents from the United States of America for a total of 206 respondents. There also was a good distribution of both genders responding to the survey: 91 male and 115 female respondents presenting their views on aging and employment practices regarding older workers.

Demographics – Female v. Male. It is very interesting to note that the preponderance of respondents from the U.S. and Jamaica are female. Given the later "scores" and comments regarding the prevalence of age discrimination, it is possible that older females may feel, perceive, or observe the presence of such discrimination more keenly than males. Perhaps this is an avenue for future research in order to see if there is a relationship between gender and the perception of age discrimination.

Table 1 - Gender of Respondents			
Country	Male	Female	Total
Afghanistan	39	18	57
Turkey	22	14	36
USA	21	50	71
Jamaica	9	33	42
Total	91	115	206

Figure 1 - Gender of Respondents

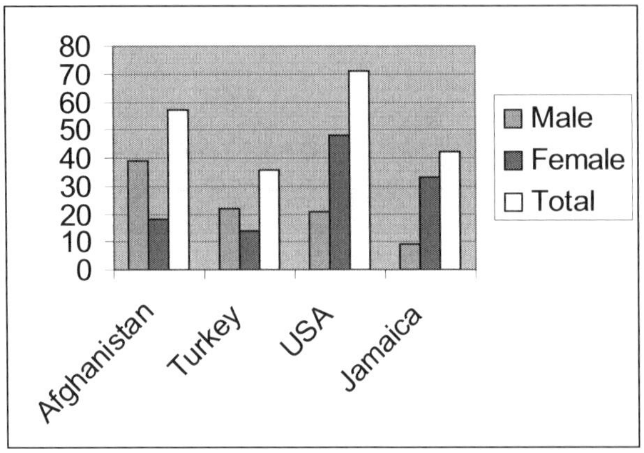

Demographics – Age. It is interesting to note that the representation among the age groups is more or less evenly balanced between "young" (the first two categories) and "old" (the second two), except for Turkey, where the "young" clearly outweigh the "old." Yet this disparity does show up in the Turkish scores, except perhaps for the category of "evidence of age discrimination against 'younger workers;" where half the respondents reported seeing evidence of such discrimination.

Table 2- Age of Respondents					
Country	16-25	26-39	40-49	50-above	Total
Afghanistan	7	27	10	13	57
Turkey	3	28	4	1	36
USA	5	33	10	23	71
Jamaica	2	15	19	6	42
Total	17	103	43	43	206

Figure 2- Age of Respondents

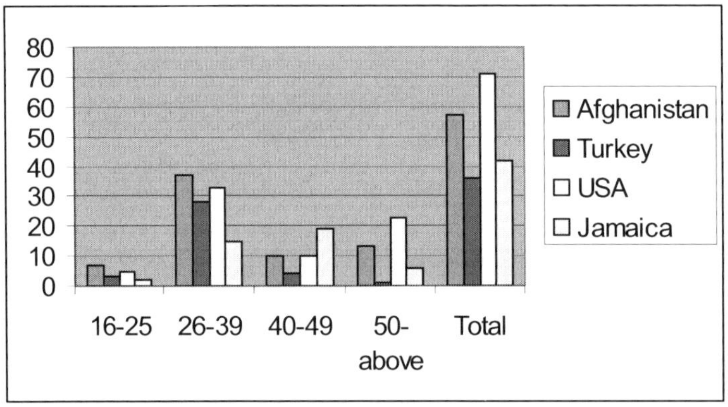

Racial background. Also, for USA, the bulk of the respondents are "White" with only 1 Hispanic, which seems surprising. Thus, the age discrimination reported for the U.S. is by predominantly white respondents, which means perhaps that the age discrimination is not "colored" by race, skin color, or ethnicity discrimination. So, age discrimination impacts people of all backgrounds regardless of each individual's unique characteristics.

Table 3 - Racial Background							
Country	Black	White	Hispanic	Asian / Pacific	American Indian	Other	Total
Afghanistan	0	20	-	9	-	28	57
Turkey	1	23	1	2	-	9	36
USA	7	53	3	4	-	4	71
Jamaica	38	1	-	-	-	3	42
Total	46	97	4	15		44	206

Education level. As can be seen in Table 4, the education level was very high for all categories, but nonetheless sizable numbers of respondents reported that they did not know whether age discrimination against older workers was illegal in their country. As a matter of fact, out of 206 respondents from the four countries, 48 "did not know" or were not sure if age discrimination was legally wrong in their country. Clearly, something may be lacking in all this advanced education with regard to hiring practices and awareness of rules. Of course, many of these so called "well educated" individuals are more likely to become managers and leaders because of their education and, thus, should receive training on age-related employment practices.

Table 4 - Education Level					
Country	High School	Bachelors Degree	Masters Degree	Doctor Degree	Other
Afghanistan	5	29	12	5	6
Turkey	3	18	12	2	1
USA	9	13	31	13	5
Jamaica	1	11	25	3	2
Total	18	71	80	24	13

Figure 3 - Education Level

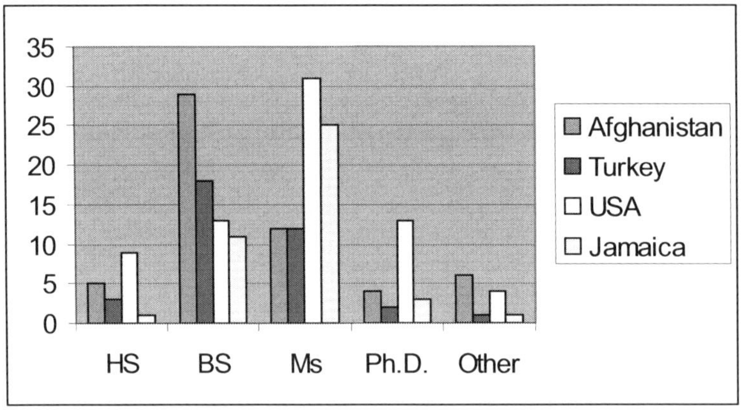

Employment history. For the USA, 63 out of 71 respondents chose "education" as their employment industry which makes the fact that the USA category reported in Age Perceptions that "older workers" by a 42-29 majority do NOT get more respect than younger workers, which cast doubt on being an "older" and "respected" academic.

Table 5 - Years with Current Employer						
Country	0-1	1-5	6-15	16-29	30 -more	Total
Afghanistan	11	27	11	8	0	57
Turkey	5	15	11	1	4	36
USA	15	27	22	7	-	71
Jamaica	2	21	13	5	1	42
Total	33	90	57	21	5	206

Table 6 - Employment Industry							
Country	Educ.	Gov.	Private	Retail	Health	Other	Total
Afghanistan	9	7	16	5	2	18	57
Turkey	2	1	18	1	3	11	36
USA	63	-	5	-	-	3	71
Jamaica	12	5	17	-	2	6	42
Total	86	13	56	6	7	38	206

Diversity training. The USA category reported by a "vote" of 42-29 that it had diversity training, and the other categories had significant minorities reporting such training, all of which makes the fact that so much age discrimination in employment was reported even more disturbing. Perhaps the diversity training should have a much stronger age component, which could be another avenue for future research.

Table 7 - Previous Professional Diversity Training			
Country	Yes	No	Total
Afghanistan	28	29	57
Turkey	12	24	36
USA	42	29	71
Jamaica	18	24	42
Total	100	106	206

Figure 4 - Previous Professional Diversity Training

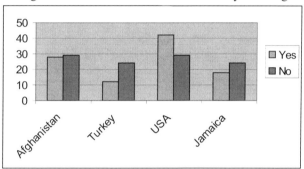

Respect. All categories of respondents reported that older workers get more respect than younger ones, except notably for the U.S.A., which reported that older workers do NOT get more respect from managers and employers. This result, again, is disturbing considering the educational levels and educational setting of the U.S.A. respondents.

Table 8 – Respect for Older Workers in the Country

Do "older workers" get more respect than "younger workers" in your country?			
Country	Yes	No	Total
Afghanistan	47	10	57
Turkey	27	9	36
USA	29	42	71
Jamaica	28	14	42
Total	131	75	206

Figure 5 – Respect for Older Workers in the Country

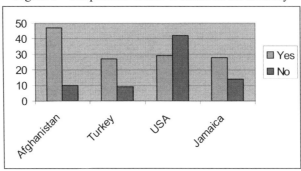

Table 9 – Respect for Older Workers from Managers

Do "older workers" get more respect than "younger workers" from managers and employers in your country?			
Country	Yes	No	Total
Afghanistan	42	15	57
Turkey	28	8	36
USA	35	36	71
Jamaica	32	10	42
Total	137	69	206

Figure 6 – Respect for Older Workers from Managers

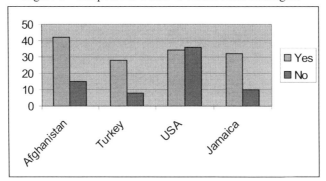

Difficulty of older workers finding jobs. Once again, the U.S.A. figures are disturbing, as more than half the respondents reported that it is more difficult for U.S. older workers to get jobs in their country. Moreover, this result occurs despite the facts of U.S. age discrimination law, the awareness of such law, as well as the respondents' thoughts and moral norm regarding age discrimination as morally wrong, and the prevalence of diversity training.

Table 10 – Difficulty for Older Workers to Get Job

Is it more difficult for "older workers" to find jobs in your country?			
Country	Yes	No	Total
Afghanistan	33	24	57
Turkey	26	10	36
USA	50	21	71
Jamaica	26	16	42
Total	135	70	206

Table 7 – Difficulty for Older Workers to Get Job

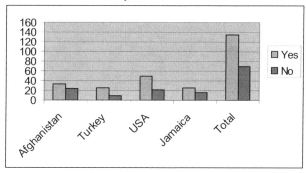

Table 11 – Difficulty for Younger Workers to Get Job

Is it more difficult for "younger workers" to find jobs in your country?			
Country	Yes	No	Total
Afghanistan	16	41	57
Turkey	17	19	36
USA	20	51	71
Jamaica	18	24	42
Total	71	135	206

Evidence of age discrimination against older workers. With regard to evidence of age discrimination, the scores were close for Turkey and Afghanistan in reporting "no," and also close for Jamaica in reporting "yes"; but yet again the U.S.A. scores were disturbing, as by a "vote" of 45-26, the U.S.A. respondents reported seeing evidence of age discrimination against older workers.

Table 12 – Evidence of Age Discrimination for Older Workers

Have you ever seen evidence of age discrimination toward "older workers" by managers in your country?			
Country	Yes	No	Total
Afghanistan	26	31	57
Turkey	17	19	36
USA	45	26	71
Jamaica	23	19	42
Total	111	95	206

Figure 8 – Evidence of Age Discrimination for Older Workers

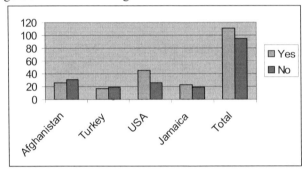

Table 13 – Evidence of Age Discrimination for Younger Workers

Have you ever seen evidence of age discrimination toward "younger workers" by managers in your country?			
Country	Yes	No	Total
Afghanistan	24	33	57
Turkey	18	18	36
USA	43	28	71
Jamaica	28	14	42
Total	113	93	206

Age discrimination against older workers as legally wrong. With regard to age discrimination against older workers being legally wrong, respondents from Turkey and Jamaica reported "no" by sizable margins, but there was a very big "do not know" "vote." Afghanistan reported "yes" by a material margin, but also with a fair "do not know" "vote." What is very clear is the USA reporting, where an overwhelming number of respondents (63) stated that such discrimination was legally wrong, with only three reporting "no" and only five reporting "do not know." Yet the fact that U.S. law prohibiting age discrimination exists, and that people are overwhelmingly aware of this law, apparently does not prevent, as reported by the respondents, age discrimination against older workers from occurring in the United States. This provides further support for the notion of cultural conditioning being a very strong "driver" of human behavior.

Table 14 –Age Discrimination Legally Wrong

Is age discrimination against "older workers" legally wrong in your country?				
Country	Yes	No	Do not know	Total
Afghanistan	31	18	8	57
Turkey	3	12	21	36
USA	63	3	5	71
Jamaica	10	18	14	42
Total	107	51	48	206

Figure 9 – Age Discrimination Legally Wrong

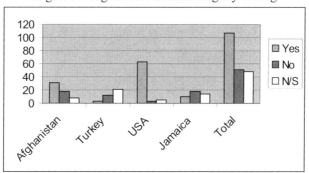

Age discrimination as morally wrong in "Your Country." In all the countries except Turkey, which had a "tie vote," the respondents reported that such discrimination was morally wrong, but with material "do not know" "votes"; but for the U.S., by a 58-7 vote, with seven "do not know" "votes," the respondents reported that age discrimination was morally wrong in the United States. Once again this presumably prevailing moral belief in the U.S. that age discrimination is morally wrong apparently does not prevent such discrimination from happening in employment. The conclusion also provides further support that cultural conditioning can be a strong influence on the behavior of individuals regarding employment practices.

Table 15 – Age Discrimination Morally Wrong

Is age discrimination against "older workers" regarded as morally or ethically wrong in your country?				
Country	Yes	No	Do not know	Total
Afghanistan	39	10	8	57
Turkey	14	14	8	36
USA	58	6	7	71
Jamaica	20	9	13	42
Total	131	39	36	206

Figure 10 – Age Discrimination Morally Wrong

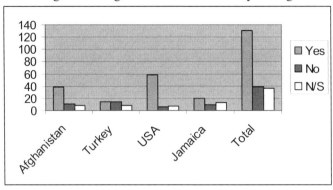

Age discrimination against older workers as personally wrong. All country categories reported by wide majorities that they regard age discrimination against older workers as personally morally wrong. The U.S. figures are especially evident, as 69 said "yes," and no one reported "no," and only two respondents said they did not know.

Table 16 – Age Discrimination Personally Wrong

Is age discrimination against "older workers" regarded by you personally as morally or ethically wrong?				
Country	Yes	No	Do not know	Total
Afghanistan	50	6	1	57
Turkey	26	8	2	36
USA	69	-	2	71
Jamaica	41	1	-	42
Total	186	15	5	206

Figure 11 – Age Discrimination Personally Wrong

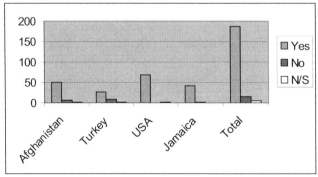

Age discrimination against younger workers as personally wrong. All country categories by wide majorities reported that such discrimination was wrong. Thus, for both young and old workers the respondents believe that discrimination against them based on their age is morally wrong. People of all countries seem to believe that an employee should be hired based on qualifications for the job's requirements rather than his or her age category.

Table 17 – Age Discrimination toward Younger Workers Personally Wrong

Is age discrimination against "younger workers" regarded by you personally as morally or ethically wrong?				
Country	Yes	No	Do not know	Total
Afghanistan	43	13	1	57
Turkey	24	10	2	36
USA	63	5	3	71
Jamaica	42	-	-	42
Total	172	28	6	206

Figure 12 – Age Discrimination toward Younger Workers Personally Wrong

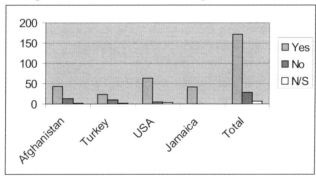

As a result of the overall review of the data from each country and the respondents' verbatim comments (included later in this chapter), one can make some observations regarding cultural views about aging and its behavioral implications in the workplace of each culture. At a general level, one can make some conclusions with regard to "unearned privileges" or "unearned advantages" to various categories of workers in different cultures. Previously, *unearned privilege* was defined as advantages given to some individuals and withheld from others, without regard to their efforts or abilities, because of their perceived difference. What is interesting to think about is that such privileges often come to one group or category of individuals at a cost to other individuals or category of workers. From a qualitative analysis of the data, one can conclude that younger workers in the United Sates of America and in Jamaica tend to receive unearned privileges simply because of their age. Such privileges to young workers mean stereotypes, biases, and discrimination to those individuals who fall in the category of older workers. So, older workers in the United States and in Jamaica are at a disadvantage when they are competing for jobs against younger individuals in the marketplace. One must reflect on the fact that all younger workers will eventually become older workers, thus losing the unearned privileges to those who are seen as young.

Similarly, because of tradition and thousands of years of cultural conditioning, older workers in Turkey and Afghanistan seem to enjoy unearned privileges. It is important to emphasize that these are simply assumptions about older workers being wise and mature until they prove themselves otherwise. It is also assumed that younger workers are not at the same level of maturity as older workers until they prove themselves otherwise. Therefore, younger workers with extremely high levels of knowledge and maturity when compared to many older workers are only given the opportunity after they have proven themselves. So, young workers might be at a disadvantage in such cultures when they are competing for jobs against older workers.

It is striking to see that the U.S. respondents, principally from the education sector, reported such a prevalence of age discrimination, and especially so considering that the U.S. has such an extensive anti-discrimination legal network, which the vast number of the U.S. respondents were aware of, and also that the U.S. respondents reported their beliefs as well as the prevailing norms that age discrimination was legally wrong, ethically and morally wrong, and, moreover, they reported that they had diversity training. So, what does the data reveal? Despite all the legal and moral norms as well as the training, the respondents still report significant age discrimination in the U.S. It is clear that national and international managers, leaders and twenty-first century professionals need to effectively prepare and deal with age discrimination issues in their workplace.

The current data supports previous data and the conclusions of other researchers with regard to the widespread presence of age discrimination in the Unite States. Raymond Gregory (2001) pointed out that "I can still state, without fear of contradiction, that age discrimination continues to be a common practice in the American business firms." Gregory ends with an optimistic view by stating that "isolated instance of enlightened thinking on the subject of age discrimination might very well be a harbinger of fairer days for older workers in the future." Gregory also stated that "Discrimination against middle-aged and older workers has long been a common practice of American business firms. Nearly all middle-aged and older workers, at some time during their work careers, will suffer the consequences of an age-biased employment-related action." While the law prohibits age discrimination in the American workplace, workers over the age of 40 are "nevertheless subjected to adverse employment decisions motivated by false, stereotypical notions concerning the physical and mental abilities of older workers" (Gregory, 2001). As such, older workers in the American workplace are often encouraged into premature retirements, denied developmental opportunities that can lead to promotions, denied deserved transfers or job promotions, terminated for causes that have little to nothing with their performance, and are excluded from long-term decision-making due to biases and assumptions. Gregory (2001) mentions that "America will be an even better country once age discrimination in the workplace is eliminated." The authors of this book also hope that the elimination of age discrimination in the workplace comes faster; and, of course, you (the reader) can be a huge factor in this process by doing your part to become aware of such biases and not letting inaccurate stereotypes and myths about older workers negatively impact your hiring decisions.

Limitations of the Study and Future Directions

Understanding cultural norms and local practices related to hiring and developing "older worker" is important for international managers and researchers. While this qualitative study focused on determining the perceptions of people about aging in Afghanistan, Jamaica, Turkey, and the United States, the resources were limited. Furthermore, the survey distribution was limited to those who could speak and read the questions in the English language since the survey was not translated to local languages. Besides having a relatively small sample size, it should be noted that the populations completing the survey are not necessarily representative of the general population in each culture. It is recommended that future researchers translate the questionnaire to the local languages and distribute to more individuals in order to secure a higher percentage of respondents that are a better representative of the local population than the current study. It is also recommended that future studies track the results of some questions using a Likert Scale, while collecting more demographical information from the respondents than included in the current survey. Such changes to the survey also will allow for quantitative analysis of the data and it will make it easier for researchers to duplicate the study with different segments of individuals and industries in the same culture.

Future studies can perhaps analyze the perceptions of male and female respondents using quantitative analysis. Other variables such as education, citizenship, education, and management experiences can also be used to determine the awareness of age discrimination practices in each culture regarding "older workers." Another interesting study might be to provide training to managers of each culture regarding "best" hiring practices in the hiring and retention of "older workers' and then conduct a longitudinal study to determine whether such education or training sessions actually make a difference in their hiring practices. The research question could be related to whether such training sessions result in behavioral changes when it comes to recruitment, hiring, retention, and development of older workers in the workforce.

Respondent Comments from Afghanistan

1. Although in Afghanistan respect comes with age but discrimination against poor and people with no ties to rich and famous is common. Even the educated Afghan-Americans who were suppose to help stabilize and reconstruct the country, when in power, offered their relatives and friends the high paying positions and other favors such as distribution of land, gas stations, all sorts of permits. As an Islamic country, youth should respect their elders for they receive God's reward for doing so and vice versa. Older people are considered blessing at home contrary to US where they are deposited to the nursing homes. Even when older people make mistakes, the youngsters would not voice to humiliate them, which sometimes is not such a good thing. At the work

environment, since Afghanistan is not fully computerized yet like many developed nations, experience is preferred. It is believed that by practice one omits making errors or perfection is achieved. Finally, elders reserve special rights over younger individuals – one should restrain from abusing them or cause any harm to them or even ignore them. The elders speak first, start eating the food first, lead the way and walk first, and set first at the top while others are standing poise. When setting, they make sure their back is not towards them. Most young co-workers respect their elder colleagues by calling them "uncle" or "aunt" to avoid calling them by their real names (surely, we are talking about decent people and decent behaviors of the majority).

2. The public sector, NGOs, UN Agencies, Donor Offices all in a row are replacing 90% of their older workers with young workers. However, in the private sector the older workers with good experience are still getting the jobs. However, the private sector has very limited job opportunities. And that is due to the fact that these experienced public servants are used to work at lower salaries. Whereas, the younger workers not only avoid working at low wages but are also ambitious to replace the managers above 40 years old.

3. In my country, Afghanistan, we are stepping in a new world and the new world starts with new technology. The older workers are not always familiar or are less familiar with them, which delays the process of accepting new system with new technology. This is one of the main reasons for age discrimination. The other reason is that older workers have communist systems in mind and this issue makes them to be discriminated from young generation.

4. Afghanistan's government officials are now restructuring their laws and should make sure that "older workers" and "younger workers" are welcomed to all jobs.

5. The older you are the lesser you are "worth" in the corporate American culture.

6. There was no age discrimination in Afghanistan against older workers, but there is age discrimination against older workers in the USA, particularly in the industrial and manufacturing sectors of economy.

7. In Afghanistan, age is not yet a big issue because life expectancy continues to be very low. The retirement age is set at 55 years, which I think is not fair.

8. I think it is wrong to discriminate against older workers, because they have knowledge, they have learned through experience. They are more laid back due to the fact that they do not need to be as aggressive in doing things as they were young, but one should not hold that against them. As for young worker, they also need to be given a chance to prove themselves. You cannot discriminate against them simply because they are young or inexperienced. You have to let them apply themselves and show what they can do. We all have to start somewhere.

9. I believe that the level of age discrimination depends in the industry or the specific organization where one works. The two different categories of work field that I have experience in are sales/business and pharmaceutical/health. In these two fields I have noticed that sales/business favors youngsters with more energy and enthusiasm where pharmaceutical/health favors older workers with more experience.

10. I think I like to work with older people and the reason is that they want to work (at least most of them), and the second thing is that they listen. But of course sometimes you see

they are useless in their job or in today's language they are not computerized. We had a few people (older guys) in our office and they were very intelligent but they were really slow which sometimes makes you crazy. But at the same time. I learned myself how to be quick or what does it mean to be quick. I like to work with younger people as well... because I can teach them how they can work and work efficiently.

11. It is difficult to for older workers in my country to update their knowledge about the modern way of management. They are hard to change and adopt.

12. I think they should give the work to someone who is able to do it best, where I work we have old coworkers who are over 60 years of age and just don't want to retire. They are paid the highest salary while us young worker do their work for them. I think just having few grey hair doesn't really make you the expert in your field of work. I do agree that experience is important but in today's society most young people are educated and much more aware of the environment around them than the old generation. I have heard of cases where a young intelligent person applied for a job and the person was told that he can't get the job because HE IS NOT OLD ENOUGH, not because he is not qualified but because he does not have those few grey hair to look smart and qualified in the eye of the employer. It is sad.

13. In my country, old age people get more respect or attention everywhere, they are listened, their ideas accepted and everyone thinks they know everything, even if they don't. I am not against respect for elders but I want younger people to be heard as well. Their ideas be accepted if they are right.

14. Personal ambition and drive is what equates to success with one's career, not age.. Discrimination is present everywhere, including with a variety of age groups.

15. It's upsetting to see that even in today's society, age and personal looks DOES play a role in getting a job. I have seen my former employer throwing away applications after seeing someone dropping off an application. The media is a good example showing women having cosmetic surgery before going for a job interview because they think it will give them a better chance. Regardless of their race, ethnicity, age, and gender. I believe if a person meets the requirements/criteria and can perform the tasks then they should get the job.

16. In my opinion, older people are an asset to the organization.

17. Discrimination of any kind, age, place and ethnicity is totally wrong.

Respondent Comments from Turkey

1. I have noticed the difference in treating younger workers between USA and Turkey. This difference is mostly in terms of Job security. Older employees in Turkey tend to keep their jobs longer than they should, and by doing that they not only play a negative role in terms of feasibility, but also they close the doors to young people to start up with no experience. Older people with experience tend to find jobs easier than younger new starters.

2. The company at which I work is trying to back everything- no matter right or wrong – that they do. I have been working at the current company for a year now and

continuously disturbed by the two women with whom I am sharing the room. I have talked about the issue with my director many times; however although he knows that I am right, he does not support me at all since the others have been working at the company more than seven years now and he just does not want to deteriorate his relationship with them.

3. As long as demand and supply is not in balance younger people will be preferred due to less cost and their ability to adjust themselves to new developments. The increase of efficiency due to technical innovations will never balance and for this specific reason age discrimination can not be avoided because of wild competition in world.

4. In Turkey, it is not pronounced but people over 35 are considered as older workers. Due to the size of the younger population, you can often see statements such as "applicants should be younger than the age of 30" in job listings. People respect older workers in terms of their experience but some older workers are not that open to change either.

5. I do not support any kind of discrimination. But in reality companies must have a choice between younger and older ones. I am not sure what should be considered to make a choice.

Respondent Comments from United States of America

1. Age discrimination against "older workers" is rampant in this country (United States). It is criminal!

2. Younger workers want to get to the top much more quickly than before. I believe they have a high sense of entitlement. Generally, the older workers that I see feel stuck in their positions and don't like change. Younger workers have little patience for this and dismiss their experience and intelligence.

3. North America is somewhat culturally diverse. See "Nine Nations of North America" or related literature. I wonder just how much diversity there is within and among the regions discussed in geographical terms. So living in the USA may not identify anything like a homogeneous population. I expect there will be more age-related conflicts as we get a substantially large older population. This conflict will become more visible toward the end of this decade when major parts of the baby-boomer generation try to retire. Both public and private pension plans will not be able to cover them. Then I expect political forces will emerge to tax the young to support the old; and contrary-wise to avoid taxes on the young.

4. Each individual should be evaluated based on their own merit and current and potential contribution to their organization, NOT age or any other improperly prejudicial criterion.

5. Age should be at the end of one's hiring criteria. Capability and getting along with others should be at the top of the list.

6. In our place of work, they hire the very young, who in turn stay to finish their education and leave. This is not good. The position they held keeps getting passed around and in the process it loses some of knowledge about that position. They need more mature people who could stay longer and give value to their job.

7. Currently, I live in the Bahamas where younger workers feel that the older workers should quite active employment and give them a chance on the social mobility ladder.

8. Several older workers perceive that they will not be hired for new employment because they are too old. I've heard several people over 50 say that they can't leave this organization because they are too old to obtain employment elsewhere. On the opposing side, I've heard opinions from younger workers dismissed because "they don't know what they're talking about." Usually followed by a comment on the lack of experience. My sense is that this is a perception problem on both sides.

9. It seems that a lot of 50-year old men lose their jobs and are the unemployable. A lot of people under 25 don't seem to be treated as though their opinion matters. Women seem to experience it more than men

10. Directors, managers and supervisors should feel good about having older workers: they are experienced, reliable, and are more loyal.

11. Female workers experience more discrimination than male workers and older female workers experience far more discrimination that their male counterparts.

12. Older workers are still "respected" in my country as is in Jamaica and most of the Caribbean. However, the situation is changing as Governments especially, are insisting that older workers SHOULD RETIRE when they have reached 'retirement' age. Also, the 'respect' for older workers appears to be "changing" as young people have different 'mind sets' with regards to "age."

13. The older worker brings maturity, experience, a sense of responsibility, and usually a stronger work ethic than younger workers. It seems like it's harder for an older worker to change jobs as the potential employer prefers a younger worker.

14. While the public philosophy in the US is that age discrimination is both illegal and immoral, when individuals are asked to submit CVs with past work history (generally for more than the last 5 years), approximate age becomes apparent to the prospective employer, making the possibility of age discrimination "easy."

15. Seniority prevails as is "paying one's dues." Younger workers, especially those without work experience have a difficult time "breaking" into corporate arena. Top jobs are opportunities for those highly educated and with connections.

16. I think that "over 40"---is too young to be considered an older worker–"over 50" would be more appropriate.

17. An employee's worth and candidacy for consideration in a new job should be based upon competence, knowledge, and experience – regardless of age.

18. I think in general, older workers are discriminated against, particularly when seeking a position. In the education field there is probably less of this going on because more experience is looked upon as something good and the pay will reflect that. In other businesses, two young people could be hired (at the salary of the one older individual) to do the work that one older person was doing and who was let go because "their position was no longer needed."

19. I certainly have heard of issues that older workers have had with employers who replace them with younger, less expensive workers, then wonder what happened to all of the quality and customer service that they had before. Older workers bring stability to the

organization (as Wal-Mart knows), while young workers take time off to go to the beach, to party, and do not have the dedication that the older worker brings to the workplace.

Respondent Comments from Jamaica

1. I find that older workers do sometimes display certain mindsets that cause them to respond slowly to changes and to be less open to the ideas posited by younger workers. However, older workers are usually more thoughtful in decision making and have the experience to aid them in considering a greater number of variables and possible adverse externalities. Younger workers usually have more fresh ideas. I believe both sides have their strengths and place in the workplace and should be treated equally and with respect and fairness.

2. Each prospective employee should be treated based on their attitude, aptitude, qualification and in some instances experience.

3. It is sometimes difficult for "older workers" to be employed especially if they are not qualified. However, if they are highly qualified, the younger workers do get some form of preference because they can be paid at the minimum of the scale.

4. The job market is very competitive. Depending on the type of jobs available and the income employers are willing to pay, they may make a decision to go for a younger person if the budget is tight. Where the funds permit qualification and experience which favors the older person takes precedence.

5. While I am unsure of the official legal position on age discrimination in Jamaica, most organizations have adopted a set of guidelines for business conduct which expressly forbids age discrimination. As such, the issue – if it exists – is not widely known or debated.

6. While older workers can offer experience not available from younger workers, younger workers are frequently more receptive to training and other opportunities that older workers disdain.

7. The views of the performance of younger workers have changed over the past 5 years or so with many "young" persons now in managerial roles.

8. Ability to perform at the required level should be one of the main criteria in determining who is employed. Far too often wisdom and experience is lost because someone has to retire as the age for retirement has arrived. This relates mainly to government employees and is felt in the area of education in particular.

9. In Jamaica, unemployment among young people is a very worrying problem. Employers all want workers with experience, which is, of course, the one thing, young people don't have.

10. Employment laws in Jamaica are not stringently upheld / enforced, therefore the issues of age and discrimination, while being felt to be morally wrong are not addressed and in some cases are not recognized for what they really are. Therefore, organizations by and large operate in whatever way suits them as they know that actions will not be brought

against them, and should that happen, the burden of proof may result in rulings in their favor.

11. It is not really discrimination but older people feel threatened that employers would PREFER to employ some younger workers with degrees, because they may be more willing to accept less salary than they would. Younger workers are frustrated because they feel that although they may have the required qualifications they lack experience and most employers request this.

12. In many cases employers are of the opinion that "older workers" are somewhat set in their work habits; which if they are not good habits, it is more difficult for them to break out of than a "younger workers". On the other hand, I some employers who regard the experience of "older workers" as of a far greater value than the youthfulness and academic superiority of the "younger workers."

13. I believe that age should not matter, as long as the individual is qualified (training, experience and aptitude and has the right attitude to learn); then age should never be any issue. It is natural that the older worker is likely to have more experience and knowledge/ training since age will allow (that though it is not necessarily always the case). And younger workers may not have enough time to gain the training and experience that may be required for a task. Though I believe that given equal opportunity in all respect age should not be an issue. The age will go along way with the right attitude whether as a cooperative follower or exemplary leader. Consequently, there should be no discrimination based on age as the only factor. Personal case of discrimination: when I just graduated from Teachers college, though I was told that I was qualified for certain jobs, I was also told that I was too young, this hurts then and it was not fair. Later the very persons required my service when I was older. Naturally I would have lost interest and zeal for such place.

14. What is regarded as discrimination? I consider mandatory retirement age of 62 or 65, as is the case in many institutions, age discrimination. The preference for older workers vs. younger workers depends on the job to be filled. In some cases, there is a preference for younger workers vs. older ones, and vice versa

15. Selection for a job is based on the capability of the person to perform in the position. This could be based on experience or education/training or a combination. Definitely some jobs will have requirements for expertise, which not many young persons have, although they have the educational background. Younger persons will therefore have to act perhaps in an 'apprentice' role until the requisite skills/expertise has been attained. On the job training is not a new concept in any culture. On the other hand, experience alone by older workers may at times not be sufficient. It would be advantageous to the older worker that job related qualifications be attained, whether he/she intends to retain present position, or change jobs/workplace.

16. Discrimination occurs in both categories of workers identified. The nature of the job will determine the level of discrimination. Some jobs prefer younger and attractive persons while others have a preference for older persons. Equally there is discrimination relating to sex and the survey did not capture that information. Age discrimination primarily occurs as younger persons are preferred for some jobs and older employees are preferred

for others. Newer companies appear to have a preference for younger employees. With established companies as well as new companies management positions may more readily be offered to older persons as companies usually ask for experience covering a certain period of time.

17. In Jamaica older people get better jobs and higher salaries than younger persons performing the same jobs. As a younger person every interview that I go on for a job which I am qualified for and have the experience and expertise to perform the interviewer questions my capabilities because of my age (or perception of youth because I don't put it on my resume and I look young). Age is revered in Jamaica because people think that older persons possess greater wisdom, "stictuitiveness" and bring status to their establishments.

18. It is imperative that we treat each worker, regardless of age, as an equal. In addition my country should ensure that benefits that accrue in your activity years are protected legally and that you are still able to access vital financial assistance despite age.

19. Now that I am one of the older workers I worry that the time will come when I will be perceived as too old for certain jobs. I know that in some jobs being older is an advantage. Some companies prefer the work ethic of the older generation, while others will not hire you because you are perceived as being too expensive from a health insurance perspective. There are advantages and disadvantages on both sides of the issue and I think smart companies recognize this and make it work for them.

General Evaluation of Comments

It is quite revealing to see the actual verbatim comments by the survey respondents, as these comments clearly indicate the challenge global managers will confront in managing a diverse workforce.

Afghanistan. One respondent from Afghanistan stressed that respect for elders is based on the fact that the country is Islamic, and thus requires that youth respect their elders. Any religious based moral norms against age discrimination would be very important to note. Another respondent stated that older workers with "good experience" can still get jobs in the private sector, but another said the main impediment was that older workers are not familiar with the "new technology." Other respondents also mentioned the technology factor as well as some older workers not being familiar with "modern" management. Another offered the very practical, and ethically egoistic, advice that it is wrong to discriminate against older workers because they have knowledge gained through experience. One respondent related that the retirement age is "set" at 55, but by whom, the private sector or the government? Most disturbing were the two comments by two different respondents. One was that "the older you are, the lesser you are 'worth' in the corporate American culture." The other comment was that there was no age discrimination against older workers in Afghanistan, but there was in the U.S., particularly in the industrial and manufacturing sectors of the U.S. economy.

Turkey. Again, the technology factor was mentioned by respondents as an impediment to older workers, as well as their perceived inability to adjust and to be open to change. However, similar to the country of Afghanistan, the people of Turkey are heavily influenced by thousands of years of cultural conditioning and history that respect the elderly and their experience.

United States of America. Once again, it was disturbing to read several comments regarding the prevalence of age discrimination against older workers from the U.S. respondents. One said that age discrimination against older workers was "rampant" in the United States. Another stressed that such discrimination was even more prevalent against older female workers. One comment revealed a particularly "machiavellian" practice; that is, an employer using an applicant's past work history and resume (or curriculum vitae) so that his or her approximate age becomes "apparent," thus leading to the possibility of age discrimination, and even making such discrimination "easy," according to the respondent. Perhaps that comment revealed how the extensive U.S. anti-discrimination law could be circumvented. One other comment by another respondent was also provocative and thought-provoking, as the respondent stated that due to the older population growing substantially, there likely will be more "age-related conflicts" in the United States. The comments reflected a consensus that although there are positive aspects of obtaining older workers, such as their experience, the negatives of so doing, such as their perceived inability to change or adapt and the lack of technological skills, outweigh the positives.

Jamaica. One comment was troubling, and that was that the respondent did not know the "official legal position" on age discrimination in the country, but "the issue, if it exists, is not widely known or debated." This comment was echoed by another respondent that said that whatever employment laws exist in Jamaica, they are "not stringently upheld/enforced." One comment indicated that the mandatory retirement age at "many institutions" was 62 or 65, which the respondent felt was age discrimination. Finally, the same negative "theme" regarding older workers was reflected from the comments. That is, the benefits of hiring experienced and mature older workers were counterbalanced and outweighed by their lack of modern skills, and as one respondent said, being too "set" in their ways and their habits, which according to the respondent may be "bad habits."

Summary. What is the purpose of having such an extensive body of anti-discrimination law, as well as prevailing moral beliefs – individual and societal and even religious-based norms – against age discrimination, and what is the purpose of having "diversity" training, which presumably includes an age component, when so much age discrimination in employment is reported by the data and the comments, especially in the United States of America. Perhaps the law, ethics, religion, and the training are superseded by perceived negative picture of older workers in the culture. Thus, perhaps, along with more specific laws or more stringent laws, or more diversity training for managers who hire, develop, and promote workers, what may help older workers the most is more technology training and relevant training as to modern techniques regarding management and business practices. Resolving these workplace issues, legally, morally, and practically, emerges as a critical task for modern day, global, business leaders.

Effective Leadership in Developing Nations

Leadership, the art of influencing others, is one of the main elements of international business. Global leaders contribute inspiring ideas and implement flourishing strategies for the success of a company. According to Thomas and Mujtaba (2004), "Leaders play a significant role in the company; therefore employing leaders or executives with appropriate leadership skills generally determines the victory of the company." Being a leader in a company is fundamentally a complicated task, and when he or she is a global leader the chore becomes more complex. Global leaders work with a vast diversity, which includes many different nations so they should have the knowledge of various cultures. Since the opportunities in international business are growing rapidly, the necessity for proficient global leaders is rapidly increasing. In different centuries the businesses were practiced differently. In order to be successful in the twenty-first century, it is necessary to change the business style from prior years. In global organizations, global leaders are usually responsible for instituting the new transformations for the company's future prosperity (Thomas and Mujtaba, 2004).

Global leadership, that is, influencing people throughout the world, is described as a blend of global business, managing diversity, encouraging employees, responsibility, and broad thinking (Mendenhall, Kuhlmann and Stahl, 2001). Thomas and Mujtaba said that global leaders and managers interact with people worldwide; therefore they should have the ability to encourage and influence people from all over the world. These managers and leaders think globally instead of locally, which is the primary method to conduct business effectively. For companies to have knowledgeable leaders in the twenty-first century, they should provide chances for the leaders to obtain extensive knowledge regarding their worldwide operations and the different processes around the world. The companies also can provide opportunities to increase the knowledge of their global leaders by letting them have real practice in overseas and by instructing the culture of those countries (Mendenhall, Kuhlmann, and Stahl, 2001). There are various ethical decisions that leaders will have to make in their daily activities. Sometimes they depend on their personal experiences and beliefs to make these decisions, which might not be a suitable method since people have different ethical perspectives and these decisions affect many people (Cavico & Mujtaba, 2005). In international business, managers and leaders can face some difficulties in making ethical decisions since those decisions have to be appropriate and acceptable for the local culture.

The global companies in the twenty-first century demand global leaders, who have the capabilities to work successfully throughout the world. Today's leaders thus should be able to change themselves according to the environment without varying their values and morality. Marquardt and Berger (2000) said that "To be an effective leader in the twenty-first century one will need to possess eight key attributes: an ability to develop and convey a shared vision, a service/servant orientation, commitment to risk-taking and continuous innovation, a global mindset, comfort and confidence with technology, competence in system thinking, recognition of the importance of ethics and spirituality in the work place, and a model for lifelong learning." The global leaders with these attributes can direct the company in a new path to achieve success.

The twenty-first century often is titled as "the global age." Businesses are practicing and people are thinking and acting globally, and these performances direct businesses and people sharing more common values and systems. There are four common elements or forces that led businesses to be in the global age, and they are technology, travel, trade, and television (Thomas and Mujtaba, 2004). According to experts "an organization is globalized when the organization has developed a global corporate culture, strategy, and structure, as well as global operation and global people" (Marquardt & Berger, 2000). More companies are globalizing, therefore the need of global leaders is rapidly increasing. Dealing with the international market means interacting with people of different ethnicities, ages, and value systems throughout the world; therefore global leaders need to be aware of the cultural and market differences between countries in order to be successful in the twenty-first century.

The new business environment is different from prior years; and there are still differences among culture despite technological convergences. While some management and leadership practices are global, there must be room for local adjustments and local practices. Local people are not as willing to accept leadership practices by foreign managers that disrespect their ways of doing things. Consequently, the global leaders have to recognize this transformation from twentieth to twenty-first century and perform accordingly. Accordingly, a twenty-first century leader should have the capability to view the world and businesses with a global mindset but with local adjustments, and it would guide them to understand the international business practices effectively. The global leaders with a global mindset have a broader way of thinking, they are aware of the cultural diversity, and they make appropriate decisions from a global perspective while acting locally. The global minded leaders think globally but act locally. They are usually open to adapt and exchange new ideas and techniques. They generally try to equalize local and global needs in order to be successful both locally and internationally (Marquardt & Berger, 2000).

In most cases, while the ultimate goal in business is to make profit; the business systems vary from country to country and culture to culture. According to Cavico and Mujtaba (2005), "when companies do business with developing countries they should not always expect the developing nation to have the same economic systems as their native country. Every country has its own economic system, political system, and other local customs that influence its infrastructure. It is the foreign company's obligation to follow the country's rules while enforcing high ethical standards and safety measures." The global leaders should try to follow the social standards of the country where they are doing the business. Following moral values of the native country in a different nation might not be appropriate for the local standards. However since the ethical standards in all the countries are similar, following those standards will be appropriate for the business success and stability in the foreign country (Cavico & Mujtaba, 2005). According to Marquardt & Berger, leaders are teachers, coaches, and mentors, who lead people in the successful business direction. It is their responsibility to teach, mentor, and coach others in the company in order for others to have effectual knowledge regarding the business. Today's leaders also must be great teachers as they need to effectively impart knowledge and develop their people appropriately. This may allow people to learn the processes instantaneously and efficiently (Marquardt & Berger, 2000) while working collaboratively with their superiors.

Leadership, the process of influencing others, is fundamentally a continuous teaching and learning process. A leader should have the capability to influence people and change their views and actions in order to improve their performance in an organization. The most effective method to have more leaders for the twenty-first century is by having the current leaders develop new leaders. The current leaders need to teach the new leaders every aspect of the business and help them to form a new and effective leadership style and this will guide company's future success. The twenty-first century business environment is very fast paced; therefore if the companies transform slowly, they might not persevere in the industry. Action learning appears to be one of the most effective methods to learn business, since it involves real practice and it would allow people to handle complex tasks (Marquardt & Berger, 2000). In global business, according to Thomas and Mujtaba (2004), global leaders need to be sent overseas and have the hands on practice to learn the culture and local business style. Globalization opens new doors that demands new aptitudes; however these capabilities are not attained in a short period of time. The need for the global leaders is increasing because of the method of the globalization (Black, Morrison, & Gregerson, 1999). Since majority of the large companies are globalized in this century, it is very important for the companies to have skilled global leaders and that they receive adequate overseas training. Such global leaders must then become effective teachers and developer so their people so they can all function effectively in the context of cultural differences (Thomas and Mujtaba, 2004). Effective leaders and teachers understand that learning is about exploring the unknown and that such exploration begins with open-ended questions and personal reflection. One also needs to remember that teachers are not there to just be passing out information. Educators are also teaching people how to think and deduce conclusions. The last thing one wants to do is stand up and tell people what to do; or give them the answers that one wants to hear. The best educators are less interested in the answers than in the thinking behind them. One final point that all leaders and educators should keep in mind is to never stop teaching, as it is the best source of learning. Effective teaching is about the quality of the relationship between the teacher and the student (or leader and employee). It doesn't end when the workday is over. One should remember that effective leaders are also effective coaches that coach their players before the game, during the game, and after the game for future successes. Teaching is a continuous learning process for both the coach and the players. Effective global leaders must become effective teachers and coaches as they lead their organizations to avoid disasters in developing countries while securing their trust and business and ultimately achieving success.

Guidelines for Fair Employment Practices

In order to create awareness and a culture of fair employment practices, global leaders and managers should institute relevant policies and procedures to bring about appropriate cultural changes in the organization. As presented in Figure 12, human resource professionals can apply the following steps to better manage various organizational-relevant cultural diversity dimensions and, thus, to avoid, eliminate and end age discrimination.

1. Understand the culture and cultural attitudes towards age discrimination.
2. Clarify cultural, national, and international laws applicable to employment practices in the organization. Measure current organizational practices.
3. Develop policies and implement procedures appropriate to the organizational values.
4. Elicit support from senior management.
5. Disseminate organizational policies and communicate expectations to all managers and employers.
6. Educate and train all managers in fair hiring, developing, promoting, disciplining, and retaining of experienced employees.
7. Consistently monitor program and enforce policies.
8. Improve the program, policies, and procedures with regard fair employment practices.

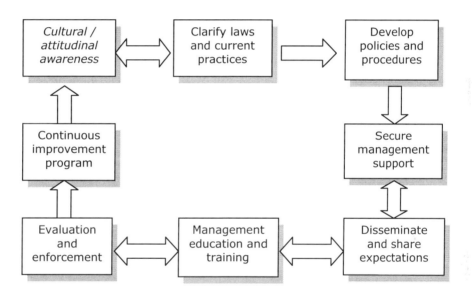

Figure 12 – Cultural Diversity Management Steps

Global leadership plays a significant role in international business. It is important to have highly skilled leaders in an organization to encourage and train employees. Since global leaders work with people throughout the world, they need to be aware of the cultural differences. Using the same business style as the parent company in another nation might not be a successful method to conduct business. Global leaders ensure that the global organization is operating smoothly and all the subsidiaries are being treated equally. Companies need to send their leaders to foreign nations for them to understand the culture and social standards. Business in the twenty-first century is completely different from prior years, and leaders need to make sure their people are adapting quickly to such changes. Due to the rapid growth of international business, companies require more global leaders and global-minded employees. To develop more global leaders, current leaders need to provide adequate training for the new leaders. The best methodology in developing global leaders is by providing more exposure to the international arena of the organization, and offering training from other experienced global leaders in the company. As stated by Albert Einstein, "Everything should be as simple as possible, but not simpler."

Compared to people working within a country or culture, those who work on international levels have to deal with greater levels of change regarding employment practices because of legal, cultural, social, economical, and environmental differences that exist within and among people of various countries. These international business and non-business people must become aware of subtle differences and nuances in other people's conversations, body gestures, sensitivities, table manners, business dealings, general contracts and agreements, gender differences and perceptions, time management styles, attitudes, values, religious beliefs, and many others that might be more prominent in some cultures than others. The authors conclude that all people deal with change to different degrees, yet everybody goes through the same process in dealing with change. However, how they move through the process may vary based on their subtle differences which could be influenced by personal, organizational, and/or cultural elements. The authors further emphasize that global leaders can use various strategies to initiate, champion, and bring about the needed changes in their employment practices regarding older workers in the right manner and at the right times.

Summary

Global thinking and local acting mindset has become the norm in today's small business world. International joint ventures, mergers, partnerships, and cooperatively working in complementary businesses have become a prevalent mode of business and are not considered anomalies anymore. All of the above has been caused by the advent of new technology, global competition, diverse global employees, and the availability of resources around the world in short periods of time. Of course, an abundant amount of information is available and can be accessed in a matter of five to ten seconds through a telephone or a computer and Internet. So, change has become a way of life, and it comes in a variety of shapes, sizes, and forms. Change impacts both young and older workers as well as the employment practices of managers in the workplace. As such, everyone must be properly prepared to effectively deal with these societal changes. Change can be passive or inactive, mandated, and self-generated or proactive. Each type of change may have different affects on people because the variable and elements may be different. However, one knows that successful implementation of international change entails both learning how people go through the stages of the change cycle and learning to get people excited about change and move them into a brighter future, perhaps more quickly and with less stress in the process. Today's environment demands that each individual becomes a change agent and take responsibility for his or her own future by mentally creating it and then working toward accomplishing it on a daily basis. Once the vision of the future is clear, then a global leader or manager can align the changing world to fit his or her goals and objectives. There is something valuable in each learning experience. At the global or national levels, having a world of wealth means nothing, having good health means something; however, having integrity and a virtuous character mean everything for both younger and older workers of all nations.

CHAPTER 6

MACHIAVELLIAN THINKING IN MANAGEMENT

The Prince was written by Niccolo Machiavelli (1467-1527), the Italian philosopher and Florentine public servant, in the sixteenth century, and Machiavelli used Caesare Borgia, a local dictator, as his "model" Princes. Instructions were provided on how a prince should rule, whose advice the ruler should rely on, and how one should conduct oneself to gain the most from one's leadership.

Research shows that there is a statistically significant difference between "high Mach" and "low Mach" respondents and that the views of respondents with different levels of education in business are similar with regard to Machiavellianism. Furthermore, research shows that Machiavellian thinking still exists in today's organizations leading many managers to take actions that are beneficial only to the organization even if it comes at the cost of discriminating toward older workers. This fact would seem to be significant given the attention that researchers and writers have given to the styles of leadership needed for effective organizations. Accordingly, the practical application of Machiavellian principles relating to management, leadership, and entrepreneurship in the twenty first century organization are presented in the context of age discrimination in employment.

Machiavellian Principles and Thinking

The term "Machiavellian" is often used to mean "of, like, or befitting Machiavelli," "being or acting in accordance with the principles of government analyzed in Machiavelli's *The Prince,* in which political expediency is placed above morality and the use of craft and deceit to maintain the authority and carry out the policies of a ruler is described," "characterized by subtle or unscrupulous cunning, deception, expediency, or dishonesty: *He resorted to Machiavellian tactics in order to get ahead*," or "a follower of the principles analyzed or described in The Prince, especially with regard to techniques and strategies of political manipulation. So, a "Machiavellian" is perceived to be someone who used manipulative strategies and tactics to benefit himself or herself.

Shameful! Dreadful! Contemptible! Detestable! Immoral! Amoral! Evil! These sample assertions have been the sort of denunciations cast at Machiavelli in direct response to his political treatise, *The Prince*, a "little" book on political theory and the practical applications thereof. Pursuant to this "immoral" interpretation, Machiavelli rightly is condemned as a "bad" and dangerous "machiavellian." This negative view, perhaps the prevailing "popular" one of Machiavelli, has engendered the most consternation and vociferous protest against "machiavellianism."

In reading "The Prince," it's very easy to see the context upon which it was written, during early 1500's. Given this reference, the mindset from the 16th century, and the politics of the time from the city state rule in Italy, one should proceed cautiously with his/her application. Many individuals agree with Machiavelli despite the fact that his writings may have been shocking and controversial, but perhaps because he dared to put into words the actions of men for his time period. Perhaps, many parallels can be made between today's business leaders and Machiavelli's Prince since, supposedly, among many others, even President Bill Clinton had made references which had their basis in Machiavelli's writings. However, perhaps the modern business person has missed a point that Machiavelli stated, and that is that leaders reflect on their actions: "Nevertheless, you should be careful how you assess the situation and should think twice before you act. Do not be afraid of your shadow. Employ policies that are moderated by prudence and sympathy. Avoid excessive self-confidence which leads to carelessness and avoid excessive timidity, which will make you insupportable." Some individuals claim that modern business has adopted only the parts of Machiavellian which suit its purpose, and as such, businesses have missed the big picture. One must keep in mind the context of Machiavelli's writings and the society in which it was written for in the sixteenth century; yet, some of what he said about men's loyalties are still true, but the present society is much different than Florence in 1500. Perhaps, just as Sun Tzu, in the "The Art of War" which is still being taught, there are valuable principles to be learned, Machiavellian concepts should be taught as well; but they must be considered in the context in which they were written, and one must be very careful to "translate" their message to today's society. Machiavelli did say that a prince is often forced to know how to act like a "beast," but he must learn from the fox as well as the lion to be effective. He also said; "A prudent ruler cannot, and must not, honor his word when it places him at a disadvantage and when the reasons for which he made his promise no longer exist." His writings still impress people four centuries after they were written; and parallels can be made between his thoughts and today's business leaders.

Research Results with Working Adults

The study of effective style of leadership has received much more attention than ever before over the past few years, and continues to grow as more and more senior executives of large corporations are making the "evening news" for wrong-doing. Over the years, research on Machiavelli has examined the actions of leaders, and the results have been controversial and interesting simultaneously. For the purpose of this book, masters of business administration students attending a weekend program were surveyed to determine the extent to which they practiced Machiavellianism. The students were 95% working professionals, and some had their own businesses. Thus, a large number of them have been exposed to "high Mach" and "low Mach" behavior. They have had an opportunity to make an informed choice about managerial and leadership behaviors.

Over eighty working adult students attending class for their first or second semester in the masters program at a non-traditional format during weekend were given the survey in their Twenty First Century Management Practices course during the discussion on leadership theories, or the surveys were administered to them in their Ethics course. The return rate was a 52% response rate with five incomplete forms leaving 37 usable surveys for the study. The Mach V Attitude Inventory Instrument was used to determine the extent to which they agreed with Machiavellian concepts. The survey includes twenty groups of statements with each group consisting of three different responses. The participants were to choose the statement that they considered most true based on their experience and personal preferences. Of the remaining two questions, they were asked to identify the statement that they considered most false. The third statement, which is considered to be average, was left unmarked. The following is a sample question demonstrating what is to be completed by each person completing the survey where *"Most True = +"* and *"Most False = -."* So, the most true statement gets a "+" sign and the most false statement gets a "- or minus" sign and they are asked to leave the remaining of the three statements unmarked.

    _____ A. It is easy to persuade people but hard to keep them persuaded.
    _+_ B. Theories that run counter to common sense are a waste of time.
    _-_ C. It is only common sense to go along with what other people are doing and not be too different.

In this example, statement B would be the one this person believe in *most strongly* and statements A and C would be ones that are *not* as characteristic of this person's opinions. Of these two, statement C would be the one this person believe in *least strongly* and the one that is *least* characteristic of his/her beliefs. Once the scores for all surveys are completed, total scores were determined by the number of high-Mach responses and low-Mach responses. The possible range for the scores is between 40 and 160 as per design of the instrument. Higher scores indicate a high mach and lower scores indicate low mach. The neutral point is 100 for the survey. From the 37 respondents, 11 (or 30%) scored at the neutral point with scores of 100 on the Mach V Attitude Inventory Instrument.

Table 18: Mach Statistics				
	Frequency	Percent	Valid Percent	Cumulative Percent
Valid Low Mach	13	35	35	35
High Mach	13	35	35	70
Neutral	11	30	30	100
Total	37	100	100	

Descriptive statistics was performed to identify those students who were "high Machs" and those who were "low Machs." Although not necessary, a t-test was conducted to determine whether there a significant difference in the mean scores of the "high Machs" and the "low Machs." As expected, there was a significant difference.

Table 19: Group Statistics				
	Mach	N	Mean	Std. Deviation
TOTALSCO	Low Mach	13	91.0	6.125
	High Mach	13	110.0	4.793

Thirteen or 35% of the respondents scored above the neutral point on the Machiavellianism scale, suggesting that they are "high Machs." Twenty four respondents or 65% scored at or below the neutral point. The mean score for the high Machs was 110 and for the "low Machs" 91 (not including those with the neutral score). From the 37 respondents, 11 scored at the neutral point with scores of exactly 100 on the Mach V Attitude Inventory Instrument. As such, their scores were not counted with Low Machs. Therefore, the final numbers for comparison are 13 Low Machs and 13 High Machs which would obviously show a significant difference. The result of the t-test, as can be seen in Table 20, shows (t= 8.88, p= .000), suggesting that there is a statistically significant difference in the mean scores. Perhaps society continues to reward and reinforce the "high Mach" behavior because it is more efficacious than "low Mach" behavior.

Table 20: t-Test: Two-Sample Assuming Unequal Variances		
	Variable 1	*Variable 2*
Mean	90.84615385	109.7692308
Variance	37.80769231	21.19230769
Observations	13	13
Hypothesized Mean Difference	0	
df	22	
t Stat	-8.882545179	
P(T<=t) one-tail	4.97874E-09	
t Critical one-tail	1.717144187	
P(T<=t) two-tail	9.95747E-09	
t Critical two-tail	2.073875294	

These results support previous research conducted by Preziosi and Gooden in 2003, who surveyed working MBA students attending their last course in the program. Preziosi and Gooden found that 41.4% of respondents scored above the neutral point on the Machiavellianism scale, suggesting that they were "high Machs," and 58.6% scored at or below the neutral point suggesting that they were "low Machs." As such, Preziosi and Gooden concluded "The research participants knew the implications of their choice of low

Mach or high Mach…perhaps their environments continue to reward and reinforce the high Mach behavior because it is more expeditious than low Mach behavior." Since the result of the current study with new (starting) MBA students are similar to the scores of graduating MBA students, one can summarize that entering MBAs and those who are near graduation are likely to be similar in their views with regard to Machiavellianism. Consequently, the approximately one year of attending MBA classes has not made much of a difference in their views regarding Machiavellianism and power-seeking initiatives.

Overall, power still seems to be driving the corporate executive, manager, and entrepreneur because power is not only a "good" end but also a "good" means. If one acquires, uses, and wields power correctly, one will be rewarded with success, wealth, fame, and ultimately glory, and thus attain the eminence of The Prince. According to Preziosi and Gooden (2003), the principles and practices of inclusion (empowerment, participation, etc.) continue to be the focus of many theorists and researchers. Many are of the opinion that most successful organizations require leadership and management built around this philosophy. They continue to suggest that less effective organizations, at least over the short term, tend to be exclusionary. Exclusion is more in line with Machiavellian behaviors than inclusion. So why do over one-third of the research study participants end up with high Mach scores? Why do such a high percentage people place a high value on authoritarianism? Is this what they see constantly in their organizational environments? This is a question, as well as a statement, of the need for continued research that will address the impact of exclusionary versus exclusionary behaviors in building a successful enterprise. Perhaps the educational institutions teaching management leadership skills, while emphasizing knowledge, skills, and techniques, may also be de-emphasizing the prospective manager's faith and trust in others which is further reinforced by visual picture of senior organizational leaders being taken to jail for wrongdoing. Perhaps, these "high Mach" scores are a reference to the authoritarian style of some professors who are classroom teachers in the colleges. Also, the current work environment may be dominated by many "high Machs" managers who will do whatever it takes, including immoral and bad means, to achieve the stated numerical objectives of the organization, including discriminating against older workers.

The remaining portions of the chapter are devoted to the business application of Machiavellian principles exemplified by *"The Prince."* The business application, interpretations and extrapolations are subjective since they are based on the personal thoughts and experiences of the authors in modern business environment and not necessarily any scientific studies.

Machiavellian Business Application

Managers "Power" Strategies and Tactics

Although the entrepreneur, CEO, or other top executive typically is thought of as The Prince of the business realm, many managers also are "princes" in their own domains. There they rule, develop their knowledge and skills, and display their ambition; and, moreover, where some very ambitious ones may be plotting to overthrow their Prince. The major difference between the person at the apex of the organization and those just beneath him or her is the extent of the realm, and perhaps, also, the degree of ambition as well as the level of success in satisfying it. In many cases, the head of the organization simply is the most ambitious and successful of its management leaders and aspiring Princes. Regardless of the domain, for a Machiavellian-based manager, power is the key – the acquisition, retention, and exercise of power; and thus the astute manager will be concerned above all else with acquiring power in his or her sphere as well as commanding greater influence within the organization. Promotion to greater spheres naturally leads to greater power in decision-making and ruling over subordinates.

In the pursuit of corporate power, the Machiavellian manager must be keenly aware that conduct within the firm readily can become truly "machiavellian." Abusive tactics, such as deception, manipulation, discrimination, and exploitation can be employed to advance selfish individual interests at the expense of others and the company. These tactics can harm seriously those who themselves possess little knowledge, expertise, or power. A "machiavellian" manager, for example, may attempt to sabotage the careers of his or her co-workers by making anonymous false charges on the corporation's ethics "hot-line." He or she may seek to acquire control of scarce resources needed by others; or may engage in the withholding or distorting of information, or may attempt to overwhelm a party with information. He or she may discriminate against older workers with less technological capabilities than younger workers, and my circumvent the law to do so. The "machiavellian" manager may feign power, expertise, friendship, concern, favor, or respect; and thereby manipulate others to show deference, loyalty, indebtedness, and trust; and persuade them to perform actions that they would not ordinarily do. He or she can exploit particular personal vulnerabilities, such as vanity, gullibility, sense of responsibility, or generosity, so as to unknowingly place a person in a position of dependency and servility. The "machiavellian" manager, of course, will associate with the influential "power-brokers," and seek to ingratiate himself or herself with them, and thereby build an image and develop a base of support to advance ideas and ambitions. Yet, if his or her policies are failing, the "machiavellian" manager will attempt to undo, obliterate, or minimize any association with nonsuccess. If one challenges the "machiavellian" manager, he or she will attack them, blame them for any failures, and denigrate any rival accomplishments as unimportant, self-serving, poorly timed, or just lucky. One always must remember, as Machiavelli stressed, that appearances are essential; and thus the "machiavellian" manager always must seem to be important, intelligent, confident, honest, moral, fair, sensitive, personable, and popular.

A manager in a position of power thus must take care to fortify his or her corporate domain in order to withstand the assailing forces of any corporate "invaders," from either outside or inside the firm. In Machiavelli's time, the Prince secured his principality with brick, stone, and mortar in the form of high and strong city walls, and manned these positions with his loyal subjects. How does a modern day "machiavellian" manager secure his or her position? Principally, by acquiring, shrewdly using, and perhaps concealing information. That is, the manager will use, release, or conceal information only if it is advantageous for him or her to do so. Thus, any time an information type decision is made, it must serve, at the very least, as another brick or stone in the rising wall around the manager's domain. Information that is essential for controlling a process, or critical to extricate the organization or an ally from a difficult situation, are examples of "solidifying" protective information.

Another excellent example of a manager fortifying his or her position can be seen in the manager's treatment of his or her subordinates. Subordinates generally should not be viewed as a threat, even especially talented ones. A wise and prudent manager always will seek out, and intelligently utilize, capable individuals in an effort to better serve the firm, as well as to inure to the benefit of the manager. An empowerment style of management, therefore, is not in disharmony with Machiavellian-based business values. Empowerment should produce more trust, initiative, and innovation among one's subordinates. Employees who are permitted to be self-supervised, and are allowed to work freely (within established guidelines, of course) to achieve identified and agreed-upon goals will feel trusted and respected as colleagues and partners; and thereby should have their potential unleashed to achieve mutually beneficial results. Values, such as communication, team-building, participation, delegation, and self-management are fundamental to successful performance; and these values do not contravene Machiavelli's counsels. At work, therefore, it will be very important for a manager to create a team of very qualified individuals, as well as an appropriate system of communication between and among them. Properly flowing communication will promote understanding, and increase knowledge. Enhanced communication clearly is conducive to achieving the "good" of profits and power.

Individuals, moreover, must be selected, and given their "team" assignments based on their strengths of course, and their weaknesses too. Such assignments should be made with a motive to providing individuals an opportunity to excel, to develop additional skills, and acquire useful knowledge. The Machiavellian manager should strive to establish a mutually beneficial career-learning and career-advancing environment; and such an environment will inure to the benefit of the manager as well as his or her subordinates. The manager's subordinate employees very well could be equated to Machiavelli's "native troops," that is, those with a sense of loyalty and dedication to The Prince. Such "troops" more easily can be managed and directed by the manager. They also will work more diligently and loyally for the manager than Machiavelli's "auxiliary" or "mixed" troops, perhaps today's part-time employees, independent contractors, and consultants. All of the latter work primarily because they are getting paid; and once the money runs out, so does their loyalty, which probably is leaning to some other personal objective anyway.

Certainly, the team-work, empowerment, and open communication style of management does entail some risks, for example, unpredictability of behavior, difficulty in supervision and control, and especially the risk of creating competitive power centers. The careful "machiavellian" manager, therefore, clearly and explicitly must indicate definite goals, establish available resources, identify degrees of authority, lines of accountability, channels of communication, and agree upon specific consequences. These managerial guidelines and channels, however, should not be so rigid or fixed to deter new ideas, suggestions, recommendations, and sources of information. Managers will need this information to understand their markets, people – employees, subordinates, and superiors, and especially their competition – internally as well as externally. Gaining a clear understanding of the power structure of the firm, and the factors that affect it, are crucial to the attainment of the manager's ultimate goals of position, power, and profits.

When a manager's methods have been proven successful, Machiavelli, of course, would counsel their continuation, but Machiavelli also advises, definitely and forcefully, to adopt new methods when a manager is confronted with conditions of change. Recognizing the need, and possessing the courage and capability, to change emerge as difficult challenges for a manager, yet indispensable to a manager's success.

Machiavelli also argues for an aggressive approach to detecting and solving problems. He thereby counsels to address problematic issues at an early, and presumably more tractable, stage, rather than temporizing until they fester into bigger dilemmas. Machiavelli, in fact, notes that problems which are difficult to perceive are frequently the simplest to cure, but those that become obvious often are the most complex to solve. Preparation and vigilance thus are important values for the manager. Machiavelli emphasizes that without opportunity, one's talents will be wasted; but without capability, an opportunity will be wasted and squandered. The astute CEO and entrepreneur, therefore, should recognize, advance, and support knowledgeable, skillful, and perceptive managers, and reward their valuable contributions. In particular, those managers who take the initiative and increase the wealth of the firm and its owners and "stakeholders" should be encouraged and honored by the firm's principals.

Interestingly, in reading *The Prince*, one almost can presume that Machiavelli had foreknowledge of management's (at least U.S. business management's) obsession with the immediate "bottom-line" focus on short-term profits, instead of concentrating on the long-term financial growth and health of the firm. Machiavelli, in fact, warned that people of little prudence will perform an action for immediate gain, without comprehending the harm this action will cause in the future. One problem that arises from *The Prince* is Machiavelli's advice to the Prince to rule through fear. This counsel, at first glance, might cause perplexity for the modern day "team-oriented" business manager. Yet when Machiavelli talks about "fear," he does not necessarily mean fear that produces immobilizing insecurity, for example, the fear of a cowered underling of arbitrary punishment by "the boss." That degree of intimidating fear would hinder open, honest, and essential communication, and clearly would be counter-productive. "Fear," rather, should be the fear of not meeting clear, specific, and reachable objectives, or the fear of doing expressly forbidden actions.

A manager following a Machiavellian-based management philosophy and style must be aware of certain significant "moral" practices – "moral" in the "pure" Machiavellian sense that they will result in power for the manager. A manager must know the people to whom he or she reports. Understanding them and being sensitive to their needs and concerns are key ingredients to success. A manager, therefore, may need to solicit, cautiously of course, advice on the more subtle aspects of the "office politics" of his or her firm. Making friends with the "power-brokers" in the firm naturally will be most helpful. Similarly, it will be essential for the manager to know well his or her own employees and staff. Treat them well, reward those who perform ably; and tactfully transfer or dismiss non-productive individuals. Maintain open, but not unlicensed, communication with one's staff, as well as one's superiors, other personnel, and clients. Remain accessible too; and keep key personnel properly informed and interested in plans being formulated and projects undertaken. Demonstrate competence, Machiavelli would counsel. Initiate programs and execute them well; and keep one's critical managerial role clearly visible and prominent. Build on programs that are already established and functioning well. Share credit with one's "team" members for the successes, but, once again, make sure that one's managerial role is perceived as an indispensable element to the process. Anticipate problems; and work to solve them early, quickly, and ordinarily "behind the scenes." Yet cultivate a reputation for helping others solve problems. Be disposed to offer one's time and advice when requested, but be realistic too. Avoid being negative and confrontational, but be prepared to vigorously defend the quality of one's work, effort, or role, if questioned. Definitely do not "burn any bridges"; and do not make any unnecessary enemies. Always seek to bring about those policies and programs that increase long-term organizational power and profits, particularly so when the manager's own recognition, reward, power and prestige are enhanced within the organization.

What will the personal life of such a Machiavellian manager look like? What characteristics would he or she display. Typically, such a person would be extremely work-oriented; and dominated by a passion to achieve and excel. He or she will work very hard at work – on the job, at home, on "vacation" – all in a focused, sustained effort to achieve success and recognition. The Machiavellian manager constantly will be studying, reviewing, learning, consulting – all with the objective of meeting certain goals. Of course, one problem with such a manager is that the truly personal dimension to one's life, that is, one's family life, may suffer, but that is a "price" to be paid for pursuing influence and power, and attaining success, fame, and riches, ultimately on a "princely" scale.

Entrepreneurs–Machiavelli's Business "Founders"

In the modern world, founding a political principality, let alone conquering a kingdom, is a problematic undertaking; but Machiavelli's philosophy also has real meaning for modern day business entrepreneurs. Entrepreneurship and corporate "empire-building" are excellent business opportunities for a person with "princely" ambitions. Machiavelli's "lessons" for the aspiring entrepreneur are evident: be a "tough," smart, single-minded, dedicated, visionary leader; work persistently and diligently; bend and break the "rules" if absolutely necessary; do not be overly concerned with traditional notions of value, ethics, and morality; achieve success and attain the ultimate goals of wealth, fame, and glory.

Entrepreneurs are a singular class of managers as well as leaders. An entrepreneur in the business realm, as Machiavelli's aspiring Prince in the political realm, must be a farsighted, highly motivated, creative, energetic, persistent, and proficient person; and a fearless one too, who is willing to take chances and to accept the risks inherent in venturing into a new business endeavor. Entrepreneurs, in fact, frequently are the creators and disseminators of new technologies or unique methodologies that change the way business and society operate.

In *The Prince*, Machiavelli discusses at length and attempts to solve the problems confronting an aspiring "founder." This examination, although in a political context, does make Machiavelli's work relevant to an enterprising individual in the business sector. The entrepreneur can start a business; the Prince could found a principality; an entrepreneur can conquer markets; and the Prince could subjugate cities.

Accordingly, many practical examples cited by Machiavelli for establishing a political entity can be translated into modern business terms. His commentary on the manipulation of people, and the orientation and tactics utilized by manipulators, certainly are subjects that the aspiring entrepreneur might be motivated to study.

Entrepreneurs definitely manifest a commensurate fundamental need for "princely" achievement and renown as well as a desire for power. They are, and they seem to know they are, grades "above" the ordinary person. To be successful, they must maintain dominion over and manage their followers, yet also inspire and lead them to attain the entrepreneur's aims. Structure, organization, and processes naturally are necessary ingredients to administration, command, and control; but the entrepreneur, like the Prince, must possess the capacity and courage to confront competitive challenges, change tactical directions and strategic objectives, as well as have the ability to make swift expeditious decisions. As Machiavelli emphasized, a "founder" succeeds by adapting one's way of proceeding to the nature of the times, and, conversely, does not succeed by rigidly adhering to a method that is out of harmony with the times. Today's founder, the business entrepreneur, whose "political" arena is the "marketplace," (at least initially!), would be wise to heed Machiavelli's advice.

Entrepreneurs need, and resourcefully strive for, the power essential to accomplish their goals. Machiavelli, however, recognized that "founders" often can become enthralled with, and corrupted by, their own power; and perhaps thereby distance themselves from the "real" issues, their true confidants, and loyal followers, or even worse, degenerate into abusive autocrats. Machiavelli, therefore, counsels that a "founder" not only select certain sagacious and sensible people as advisors, of course make them dependent upon and obligated to the "founder," but also allow them the openness to provide honest opinions, and reward them for so doing. Such trusted counselors will aid the entrepreneur's deliberations, and also, vitally, will serve to keep the entrepreneur centered on the legitimate needs, ends, and means of the enterprise, rather than on any potentially ruinous personal cravings for strict control and absolute dominance.

Entrepreneurs, finally, must attract and select faithful and competent people whose vision, attitudes, attributes, and work ethic are compatible with the entrepreneur's. Such congruity will help to build a cohesive, unified, and energized work force, which surely is indispensable to the enterprise's ultimate success. The entrepreneur must recognize their capability and loyalty; reward them accordingly, and as a result keep them faithful and motivated. In the long run, followers and employees need to "buy into" the entrepreneur's personal vision, as well as ambition, and truly must want to build a great enterprise together with the entrepreneur.

Surely there are messages for entrepreneurs to be found in Machiavelli's work. Entrepreneurs will be aided in establishing great enterprises, achieving huge financial gains, and acquiring lasting fame, by adopting some of the strategies and tactics spelled out or suggested in *The Prince*. Yet, the astute entrepreneur must consider carefully the ramifications to the more "machiavellian" aspects of Machiavelli's methods. The risk and severity of legal punishment, especially pursuant to U.S. anti-discrimination in employment laws, the negative reaction from society as well as a company's constituent groups, and the existence of potentially like-minded competitors, all serve to bound the entrepreneur, even a "princely" one, to "mainstream" as opposed to more "machiavellian" methods. Machiavelli's Prince was in essence a "law unto himself," but the modern entrepreneur confronts an extensive, pervasive, and powerful legal system, which makes it very difficult for an individual, even a shrewd and ambitious entrepreneur, to consistently and persistently utilize immoral means which the law also proscribes as illegal. Yes, it is quite possible to achieve power, riches, and fame by employing the full range of Machiavelli's tactics and weapons, but it is also very unlikely for the entrepreneur to maintain this level of ascendancy and success.

Certainly not all of Machiavelli's theories and counsels are appropriate for modern day entrepreneurs, but some do merit very close attention by the aspiring entrepreneur. For the entrepreneur, these recommendations include the importance of strong visionary leadership, the value of participative, empowered, and loyal management, the advantages of a cohesive and committed work force. Vitally, the entrepreneur needs to possess the intelligence of mind, strength of character, and boldness of heart to change course in whatever direction the winds of prosperity and the variations of affairs demand for the attainment of the objective of success.

One of the most critical elements in building a successful enterprise is the strength of its leadership. As an entrepreneur strives to secure power and become an effective leader, he or she must obtain the loyal support of others and convert them into dedicated followers. To accomplish this object, the entrepreneur must convince others that his or her vision is worth following; and that the he or she has the talent and the will to realize the vision. To emphasize these "good" values of strength and talent, Machiavelli would contend that the entrepreneur, to be a leader, must publicize significant aspects of his or her business career, or important aspects of one's work, which the entrepreneur has executed in an outstanding manner. The entrepreneur, moreover, must demonstrate that he or she can anticipate problems, resolve difficult dilemmas, and remove or circumvent impending "roadblocks." As for any other less auspicious or successful aspects of one's work and career, Machiavelli would counsel that one maintain the outward appearances of power, control, success, and, of course, morality.

Machiavelli, as well as the leadership of his day, strongly emphasized the value of loyalty; and concomitantly possessed very little tolerance for disloyalty. Thus, in today's business world, any perceived disloyalty typically is dealt with promptly, and harshly too, for example, by the loss of a raise or promotion or even the loss of one's position. "Whistle-blowing," moreover, easily could be construed as a "mark" of disloyalty. Yet, "whistle-blowing" by employees or followers, solicited by, and properly channeled to, the entrepreneur, executive, or manager is permissible. A wise person, and aspiring Prince, in order to attain and maintain power, needs to secure information and gain knowledge. He or she as well needs to seek the advice of competent and trustworthy counselors. Unsolicited or improperly given information or suggestions, however, ordinarily should not be tolerated as it undercuts the entrepreneur's status and power.

Machiavellian-Based Business Leadership

A Machiavellian leader, whether acting in the capacity of a business manager, executive, or entrepreneur, strives to attain power, riches, rank, fame, and above all, personal eminence and grandeur. In order to achieve these lofty and exalted goals, the Machiavellian leader first must be cognizant of the true nature of people. Most people are, stressed Machiavelli, ignorant, unmindful, and stupid, self-interested, selfish, and petty, suspicious and envious, ungrateful, disagreeable, and malcontented, readily deceived and misled. They merely are satisfied by, and even impressed with, superficial appearances and outward show, rather than substance and reality; and they are too weak, fearful, and stupid to be either completely good or bad, though venal and easily corruptible and readily prone to evil. If anarchy is to be avoided, and order and progress to be secured, the majority obviously cannot rule; but rather the people need a strong leader to discipline and control them and to convince, persuade, manipulate, command, or frighten them into acting prudently and properly for their own common good.

In order to be a successful leader of the people, and to gain one's own position, wealth, and glory, the Machiavellian leader must be well aware that leadership definitely does not consist of adhering to any objective, universal, veritable, or ethical code, law, or principles of leadership. True leadership, rather, is a relative, situational, contingent, suitable, adaptive, and amoral conception; that is, the leader must do, and has the right to do, depending on the circumstances, whatever the leader deems necessary, fit, and efficacious to get the people to perform correctly, to maintain the leader, and advance the leader's objectives, and achieve the leader's greatness. The leader, moreover, must do whatever it takes to fulfill these purposes, repudiating any notion of "higher law," as well as ignoring any questions as to the conventional rightness or wrongness of the means utilized. Leadership, therefore, is simply a matter of expediency, which Machiavelli extols as the only one true and inviolable principle of leadership.

In purely private matters, for example, dealings with family and friends, the conventional virtues, values, and moral standards can be sustained; but when one enters the domain of public affairs and concerns, one must leave behind any notions of conventional morality, goodness, or rightfulness, because such "good" thoughts and precepts are irrelevant, and perhaps even "bad," for the ambitious leader, who instead must take on a morally neutral approach, even to such "moral" issues as discrimination in the workplace.

The overriding issue for the leader, therefore, plainly is not whether a particular action is consistently good, right, or moral, or bad, wrong, and immoral; rather, the superseding principle is whether the circumstances require the use of a specific, expedient, efficacious means. Any traditional "badness" of the proposed method must be weighed carefully against the anticipated, desirable, good consequences of achieving the objective. It is thus quite possible that a customarily "bad" means will be outweighed by the prospects of securing a sufficiently good end, as defined and calculated by the leader, of course. Immorality and vice, as well as morality and virtue, all have their uses; and the sharp leader cleverly can alternate between good and bad. Such actions as fraud, deceit, dissimulation, manipulation, cunning, intrigue, disrespect, and abuse are not necessarily "bad"; rather, they are merely instruments to be utilized if the situation demands their use; and they actually may rise to the level of laudable "virtuous" actions, depending on the good ends they further. If the situation requires, for example, that the leader's followers be discriminated against, lied to, misused, or even betrayed, and these "bad" actions are indispensable to the leader's success, then so be it! Machiavelli counseled, for example, that a reputation for morality is a very important ingredient to the leader's formula for mastery; and if it is necessary for the leader to deceive the people as to the leader's true character, such deception not only is permissible, but good too! The goodness or badness of any action just depends on the particular circumstances and consequences involved; traditional moral norms are irrelevant; and actions become disassociated not only from moral standards but also from the actors performing them. The leader thereby is "licensed" completely to perform actions that do not conform to the exemplar of the classic virtuous ruler; and the leader also is enjoined not to render conventionally "good" deeds if to do so would thwart the leader's good purposes. "Good" and "bad" are merely seemingly good or bad; and the leader is not bad by using an expedient "bad," that is, an actually good, effective means.

Intelligence, reason, and judgment accordingly emerge as truly virtuous qualities for the successful leader. Realizing that traditionally "good" acts may serve neither the public nor the "princely" good, the astute, calculating, and perceptive leader cautiously will alternate between good and bad, virtue and vice, and moral and immoral. The leader may have to utilize a means, traditionally classified as "bad," which due to its efficaciousness in a particular situation now may be deemed a "good" action. In certain circumstances, for example, it may be counterproductive and "bad" to be kind and compassionate, and instead "good" to be severe and cruel. If innocent people have to be discriminated against, dishonored, betrayed, or abandoned for a greater good, so be it. Yet, Machiavelli warns that the leader must be very careful, circumspect, and proportionate in employing conventionally "bad" means. Do not indulge or tolerate disproportionate or pointless badness, admonishes Machiavelli, or else one will become subject to hatred and contempt and one's purposes ultimately will be frustrated. "Bad" means are temporary, necessary expedients which must be used in appropriate, direct, and expeditious ways, and always to accomplish great goals, of course. The leader, moreover, who is obliged to apply "bad" methods, naturally should attempt to appear as conventionally "good"; and otherwise actually may be quite conventionally good, but always ready and willing to change to the contrary if circumstances dictate.

Carefully alternating between good and bad and eschewing extremes, however, do not mean that the leader should give way to feeble half-measures, weak compromises, and generous concessions. Irresolution, vacillation, and continuously choosing the "safe" middle course must be rejected. Such signs of weakness and indecision surely will undermine the leader's power. The leader, instead, may have to opt for the bold course of action; and execute it well. Such a Machiavellian leader hence will be able to successfully effectuate change. Whether by reason and common sense, persuasion and manipulation, or command and coercion, the Machiavellian leader must act, act decisively, and act well..

A fundamental question concerning a "machiavellian" approach to leadership is whether Machiavelli really is teaching evil. Machiavelli, in fact, at times does abjure traditional moral virtue and goodness; and instead seems to sanction the "machiavellian" virtues of egoism, ambition, expedience, and the shrewd use of good and bad. Yet, for the leader to attain and maintain power and authority, and ultimately to achieve great glory, must not the leader also consider the needs and aspirations of the leader's followers, the community, as well as society as a whole? That is, must not the leader's personal ambitions and "princely" goals be advanced and achieved fully in the context of benefiting the public; and, therefore, does not the common good become the ultimate, almost utilitarian, criterion for even the "machiavellian" leader?

Perhaps the arrival of a crisis allows a leader to act in an absolutely "machiavellian" manner. A leader confronting an emergency may be impelled to take swift, decisive, strong, even draconian, measures to save the organization; and in such a situation the leader must do quickly whatever is necessary to ensure survival, without the consultation, participation, or approval of followers or managers, even though the leader's determination directly affects them. The leader must be allowed to act, moreover, without the "niceties" of ethical evaluation or moral justification. Yet, if there is a true crisis, and the leader has forged bonds of trust with his or her followers, then one's followers should be willing to rely on the leader's judgment, and accept, and perhaps welcome, the leader's prompt, unilateral, forceful exercise of power.

In the short term, however, it may be expedient for a leader to be "machiavellian"; but is it efficacious in the long term for a leader to be "machiavellian" in the sense of being deceptive and manipulative and discrimination, disrespectful and abusive? Dissimulation and discrimination cannot be concealed forever; and eventually one will run out of people to mistreat; and thus this exercise of "raw power," and coercive, intimidating leadership, ultimately will fail as it cannot sustain itself indefinitely. People simply neither will follow nor labor for individuals they mistrust or detest; and thus such a "machiavellian" immoral or amoral "boss" will confront insuperable impediments in attempting to motivate, direct, or sustain such activity.

A leader, therefore, must be very careful in asserting Machiavelli's rationales as the pretense for expedient, short-term, or crisis-caused authoritarian conduct. Once one acknowledges that "machiavellian" behavior is at any time or period acceptable, one risks falling into the trap of portraying present circumstances as fittingly critical, problematical, exceptional, or tactical for swift, arbitrary, "tough," "machiavellian" handling; and one thereby steadily sanctions autocratic conduct. Moreover, regardless of the unsettled, troublesome, or exiguous nature of a situation, is it ever morally permissible or appropriate for a leader to act in such a despotic and tyrannical manner?

It is never ethically permissible nor appropriate, one can strongly argue, to discriminate against, mistreat, disrespect, betray, deceive, manipulate, or exploit people. It is always immoral to behave in such a wrongful manner and to contravene fundamental natural rights; and no crisis, real or perceived, no short term advantage, can ever justify such misconduct. True leadership, as well as successful long-term leadership, are said to be built on certain, fundamental, inviolable ethical principles, such as integrity, honesty, trust, fairness and respect, which are constant, permanent, non-contingent, and categorical norms. Effective leadership, of course, will require at times course "corrections" and changes in strategy and tactics; but true leadership also will demand steadfast adherence to ethical principles and moral rules.

A person who is ethically deficient may lack a necessary predicate for successful, long-term leadership; and when such a person confronts a crisis or is tempted by short term advantage, or for that matter, simply faces the unavoidable problems of authority and administration, he or she may act in such an immoral way so as to destroy any leadership effectiveness. A leader who is demanding, and even exacting, very well can be acceptable and even necessary; but one who is abusive and coercive is never acceptable; and in the long term such leaders will be failures. Trying to lead by fear, suspicion, and manipulation hinders genuine communication and interaction, breeds apathy and mistrust, suppresses motivation, undermines commitment and loyalty, prevents empowerment, and eventually engenders serious problems and wrong decisions.

If leading by fear, manipulation, and discrimination are neither morally acceptable nor practically efficacious, are there feasible leadership techniques for the results-oriented individual? Truly effectual, successful, and long-term leadership always comes down to certain essential attributes – fairness, morality, honesty, and integrity. Treating one's followers and one's employees with dignity and respect, trusting and empowering them, as opposed to coercing and controlling them, will create not heedless, mindless, enervated automatons, but knowledgeable, energetic, and motivated associates who wholeheartedly believe in the leader and who are enthusiastically committed to achieving the leader's vision. Such leadership is principle-centered, values-based, and vision-inspired; and the only type of leadership capable of producing and sustaining transformational and beneficial change.

Challenges and Problems with Machiavellian Values

The value of power is the key value – instrumental and intrinsic – emphasized by Machiavelli. Yet, the serious risk of so underscoring the value of power is that power will become an end in itself. This object of power, however, may be unattainable. Acquiring, possessing, and maintaining power over others may require one to strive continually to increase the power that one possesses. The power that one does have, therefore, may not be able to be used to achieve any constructive, let alone notable, purpose; rather, power is merely the means to obtain more power, which is the vehicle to secure even further power, and so on indefinitely. The obvious negative result is an incessant, repetitive, "naked," power struggle, with an endless deferring of goals. The Machiavellian liberation from traditional values and moral restraints, and the granting of moral legitimacy to self-interest and "bad" conduct, may make some people more energetic and creative, but a concomitant decline in moral standards might engender increasing malaise, suspicion, distrust, perfidy, social disunity, and perhaps anarchy.

Machiavelli counsels that a person acting in a public affairs capacity ought to be able to do whatever he or she desires, so long as the action is for the community as a whole, and not merely for that person's own, sole, personal satisfaction and aggrandizement. Yet how realistic is such a scenario? Machiavelli himself saw the problem with his own advice. He notes how difficult it is to find a good person willing to employ bad means, even though the ultimate goal is greater good; and he also observes how infrequently a bad person, after having acquired power, is willing to use it for good ends. If a person cannot succeed by moral means, perhaps it is preferable that he or she not succeed at all, because if successful, the objective would no longer be the same cause for which the person initially sought to attain.

Perhaps Machiavelli is too much the realist, and gives too much attention to material and "scientific" elements. His "crime" may not be one of immorality or amorality, but rather an underestimation of the moral factor in public (including business) affairs. One must consider, moreover, the long-term consequences of utilizing "machiavellian" tactics on oneself, others, and one's organization. Prolonged use of such tactics could engender debilitating outcomes. One who exercises power in such a manner, and aggressively seeks to secure and use even more power, may find that he or she is corrupted thereby. The use of power can establish a regimen not only of control over less powerful individuals, but also their abusive and undignified treatment. Those controlled and so treated may feel like failures, and perhaps may regress to a depressed and apathetic state, or even may feel frustrated and become aggressive and hostile. In the business context, capable employees might leave the corporation, or their performance could deteriorate, in response to a manager using demeaning and unscrupulous tactics. An organization might become plagued by ruthless competition, antagonistic rivalries, and actual conflict. A society's economic and social health, as well as the livelihoods of many individuals, are too dependent on business to regard business as some type of "pure" "machiavellian" "power-game."

Admittedly, building a power-base is important in establishing or conducting a business, but gaining power as one's ultimate goal is not a license for adopting an inverted value system or practicing a spurious or specious code of ethics. There neither is a separate set of moral standards for business, nor for an executive, manager, or entrepreneur acting in a corporate or entrepreneurial capacity. One is not relieved of moral responsibility by acting "merely" in a public affairs or business capacity. One cannot hide behind and attempt to operate under a separate, unique, and dual system of ethics and values applicable only to business and public affairs. There is, and should be, one system of values and ethics, one set of moral rules, and one ethical code that apply to everyone alike, including businesspeople. Otherwise, a pernicious potential consequence of the duality mode of thinking is the acceptance or acquiescence by some in the political and business communities that the "public" system or code can be, is, and should be, morally "inferior" to the private code.

In many ways, moreover, society today, and especially its "background" institutions of law and morality, have improved since Machiavelli's time. Consequently, a ruthless, determined, and ethically publicly empowered individual would find it considerably more difficult to utilize consistently and extensively Machiavelli's more "machiavellian" precepts in a modern business setting. In addition, enhanced awareness and scrutiny, the greater availability of information, as well as increased competition, render it practically impossible for anyone to act successfully in the "marketplace" in such a "machiavellian" manner on a large scale and for a lengthy period of time. In particular, the relative level of knowledge and access to information enjoyed by people today, as compared to the citizens of Machiavelli's Italian city-states, should act to expose and to deter any persistent "machiavellian" behavior, particularly in the context of discrimination in the workplace.

An entrepreneur, executive, or manager cannot expect, unlike The Prince, to have his or her every wish carried out with the force of law, deceiving and manipulating some, and compelling, coercing, and punishing others. The Prince no longer is the only reigning ruling power, with no other "higher" authority to obey. Machiavelli's Prince may have had the license to commit expedient wrongful acts, but today the government and legal system, as well as society as a whole, will constrain the scope of activities of even the most ambitious and relentless aspiring Prince. The dispersion of power throughout the system, politically, legally, economically, and the existence of competition and public pressure, serve as serious obstacles to a modern day entrepreneur who tries to emulate Machiavelli's Prince.

A modern day entrepreneur, for example, can be prosecuted criminally pursuant to anti-trust law for committing monopolizing practices in an attempt to "corner the market" or to maintain a monopolistic "principality." An advertiser who lies, or even misleads, can be fined heavily for its deceptions and forced to cease these practices. An employer who discriminates against employers based on their age can be sued under U.S. Civil Rights Laws. A wide array of powerful government regulatory agencies as the EEOC, has been established for the express purposes of overseeing business, investigating possible wrongdoing, preventing these abuses from happening, and punishing their occurrence, criminally as well as civilly.

A government system and structure based on the law, rather than the dictates of an arbitrary decision-maker, should minimize considerably the risk that a completely unscrupulous and aggressively ambitious person will "make it to the top" of the business world; and even if so, that he or she will stay there. The legal system will help to protect society from such people and the "machiavellian" "shortcuts" they might employ to achieve success; and "shortcuts," one should note, pointed out plainly in *The Prince*, and thus conceivably warned about therein by Machiavelli! The law now proscribes most of these "shortcuts"; and punishment is a real contingency; and thus all actors and participants in business endeavors and dealings should be cognizant of the legal limitations and consequences to their actions. Unlike Machiavelli's Italian city-states, business corporations today are not powers in, of, and amongst themselves; rather, there are "higher" powers to answer to.

There also are serious problems with Machiavelli's conception of human nature. Machiavelli claimed that most people are selfish, gullible, treacherous, and above all, stupid. Granted, the world is filled with ethical "traps" as well as ruthless people; and one surely would be wise to exercise caution with regard to both. Yet, so long as there are choices to be made in life, and the freedom to make them, the frailty of human nature, combined with the randomness of life, will lead some to choose, perhaps even grasp at, the "wrong" option. The traits of lying, cheating, discriminating, and stealing, for example, are said to be an inherent part of human nature. Yet most people are not so depraved; there also exists some degree of control over one's "baser" nature. The majority of people generally follow the conventional moral path, though people, as fallible human beings, sometimes stray.

Society, today, and its supportive institutions, such as family, church, and school, strive to teach people "right from wrong." Ethical principles and moral standards certainly are not overlooked, let alone traduced. Societal norms, and people as well, obviously have changed from Machiavelli's more aristocratic and brutal time of the few lordly princes, their regal principalities, and their many "inferior" subjects. Immoral individuals and organizations, therefore, cannot so easily fool, seduce, or overawe the "public," because people have become more knowledgeable, intelligent, ethical, and emboldened. Aspiring "machiavellian" Princes fail to comprehend that many sensible, capable people, and equally ambitious ones too, regardless of their age, not only possess the ability and strength equal to or greater than the Prince's own, but also have chosen to behave in a manner consistent with moral norms; and they very well will use their power to defend themselves and society from others who would use their skills and "smarts" in harmful ways.

No modern business person, whether entrepreneur, executive, or manager, realistically can expect to subscribe to and practice all the objectives and tactics discussed in *The Prince*, at least not without encountering justifiable personal and public outrage as well as societal sanction. Despite what has been documented in history, a "machiavellian" person or business today would not be able to sustain itself for long.

One major factor militating against "machiavellianism" is that entrepreneurs, executives, and managers are dependent upon people, especially employees in a business context. These employees very well could possess different virtues and morals than the Prince. There actually may be a few people who are consciously and morally aware of what transpires in the business; and who courageously will object to, refuse to participate in, and even "blow the whistle" on perceived wrongdoing. People who do possess the awareness of ethics and the concomitant desire to act morally, may feel that they may have an obligation to incorporate ethical analysis into their daily lives and to choose accordingly. They also may feel that it is incumbent upon them to use this "virtuous" knowledge to encourage, and even insist on, moral behavior in the business world and in all human activity. There is one more possibility for the downfall of the "machiavellian" prince, and one that Machiavelli surely would recognize and appreciate; and that simply is "bad luck." Someone, such as a government or media representative, randomly may choose to look into the Prince's dealings, and thereby find illegal and immoral activities, or perhaps a random event may expose "machiavellian" activities to scrutiny. Nonetheless, Machiavelli does seem convinced that satisfying one's self-interest, accumulating power, and achieving lasting personal success and fame, through expedient means if necessary, are the paramount justifiable goals in life. Still, the true "machiavellian" entrepreneur or manager, in order to achieve these complimentary goals of maximizing organizational and individual power, must be astutely aware of the needs, and be prepared to satisfy the legitimate claims, of the enterprises' "stakeholders." Doing the best possible job to provide real value to all constituents, on a long-term, sustaining basis, will best ensure the Machiavellian manager's survival, success, and "princely" rewards.

One cannot truly attain lasting success and distinction by following a narrow, self-serving, and egotistical "machiavellian" philosophy. Founding and managing a successful enterprise certainly are measures of accomplishment; but does not real success and renown include the values of morality and social responsibility. Creating a morally abiding and socially responsive enterprise, as well as an economically productive one of course, are the veritable "tests" of enduring "princely" eminence. Achieving power and profits, and then utilizing these resources efficaciously in a constituent-based manner, will ensure that the business person will be respected and admired for his or her "princely" achievements, rather than merely being held in awe due to his or her power, wealth, and individualistic feats.

The acquisition of power and the assumption of a business role afford the executive, manager, or entrepreneur the opportunity to change others lives on a large scale. Since power, pursuant to Machiavelli's scheme, possesses instrumental as well as intrinsic value, the business person can use power for good ends, such as creating and distributing wealth. One also can establish one's authority in moral matters, develop Codes of Ethics, treat employees and stakeholders fairly, and prescribe and administer standards of right and wrong in a business setting. Business affairs, especially in the modern corporate context, entail enlarged responsibility, accountability, and gravity in the use of power. The likelihood of significant "real-world" consequences, therefore, compels the Machiavellian executive, manager, and entrepreneur to formulate carefully and seriously, calculate cleverly and accurately, justify sensibly and shrewdly, and implement prudently and carefully business policies.

Reflections, Implications, and Summary

Machiavelli is regarded as the well-known exponent of "public" morality, power objectives, and "machiavellian" tactics. Machiavelli's name also is used popularly to symbolize a sinister "real-world" "moral jungle" view. Machiavelli does expose the supposed distinction many people assert between traditional values, morality, and ethics and the "true" business ethics of immorality or amorality. Comprehending this contradiction, and resolving it are not merely abstract theoretical challenges, but very concrete and practical ones too. It is much too simplistic, however, to use Machiavelli as the synonym for wicked realism. Machiavelli does recognize traditional moral values and standards; he does not deny the intrinsic value of conventional moral rules and values. Yet, he also recognizes, and wants his readers to understand, that the real world of "values" is not a homogeneous one. There is not just one world of values, which alone exists in reality. Discerning this reality does not mean that the Machiavellian solution is simply a matter of recommending "machiavellian" tactics. Machiavelli, rather, is urging people to confront the real world, know what "real-world" tactics they and others are using, and realize that some of these tactics are in fact "bad." Yet even Machiavelli never regards "badness" as a tactic to be used continually and regularly; but rather only as a temporary, expedient, necessary means to attain, secure, and maintain power even more firmly. In the "real" world, Machiavelli believes, it will be impossible to act always in compliance with traditional moral standards and values, at all times, in all places, and in all situations. Such consistent compliance may be contrary to human nature, and hardly a new discovery. Machiavelli's point, however, is that the contravention of traditional morality, although in a conventional ethical sense adjudged as "bad," can act as a "good" means in certain concrete, actual circumstances in order to effectuate a greater good.

Machiavelli clearly recognizes, and wants his readers to be keenly aware, that certain means, although deemed to be necessary, are in fact bad and immoral. The moral character of the means thus remains unchanged, even though they are used for an overall greater good. One not only must be cognizant of the fact that a bad means is a bad means, but also that the bad means must only be employed in the most delimited manner. Then, as soon as the greater good end is achieved, one can dispose of the bad means. One, moreover, must be true and honest to oneself and others; admit that one does not always have "clean hands" by having used such means; and one ought to confront directly and accept forthrightly that reality.

So, are there any redeeming qualities to Machiavelli's message for the modern day executive, manager, or entrepreneur? As a political philosophy as well as a collection of practical political techniques, certain of the more "machiavellian" aspects may be condemned as morally deplorable; and very few contemporary political or business people would countenance following strictly and completely all of Machiavelli's counsels. Yet, one should not disregard summarily *The Prince* as lacking worth or merit; and certainly not view it as not having applicability to modern day business management and entrepreneurship. Much can be learned from Machiavelli's theories, principles, and methods. The wise, decent, yet practical, person, who wishes to be a successful business entrepreneur, executive, or manager, but who may be compelled to function in an environment where not everyone is acting morally, should use *The Prince* as a defense mechanism (which actually could be the manner which Machiavelli intended!). Therefore, *The Prince* could be construed as a means to become aware of, and devise counter-measures to, the potentially abusive, exploitative, manipulative, immoral actions of one's dangerous "machiavellian" opponents. The wise person neither ignores nor minimizes determined, resourceful, unscrupulous adversaries; but rather seeks to discern their selfish motives and deplorable methods; and learns how to deal with them effectively. Machiavelli's apparent cynicism about human nature and people's capacity for goodness can produce a very pragmatic "worldly" view of public affairs; and one that an astute, enterprising, good person would be hard-pressed to refute, despite the many "good" exceptions to the "bad" general rule. With this recognition of potentially immoral ambitions and actions in others, and perhaps temptingly lurking in oneself too, a well-intended individual can gird himself or herself to resourcefully do battle with the ruthless "enemy" without or within. Moreover, a political entity or politician, who attempts to behave morally in an otherwise immoral society, may suffer adverse consequences at the hands of immoral or amoral adversaries. The business firm and business person, whether entrepreneur, executive, or manager, similarly may be forced to accept some short-term disadvantage or defeat in order to live and stand by ethical principles. The moral businessperson and firm thus must be patient and steadfast; and allow the proper institutional safeguards and society as a whole to deal with and rectify immoral behavior.

Where safeguards do not exist, one can work assiduously to create them; and when society is disinterested or dull, one can agitate to arouse, elevate, and unite individuals.

Overall, there is a great deal of practical, substantive, and good material in Machiavelli's *The Prince*; and one can find many good examples of right and fair conduct which are ethical, admirable, and efficacious. Yet, one must be very careful to ensure that only the positive aspects of Machiavelli's work are emulated; and that the distinctly "machiavellian" offerings are learned only in a defensive sense. As intelligent, rational, and presumably moral individuals, business entrepreneurs, executives, and managers must possess the capability and character to choose the appropriate parts of Machiavelli's teachings, and to use them sagaciously and ethically to achieve success, both in business and in their personal lives. One can act eruditely, properly, and practically, and pick the right parts of *The Prince*, and use them in a moral manner to attain one's good objectives; or one can act in an ignorant, foolish, and impetuous fashion and condemn the work in its totality as merely an outbreak of virulent ambition and moral depravity. A careful reading of Machiavelli's *The Prince* (and especially in the context of his other more democratic and republican works) will indicate that Machiavelli himself did not necessarily believe that his "machiavellian" means are always necessary, let alone moral; and that perhaps his true political and ethical beliefs were more moderate and noble. Hopefully, an open-minded and reflective reader of *The Prince* can give some credence to this more positive Machiavellian outlook to Machiavelli.

This chapter has attempted to show that Machiavellian thinking still exists in the minds of working adults as well as in the workforce; and, it further attempted to apply to real-life, modern day, business dilemmas to the teachings of one of history's great philosophers, Niccolo Machiavelli, as described in his seminal Renaissance work, *The Prince*. Executives, managers, entrepreneurs, and leaders who wish to maximize their positions, secure power, and attain success and prosperity, should be roused by, learn from, and perhaps be beguiled by, the frankness, directness, and evident practical applicability of Machiavelli's provocative thoughts and precepts to the 21st century business world. Managers and leaders should also proceed cautiously as they adopt these philosophies written for the 16th century mindset and environment while applying them in the twenty first century business world. Machiavellian thinking and practice should not come at a cost to older or younger workers or at the expense of discriminating based on age.

CHAPTER 7

ACCOMMODATIONS AND SKILL BUILDING

*T*he United States of America has about 60 millions individuals that have some sort of a recognized disability, and there are over 50 different legally recognized disabilities. More specifically, there are approximately 32.1 million or 18.7% of the American population, working-age people with disabilities (Stoddard, 1998). Some of these individuals with various disabilities also fall in the category of "older workers," and thus need to be accommodated accordingly. In today's diverse workplace managers in an organization must learn how to deal with employees of all ages that have disabilities to remain competitive as an employer of choice. Title I of the Americans with Disabilities Act (ADA) makes it unlawful to discriminate against a qualified applicant or employee with a disability. This law covers private employers who employ 15 or more people. The A.D.A also applies to state and local government employers.

It is important to understand that just like any other applicant, a person with a disability must meet the employer's required qualifications for the job. Some examples include education, training, skills, or licenses. The candidate with a disability must be able to perform the essential job tasks with or without reasonable accommodations.

In today's work environment, social responsibility of managers and corporations goes beyond ensuring that people with disabilities are not discriminated against in the job application process, hiring, discharge, promotion, as well as training opportunities. Social responsibility and reasonable accommodations are about providing resources, if necessary, and training all employees on how to appropriately treat and interact with "differently-abled" employees. An organization that creates an inclusive environment for individuals of all ages, genders, races, sizes, and ethnicities will benefit in many ways from having diverse employees and diverse customers.

The Hiring Process for Workers with Disabilities

Complying with the American with Disabilities Act of 1990, starts with the job application process, and the understanding that employers should provide reasonable accommodations to any applicant with a disability. Accommodations could include such things as providing written material in alternate formats such as audiotapes, Braille, or large print. An applicant, if needed, should be allowed the opportunity to have a sign language interpreter in the interview process. An employer must be willing to provide testing materials in alternate formats or allow an applicant additional time to complete a test if necessary. Leaders and managers must understand what they can and cannot say in the interview process. Training leaders will benefit an organization in the long run by avoiding the potential of being charged with discrimination based on an applicant's disability.

In an article outlining guidelines for interview questions, Nail and Scharinger (2002) advise that managers cannot ask an applicant whether or not he or she has a particular disability. The question that one can ask is whether or not the applicant can perform the duties of the role for which they are applying. The authors also say that the Equal Employment Opportunity Commission does not specifically disallow any questions but they do not favor questions that relate to disability, race, religion, age, color, national origin, gender, or veteran status.

Making Reasonable Accommodations

As previously mentioned, it may be necessary to provide reasonable accommodations during the application process. An employer is also required to provide reasonable accommodations once an applicant has been hired. According to the United States Equal Employment Opportunity Commission (The ADA: Your Responsibilities as an Employer): Reasonable accommodation is any change or adjustment to a job or work environment that permits a qualified applicant or employee with a disability to participate in the job application process, to perform the essential functions of a job, or to enjoy the benefits and privileges of employment equal to those enjoyed by employees without disabilities.

According to Nail and Scharinger (2002), failing to provide reasonable accommodations for the known physical or mental limitation is a violation of the American with Disabilities Act. The only exception would be if the accommodation creates an undue hardship (severe expense or difficulty) on the operation of the business. Reasonable accommodations according to the Equal Employment Opportunity Commission is defined as making existing employee facilities accessible by making persons with disabilities, modifying work schedules, restructuring a job or modifying equipment, materials or policies. According to an HR Focus article (June 2003), employers often are afraid of the costs of providing reasonable accommodations. Yet according to a survey, the average cost is less than $500 in the United States.

Becoming Aware of Disabilities and Accommodations

The Equal Employment Opportunity Commission (EEOC) defines an individual with a disability as one who "has a physical or mental impairment that substantially limits one or more major life activities; has a record of such impairment; or is regarded as having such impairment." Some examples of major life activities include caring for one-self, walking, seeing, hearing, speaking, breathing, learning, and working. Physical disabilities are those things that cause a loss of physical movements or a weakness in normal motor control. Not only are people with physical disabilities protected, those with mental disabilities may also be included.

Stephen Sonnenberg (2002) explains that a mental impairment is defined as any mental or psychological disorder such as mental retardation, organic brain syndrome, emotional or mental illness, and specific learning disabilities. In the opinion of one author, workers with hidden or invisible impairments are often "lost in the shuffle" (Cheng, 2003). Kipp Cheng also says that it is difficult for some people to get past the preconceived notation that mental-health impairments might keep a worker from being able to perform the job.

Providing reasonable accommodations for employees may be a challenge, but according to Angela Johnson (October 2003), the attitudes that managers and co-workers have towards people with disabilities may pose an even bigger challenge. Her advice is to train leaders to treat people with disabilities the same as you would an able-bodied employee. Employees with disabilities should not be given special considerations with regards to being held accountable for the work they are required to do. Employees with disabilities are not looking for special treatment; rather they want to feel they are on the same level playing field as able-bodied employees. Equally as important as insuring consistency in holding able-bodied and employees with disabilities is day to day interaction. Most people don't grow up interacting with people with disabilities so it is the organization's responsibility to design training to cover disability etiquette and interaction. For example, it is important for leaders to know how to interact with persons' with disabilities as well as how to talk about them. When talking about a person with a disability, it is only appropriate to mention the disability if it is relevant to the situation. Also, one should mention the person first, then the disability. This type of training is beneficial in breaking down myths and stereotypes of persons with disabilities.

The Family and Medical Leave Act Compliance Guide (2003) provides some great tips for organizations to follow to ensure compliance with the Americans with Disabilities Act. Senior leaders in an organization should read the law and determine the impact it has on their organization. They should review their hiring processes and human resources policies to ensure adherence. Leaders' should implement any changes needed within the organization. Another tip is to utilize employees with disabilities as subject-matter-experts when dealing with working to provide reasonable accommodations. It is critical that all leaders in an organization understand the Americans with Disabilities Act and what they should and shouldn't do. But even more important is that they receive training on how to interact with people with disabilities.

In her article *Americans with Disabilities Act: Is Your Company Compliant?* (June 2003), Angela Johnson advises that many of the 174,000 charges filed with the Equal Employment Opportunity Commission over the past ten years could have been avoided if companies had made sure the policies and procedures of the company were compliant with the American with Disabilities Act. The cost of settlements and fines for non-compliance over the past decade has totaled $464.1 million. Ensuring compliance with the A.D.A will prevent a company from having to pay fines or settlements. Not only will a company benefit from being compliant, hiring people with disabilities often sends a message to the public that people with disabilities are welcomed in their business. This has the potential to attract the business of consumers with disabilities and their family members. Along with increased revenue from consumers a company that welcomes people with disabilities will have the opportunity to attain them for long-term employment.

Summary

Creating an inclusive environment where all people are respected, appreciated, and made to be valued should be a business objective of all companies. With approximately 32.1 million people with disabilities in the workplace today, and the likelihood of this number increasing as more people are falling in the category of older workers, companies should build a business case for diversity and create an environment where all are welcome. From the application process through promotional opportunities, people with disabilities are expected to have the same opportunities as able-bodied workers. The Americans with Disabilities Act protects these rights. Companies must focus on more than just being compliant. Creating an inclusive environment requires training of leaders as well as co-workers. Elements of training are wide-spread, ranging from understanding the Americans with Disabilities Act, to making reasonable accommodations, and learning how to treat and socially interact with people with disabilities. Providing a great experience for workers with disabilities gives employers a competitive edge – not only as an employer of choice but also in the consumer market.

Older Workers as Coaches and Mentors

Due to the changing demographics of the business world, such as more competition and the introduction of new technologies, organizations are discovering that traditional tactics of management are no longer enough to remain competitive. As such, coaching is becoming to be recognized and practiced as an effective tool to increase morale, performance, and the "bottom-line" through the success of each individual associate. For example, about 90% of employees who received coaching in their jobs say that it improved their job performance and professional success. In organizations where coaching is effectively practiced as a management style, the bottom-line performance is two to three times better than the traditional "command-and-control" type of organizations. Furthermore, it has been proven that employee commitment increases when there is a strong, positive relationship between the manager and his/her employees. These types of relationships are developed best as a result of effective coaching. Since older workers are the ones with most experience, skill, management, and leadership experience they can make great coaches and mentors to younger employees. Consequently, they should receive training, education and proper development to effectively serve in such capacities.

Effective relationship-oriented coaching creates more knowledgeable and competent employees, reduces errors and rework, and greatly assists in bringing new changes to the culture. Both effective and ineffective managers tend to know what makes a good coach. The difference lies in being able to transfer this knowledge into successful actions with employees to increase their performance and success. Effective coaching skills make a manager's job easier as it enables greater delegation leaving him/her time to take on bigger projects. It builds the manager's reputation as a developer of people while increasing productivity since everyone will know the expectations and the fact that what they do matters. It also can develop trust and a good relationship between managers and employees. Last but not least, good coaching skills can increase creativity, innovation, morale, and teamwork since everyone will feel safe working in an inclusive environment.

So what is coaching? Simply stated, *coaching* is about developing a trusting relationship with your people, so one can jointly clarify expectations and departmental goals thereby leading to specific action plans for their achievement. Accordingly, there are many situations where coaching skills will be very effective, and the following list presents some of them.

- Reinforcing good performance.
- Motivating employees to new heights and peak performance levels.
- Orienting a new employee into the department or organization.
- Providing new knowledge to individuals about changes and tactics.
- Training a new skill for a new task that needs performing.
- Following up on competencies passed on during a training session.
- Explaining the current or new standards and how they can be achieved.
- Setting priorities for effective time management with those employees who need it.
- Inculcating someone into the cliques and groups which may exist within the political circles.
- Clarifying expectations and correcting poor performance.
- Increasing the self confidence of an employee about the task or new responsibilities and challenges.
- Conducting a performance review.

Coaching is not an innate skill, but rather it is learned. It occurs through one's life personally and professionally. Effective coaching is the process of letting people know that what they do matters to you and to the organization. Furthermore, it is about letting them know that you are there to help them be the best they can be as their success is important because it matters to you. It also is about being sincere, specific, and to-the-point about both good and poor performance so they can take personal responsibility for their achievements. From this perspective, coaching is and it can be one of the most important functions managers perform because it communicates performance levels, expectations, importance of the tasks and responsibilities, and it communicates a caring attitude. The following list summarizes some of the main elements involved in coaching.

1. Before beginning the coaching session, be sure to plan exactly what you want to achieve, and the potential benefits for the other person.
2. Start on a positive note and establish a common ground by having a supportive environment.

3. Communicate clearly, listen effectively, show that you care, and do not "beat around the bush." Clearly and caringly state the challenge, opportunity, and/or expectations.
4. Be respectful of the other person's feelings, honor and dignity. Create a non-threatening environment for the interaction, dialogue and discussion.
5. Be culturally sensitive by getting to know the other person's background, values, and anticipate his/her reactions.
6. Avoid value judgments, stereotyping and labeling the behavior of others.
7. Use empathic listening skills to clarify your understanding and the other person's perspective.
8. Stay with the point and do not get side tracked with other issues. Restate the purpose of the session and ask what specific things can be done to increase or improve performance. You can offer assistance but avoid providing solutions – let the individual come up with the solutions. Your job is to lead them in the right direction.
9. Document and clarify the specific plan suggested by the employee, the expected level of performance and how the plan will improve performance. Seek agreement and summarize the conversation.
10. End on a positive note and thank the person for coming up with the specific plan.

Older Workers as Mentors

Mentoring can be seen as an art since it requires experience and leadership traits. Mentoring can also be seen as a science since it can be formalized, structured, and taught. *Mentoring* is a continuous process of sharing relevant information with selected others in the organization that can maximize the success of the institution, while guiding and supporting each person toward individual and collective achievement opportunities. *Mentoring* is a developmental, caring, sharing, and helping relationship where the mentor helps the mentee. A mentor can be a person who offers knowledge, insight, perspective, or wisdom that is helpful to another person in a relationship which goes beyond duty or obligation. A mentor also creates opportunities for exposure, provides challenging and educational assignments, and serves as a role model and advisor to the mentee. Such relationships often evolve informally, but managers can encourage and formalize them. Effective mentoring requires listening, caring, and other forms of involvement between mentors and mentees. According to experts, mentoring is often used to achieve the interests of special groups and populations, conserve and transfer special know-how, encourage mentee contributions, bring employees together in a new social environment, help people reach their full potential, enhance competitive position of a person or department, and develop better relationships around the globe. Mentoring is a collaborative effort on the part of the mentor and the mentee. Effective mentoring is a relationship built on trust where the mentee confides personal information and characteristics to the mentor, and the mentor guides the mentee toward growth and learning opportunities. A good mentoring program usually is focused on specific learning objectives where both the mentor and mentee receive training. There are many deliverables from a mentoring program which can include easier recruitment of the best talent, more rapid induction of the new recruits, improved staff retention, improved equal opportunities, performance and diversity management, increased effectiveness of formal training, reinforcement of cultural change, improved networking and communication, and reinforcement of other learning initiatives.

Successful organizations recognize the value of mentoring and mentoring programs as an effective way to address diversity, manage organizational knowledge, retain stellar performers, and prepare for succession. There are many organizations with good experiences in mentoring individuals from under-represented groups, specifically women, Asians, Hispanics, Native Americans, and African Americans in the fields of business and education. Great mentors are great leaders as they share similar characteristics. Just like leaders, mentors are not limited to influencing others only professionally at work since mentors can guide people at home, in the community, at places of worship, at the soccer field, in the Tae Kwon Do classes, and other such interactions. According to experts, there are many roles that professional mentors play including: teacher or tutor, coach, befriender, counselor, information source, nurturer, advisor, net-worker, advocate, and role model. Regardless of the mentoring location, some specific elements of highly effective mentors and leaders are that such individuals:

- Are experienced, and respected in the field.
- Have current knowledge and are professionally confident.
- Are trustworthy, confident and show high self-efficacy.
- Use transformational leadership skills.
- Willingly share their knowledge and guide others.
- Remain approachable.
- Have great passion for their work.
- Know what to communicate, how to communicate, when to communicate, and how to help improve the mentee.
- Excel at creating exciting learning environments for mentees.
- Connect exceptionally well with others.
- Challenge mentees to reach their full potential.
- Get extraordinary results using a variety of skills to get their points across and to bring about the needed behavioral changes in their mentees.

The goal of a mentoring program should be to help leaders, managers, coaches, and senior employees in the firm be highly skilled, self-aware, inclusive, energetic, and creative, and to carry a zest for mentoring into the organization every day. Mentoring is not an easy task, but such is the obligation bestowed on the fortunate ones. Highly effective mentors and leaders understand that developing others requires self-reflection, sensitivity, risk taking, interdependency, and teamwork among all parties (mentors, mentees, managers, peers, and senior officers). They also understand that such a synergy requires forging a partnership, inspiring commitment, growing both the mentor and mentee's skills, promoting persistency, and shaping the environment so all parties can achieve their goals. Often mentors (managers, leaders, and coaches) cannot influence the working environment for the entire organization. However they can control the area in which they are responsible for by applying the following tactics:

- Build visibility as a role model.
- Strengthen the learning climate in the department.
- Leverage organizational culture and systems.

Mentoring programs, using older workers, can help companies share knowledge, success, network, and build strong relationships with peers around the globe. It is a work-related partnership for the purpose of professional development between two or more individuals that allows an individual with more experience (the mentor) to share his or her skills, knowledge and experience with the mentee who has less experience. Mentoring is also an effective strategy that can contribute significantly to overall professional development of all employees. The use of mentors should also be considered and strongly encouraged when designing an effective repatriation program for international employees.

Mentoring is a growing strategy used today for developing the talent of employees in professional positions. Mentoring programs in large organizations tend to be formal, while allowing a great deal of flexibility and informality in the relationships. Effective mentoring programs should benefit the mentee, the mentor, and the organization. A mentoring program can develop the leadership, management, and coaching skills of managers to create a productive culture. Effective mentoring in the twenty first century organization requires the skills of management, leadership, and coaching which are critical to the new employee's development. Mentoring relationships are helpful for most new and veteran employees, and they are especially helpful for employees working in different cities and cultures. One best way to reduce the negative impact of a strong culture in a new organization can be to have one or more experienced mentors who help one understand and effectively assimilate into the organization.

Coaches and Mentors Resolving Conflict and Rumors

Older workers, as coaches and mentors, can be great "change agents" and catalysts for effectively handling conflict in the workplace. Because of their experience and earned respect, older workers that are educated in the art of handling conflict and effectively settling rumors can serve in the capacity of conflict resolution agents. Philosopher Blaise Pascal once said, "never speak well of yourself." It is better to let one's actions, as a leader, do the talking. Philosophers encourage leaders to "Live a life that will earn you the kind of reputation you desire. People will notice; be humble and you will be lifted up; demanding respect and admiration is like chasing an elusive butterfly; chase it, and you'll probably never catch it; sit still, be quiet, be confident, and it may land right on your shoulder." Actions speak louder than words and a leader's overall behavior will certainly communicate much about his/her character to others than anything s/he says.

Sharing information with others is a fact of life and spreading misinformation with others is also a reality, especially when there seems to be years of animosity and distrust of corporate leaders due to job insecurity, layoffs, bribery, and other such actions caused by selfishness or corporate greed. As such, it is necessary that educated individuals not spread misinformation about leaders, politicians, or one's colleagues in the workforce. Effective leaders can benefit from the facilitation skills and wisdom of Socrates about why rumors or certain messages should not be shared with others especially when the message has not been verified to see if it is true, important or even useful. Perhaps one can use this story to take a stand and hopefully influence others to "stop" and think about "the spoken words" and its impact on the person. People often wonder why some people have such great friends and manage to keep them. If one successfully applies the "Triple Filter Test" in one's conversations, the same could work for everyone. The following is the story behind the "Triple Filter Test" coming from Socrates as he saw an appropriate opportunity to teach a great lesson in the given situation.

In ancient Greece, Socrates was reputed to hold knowledge in high esteem. One day an acquaintance met the great philosopher and said, "Do you know what I just heard about your friend?" "Hold on a minute," Socrates, the great situational leader, replied. "Before telling me anything I'd like you to pass a little test. It's called the "Triple Filter Test." "Triple filter?" said the acquaintance. "That's right," Socrates continued. "Before you talk to me about my friend, it might be a good idea to take a moment and filter what you're going to say. That's why I call it the triple filter test."

1. *"The first filter is Truth*. Have you made absolutely sure that what you are about to tell me is true?" "No," the man said, "actually I just heard about it and..." "All right," said Socrates. "So you don't really know if it's true or not."

2. *"The second filter is the filter of Goodness*. Is what you are about to tell me about my friend something good?" "No, on the contrary..." "So," Socrates continued, "you want to tell me something bad about him, but you're not certain it's true. You may still pass the test though, because there's one more filter left."

3. *"The third one is the filter of Usefulness*. Is what you want to tell me about my friend going to be useful to me?" "No, not really."

"Well," concluded Socrates, "if what you want to tell me is neither true, nor good, nor even useful, then why tell it to me at all?" This is why Socrates was a great philosopher and held in such high esteem. Rumors, which seem to flow often among people, should be stopped and corrected instead of spreading them when they have no reality but can damage an individual's reputation or morale in the department. So, one should always remember the application of the "Triple Filter Test" by passing ones' messages through the filters of "truth," "goodness," and "usefulness." It is a moral imperative for leaders to always make sure what is said is true, good, and useful before it is passed on to others. Leaders can certainly use similar strategies to influence their followers, and hopefully stop people from passing on rumors and misinformation in their workforce.

During an interpersonal conflict with a team member or colleague, one can remain focused on stating the facts, their feelings and future expectations rather attacking the other person. For example, when hearing an offensive comment or joke about minorities or women in the workplace, one can immediately use the 3-F model (facts, feelings, and future expectations) by calmly saying: "When you make comments like that about women..., I feel angry and disappointed because...they are false and inappropriate in the workplace. Please don't make comments like that again." In most cases, repeating the facts of what was said by the person, one's feelings as a result of hearing what was said, and future expectations would take care of the situation as it brings this concern to the attention of the person making the comment. The person is likely to either clarify the misunderstanding, if that was the case, or change his or her behavior as a result of this awareness. As such, there may not be a need to place an official complaint with the human resources department or the company's lawyers since the goal is to have a healthy work environment. This is a very effective method used by skilled individuals to bring about positive changes in their departments one person at a time thereby eliminating the existence of a hostile work environment. Of course, if the candid discussion, based on the 3-F model, does not work and there is a repetition of inappropriate comments then one must take appropriate actions to inform the organization. After all, the best way to resolve conflict is to seek cooperation from all parties involved and to create a win-win solution for everyone. Of course, with training and development, most "older workers" can be perfect candidates for the creation of win-win situations.

Developing and Involving Older Workers in Technology

Older workers may feel alone in the struggle to keep up with the world of technology since most people in the United States assume that they are not interested in new skills. It may seem like a difficult concept to accept the myth that older workers will never learn computers or get involved with technologies such as the internet. Elderly people, in general, are at a lack of knowledge when it comes to technology because it is so new and different to many of them. Since we are all creatures of habit, it is true that as individuals age they get comfortable doing things a certain way. When new and more effective ways are presented to them they may feel as though they don't need to learn it. They wish to do things as they always have. This is a valid belief but not understanding that technology can really benefit older workers is a mistake. There is extensive information available to older workers who wish to learn, it is tapping the resources to find these new methods. Luckily, there are many resources available to elderly at their fingertips. Some of the resources available are supported by the American Society on Aging (ASA), American Association of Retired People (AARP), Gerontological Society of America, and the Silver Surfers from the United Kingdom. These organizations strive to help the elderly population learn and be able to effectively use technology to their benefit. They use tools such as extensive libraries of information, how-to guides, and assistive technology that are specially tailored to the needs and desires of older people. Of course, older workers are not alone in this struggle to integrate technology into their changing lives. There are many organizations that assist older people in learning about not only technology but also continuing in any education that they desire.

American Society on Aging. The American Society on Aging (ASA), founded in 1954, is an association of diverse individuals bound by a common goal: to support the commitment and enhance the knowledge and skills of those who seek to improve the quality of life of older adults and their families (ASAging.org, 2004). The ASA offers services of professional education, publications, resources, educational products, and award programs that aid in the advancement of elderly education. A section in the professional education is the ASA's Web-Enhanced Seminars where, via the internet, people can view recorded and live seminars on various topics concerning aging. Web Seminars are a cost-effective, high-quality training option for professionals working with aging issues and older adults (ASAging.org, 2004).

In addition to the Web-Seminars, the publications that ASA offers are far more extensive. The ASA's mission states "Insightful, timely and widely respected, ASA's print and electronic publications are a premier resource for thousands of professionals in the field of aging," for its publications section. Let us focus on a particular publication that relates to older people and technology in the Generations Journal of the ASA. The article is named "*Aging and Information Technology: The Promise and the Challenge*," discusses some of the advancement technology has made and its conformity to elder needs. The article talks about the increase of web sites and resources available and useful to older people. Jeffery Finn, the author of the article states, "Unquestionably, the Internet and the World Wide Web are the driving forces prompting professionals in aging to reexamine their delivery of services and prompting consumers to rethink the relationships with these professionals...By mid 1998, more than 2,000 aging-related Web sites are expected to exist, up from 25 in mid 1995" (Finn, 2004, ASAaging.org). This article shows the dramatic increase in support for getting the elderly to work more closely with technology. Older people are captivated by the promise of information technology to keep them connected to their past, their present, and their future. They realize the wealth of knowledge that the internet has to offer including endless medical information and studies, news reports, history information and many other things that may come of interest to the elderly. Another point that they can relate to is that much of the new technologies today are directly related to them. In hospitals and care centers, new technologies assist in the health of human beings. An example of this is health monitoring systems that do not require someone to be present for it to be monitored. It can be monitored remotely from a central location. "ASA is a valuable resource to anyone interested in aging issues...Through our constituent groups and numerous special projects ASA carries out its commitment to education, diversity, and quality of life for older adults" (ASAging.org, 2004). They also provide specialized educational products that customers can order from their "E-Store." These products include books, journal issues, videos, and multimedia packages geared towards the education of the elderly.

Also, for involvement in the elderly community the ASA offers award programs that recognize elderly achievement such as Best Practices in Human Resources and Aging, Business and Aging awards, Graduate Student Research awards and Healthcare and Aging awards. The Best Practices in Human Resources and Aging is described as, "For model staff recruitment, training and/or management" (ASAging.org, 2004). This award encompasses success in an organization's diversity training programs and how the company performs its staffing. Business and Aging awards program is described as, "For exemplary programs and services in the private, for-profit sector, in two award categories: large company; and small company" (ASAging.org, 2004). This award is for for-profit companies that show outstanding performance in accommodating older people and their families. The Graduate Student Research award is presented annually to a graduate student for research relevant to aging and applicable to practice. A review panel judges the research on the quality of its conceptual framework, methodology, presentation and analysis of findings, as well as its significance to practice in the field of aging. The Healthcare and Aging award is given to organizations that have demonstrated high-quality, innovative programs that enhance the health-related quality of life in older adults (ASAging.org, 2004). The ASA annually presents these awards to recognize excellence in the studying in the field of aging. The ASA gives offers broad services that help elderly people.

American Association of Retired People. The American Association of Retired People (AARP) also provides great resources for the elderly interested in advancing their technological skill levels. The AARP website under the Computer and Technology section offers news updates concerning technology tailored to the older generation. It introduces concepts that have been proven difficult to learn by older generation in an easy to learn format. One example is their "Gadgets and how to Guides" section of Computers and Technology which has reviews of new products on the market that have the possibility of benefiting older people through step by step instructions on commonly accepted principles such as getting started on email and how to find files on your computer. In the how to find files article it starts off easy such as, "Here's a common scenario. You know you saved a file, but it isn't where you thought it would be. How can you find your errant file? It's fairly easy if you use a simple feature that is built into Windows" (Berger, AARP.com, 2004). Among the younger generations, this knowledge is given but since the older generations are just starting to use computers this is an excellent starting guide that isn't belittling. A separate section is how to use the internet in the favor of older people. In this section, AARP presents several options for learners of different skill levels. For beginners it starts it's learning by saying, "Congratulations! You're on the Internet! Now you will probably want to learn a little more. You've come to the right place. By working through this Learn the Internet program, you will find out how to do many useful things. You will learn how to create and organize Favorites, how to make text larger, how to customize your browser, how to capture Internet information, and much, much more" (AARP.com, 2004). Over time the factor that affects older people from learning technology related things is due to the diminishing of their motor skills over time. The product review show how products can assist elderly people in everyday functions. For instance a product review is on the Bose QuiteComfort 2 Headphones is described as: "The first QuietComfort headphones were comfortable, produced excellent sound and greatly reduced outside noise making them extremely useful for air travelers and those who frequent noisy environments. Bose kept all these great features in the QuietComfort 2. Bose, then tweaked the headphones with small changes that turned them into an all-around excellent product" (Berger, AARP.com, 2004). Although this product was not necessarily geared toward older people it can greatly help them. The AARP is a great resource for older people who want to learn technology. It proves as an excellent resource that is specifically for the elderly.

Gerontological Society of America. The Gerontological Society of America (GSA) does not offer such a wide range of services however it does offer some interest groups that educate older people. The *"Technology and Aging"* forum is an area discussing training issues in communication and information technology (particularly the Internet) by senior citizens. This forum provides information on using the Internet in the interest of senior citizens including areas of focus such as searching for trustworthy health information on the internet which is an important concern that involves age-specific, well-planned curriculum development. Also, this group discusses how generations relate in their understanding of technology and the trends that relate.

Silver Surfers. The Silver Surfers is a charity organization whose mission is to promote internet usage with elderly people in the United Kingdom. Currently 62% of British people have tried the internet and only 15% of British people aged 65 or over have been online. This was an area that needed to be improved. However, because of many of their efforts the number of British people age 55 and over that use the internet increased 90% in 2001. Studies also show that older surfers are keen to keep their finances in order over the net, which accounts for more than 40% of online banking in the U.K. There are various events to promote Silver Surfers including Silver Surfers Day. Silver Surfers' Day is managed by Hairnet, the company that makes learning technology simple and effective — whether you're a large organization or a private individual. Monthly and annually a Silver Surfer is nominated to be the "silver surfer" of the month/year where eligible individuals are to submit a picture of an elder of the age of 50 enjoying the internet.

Technology Benefits for the Elderly and Older Workers

Assistive Technology. Many of these technologies require little intervention or knowledge of technology by the operator but they help a great deal. Assistive Technology is defined as technology that supports, bolsters or helps a person do something. Assistive Technology has helped work with the elderly. One example is the volume control technology found on common things such as phones, TVs, and stereos so someone with a hearing loss can keep up with the information they need to be part of the community (ILTech.org, 2004). For those with vision disabilities Assistive Technology has helped with things like magnifiers on computers. Also for magazine, journals and subscriptions people can call the publisher to see if they have versions available to suit your needs. Assistive Technology can be expensive but there is government assistance available to those who need it.

The reason that the elderly have a more difficult time with technology is because most of the technology made, is made for young people and by young people. However on the American Association of Retired People's website it helps elder people connect with one another and explains how to do this in its guide to meeting people on the internet. It starts by saying, "The approach of Valentine's Day may make you feel lonely. No mate? Not a soul to talk to? No valentines coming your way? Don't feel bad. You're not alone" (Berger, AARP.com, 2004). This presents that there are many elderly people who are alone and at a lack of resources in meeting people. Using the method of the internet to come together with people with similar interests has endless possibilities. Some of the interests that AARP supports on their message boards are described as, "The AARP Computers & Technology message boards have many "regulars" who ask and answer questions and interact with each other. Other popular AARP message boards are Grief & Loss, Health & Wellness, and Travel. If you are a movie fan, look into message boards and chats at movie-related Web sites. No matter what your hobbies or interests, there are sure to be others on the Web who share your enthusiasm" (AARP.com, 2004). These message boards are of great benefits to the mental health of elderly people.

There are many resources available to use towards assisting elderly people in learning and using technology effectively. The ASA, AARP, GSA, and the Silver Surfers present endless options to older people who have the desire to learn technology. Many of these technologies as older people learn them show to be of great benefit. The ASA offers products such as professional publications and educational opportunities. The AARP provides a "Gadgets and how to Guides" section in their website which can help the elderly in learning and understanding technology. The GSA provides special interest groups that help elderly people come together to talk about their interests. The Silver Surfers is a charity organization in the United Kingdom for the purpose of promoting the use of the internet by older people. Significantly, the research conducted for this book indicates that learning technology skills may be just as important to older workers in securing and maintaining jobs as age anti-discrimination laws.

CHAPTER 8

RECRUITING AND RETAINING OLDER WORKERS

*M*any of the best firms in the world are in search of wisdom, more specifically, the type of wisdom that comes with age and experience which make companies and organizations successful. Jamrog and McCann (2003) mentioned that about 43 percent of the civilian labor force will be eligible for retirement within the next ten years (by 2013). Therefore, there will be a shortage of talented and skilled professionals that accompany top leadership. So, companies will have to implement effective strategies for attracting, hiring, developing, and retaining an experienced workforce.

There are many excellent practices in attracting and hiring senior citizens, and the process often starts with the elimination of behaviors stemming from one of the most common barriers which are traditional biases and stereotypes toward older workers.

Hiring Practices for Older Workers

Many organizations and individuals believe that the education system in the United States has failed to deliver graduates who are fully qualified to enter and meet the demands of today's labor market. Consequently, more and more organizations are trying to retain, recruit and hire older workers because of their skill, professional expertise, and accumulated knowledge. Plato, the philosopher, said 2000 years ago that "It gives me great pleasure to converse with the aged. They have been over the road that all of us must travel and know where it is rough and difficult and where it is level and easy." The demand for the aged and the wise with corporate management and leadership is on the rise. While there seems to be a global decrease in the professional labor supply, there is a rise in demand for experienced professional workers. According to the Bureau of Labor Statistics (2002), about 50 percent of the workforce in the United States will be made up of individuals forty-five years or older and the same workforce age trends are occurring in most developed nations. The increase of older workers in the workforce are caused from the aging baby boomer generation, low birthrates in the last third of the twentieth century, and discouragement of early retirement caused by economic conditions (Kanfer and Ackerman, 2004). Kanfer and Ackerman state that "In the United States, aging is often associated with general decline—particularly in cognitive and intellectual capabilities. Increasingly, however, researchers in a number of domains have shown that the assumption of general decline with age is simplistic and misleading." Age is one dimension of diversity, and "diversity is a complex and challenging reality for most managers and employees in today's world" (Jones et al, 2002). The best way to use this diversity toward organizational objective is to learn about it, make sure everyone is treated fairly, and appreciate the increasing diversity of the workforce. Unfortunately, as Jones et al. (2003) state, "We are the land of diversity and yet we are seemingly without the conceptual ability to take that reality in, accept it and work effectively with it. Of course there are many historical reasons for bias and deeply seeded reasons of prejudice that we don't even understand, but even so, we must manage them." According to the 2000 Census, the median age of a person in the United States is the highest it has ever been (35.3 years), and this fact has certain implications for the workers and managers. Furthermore, those who fall between the ages of 45-54 years old had the greatest population growth.

The elderly professionals are often in the position of being fairly healthy, wealthy and selective in terms of what they would like to do in their later years. As a result of their years of productive work in society, they tend to live in better neighborhoods and often have hobbies or community roles. As such, one barrier for attracting the elderly is that they can be selective in determining where they would like to work. Often times, they would like flexible hours with options to come and go to pursue their avocations and personal community obligations. So, the fact that they do not apply to all organizations is one barrier. Another barrier is the fact that they want flexible hours with jobs that offer the opportunity to fulfill their socialization and other higher order needs for self-actualization. Some of them may also want to work in positions that do not require too much new learning or physical activity since they have been through all this before and would rather not deal with it again. So, wanting selective jobs is yet another barrier in entering the workforce. However, the most common barrier for those older workers who do apply for specific jobs in the workplace is probably the widespread stereotypes and biases on the part of interviewers which result in not hiring the elderly. Increasingly, older workers are claiming that opportunities have been limited for them due to stereotypes, biases, and structures that are designed to discourage them from the work environment.

An "older worker," according to the laws in the United States, is a worker that is 40 years of age or older. Unfortunately, there have been many firms that have shown patterns of discrimination against "older workers" in the United States' work environment. When such discrimination becomes an "unseen" part of the culture, it can hinder the organization's morale, productivity, and may possibly cause many legal problems for the firm. Creating an effective organizational culture that avoids age discrimination requires long-term commitment and resources since there are no panaceas. Organizational leaders and managers must be concerned about age discrimination, since an increasingly larger percentage of the workforce is coming, and will continue to come, from the older population as "baby boomers" continue to age. According to the United States Census Bureau and the Administration on Aging, the number of Americans who are 65 years of age or older has increased by a factor of 12 since the early 1900s.

Table 21 – Statistics on Older Workers

Year	Americans 65 Years of Age or Older
1900	3 million (4%) older workers.
2000	35 million (13%) older workers.
2011	First baby boomers will turn 65 years of age!
2030	Estimated at 70 million people (20%)

In contrast to intentional age discrimination, covert discrimination against older employees seems to be subtler in nature, and human resource managers should be aware of such subtle forms of discrimination. Further research has revealed that unintentional code words often are used during the interview process, such as, "we're looking for go-getters" and people who are "with-it" to describe desirable employees. Generally, "buzzwords" seem not to apply to people who are seasoned and experienced. According to a U.S. News article (Clark, 2003) titled "Judgment Day," about two thirds of all U.S. companies use performance as at least one factor when deciding whom to lay-off during these tough economic times. Many firms use the "forced ranking" system since executives like them because they seem to be the "fairest and easiest way to downsize." Unfortunately, "older workers" seem to get the worst of it as larger portions of them lose their jobs possibly due to biases and because they earn more income and earn more benefits compared to their younger counterparts. For example, in 1999, Ford wanted to increase diversity in its work environment and change Ford's culture to be more change oriented while embracing new technology, and new markets. As such, Ford created a new performance appraisal process for its 18,000 salaried, white-collar employees in which supervisors were required to give a yearly grade to each of their subordinates of A, B, C (Jones et al, 2002). If an employee received a C, that employee could not receive a pay increase and if this happened two years in a row, the employee was either demoted or fired. In 2000 the management told the supervisors to give only 10% As, 80% Bs and 10% Cs in their overall performance appraisals. The following year it was the same except 5% was moved from C (5%) to B (85%). The new process supposedly negatively affected some older managers, since it has been a very negative experience with 42 employees filing two class action lawsuits against Ford claiming that the new process was used to terminate older managers. Their attorney had suggested that Ford stereotypically assumed that older workers were slow to change or learn new things and so tried to diminish their numbers.

In another situation, Schering-Plough, a New Jersey based firm, was ordered to pay one of its ex-employees the amount of $435,000 in punitive damages and $8 million in compensatory damages based on evidence that his managers engaged in age discrimination by firing him (Jones et al, 2002). This employee, named Maiorino who was a salesperson, had worked for the company about 35 years and had several times been commended for his sales performance. While in his 60s, Maiorino had repeatedly declined enticements of early retirements. Then, he reported that management had instituted unfair practices against him to make him look bad on paper, and to build a paper trail to justify firing him. These unfair practices included very difficult tasks, higher standards than others were held to, and being spied on (Jones et al, 2002). The company had his direct boss meet him at dinner and gave him his termination letter.   Some of the former customers who sided with the employees were boycotting the company for such unfair practices.

Unfortunately, age discrimination in the workplace impacts people of all sizes, races, colors, religions, and ethnicities. Segrave (2001), in his textbook titled '*Age Discrimination by Employers*' wrote "…consistent across the period, and from country to country, it is apparent that age discrimination in employment creates more difficulties, and begins earlier, for women than for men." Such discriminations which can be highly unethical and totally illegal in the United States, is causing many managers anxiety and are forcing many of them to court. One of the greatest fears of company officials and individual managers is the likelihood of either being sued for something they have done intentionally or unintentionally, or for something they should have considered doing but did not. It is no secret that age-related lawsuits are proliferating, and more recently age related claims have been on the rise due to layoffs, which seem to be targeting older workers.   Juries often side with aggrieved employees, even if the evidence is flimsy. Because of these trends, companies and their managers are realizing the need to protect themselves by periodically reviewing workforce diversity and analyzing for latent signs of discrimination (Administration on Aging, 2001).   Facts show that it is imperative that older workers are kept in the workforce as long as possible since there will be a shortage of skilled labor starting as soon as the next few years if eligible older workers decide to retire early (Harvey & Allard, 2002).

The Age Discrimination and Employment Act (ADEA) of 1967 prohibits discrimination in all terms and conditions of employment against all persons 40 years of age or older.   This federal law covers employment practices, including hiring, discharge, pay, promotions, benefits and other terms of employment, to include forced retirement.   The focus of ADEA is to promote fairness in the employment of older persons where they are evaluated based on their ability rather than their age.   ADEA also helps employers and workers seek ways to combat problems resulting from the impact of age on employment. The Age Discrimination and Employment Act is enforced by the Equal Employment Opportunity Commission (EEOC), which provides the same protection to age protected individuals as provided under Title VII of the Civil Rights Act of 1964.

According to EEOC, in 2004 fiscal year, they received 17,837 charges of age discrimination; resolved 15,792 age discrimination charges; and recovered $60.0 million in monetary benefits for charging parties and other aggrieved individuals (not including monetary benefits obtained through litigation). The Equal Employment Opportunity Commission reports that age discrimination claims are still a major factor; however the percentage of such claims declined in the mid 1990s compared to previous data. However, it did increase again in the turn of the new century. One reason for this decline in the mid 90's is attributed to the over 40 population as being one of the fastest growing demographic segments in the United States.   Age discrimination settlements and jury awards are substantially higher than those awarded for race, sex, or disability cases.   Individuals claiming discrimination based on age were awarded an average of $219,000 compared to the low to mid $100,000 for race, sex and disability (Mujtaba et al, 2003). An increasing number of corporations have been accused of age discrimination in the years 2001 to 2003 since there have been many layoffs due to the downturn of the economy. Even before the downturn of the economy, there were accusations of age discrimination by major corporations. For example, in 1997, First Union Corporation, a major banking institution agreed to pay $58.5 million to 239 former employees to settle an age discrimination suit, and Continental Airlines paid between $7 and $8 million to 207 employees (Steinhauser, 1998). Kelly (2003) states that many employers in the past few years have reduced their operating costs and the number of their employees by specifically targeting highly compensated employees that, more often, tend to be the "older workers." EEOC, which administers the ADEA, provides updated information on charges of age discrimination cases that have been filed with them. For example, Table 22 provides some of the data and these statistics that show a rise in age discrimination cases during the past five years.

Table 22 – Age Discrimination Charges (EEOC Data, 2005)

Year	Charges of Age Discrimination Filed with EEOC	Percentage of Total EEOC Charges
1992	19,573	27.1%
1993	19,809	22.5%
1994	19,618	21.5%
1995	17,416	19.9%
1998	15,191	19.1%
1999	14,141	18.3%
2000	16,008	20.0%
2001	17,405	21.5%
2002	19,921	23.6%
2003	19,124	23.5%
2004	17,837	22.5%

Updated information and data can be retrieved from the Equal Employment Opportunity Commission's website (www.eeoc.gov/stats/charges.html) which is compiled for each year. While reviewing the EEOC data on July 25, 2005 for a longitudinal observation, it showed that the percentage of race related charges have decreased between 1992 (from 40.9%) and 2004 (to 34.9%). The percentage of charges filed on the basis of religious discrimination has increased from 1.9% in 1992 to 3.1% in 2004, showing a huge increase. Similarly, the number of complaints or charges related to Title VII has progressively and steadily increased from 14.5% in 1992 to 25.5% in 2004. At the same time period, the data revealed that the percentage of sex, national origin, and disability related charges have remained very similar from 1993 to 2004 with small changes in between the years. While age related charges have increased in the first five years of this decade, when compared to the last five years of the previous decade, many managers still remain skeptical and believe that age discrimination is not a major problem. Yet, the data shows that it really is, as such discrimination adversely impacts people of all races, ethnicities, body sizes, genders, and disabilities.

It is critical that employers exercise extreme caution within their corporate culture to minimize any inferences of older workers being mistreated. How can this happen one might ask? It actually starts at the top. Corporate culture is shaped at the top of the corporate "ladder" by the senior executives and managers who determine how human resources are to be utilized. If key executives are entrenched in a culture that views younger people as being more successful and aggressive and older people as being more complacent, then those beliefs will create a negative climate that will permeate throughout their organization, thereby, causing subordinates to buy into the same type of behavior. Given this, senior executives and managers, as well as the entire workforce within organizations should make every effort to ensure their corporate culture is positive and free of illegal discrimination, thereby avoiding any instances that may make older workers feel uncomfortable.

Changing Paradigms of Aging

The United States of America (U.S.A.) has a diverse population of nearly 300 million people. The perspective on aging in the U.S.A. can be seen from the high level of discrimination against older workers due to biases and stereotypes against older workers. An American by the name of William Osler in 1905 had said "Take the sum of human achievements…subtract the work of men above 40 … we would practically be where we are today" (Segrave, 2001). Segrave mentions that an anonymous personnel executive in 1910 stated that "A man who has failed to make good at 45 is not wanted today; he will never make good." Daniel Motley, in 1915, is quoted as having said "It is more delightful to be surrounded by the young, with hopefulness, gladness, and outlook in their eyes." Yet, a statement appearing on the New York Times editorial page in 1916 read as "That disinclination to hire old workers is actually a decent thing, proportional to the employer's kindness of heart." Such views, expressed today by citizens and the American comedians, associated with aging are common in the United States. They are representative of how the American society feels about aging, and, as such, youthfulness is valued and "older age" is not. These mindsets are causing an increasing number of the aging "baby boomers" to constantly search for the "fountain of youth," when in reality there is no such panacea. Nonetheless, such societal views tend to impact the workplace since senior executives and managers that make hiring decisions do come from the society.

The American culture seems to be obsessed with youth (Kelly, 2003), as can be seen from the increasing number of cosmetic surgeries while members of the media are fully capitalizing on such obsessions in their ads and selling efforts. Such youth-mindedness is also accompanied by a negative perception of aging in society, which is inclusive of the workplace. While many of the Asian and Middle Eastern cultures value and respect older individuals (both in their personal and professional lives), Americans view aging from a negative perspective as if it was a "bad thing." These negative perceptions tend to convey the message that older workers are not able to keep up with new technology or new ways of doing things because they are not open-minded. These negative perceptions regarding older workers and technology also were clearly revealed in the research results and participant comments in the survey study conducted for this book. Besides the perception of not being up-to-date on technology, older workers in American society are seen as: "deadwood, incompetent, closed minded, un-trainable, and less productive" (Kelly, 2003). Of course, as mentioned before, these are stereotypes and myths that are not factual and individuals disproving these myths are ubiquitous in today's workplace. Nonetheless, such views tend to put older individuals at a disadvantage as they attempt to compete in the job market with their younger counterparts. On the other hand, young Americans tend to have this "unearned privilege" or "unearned advantage" that comes to them at a cost to "older workers." Older workers tend to possess the qualities of functioning well in crisis; possessing basic skills in writing, reading, and arithmetic; being loyal; functioning as solid performers; and having good interpersonal skills. Older workers have various talents that are vital to multinational businesses in today's organizations.

The presence of more "older workers" being active in the workforce presents many challenges and opportunities for organizations. The challenges are stereotypes and age discrimination that are widespread in the American workforce. Organizations must effectively transcend such challenges and proactively take advantage of the experienced workforce as they attempt to be globally competitive. There are many proactive firms such as Publix, based in Lakeland, Florida which employed about 130,000 employees in 2005, that need to be congratulated for their efforts to reduce/eliminate age discrimination in the workplace. As a matter-of-fact, Publix leaders and executives need to also be congratulated for their national award as one of the country's Top Employers of older workers, which was presented to them in September (2002) in Washington D.C. through the Experience Works Prime Time Awards Program. Of course, there are many other such proactive organizations that value employee loyalty and experience, which eventually either reduces age discrimination in the workplace or, in ideal scenarios, eliminates it.

Preventive Measures in Avoiding Age Discrimination

How and at what point does one step in to eliminate biased strategies that drive older people out of the company? One solution is to audit diversity ratios of the organization carefully and on a regular basis. It is essential to ensure there are nondiscriminatory reasons for whatever decisions managers make. When there is a reduction in the workforce, it is necessary for management to do a careful analysis prior to implementing decisions about who will be laid-off. This act can be done through scenarios planning in order to see the impact of decisions before they are implemented. Before implementation of significant changes, managers should perform statistical analysis and review demographics, then compare this information to what the expected results would be if implemented. Occasionally, indications of an effect on certain age groups will surface. When that happens, managers have to begin asking some "tough" questions, such as why is that happening. If the people one retains require certain skill sets, what are those skills? In addition, why is it that these people over 40 years of age do not meet the requirements? It could just be the way the chips fall, but one would have to look carefully at planned separations. First and foremost, one must make sure to be using nondiscriminatory criteria for the decisions and older workers are not disproportionately affected. Once determined, ensure that performance issues of affected employees are carefully documented and communicated prior to separation (Bennett, 1988).

There are several other ideas that might prove helpful in dealing effectively with age bias and discrimination in order to recruit, hire, and retain an experienced workforce. The following are a few helpful suggestions used by various consultants and organizations (Steinhauser, 1998; Mujtaba et al, 2003).

- *Periodic research.* Conducting periodic research on how employees feel about older workers and how those feelings manifest themselves in the workplace;
- *Educational programs.* Formulating educational programs designed to dispel myths and providing the facts concerning retirement, healthcare and retraining;
- *Support mechanisms.* Reexamining what it takes for individuals to progress within the organization and providing whatever support mechanisms are needed in order for them to progress;
- *Benefits.* Developing a friendly environment for older adults as part of work-family benefits;
- *Appreciation.* Building morale and higher productivity by demonstrating to older workers that they are valued and appreciated; and
- *Management commitment.* Making sure senior managers and human resources staff are committed to the success of these efforts.

So, how can managers avoid the nightmare of being on the "wrong end" of a deposition? In most organizations, human resources professionals are unable to stay abreast of all staffing details. This is where managers' everyday decisions come into play, and especially where they are most likely to carry out decisions that leave them legally vulnerable. Not all instances of discrimination and harassment are easy to detect, and the laws are not always easy to interpret. In addition to the aforementioned preventative measures, of course, there are common sense and good judgment solutions that must be considered as well, such as:

- First, avoid both blatant and subtle forms of age discrimination as well as inappropriate comments.
- Second, maintain candid one-on-one conversations with older workers regarding how they perceive the situation.
- Third, managers should ensure training opportunities are available to everyone and encourage older workers to keep their skills current.
- Fourth, provide good benefits suitable for the needs of older workers.
- Fifth, consciously recruit older workers from their places of socialization and invite them to the organization.

- Finally, avoid unexpected lawsuits. This result might be the most common category of "everyday management," that is, managers must remain cognizant of common cultural and socioeconomic misunderstandings and important developments regarding age discrimination.

Personal Responsibility

While individuals who are considered to be "older workers" may not always be able to reduce or eliminate the presence of age discrimination during the hiring and recruitment process, they should and can take certain steps to make sure they are not victims of such stereotypes and biases. One challenge many older workers, especially senior citizens, face is finding interesting jobs that pay well after retirement (Jamaican Handbook, 2001). Yes, good jobs are "out there" and, with some searching, they can be found. There are many helpful suggestions which can be used by everyone at a personal level to increase one's chances for a successful job hunt. The Jamaican Handbook (2001) and other researchers offer many tips for being prepared and getting a suitable job; and the following are a few of them for consideration:

- What is more valuable to a company, someone with the skills and education, or someone that has the skills, education, and experience? Market your skill, education and experience with pride.
- What if you only have the experience but lack the skills and education? Could you still be hired? The answer is yes. Show them that you can learn the new skills and you are willing to get the required education.
- At the personal level, one should always have an updated resume, get the new skills needed to effectively compete in the job market, continue one's professional development, network with professionals in the field, stay current on organizational changes, and use one's experience not only to assist the organization but also the community to the furthest extent possible.
- Take an inventory of yourself. Assess your physical, mental and emotional conditions and determine what you would like to do while earning the kind of income you would want for your services. Take personal initiative to update your skills. Keep current and marketable in your field. Things change quickly, you can change with them or you can get left behind complaining that life is not fair.
- Realize that you might need help. Job hunting is not easy and many of the rules may have changed since the last time you looked for a position. It is fairly common to get assistance from support groups and employment offices.
- Be prepared to take no for an answer. While you may see the job as a perfect position for you, the boss and the culture of the organization might not be for you and they might need someone with a different skill set or personality based on their needs (and not necessarily always because you are not qualified).
- Learn to read the signs. When someone says "we will call you," often times this can mean that we don't have anything open for you. As such, there is no reason

to wait by the phone for their call. Instead, keep on moving to the next organization or company to see who else might be able to use your skills and service.

- Do not take rejections personally. People hire individuals based on many reasons and qualifications might not always be the only determining factor. So, no need to worry about why people did not select you for the job. Let it go and move on. It is always a good practice to send "thank you notes" for all interviews.

- Search for the right jobs in the right places. Once you know the kind of job you would like to perform, then searching through the classifieds might not always be the best resort. As a matter of fact, newspaper ads are probably the least effective for professional jobs (unless they are in the trade magazines and journals). It is fairly normal to call the company of your choice, visit their website or even visit the human resources department to see what possibilities exist and if they have a need for the type of service you can offer to them.

- Overall, the suggestion is to keep learning, stay current, and you will always have a place in the job market. If an employer is biased in respect to age, point it out to them so they can learn and it will be their loss not to have you working with them. Take an interest in the success of your company (regardless of your age) because their success is your success.

Life is not always "fair," and the "right" thing is not always done; yet, one needs to keep a positive outlook toward being fairly treated while expecting the best. The job market and pay scales may vary greatly from place to place. Innocent individuals may even at times be victims of politics since some of the hiring practices are a result of political initiatives. For example, one should make every attempt not to play the victim of age discrimination. Sometimes people get "lucky" and secure the jobs they want with a salary that is generous. Sometimes one has to work extra hard to earn it. This may require additional education, relocation, and starting at a lower salary to get into the door. One may not get the desired job right away, but once one gets into an organization and network with the right people, and that position becomes available, one will have a good "shot" at it. There are opportunities; one just has to look hard enough, long enough, see the right individuals, and one needs to be in the right place at the right time for the jobs one wants. So, if one is an older worker, then one should do the required homework about the company and go to the interviews with the attitude of "here is what I can bring to the organization and this is how I can help the department be more competitive." Avoid the tendency of "give me any job and I'll do it to the best of my abilities." Know your competencies and what you can offer; then go after getting the job you want with total dedication and commitment. Persistence "pays off," and one should also use his/her age and experience to determine the best way to move forward in serving a specific market with one's accumulated competencies.

Managers must remember that older workers are one of the valued categories of employees because they are stable, experienced, and consistent. Companies have recognized that older workers value stability and quality in their work. "We are now targeting and hiring alternate profiles. This industry is customer service–driven and older people are sensitive to customer needs" said Khan (2003). It is clear that some companies are tapping into the advantages of having highly skilled older workers within their organizations. Another example of a company that has utilized older employers while still exploring better ways of managing older employees is McDonald's. Michael O'Shaughnessy, employee relations director, McDonald's Australia, said that fast food chains regularly target older employees. He went on to say that a program aiming at recruiting more "older workers" was in the works (Comtex, 2003) in their area.

Job Opportunities

Senior employees looking for jobs can visit the website "Seniors4hire.org" (www.Seniors4Hire.org) which provides a list of companies that recruits and hires older workers. This is an online career center geared to promote businesses that value a diverse workforce and actively recruit and hire those who fall in the category of "older workers." In most cases, the jobs offered to older workers are of the nature that usually require mature, experienced and knowledgeable individuals, says Renee Ward-founder of www.Seniors4Hire.org (Senior Journal, 2004). According to the Senior Journal, there are at least 70 small businesses that are good places for older workers to be employed and some of the firms recently added to list are Regal Entertainment Group, Mayo Clinic-Jacksonville, General Nutrition Centers, NewYork Presbyterian Hospitals, Cost Plus World Market, Allina Hospitals and Clinics, RadioShack Corp, UCLA Healthcare, News America Marketing, FleetBoston Financial, Ryder System, Inc., and Providence Health System. Job seekers can become members with this center through their website, and membership is free.

Hiring seniors for project assignments or on a part-time basis saves on healthcare costs (Recruiting Seniors, 2004). According to a survey conducted by Thomas Regional, of the nearly 2,500 industrial small businesses owners surveyed nationwide, 63% stated that healthcare coverage is their biggest challenge. Hiring seniors to work part-time or on temporary assignments in most cases saves health care benefits costs (Recruiting Seniors, 2004).

A 2003 survey from the Society for Human Resource Managers (SHRM) indicated that 68 percent of organizations employ older workers; however only 41 percent specifically target older workers in their recruitment efforts. The survey also indicated that reasons for hiring older workers included their willingness to work a flexible schedule, their ability to serve as mentors, and their invaluable experience. Of course, other important reasons included the reliability and strong work ethic which often comes with older workers. Generally, firms recruit and hire older or retired workers because they offer:
1. Leadership and coaching skills for younger or new employees.
2. Superior customer service experience.
3. Stability.
4. Ability to initiate sales and transaction dependability.
5. Eagerness to provide support and guidance.
6. Superior communication skills.
7. Varied work experience.

8. Better ability to work with mature clientele.
9. An "old-fashioned" work ethic.

Overall, a mature employee's greatest assets (compared to younger demographics) are likely to be lower absenteeism, punctuality, less likelihood to change jobs, commitment to quality, superior customer service skills, better people skills, more eager to learn new skills, positive attitude, and the willingness to speak their minds and to point out the flaws of the organization. The Secretary of Labor, Elaine L. Chao, said, "Nowhere is the case stronger for tapping the strengths of older workers than with employers facing the skills gap. Everywhere I go, employers tell me they are having difficulty finding workers with the right skill sets for the jobs they have to offer." This provides a golden opportunity to turn a challenge—the approaching retirement of an unprecedented number of Americans—into a "win-win" scenario for the economy and one's workforce.

According to various writers and articles, part of the problem for older job seekers today lies in a number of persistent myths that prejudice some employers against them. Some employers feel that older workers use medical benefits more than other groups and raise the cost of medical insurance premiums for everyone. This is false because, in reality, seniors often use medical benefits less than some other age groups. Parents of younger children are the most frequent users and contribute more directly to increased premium rates. Some employers feel that older workers miss a lot of work. The fact is that senior workers have excellent attendance records, because they seldom miss work for personal reasons other than legitimate illness. Yet, others may feel that older learners can not learn new techniques and new technologies. Again the reality is that the capacity to learn isn't a function of age. If one is skeptical, ascertain the growing number of senior citizens going back to college and getting advanced degrees every year. Companies hire older workers because they have certain characteristics that other generations of employees may not always have and the following are some elements cited by authors:

- Older workers thrive on quality and hard work. They believe in putting in a full day's work for a full day's pay.
- Older workers are loyal. They appreciate the opportunity to work and stick with those who give them a chance to perform and produce.
- Older workers take great pride in their accomplishments. They care about doing a good job.
- Older workers are dependable. They show up on time all the time. They take orders seriously, keep their promises and do what they say they will do.
- Older workers do not always get involved in politics. They don't play political games, have hidden agendas or harbor secret ambitions. They are not interested in climbing the corporate ladder, so they don't have to resort to manipulation, dirty tricks or one-upmanship.
- Older workers have more than their share of "emotional maturity" and common sense.

Statistics show that about 10,000 Americans turn 55 years of age every day. As such, tapping into the strengths of these older workers is an excellent way to save on training and benefits costs. According to the U.S. Bureau of Labor Statistics, since January 2001, the biggest job growth has been among those 55 and older, with 3.2 million new workers from this group. Table 23 presents the percentages of change in the U.S. older population, by age group as reported by the U.S. Bureau of the Census.

Table 23 – Changes in the Population of on Older Population

Time Period	Under 60	50+	55+	60+	65+	75+	85+	100+
1995-2000	4.6	11.1	7.3	4.1	3.5	12.1	17.2	33.3
2000-2010	5.6	27.0	27.3	22.6	13.5	10.7	33.2	81.9

Figure 13 provides estimates and projections of the older population, by age group from 1995 – 2010 as gleaned from U. S. Bureau of the Census in 1996.

Figure 13 – Projections of Older Workers

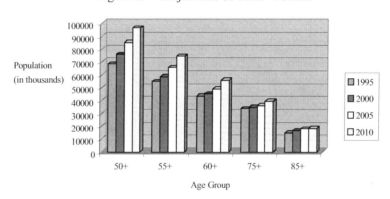

In terms of gender, the labor force participation for ages 55 to 64 in 2002 consisted of 69% males and 55% females. These numbers are expected to be 75% males and 64% for females in 2012. So, an increasing number of older males and females will be working after their retirement years; and thus firms wanting to recruit, hire and retain them must have specific strategies geared toward the older generation in order to get them. Experts state that older workers are likely not to apply for positions open to the general population because they fear they will not be considered for the job because of their age and biases toward them. Some of them also may wrongly feel that their experiences, skills and abilities do not qualify them for the twenty first century employment opportunities. So, employers wishing to take advantage of the experience and reliability that seniors provide must communicate to this group that they are specifically targeting them for employment. Furthermore, these employers must go where they can find such experienced older workers in their communities and educate them about the available benefits.

According to researchers, 60% of workers between the ages of 50 and 70 plans, to work during their retirement or never retire at all. Thus, for companies, it is "simply" a business decision. With a worker shortage in most industries, companies need to do more to attract skilled older workers and retain current employees as they age. Many companies are finding themselves in the same position of needing more skilled employees, and accordingly among the benefits offered by employers to recruit older workers are:

> *Financial Services* - Most companies offer some sort of retirement plan, but the best ones provide workshops, seminars, and counseling. First Tennessee National Corp., a financial services firm in Memphis, assigns advisers to help employees devise retirement plans, and retirees have their own dedicated financial specialist.

> *Health Benefits* – Most employers offer not only basic benefits-prescription drugs and health, vision, and dental care but long term care insurance and short and long term disability insurance. Some even offer wellness programs. Roche Inc., a New Jersey-based pharmaceutical company, offers a program that includes free health screenings and customized fitness programs.

> *Training Opportunities* – This includes everything from skill development to career counseling. The Massachusetts Institute of Technology offers career training to all employees and courses specifically for workers over 50.

> *Mentoring* – Ideally it works two ways: 1) Experienced employees help train younger workers and 2) Older workers return to the company and receive a mentor to help re-train them. At Baptist Health, older employees receive bonuses for mentoring new employees.

> *Flexible Schedules* – Forget the punch clock: 28.8% of American workers now have a flexible schedule, nearly twice as many as 10 years ago. SSM Health Care in St. Louis, Missouri, offers time off for dependent care, and spouses of retirees can take summers off to travel.

> *Phased Retirement* – Rather than quit cold turkey, many employees prefer to ease into retirement. Bon Secours Richmond Health Systems in Richmond, Virginia, lets workers shift to part-time or on-call status and they have to work only 16 hours per two week pay period to retain benefits.

> *Welcome Back Policies* – Some companies allow retirees to return to work after they have left the job. The MITRE Corporation, a not-for-profit systems engineering and information technology company based in Massachusetts and Virginia, offers Reserves at the Ready, a program that allows retirees to be on call for part-time work.

In many cases, a company's attitude towards older workers has a lot to do with the industry. Age bias is especially pronounced in youth-oriented sectors, such as advertising, technology, and securities. The entertainment industry is notorious for its youth obsession. In a company like a dot-com with predominantly younger workers and very little training on cultural competency and diversity issues, one tends to find more age bias. Inexperienced young managers often have a difficult time supervising older workers due to their own inexperience and lack of effective management and leadership skills. There are many firms that attempt to differentiate themselves from their competitors through quality service by treating customers with respect and dignity. These firms are finding that an older workforce has the experience to treat customers like "kings and queens" while taking care of them with pleasure. As such, firms like Wal-Mart, Publix, Target, Wegmans, Stu Leonard, McDonald's, and many others do target older workers to help them create a culture of satisfying and delighting customers. More important than formally recruiting older workers is the organizational culture of these firms as they focus on serving quality products, offering excellent service, providing flexible hours and benefits to part-time employees (mothers, fathers, older workers, individuals with disability, etc.), being involved in the community, and making charitable contributions. This type of an organizational culture makes employees proud of their firms and tends to not only attract but also retain older workers since they too would like to be involved in such activities in the community. As such, the firms selected here for exploration are successful, at least partly, because they have created such an organizational culture that attracts and retains competent and experienced workers.

Wal-Mart Corporation Becoming a Giant Success

At the core of every organization is its most important asset, valued employees. Wal-Mart is one of the leading employers for senior citizens in the United States. In 2004, Wal-Mart had more 170,000 associates who were 55 years of age or older. Naturally, their number of older workers (40 and above) would be much larger. Wal-Mart employees pride themselves on providing good customer service which they say has made them a great company that is able to retain employees, have low costs and provides low prices for its customers. Wal-Mart's history started at the hands of Sam Walton in 1962, but his unfortunate passing led to successor Robert Walton as chairman who has continued to cherish the founding principles of the organization. Sam Walton once said "customer service distinguishes our Company from all others." In his words, "Give customers what they want - and a little more. Let them know you appreciate them. Make good on all your mistakes, and don't make excuses, apologize. Stand behind everything you do." The two very important words making them successful were on the first Wal-Mart sign, "Satisfaction Guaranteed." Sam wanted to make sure every employee understood the importance of satisfying the customer because they worked for the customer. Wal-Mart defines success on how well they please their customers, and one of the ways to do that is to have customers be 100% satisfied whenever they shop or hear the name Wal-Mart. It is apparent that in most cases Wal-Mart employees go above and beyond the call of duty to assure their customers' satisfaction, and they do this by offering customer repair, exchange, or a refund of goods with a "thank you" and a smile. Statistics show that if a company exceeds the customer's expectations then the customer will come back again and again, thereby creating a brand loyalty between the customer and the company. Wal-Mart's customer rules state:

- Rule #1: The customer is always right!
- Rule #2: If the customer happens to be wrong, refer to Rule #1.

Most individuals understand that Wal-Mart is in the business of making money; thus they hire older workers because they want employees to treat customers with respect, sell products at low prices, and offer good service. As such, Wal-Mart delivers superior value to customers by making their shopping experience pleasant, productive, fast, and convenient. With more than one million "associates" nationwide focused on low prices and over four hundred thousand employees internationally, Wal-Mart is the fastest growing and largest private employer in the United States. It is expected to be the first trillion dollar retailer in the world as it crushes other retailers by offering low prices to consumers around the globe. Total sales for 2003 at Wal-Mart were $256 billion. Wal-Mart's annual profits are about $9 billion and they have a market value of $244 billion with assets worth over $105 billion as of 2004. As of April 2004, in addition to its 3,550 stores in the United States, Wal-Mart had 640 stores in Mexico, 404 stores in Japan, 267 stores in the United Kingdom, 236 stores in Canada, 92 stores in Germany, 53 in Puerto Rico, 34 in China, 25 in Brazil, 15 in South Korea, and 11 stores in Argentina while expanding into other countries on a continuous basis. As of early 2006, they had over 5289 stores and over 1.6 million employees. It ranked 10th on Forbes Leading 2000 Companies in the World based on composite scores for sales, profits, assets, and overall market value. As a matter-of-fact, Wal-Mart ranked first in sales, ranked sixth in total market value, and they ranked eight in overall profits in Forbes April 12th issue. Wal-Mart's organizational culture has been built around very important rules founded on Sam Walton's three basic beliefs.
1. Respect for the individual,
2. Service for the customer, and
3. Striving for Excellence.

These beliefs have been what made them successful and management has decided to stay true to them. *Respect for the individual* is critical because Wal-Mart believes that people make the difference. The company hires ordinary, hardworking, dedicated employees from diverse backgrounds, education, ethnicities, and beliefs. When this diverse group of people is treated with respect and dignity, they will do extraordinary things for the organization. *"Service for customers"* is where they get serious about their low pricing philosophy. They want to offer the lowest prices with the best possible service to customers. Most people know that customers are not just external, but internal as well. Wal-Mart's culture stresses the importance of empowerment, participation and good service to each of its employees. *Strive for excellence* is Wal-Mart's culture to empower its employees to serve their customers and to stretch to new boundaries. They want to continually improve and stay ahead of the competition. Sam Walton's philosophy included fun in the workplace and he believed that while employees work hard there is no need for them to go around with long faces. He believed in the "whistle while you work" philosophy which is attractive to older workers.

The Walt-Mart Philosophy

With Sam Walton's philosophy and leadership, Wal-Mart has become a national success due to effective application of management concepts in its day-to-day operations. In a short span of about forty years, this company has become the envy of any and every major corporation in the world.

By maintaining its promise to customers of "everyday low prices," Wal-Mart has harmed many of its competitors. Although Wal-Mart, like any other firm, experiences problems and challenges in the workforce, it continues to thrive because the company learns from its experiences. Wal-Mart, in 1962, opened its first Wal-Mart Discount City and now it sells more toys than Toys "R" Us, more clothes than the Gap and Limited, and more food than Kroger and a few other supermarkets combined (Upbin, 2004). If Wal-Mart was its own economy, it would rank 30th right next to Saudi Arabia while growing at the rate of about 11% each year. With $47.5 billion in international sales making up one-fifth of its overall revenues, Wal-Mart has enjoyed an enormous success and does not seem to be losing momentum, despite some temporary challenges and setbacks. With more than one million associates nationwide and over four hundred thousand employees internationally, Wal-Mart is the fastest growing and largest private employer in the United States. The "Wal-Martization" of the world is bringing about good and bad changes to commerce around the globe. Wal-Mart is expected to be the first trillion dollar retailer in the world. Total sales at Wal-Mart were $256 billion with 68% from Wal-Mart Stores, 19% from its international operations, and 13% coming from its Sam's Club. Wal-Mart's annual profits are about $9 billion and they have a market value of $244 with assets worth over $105 billion during of 2004. As of April 2004, in addition to its 3,550 stores in the United States, Wal-Mart had 640 stores in Mexico, 404 stores in Japan, 267 stores in United Kingdom, 236 stores in Canada, 92 stores in Germany, 53 in Puerto Rico, 34 in China, 25 in Brazil, 15 in South Korea, and 11 stores in Argentina while expanding into these countries on a continuous basis. Currently, it employs over one million people in the United States and nearly half a million individuals internationally. Furthermore, it ranked 10th on Forbes Leading 2000 Companies in the World based on composite scores for sales, profits, assets, and overall market value. As a matter-of-fact, Wal-Mart ranked first in sales, ranked sixth in total market value, and they ranked eight in overall profits through Forbes ranking of World's 2000 Leading Companies in Forbes April 12th issue.

Management Practices at Wal-Mart

The four functions of planning, organizing, leading, and controlling are all part of management's responsibilities at Wal-Mart in their day-to-day operation as they serve thousands of customers every day. Wal-Mart managers use some of the administrative management theories in their organizational structure that has helped them to be efficient. Examples are the widespread use of cross-departmental teams and empowerment concepts to decentralize some of the decision making to the lowest levels. Wal-Mart practices the concept of empowering employees and, similar to Nordstrom, Wal-Mart uses an inverted paradigm approach whereby employees are on top and often participate in decisions that impact them and their customers. Senior managers understand that the persons who are in direct contact with customers on a day-to-day basis are the frontline employees, and they hear the positive and negative feedback from customers and, therefore, are best equipped to serve them well.

Managers also practice the behavioral management theories as they seek to promote each employee's desire to be innovative and create a team-oriented atmosphere that leads to high morale, cooperation and synergy. At Wal-Mart, like most other successful organizations, the relationship between managers and employees is more of a partnership rather than an "us and them" mentality. The managers inspire employee loyalty and reap the rewards of paying attention to the people at the front lines as they have grown into a giant. A strategy used at Wal-Mart for employee motivation is offering employees an opportunity to participate in the profit sharing. By sharing profits with employees, Wal-Mart instills loyalty and inspires them to do well as they join in the success and failures of the store. Sam Walton, like many other retail experts, believed that the more you share profits with associates – whether it is in salaries, incentives, bonuses, or stock discounts – the more profit will accrue to the company as everyone treats the organization like their own personal business thereby becoming intrapreneurs. Basically, the way management treats their associates is how the associates will treat customers. So, if managers treat employees well then the associates treat customers well and the customers will return. This is a relationship-based marketing, and this is where the real profit lies – not in trying to always recruit new customers for one-time purchases. Satisfied, loyal, and repeat customers are at the heart of Wal-Mart's success. This fact is emphasized in the principle that "the most important contact ever made at Wal-Mart is between the associate in the store and the customer" (Walton, 1992). Accordingly, employees are expected and motivated to treat their customers like kings and queens.

Hiring Practices at Publix

At Publix, the company's goal is go above and beyond "the norm" to create extraordinary "shopping experiences" that shine in the industry. In order to create "raving fans" from customers, they must, at a minimum, satisfy the needs of customers better than competition. They know that many organizations can offer competitive prices and quality products. Publix wants to stand out in the customer's mind because the company is willing to go "beyond the norm" by providing *delightful* customer service with every shopping experience. *Customer Service* is about providing consistent, high quality attention to the customers who come to their stores for some sort of a service and/or product. The company's aim is to satisfy their customers all the time through their culture of customer intimacy and experienced workforce. Because of their stellar performance through an experienced workforce and a culture that is focused on customer intimacy, the company has had excellent performance, even during the past few years' of poor economy. Such success starts at the top and from the vision and mission of an organization. Their mission at Publix is to be "the premier quality food retailer in the world...To that end we commit to be Passionately focused on *Customer Value;* Intolerant of Waste; Dedicated to the *Dignity,*

Value and *Employment Security* of our Associates; Devoted to the highest standards of stewardship for our Stockholders; and Involved as Responsible *Citizens* in our Communities."

Publix, a direct competitor for Wal-Mart in the grocery business, employs about 125,000 employees in the states of Florida, Georgia, South Carolina, Alabama, Tennessee, and a few others. The company generated about $20 billion in sales during 2005 and this number is expected to grow at a rate of about 5%-10% annually. Publix employees take pride in creating an environment "where shopping is a pleasure" for their customers. Publix received national recognition for being one of the country's Top Employers of older workers and the award was presented to them in September (2002) in Washington D.C. through the 'Experience Works Prime Time Awards Program.' The first author, one time retail managers, had hired many older workers because they bring a focus on quality and service. They also make great team players and are able to treat customers as they would like to be treated. Hiring seniors can attract other seniors and bring in more local customers since older workers tend to be very involved in the community. As such, when older workers are treated with dignity and respect, their word-of-mouth advertising then can generate good human relations publicity and more candidates for prospective positions. Recently, for the sixth year in a row, Publix was named one of the country's best places to work by Fortune magazine. Publix was ranked 87th on Fortune magazine's annual list of the "100 Best Companies to Work For." The ranking was determined from formal responses from randomly selected employees, evaluating trust in management, camaraderie, and pride in the company. Furthermore, each company is required to complete a questionnaire on its benefits and practices offered to employees. Publix CEO Charlie Jenkins Jr. said, "I'm proud that our associates continue to consider Publix to be one of the best companies to work for in America. They are the reason we're one of the best." Publix associates go above and beyond the call of duty to make sure a customer's shopping experience is a pleasure while s/he is at one of their stores. More information about the survey and how companies were ranked can found at Fortune's Web site (www.fortune.com/bestcompanies).

It is easy to see why Publix has been recognized by Fortune magazine as one of the "100 Best Companies to Work For." Among the benefits of working at Publix listed at their corporate website (Publix Careers, 2004) are:

- *Unparalleled stability.* There's never been a layoff in the company's history. They have virtually no debt. Their stock price has remained remarkably stable (with a 38% increase in 2004) during periods of economic volatility. And the company is building about 50 stores per year at a time when many other companies are shrinking, merging or folding.
- *Sense of ownership.* Publix is the largest employee-owned supermarket chain in the country. Their associates benefit from that ownership through profit sharing and, as such, many become life-long employees or "lifers."
- *Opportunities to grow.* Publix has a strong tradition of promoting from within. They value extended service to the company, which is why they have so many "lifers" at Publix. And, it is why there are lots of opportunities to grow a career at Publix, not just earn a paycheck.

- *Friends and fun.* In survey after survey of associate, Publix employees express strong job satisfaction, in part because of the teamwork they experience - in stores, manufacturing plants, warehouses, corporate offices and on the road with a fleet of nearly 2,000 vehicles.
- *Innovation.* Dozens of pilots are underway at any given time to test new technology, improve products, devise more efficient processes, and pioneer new ways to help associates reach their potential.
- *Close relationship with customers.* Sophisticated research puts them directly in touch with more than 25,000 customers a year, allowing Publix to customize the product mix in every market and in every store. That's one reason Publix had the highest customer satisfaction rating of any supermarket chain for the past eight years.
- *Excellent benefits.* Publix wants to safeguard the health of their associates and their families and help them prepare for retirement.
- *Commitment to diversity.* Publix is committed to ensuring diversity in its workforce. Publix believes having a diverse workforce provides a competitive advantage in their ability to meet the needs of diverse customers.
- *Community spirit.* Publix and its associates contributed $24.5 million to United Way in 2002. Other agencies benefit from untold hours of volunteer work by their associates. They have many heroes on their team.

Publix is proud of its accomplishments, and has been honored with many other awards and recognitions from various organizations (Publix Awards, 2004). For example, as a caring employer, they have received the following awards:

- Named by Child magazine as one of the Top 10 Family-Friendly Supermarkets (2003)
- One of the top companies in FORTUNE's list of "100 Best Companies to Work For" (1998 - 2004)
- One of Jacksonville Magazine's top 25 Family Friendly Companies (2002)
- One of the nation's Outstanding Employers of Older Workers, according to Experience Works (2002)
- One of BestJobsUSA.com's "Employers of Choice 500" (2001)
- One of Central Florida Family magazine's top companies for working families (1999)
- One of the top 10 companies to work for in America in the book, "The 100 Best Companies to Work for in America" (Currency/Doubleday, 1993)

Also, as an industry leader, Publix has received the following awards:
- Received the 2004 "Outstanding Business" award for recycling efforts from Recycle Today, Inc. (2004)
- The Governor's Business Diversification Award - Business Expansion (2003)
- Rated top pharmacy in the WilsonRx Survey of supermarket pharmacies (2003)

- Scored higher than any other supermarket for customer satisfaction in a national survey conducted by the American Customer Satisfaction Index, a joint project of the University of Michigan Business School and the American Society for Quality Control (1995 - 2003)
- One of FORTUNE's "Most Admired Companies" (1994 - 2004)
- Voted "Best Grocery Store" by Florida Monthly magazine (2003)
- Catalyst Blue Ribbon Board of FORTUNE 500 Companies with Multiple Women Directors (1998 - 2002)
- One of PlanetFeedback's "A-Rated Companies" for customer satisfaction (2001)
- United States Environmental Protection Agency's Environmental Merit Award 2000 (2000)
- Progressive Grocer "Retailer of the Year" Award (1998)
- And, as involved members of the community, they have received the following awards:
- One of Jacksonville Magazine's top 25 Companies That Care (2000 - 2003)
- Executive Technology Magazine's Community Service Award (2002)
- Inducted into the Special Olympics Florida Hall of Fame (2001)
- America's Second Harvest Grocery Distributor of the Year Award (2001)
- Outstanding Industry Partnership Award for contributions to the Food Industry Crusade Against Hunger (1999)
- March of Dimes Million Dollar Club Award (1999)
- United Way of America national Spirit of America® Award (1996)

Publix both encourages and recognizes its associates for community involvement. For example, on May 16, 2003 as is done each year, five Publix associates received the Mr. George Community Service Award at Publix's Annual Meeting of Stockholders. Each year the Mr. George Community Service Award honors at least one retail associate in each division and one support-area associate. The winners represent characteristics that the late George Jenkins instilled in associates when he founded Publix: passionate volunteerism, active community involvement, and personal integrity. The winners receive the Mr. George Community Service Award trophy, three days off with pay and a donation of $5,000 to the charities of their choice (Publix, 2004). The following is a sample description of some of their 2003 award winners.

- Key Largo Store Manager Tom Moore is the winner for the Miami division. Moore is vice president for the Upper Keys United Way and is actively involved with the Upper Keys Athletic Association. He also assists the Monroe [County] Association of Retarded Citizens (MARC) by employing several MARC students in his store.
- Dan Maloney, the Business Development Director, was selected to receive the honor from the company's support area. Maloney volunteers for VISTE (Volunteers in Service to the Elderly). Dan is a board member for Camp Fire USA and has assisted the organization in many fund-raising activities to help

local youth. Also actively involved with the United Way of Central Florida, Dan is chairman of the community investment of basic needs committee, which allocates funds to 11 major United Way agencies in Central Florida.

- Tiki Vietri, store manager in Mt. Pleasant, S.C., received the honor for the Atlanta division. Seeing a great opportunity to help people in need, he serves as a board member and chairman of the operations committee for Goodwill Industries of Lower South Carolina. He was also instrumental in establishing The Bread Basket, a food pantry, and is heavily involved in his store's partner in education school, Windsor Hill Elementary.

- Store Manager Tim Bryant, of Crestview, Fla., is the winner for the Jacksonville division. Bryant helps bridge the gap between civilians and military personnel in his community. Bryant has been involved with March of Dimes, the Okaloosa/Walton United Way, the Crestview Rotary Club, the American Cancer Society of North Okaloosa and is a member of the ambassador team with the Crestview Chamber of Commerce.

For years, Publix has attempted to differentiate itself by offering "an environment where working and shopping is a pleasure." They have been able to create and maintain such an organizational culture by recruiting the right individuals and retaining them for life. Most Publix employees stay with them for a long time because the organization seems to be loyal to their employees. Publix thus is able to retain an experienced workforce and create a culture that is focused on highest standards of quality and excellence to customers. The organizational culture of employee loyalty while retaining an experienced workforce has lead to their steady and incremental growth over the past sixty years. Of course, besides Publix, there are other super markets such as Wegmans and Stu Leonards that have earned a good reputation because they retain a workforce that is focused on quality and good customer service.

Wegmans Food Markets, Inc. located on the east coast, believes that employees need to make an affordable living and if employees are making a good living then they will be more productive in the workplace. Wegmans and Stu Leonards are both east coast grocery retail companies; and they have chosen to really focus on taking care of their employees and customers as "guests" in their homes, believing and proving that satisfied employees take good care of customers. For example, the successful realization of this philosophy for Wegmans and Stu Leondards is raking in big profits and both companies have been listed as one of 100 of the best places to work. The philosophy of taking care of employees in terms of pay and benefits is "bucking" the system. Healthcare costs are rising, but Wegmans still provides free single healthcare coverage to full and part time employees. With this philosophy, Wegmans is working with employees to reduce costs. Working woman honored Wegmans by listing it as one of the top 100 best places to work in the U.S. for working mothers. Another company that is taking the same approach of putting employees first is Stu Leonards. Fortune magazine named Stu Leonards as one of the 100 best places to work. In the theme of "*In Search of Excellence*," Tom Peters (1979) also mentions Stu Leonards as an excellent firm that has been able to "wow" customers, generate high volume of sales per square footage, and provide a fun shopping experience. Stu Leonards still provides free healthcare coverage to all full time employees including medical, dental, vision, legal plans, and retirement plans. These companies have gone through great lengths to communicate with employees in terms of prescriptions drugs. They have promoted generic brands to their employees and the end result is that they have saved money and created a more loyal workforce. Wegmans saved about two million dollars because of this technique. Both companies have well above average number of sales in one year over industry standards. Both companies are projecting growth and new stores over the next several years and their philosophy appears to be working very well.

Target Corporation

"At Target, we strive to be a Fast, Fun and Friendly place to work and shop" said Bob Ulrich, Chairman and Chief Executive Officer. According to their employee handbook, Target is a quality-focused "discount retailer" offering fashion-forward, trend-right merchandise at great prices. It further states that "we treat customers as guests. We want them to feel at home when they shop at Target. After all, that good feeling will keep them coming back again and again, which will lead to greater sales and a strong, successful company." Managers teach their employees about the "moments of truth," like having clean stores, a safe shopping environment, being friendly, being good team players, offering quality products and services, having full shelves, being fast, friendly and fun with guests. The company installed electronic cash registers storewide enabling better monitoring of inventory and quicker guest service. Target became involved in community service by hosting annual shopping events for seniors and people with disabilities, and also began a toy safety campaign. Currently, there are about 305,000 employees serving Target Corporation. The value focused strategy ("expect more and pay less") enables Target to optimize, communicate, and deliver customer value through the use of superior customer service, innovative marketing campaigns, and organizational responsiveness. This value proposition is consistently linked to the company's customer service and product offerings. Target wants their customers to expect upscale department store service at a significantly lower price. The company strives to provide an inspiring shopping experience for its customers in various ways. Employees are enthusiastically willing to answer customer's questions. Customers can expect low prices and unbeatable customer service showing that the goal is to optimize customer service and overall value. Target aims to deliver a "personal touch and feel" particularly "through communication, through their products, through the design of their stores and their people" (Rowley, 2003, p. 40).

Target provides great service and value through the creation of a work environment where the customer is treated like a guest. Providing an exceptional customer experience is Target's main goal. The store is designed to support a welcoming shopping experience as the aisles are wide, the floors are shinny, the merchandise is innovative, the shelves are well stocked, the atmosphere is bright, the prices are low, and the customer service is magnificent. Customer value is provided through trendy products, novel designs, ground-breaking campaigns, and low prices. Ensuring quality products is another way Target adds customer value. Quality can signify sacrificing products and money. Target, however, believes in ensuring a quality product at a fair price. When a shipment of shoes fails the quality test in the quality control lab, immediate action is taken to make sure customers only receive the finest products. This case actually did happen once and each store was called and told to remove the shoes from the store and have them thrown in the dumpster. This was the right thing to do even if it cost the company money (Rowley, 2003, p. 148). Target is the second largest retail store because it does the right thing, and because it provides exceptional customer service through knowledgeable and experienced employees who eagerly assist customers (their "guests") in their shopping experience.

McDonald's Corporation[1]

McDonald's leaders believe that people are their most valuable resource as they compete with other fast-food locations throughout the world. They invest in their employees' growth and job satisfaction because it's the right thing to do and, perhaps, because their success as a business depends on their commitment to delivering outstanding value. The McDonald's system provides employment and growth opportunities to a vast number of older workers in the United States. Their commitment to opportunity also includes support for their employee's education and job-related development (Mujtaba, 2005). For example, McDonald's Hong Kong offers employees free continuing education courses in business. McDonald's Argentina provides scholarships for employees to study in a degree-granting program that was developed in partnership with a national university. McDonald's UK offers approximately $1,800 to each employee to invest in their education, training, or ongoing involvement in sports or the fine arts. The McDonald's Corporation invests significant resources in training and retaining employees of diverse backgrounds. Every day, around the world, restaurant crewmembers receive structured on-the-job training and coaching in workplace skills and values. As a matter of fact, diversity initiatives had begun at McDonald's back in the mid-1970s, under the guidance of former chief executive Fred Turner, who currently is senior chairman of McDonald's and a member of the board. It all started when Turner's daughters who were working at McDonald's shared some things with him about what was happening on their jobs. That led to the introduction of another initiative around diversity education in the late 1970s known as the "Changing Workforce Seminars." Supported by Turner and upper management, the seminars included education about the overall changing workforce, followed by career development seminars for women, African-Americans, and Hispanics.

While the seminars were one of the first diversity directives taken by McDonald's, their employees themselves had started informal networking activities on their own. Many of the employee networks were formed in the mid-1970s. McDonald's managers recognize not only a responsibility to provide opportunity to experienced individuals that want to work with them, but also the advantages of having diverse backgrounds and perspectives in their system. It has been said that McDonald's commitment to inclusion of workers at all levels

---

[1] - Ms. Courtney Smith, MBA candidate at Nova Southeastern University, contributed as a co-author to this material on McDonalds.

of its workforce has provided the company with the competitive edge to continue to excel as the number one restaurant chain in the world.

Since the founding of McDonald's Corporation over 50 years ago, the company has worked to be a good corporate citizen in its local communities. To assess how the company is doing, McDonald's in 2002 launched a comprehensive evaluation to measure its social responsibility. "The company works diligently to keep community values "front and center," says Ken Barun, corporate senior vice president for social responsibility at McDonald's. "We're very humbled by our responsibilities. We do work hard for continuous improvement" (Wilson Web, 2005). Social responsibility is especially important in the franchisee community. Corporate responsibility is striving to do what is right and may mean something different from one franchisee to another. One such franchisee is Lee Adams of Adams Tri-Cities Enterprises, which owns and operates 14 McDonald's units in Kennewick and Richland, Ore., and Pasco, Wash. Among the many local organizations Adams' company supports are the March of Dimes, Girls and Boys Clubs, the Girl and Boy Scouts. Internet safety for kids, Habitat for Humanity, churches and a health program called "Get Active Tri-Cities" with the local health clubs (Wilson Web, 2005).

Over the years, the way McDonald's defines social responsibility and corporate citizenship has changed. This change is a direct result of the global market and expectations changing- technology, government, politics, culture, people, and people's access to information. The public has become more sophisticated in getting and using information. The stakeholder community is much more developed in terms of what they have access to and what they want to know. It is McDonald's obligation, therefore, to do what is right, and to be a trusted company (Wilson Web, 2005).

The motivation for McDonald's is to create more trust with consumers. There are many ingredients in trust: at a minimum, it includes getting customer orders right and having clean bathrooms. But over time, customers in various parts of the world expect McDonald's to be a leader in corporate responsibility issues as well. Major areas that McDonald's addresses in corporate responsibility include: community, environment, people, responsible purchasing, an appropriate menu and balanced lifestyles (Wilson Web, 2005).

Community

McDonald's feels that they have an obligation to give back to the community that gives so much to them. McDonald's and their independent owner/operators contribute to their local communities in countless ways. Together they support: education and youth development programs, local and regional sports programs and events, neighborhood beautification initiatives, health care efforts, cultural events, and fundraisers for Ronald McDonald House Charities and other children's programs. McDonald's in the community also means: Development and Help in Need (VSA Partners, 2004). Development focuses on their restaurants around the world being locally owned and operated. They provide opportunities for local suppliers, jobs for local residents, and revenues for local projects and services. McDonald's has helped restore historic sites and contributes to neighborhood revitalization. Help in Need targets disaster relief. Working with the American Red Cross and the International Red Cross Network, their independent owner/operators provide food and other support to disaster victims, rescue workers, and others helping in the crises (VSA Partners, 2004).

Within hours after the devastating tsunami in South East Asia, McDonald's local restaurants reopened to begin providing water, food, and other assistance to relief workers and victims. When the Elbe River Flooded in Summer 2002, McDonald's Czech Republic and Czech owner/operators rose to the occasion, despite damage to many of their restaurants. For several weeks, they provided food for the local crisis teams, fire brigades, police departments, and evacuation centers, clothing and toys for victims in the centers, and support for a fundraiser to restore Prague's cultural treasures. Employees affected by the disaster also received financial and other assistance (VSA Partners, 2004). During the 2003 epidemic of Severe Acute Respiratory Syndrome (SARS), McDonald's China donated food and masks to hospitals and sponsored public education in cleanliness and personal hygiene. In 2003, after a massive flood of the Badger River in Western Canada, owner/operators Peggy and Barry Bartlett established a relief fund. They contributed approximately $25,000 in supplies and other in-kind donations to affected families, and the Newfoundland owner/operators association made a matching contribution (VSA Partners, 2004).

In the aftermath of 9/11: More than 750,000 free McDonald's meals were provided, around the clock, to rescue workers at the Pentagon and World Trade Center; An estimated $2 million was collected in Ronald McDonald House Charities in-store canisters; McDonald's Corp. and RMHC pledged an additional $1 million each for recovery efforts; and McDonald's cookies and juice were delivered to blood donation centers throughout the U.S. (VSA Partners, 2004).

The first Ronald McDonald House opened in Philadelphia in 1974. It began as one family's misfortune and millions of family's good fortune worldwide. In 1974, Kim Hill, the 3-year old daughter of Philadelphia Eagles tight-end Fred Hill, was diagnosed with leukemia. During Kim's treatment, her parents often camped out on hospital chairs and benches and ate makeshift meals out of vending machines because they couldn't afford hotel rooms. Fred and his wife began to think that there had to be a solution (RMHC, 2005). Fred rallied the support of his Eagles teammates to raise funds and help other families experiencing the same emotional and financial traumas as their own. Together with Dr. Audrey Evans, head of the pediatric oncology unit at Children's Hospital of Philadelphia, who dreamed of a home-like temporary residence for families of children being treated at her hospital, and Jim Murray, the Eagles' general manager, they opened the first Ronald McDonald House. By 1979, ten more Houses had opened. By 1984, McDonald's restaurants and local communities founded 60 more Houses; then 53 more opened by 1989. Today, there are nearly 240 houses in 25 countries around the world (RMHC, 2005). To date, they have granted over $300 million in grants worldwide to help kids immediately. They have been involved in 171 charities in 44 different countries. They have granted people $2 million dollars in surgeries and have helped with the Children's Hospital in areas of healthcare and to promote a good environment in the hospitals. The foundation has also helped with scholarships, children abuse prevention, suicide prevention, and refuge assistance (Cook, 2005). Participating McDonald's restaurants in more than 100 countries worldwide also celebrate World Children's Day every year, which is an annual global fundraiser benefiting Ronald McDonald House Charities and local children's causes (RMHC, 2005).

In order to save money in their budget, some Ronald McDonald Houses have merged. The four Chicago-area Ronald McDonald House Charities organizations have merged in an attempt to eliminate redundant costs and boost their profile. Executive Director Doug Porter says the merger should cut annual costs about $300,000, roughly 13% of the budget of the newly formed, Oak Brook-based Ronald McDonald House Charities of Chicagoland and Northwest Indiana (Mullman, 2005).

Environment

McDonald's believes it has a special responsibility to protect the environment for future generations. This responsibility is derived from their unique relationship with millions of consumers worldwide, whose quality of life tomorrow will be affected by their stewardship of the environment today. They share the belief that the right to exist in an environment of clean air, clean earth and clean water is fundamental and unwavering. They believe that in today's world, a business leader must be an environmental leader as well. Hence their determination is to analyze every aspect of their business in terms of its impact on the environment and to take actions beyond what is expected if they hold the prospect of leaving future generations an environmentally sound world (VSA Partners, 2004).

McDonald's environmental commitment and behavior are guided by the following principle: effectively managing solid waste. They are committed to taking a "total life cycle" approach to solid waste, examining ways of reducing materials used in production and packaging, as well as diverting as much waste as possible from the solid waste system. In doing so, they also follow three courses of action: reduce, reuse, and recycle.

The focus of "reduce" is to take steps to reduce the weight and/or volume of the packaging the company uses. This may mean eliminating packaging, adopting thinner and lighter packaging, changing manufacturing and distribution systems, adopting new technologies or using alternative materials. The focus of "reuse" is to implement reusable materials whenever feasible with their operations and distributions systems as long as they do not compromise their safety and sanitation standards, customer service and expectations and are not offset by other environmental or safety concerns. The focus of "recycle" is to maximize the use of recycled materials in the construction, equipping and operations of their restaurants (VSA Partners, 2004).

The second principle of McDonald's environmental commitment is conserving and protecting natural resources. They continue to take aggressive measures to minimize energy and other resource consumption through increased efficiency and conservation. They don't permit the destruction of rain forests for their beef supply. It is McDonald's policy to use only produced and processed beef in every country where they have restaurants, but in the areas where domestic beef is not available in sufficient quantities to meet their needs, McDonald's imports beef from approved suppliers and other countries (VSA Partners, 2004).

The third principle is encouraging environmental values and practices. They believe that they have an obligation to promote sound environmental practices by providing educational materials in their restaurants and working with teachers in the schools. The final principle is ensuring accountability procedures. They understand that a commitment to a strong environmental policy begins with leadership at the top of an organization. Therefore, their environmental affairs officer is given broad-based responsibility to ensure adherence to these environmental principles throughout their system (VSA Partners, 2004).

People

At McDonald's, they believe that people are their most valuable resource. They invest in their growth and job satisfaction because it's the right thing to do and also because their success as a business depends on them-their skills, energies, diverse perspectives, and commitment to delivering outstanding customer experience. The McDonald's system provides employment and growth opportunities to vast numbers of people. In their restaurants, people can learn what it takes to succeed. Many move on to careers in other fields, taking with them essential workplace skills and values and others move up within the system (VSA Partners, 2004). More than 33 percent of U.S. owner/operators and 40 percent of their top 50 corporate officers formerly worked in their restaurants. Some crewmembers at McDonald's later became Chief Restaurant Officers for the worldwide System and U.S. Division Presidents. Vice Chairman and CEO Jim Skinner joined the System as a restaurant manager trainee (VSA Partners, 2004).

Their commitment to opportunity also includes support for their employee's education. McDonald's Hong Kong offers crewmembers free continuing education courses in business leading to certification at three successive levels. McDonald's Argentina provides scholarships for employees to study in a degree-granting program it developed in collaboration with a major national university. McDonald's UK offers 100 grants of approximately $1,800 (USD) each for crew employee to invest in their education, training, or ongoing involvement in sports or the fine arts (VSA Partners, 2004).

McDonald's invests significant resources in training at every level. Every day, around the world, restaurant crewmembers receive structured on-the-job training and coaching in workplace skills and values. Hamburger University provides operations and business management training for restaurant managers, owner/operators, mid-level managers, and corporate executives. A new computer-based training system is bringing rigorous, interactive learning experiences to crewmembers and managers right in the restaurants (VSA Partners, 2004).

These efforts have given McDonald's a long-standing and distinguished record for diversity-as an employer, franchiser, and purchaser of good and services. They recognize not only a responsibility to provide opportunity, but also the advantages of having diverse backgrounds and perspectives. Approximately 40 percent of McDonald's U.S. owner/operators are minorities and women of various age categories. In 2004, they purchased more than $4 billion in food and paper products from U.S. minority and women suppliers. In their corporate headquarters and U.S. company, approximately 26 percent of the managers, not including managers of company-owned restaurants, are minorities and 46 percent are women (VSA Partners, 2004).

Responsible Purchasing

McDonald's works with suppliers to incorporate socially responsible practices throughout the company's operations, and to build capabilities for continuous improvement. McDonald's is also an industry leader in animal welfare. Their animal welfare program is global and is based on guiding principles that apply to all the countries where they do business and includes onsite audits of their suppliers' facilities. McDonald's consults with advisers to make recommendations on animal handling practices, uses of antibiotics, the quality of safety of products and restaurant resources and suppliers' employment practices (Wilson Web, 2005).

To help preserve the effectiveness of life-saving antibiotics, McDonald's has issued a Global Policy on Antibiotic Use in Food Animals. This initiative calls for McDonald's suppliers worldwide to phase out use for animal growth promotion of antibiotics used in human medicine and to follow specific guidelines for uses in preventing, controlling, and treating animal diseases. They also recognize a profound responsibility to ensure the highest standards of quality and safety in their products in their restaurants environments. The toys and promotional items their restaurants distribute are extensively reviewed and tested before, during and after production by independent experts using state-of-the-art technologies. As reported by employees and experts, equipment for their PlayPlace areas is also subject to stringent safety standards.

At McDonald's, they believe that employees should be treated with dignity and respect in every aspect of the employment relationship. They also believe that, in this area as well as others, their suppliers should share their commitment to socially responsible conduct. This belief is institutionalized in their Code of Conduct for Suppliers and their supplier social accountability program. Continuous improvement is encouraged by training and by onsite assessments, with enhancement plans required to address opportunities for improvement. They have launched a cooperative monitoring project to help their suppliers achieve sustained improvement and self-reporting (VSA Partners, 2004).

Menu and Balanced Lifestyles

Across McDonald's global system, in more than 100 nations, new menu items, physical activity programs and education initiatives have been introduced or expanded for customers. Their menu items offer a variety of safe, high-quality food products that can fit into balanced, active lifestyles. Their restaurants serve several types of hamburgers, grilled and fried chicken products, and fish and, in many cases, salads, fruits, and additional sandwich options. McDonald's recently rolled out a new fruit and walnut salad in U.S. restaurants and has introduced more salads in Europe as well as items such as chicken flatbread and fruit smoothies (Colias, 2005).

As with other menu choices, new Happy Meal options reflect the tastes and customs of McDonald's local markets. McDonald's UK has broadened Happy Meal choices to include semi-skimmed organic milk, non-carbonated no added-sugar fruit drinks, and fruit bags. Happy Meal options in China now include a cheese and egg sandwich on a steamed bun. In Spain and Germany, McDonald's customers can create their own Happy Meals by selecting among main course, side and beverage, and optional add-on desert offerings.

Happy Meal beverage choices in Japan include two 100% fruit juices and a fruit-vegetable juice blend, as well as milk, carbonated beverages, and oolong tea (Scrivano, 2004). At McDonald's, they care about the well being of children and families everywhere they do business. They want to help them achieve their goals. With their balanced, active lifestyles initiatives, they aim to make a real difference on an issue that's important to their customers and the worldwide communities they serve.

McDonald's balanced lifestyles initiatives support the goal of providing leadership to their industry on the health and well being issues that so many of its customers care about. The trends in overweight and obesity, especially among children, require attention, innovation and partnership by many sectors. McDonald's global Go Active Program includes its owner/operators' continued support for grassroots sports, promoting walking as an entry point to fitness, Ronald McDonald serving as a motivational advocate to get children moving and utilizing the sponsorship of the Olympic Games, Olympic Day Run and FIFA World Cup as opportunities to promote physical activity (Jacobs, 2004). A team of Olympic Athletes, Hopefuls and Moms-athletes who are moms themselves or are "life coaches" to their own Olympic hopefuls-will bring this effort to life in countries throughout the world. The McDonald's Olympic Run 2005 showcases the ongoing commitment to a balanced active lifestyle and the spirits and ideals of the Olympic Games. The run focuses on promoting the importance of an active lifestyle. This event joins the general public, athletes, sporting bodies and those who believe and practice sport to help promote an active lifestyle (di-ve.com, 2005).

New advertising and creative approaches to balanced lifestyles have been focused on bringing the energy balance message to life through the expression, "it's what i eat and what i do...i'm lovin' it." The creative approach is reflected in television commercials, print and outdoors advertising, packaging tips, trayliners, education brochures and a variety of other communications as it is rolled out around the world. Last year, McDonald's phased out its extra-large "Supersize" fries and drinks amid pressures to cater to Americans' growing preference for healthier food options (Colias, 2005).

Ronald McDonald will continue to expand his role as a major advocate for balanced, active lifestyles. He will help inform children and parents around the world in a fun and meaningful way to eat well and stay active. McDonald's released the first two in a series of Ronald McDonald videos intended to show kids how much fun they can have when they activate their bodies, their minds, and their imaginations. The videos were launched in more than 50 countries and featured a dozen different languages (Howard 2004).

McDonald's has refreshed its GoActive.com website with a new look and feel developed in partnership with the International Olympic Committee and the American College of Sports Medicine. GoActive.com encourages and provides specific steps to help people around the world incorporate physical fitness into their daily lives. Visitors to the site, soon to be translated into seven languages, are able to get a behind-the-scenes look professional athletes prepare for competition and can create their own customized plans to meet their specific fitness and nutrition goals (Howard, 2004).

Summary

Over thirty-three years after Congress enacted the Age Discrimination in Employment Act, some employers feel as though they have solid economic reasons for not wanting to hire and train employees who may soon be retiring. Furthermore, others rationalize that people do "slip" with age. Some writers have stated that reasoning skills may decline with age. While some of these myths/opinions might have been based on a few factual occurrences with some individuals, they are not representative of an individual's ability to successfully complete a task based on his/her age. For example, older workers are one of the desired categories of employees in New Delhi, India. Some of the reasons why older workers are among the sought after workers in India include: job stability, experience, and consistency of work. Companies have recognized older workers value stability and quality in their work, so they are taking advantage of it. There is a mutual benefit here because the companies offer older workers the stability that they desire, and in return, the older workers utilize their expertise and stability to the benefit of the organization (Khan, 2003).

As more and more companies downsize, merge, and are bought out because of economic reasons, layoffs and cutbacks are inevitable. This fact concerns all managers because with these cutbacks, one cannot help but to think that the employment of older workers will be impacted significantly. The general feeling is that many more employers are going to focus on a more youthful workforce, rather than one that is mature and more experienced because of the stereotypes, myths, and costs associated with "older workers." It has been witnessed that individuals have lost their jobs over the past several years because of layoffs, and have always wondered why certain employees with similar characteristics (such as being over the age of 40) were selected rather than others. Many of these people have had a number of years invested in their organizations, but were dismissed regardless of their seniority. It has also been witnessed that younger workers have consistently been brought into organizations, and this consistency of the age characteristic makes one wonder "why"? For these reasons, among many others, managers should consciously decide to increase their knowledge in human resources and age discrimination issues in order to become more aware of the laws governing unfair employment practices, in hopes of making a positive difference in the lives of many experienced, honest, loyal, able, knowledgeable, and willing workers in order to recruit and retain them. Therefore, in this chapter, examples of best practices and suggestions for retaining an experienced workforce were explored.

CHAPTER 9

JOB SATISFACTION AND ORGANIZATIONAL COMMITMENT[2]

*W*hile multinational corporations continue to seek profits from all trade-related areas in host nations, one common denominator that unceasingly precipitates in the final outcome of business strategies in those host nations is their culture. Multinational organizations need to consider cultural variables such as values and languages (Firoz & Ramin, 2004) when considering possible trade relations with host nations. Faroz & Ramin (2004) further added that, "cultural adaptation and flexibility are two international guiding principles for foreign trips whether for business or for pleasure" (p. 307). Adaptation and flexibility make it possible for employees of multinational organizations to function in another country because as Faroz & Ramin (2004) notes, "each country is unique with its own customs, business manners, jokes, and religious practices" (p. 307). Even cultural variables, such as perception of age, gift giving, negotiating, greetings, and punctuality can vary significantly across countries.

The implication of these cultural variances in these countries where multinational corporations operate is the inevitable and consequent injection of variances in the extent of the job satisfaction and organizational commitment of its employees, whether expatriate or local. This chapter hypothesizes that the job satisfaction and organizational commitment of expatriate or local employees of any specific multinational corporation will differ either across countries or continents where the multinational corporation operates. If so, in which continents or countries are the employees of a specific multinational corporation the most satisfied and committed. Of course, the implication of having dissatisfied and uncommitted employees is the potential for employee turnover, and in worst cases sabotage and commercial espionage.

Employee turnover, especially with regard to older and experienced workers, has consistently been noted as a costly activity. The move also has the potential to disrupt the operations of a firm, thereby defeating the ultimate purpose for establishing a multinational corporation and business in the host nation, which is principally to make profit. When

[2] - This material is written by **Ikwukananne I. Udechukwu**, *Clayton State University,* and **Bahaudin G. Mujtaba**, *Nova Southeastern University*.

multinational corporations are able to identify their most turnover-prone locations and employees, then they can strategically allocate resources to ensure that well-qualified and promising employees (expatriate or local) are either recruited, developed or retained as a strategic objective of the multinational corporation. This way, strategic human resource is brought to bear on the global operations of the organization.

Historical Perceptions of Employee Turnover

Attitudinal and behavioral variables such as job satisfaction, organizational commitment, and turnover intentions have been shown to be related to turnover (Bluedorn, 1982; Arnold & Feldman, 1982, Michaels & Spector, 1982; Porter, et al, 1974, Mobley, et al, 1979). However, in the discussions of such relationships, a review of the turnover concept is essential for managers and human resource professionals. To do so, the model on which the research is based is presented in Figure 14 (Michaels & Spector, 1982).

Figure 14 - Illustration of Path Analysis Turnover Model (Mobley et al., 1979)

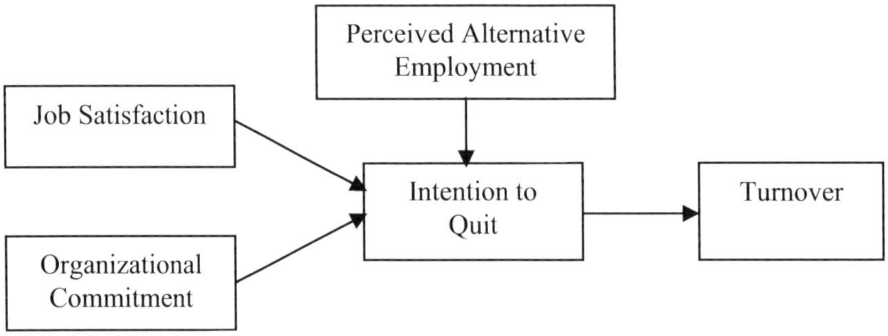

Employee turnover is an area of great interest and major relevance to most organizations. One reason for this interest is the cost associated with turnover. These costs are generally categorized as separation costs, learning costs, and acquisition costs (Mobley, 1977). They are further categorized into direct and indirect costs. Unfortunately, many organizations have failed to assess effectively the impact and consequences of the direct and indirect costs of turnover. For multinational corporations, it is no different. Porter and Steers (1973) vindicate these lines of thought by noting that the two prominent forms of withdrawal, employee turnover and absenteeism, are "clear-cut acts of behavior that have potentially critical consequences both for the person and for the organization" (p. 151).

Another reason that turnover is important is that individual characteristics/behavior, job/task related characteristics, and organizational characteristics are not set in stone. These characteristics are hypothetically in a state of flux because individuals and organizations either evolve or yield to various forms of change or stimuli in their environment. Porter et al. (1974) notes, "attitudinal measures of factors associated with turnover do not remain constant over time" (p. 603). These characteristics consequently lead to or affect the level of satisfaction and commitment employees have within their organization, and thus, produce a final outcome, turnover.

Finally, employee turnover cannot be studied by itself. Turnover exists because employees have exhibited behaviors and attitudes, expressed in their levels of satisfaction or commitment to their organization. For multinational corporations, the cultural variances in the host countries cannot be discounted in terms of the levels of satisfaction and commitment of their employees. The chapter attempts to link job satisfaction, organizational commitment, intention to quit, and perceived alternative employment opportunity to turnover. From a management perspective, three core models in the last four decades have dominated the study of employee turnover. In fact, many contemporary models, as with the model presented in this chapter, are derivatives of these core models. They are the March and Simon (1958) model, Price (1977) model, and the Mobley (1977) intermediate linkage model. These models are briefly described below.

March and Simon Model

This model, labeled the "decision to participate" model, embodies two unique concepts, "perceived desirability of movement from the organization and perceived ease of movement from the organization" (Mobley, 1982, p. 116). The model suggests that perceived desirability of movement from the organization is affected by job satisfaction and perceived possibility of inter-organizational transfer (Mobley, 1982). Ease of movement from the organization was linked to the availability and visibility of jobs in the organization for which they were qualified (Mobley, 1982, p. 117). Mobley, et al. (1979) clarified the issue of alternatives by noting, "it is not merely the visibility of alternatives but the attraction of alternatives that are most salient" (p. 519).

The Price Model

This model suggests that pay levels, integration (extent of participation in primary relationships), instrumental communication, formal communication, and centralization were primary determinants of employee turnover (Mobley, 1982, p. 66-91). The model notes that the intervening variables between turnover and these determinants were satisfaction and opportunity. While satisfaction addressed the issue of positive attitudinal orientation towards membership in an organization, opportunity reflected availability of alternative jobs in the environment (Mobley, 1982, p.121). Satisfaction was noted as interacting with opportunity in that dissatisfaction resulted in turnover only when opportunity was relatively high (Price, 1977). Bluedorn's (1980) review found no interaction between satisfaction and opportunity. Price (1977) further defined turnover as "the degree of movement across the membership boundary of a social system" (p. 3). This definition suggests a dynamic approach, which Bluedorn (1982) articulated as the inclusion of the act of entering an organization as well as the act of leaving the organization. Bluedorn (1982) further described this definition as a means by which the individual's personality intersects with the organization, with consequent increases in this intersection process, from zero state, upon organizational entry.

Rice, Hill, and Trist (1950) found that if the intersection process does not elevate to an adequate level, the process of increased intersection reverses itself (reduced intersection) and the individual, consequently, leaves the organization (Rice, Hill, & Trist, 1950).

The Mobley Intermediate Linkage Model

This model focused on the cognitive and behavioral processes, which occur between satisfaction and actual turnover (Mobley, 1982). According to the model, individuals constantly evaluate their existing jobs, and when they experience some dissatisfaction, they think of quitting, search for alternatives, evaluate the alternatives, compare alternatives to present jobs, think of quitting, and ultimately they quit (Mobley, 1982). Because of the behavioral perspective, the model depicts turnover as a process rather than an interaction of variables in contrast to the two preceding models noted earlier.

Other theoretical framework on turnover is discussed by Bluedorn (1982). Bluedorn provides an equally appealing theoretical construct of employee turnover, drawing from previous research. Bluedorn (1982) succinctly noted:

> One of the more general views of turnover is its definition as one of many manifestations of a more general phenomenon called withdrawal from work. When turnover is conceptualized in this way, two fundamental issues must be addressed. First, what is the nature of withdrawal (what is being withdrawn)? Second, what is the relationship between turnover and other forms of withdrawal? (p. 76).

Bluedorn (1982) discusses turnover studies on previous research from a behavioral perspective (withdrawal), which are either depicted as progressive (continuum model) or regarded as alternative behaviors (alternative forms). Generally, the continuum model, which was pioneered by Melbin (1961) and others, suggests that individuals progress in their state of withdrawal from low to moderate and then high forms of withdrawal. Quitting, like turnover and absenteeism, is one form of withdrawal (Bluedorn, 1982). The alternative forms, as suggested by Price (1977), presuppose that various forms of withdrawal, such as quitting and absenteeism, are not a result of progressive withdrawal attitudes and behaviors. Price (1977) argues that they are consequences of reducing the opportunity to embody one form of withdrawal, while keeping the withdrawal pressure consistent, the frequency of other withdrawal behaviors become elevated. These withdrawal behaviors (quitting, absenteeism), are generally associated with, and reflected in, turnover either as voluntary or involuntary turnover; thus laying the framework for the nature of withdrawal on voluntary turnover. Lambert (2001) notes that voluntary turnover occurs when the employee initiates termination of the employee-organization relationship. For example, the employee quits. Conversely, involuntary turnover is not initiated by the employee, but by the employing organization (Mueller, Boyer, Price, & Iverson, 1994), for example, layoffs, mandatory retirements, and discharges (Lambert, 2001).

Job Satisfaction

Because employees in organizations will either like or dislike their jobs, it is intuitive to suggest that, given the right conditions unique to the employee, some employees may stay or leave the organization (thus causing turnover). The study of job satisfaction attempts to explain this behavior and it is important from a humanitarian and utilitarian perspective (Spector, 1997). The humanitarian perspective suggests that people deserve to be treated fairly and appropriately, and that the level of satisfaction or dissatisfaction of employees may reflect the extent to which they experience good treatment in an organization (Spector, 1997). Satisfaction may also be indicative of the emotional and psychological well being of the employees (Spector, 1997). The utilitarian perspective presupposes that the satisfaction or dissatisfaction of employees can lead to behaviors that affect the functioning of the organization (Spector, 1997). For example, increased productivity within the organization is a reflection of one of many positive outcomes of satisfied employees, while absenteeism and sabotage are well-established negative outcomes of dissatisfied employees.

According to Spector (1997), "job satisfaction is simply how people feel about their jobs and the different aspects of their jobs. It is the extent to which people like (satisfaction) or dislike (dissatisfaction) their jobs" (p. 2). It is an attitudinal variable. Much of the contemporary research in job satisfaction has focused on the cognitive process of satisfaction rather than the employee's physical and psychological needs (Spector, 1997). The concept of job satisfaction is typically studied either globally or component-wise. Cook, et al, (1981) suggests that the choice of global or component approach depends on the goal of the project at hand. They further note, "A good solution in many cases is to include measures of both overall job satisfaction and specific satisfaction" (p. 2).

Satisfaction may encompass components such as work, pay, promotions recognition, benefits, working conditions, typically described as events or conditions (Locke, 1976). Other components of job satisfaction may include supervision, coworkers, company and management, typically described as "agents" (Locke 1976). However, some contemporary researchers have conceptualized job satisfaction as either intrinsic or extrinsic. This approach is based on the definition that describes job satisfaction as the extent to which workers feel positively or negatively about their job (Bhuian, et al., 1996; Locke, 1976). Intrinsic job satisfaction reflects the employee actually performing the work and the feelings of accomplishment and self-actualization experienced by the employee (Bhuian et al, 1996). Extrinsic job satisfaction refers to the rewards extended to an individual by the organization, which may be any form of compensation and job security (Bhuian, et al., 1996). Locke (1976) further distinguished the fundamental theories governing the understanding of job satisfaction into process theories and content theories.

Motivation Theories and Satisfaction

Motivation is one of the most important topics managers and leaders study in the field of human behavior. Everyone wants to know how to motivate their colleagues, bosses, friends, and, of course, employees. The term "motivate" comes from the Latin verb, *movere*, which means to cause movement. Basically, motivation is about causing others, such as employees, to move toward some predetermined objective or goal. Psychologically, motivation deals with others' (employees') needs. Unsatisfied needs cause a tension which leads to a drive to satisfy the need. The drive leads to search behavior and an examination of alternative ways of potentially satisfying the need. The need is either satisfied or frustrated in which case the search behavior continues.

A good starting point in the study of motivation is an understanding of Theory X and Theory Y popularized by Douglas McGregor. According to the Theory X model, managers believe that people disliked work and are basically lazy. Therefore, they need to be told what to do and how to do it. As such, they need autocratic managers as such a style would best fit with Theory X employees. Theory Y is the contrast to this theory. According to Theory Y, workers enjoy work and especially crave involvement and meaningful work. Workers want responsibility, and thus the correct way to lead is through delegation. While Theory Y is widely believed to be the better operation system, it must be noted that not all workers want responsibility and autonomy. This dichotomy between autocratic and participative leadership, however, permeates the motivation and leadership literature.

In general, motivational theories can be grouped under the categories of content and process theories of motivation. *Content theories* of motivation answer the question, "*What things motivate people*?" Content theories look for external or extrinsic motivators. Process theories of motivation answer the question, "*How are people motivated*?" *Process theories* look at internal or intrinsic processes of motivation. What is the cognitive process by which people become motivated. *Content* theories of motivation generally include: Maslow's Hierarchy of Needs, Herzberg's Two Factor Theory, McClelland's Achievement Theory, and Alderfer's ERG Theory. *Process* theories of motivation includes: Vroom's Expectancy Theory, Adams' Equity Theory, and Reinforcement Theory.

Abraham Maslow was a practicing psychologist who noted through his experience that people have certain categories of needs. In fact, Maslow identified five specific levels of needs that were organized in a hierarchy. The needs are as follows starting from the bottom (physical) and moving up to the top (self actualization):

- Self-Actualization
- Self-Esteem
- Social
- Security
- Physical

Starting with physical needs, initially workers and people in general are motivated by the acquisition of items that assures them of food and shelter. Once these needs are satisfied, they needs of workers "move up" the hierarchy as they become motivated by security issues. Once satisfied with the security needs, the worker again moves up the hierarchy to the "social needs" level where interpersonal relations are motivational. Many of the social needs to belong and feel needed are played out at work where workers spend so much of their time interacting with others who have similar needs and professional aspirations. When these needs are met, the individual becomes motivated by self-esteem which considers such things as recognition, opportunity for growth and autonomy. Even the keys to the proverbial executive washroom may be an element of self-esteem as they demonstrate recognition. At the top of the hierarchy, often depicted as a pyramid or ladder, is self-actualization. At this level, the individual is free from all mundane concerns and may pursue his or her dreams, become all that s/he can be. Maslow's theory is the most popular motivational theory and most other researchers have used it as a stepping stone. Maslow's theory does provide two important insights that are extremely important to researchers and managers:

1. The theory states that not all people are motivated by the similar things.
2. It states that the same person is not always motivated by the same thing since his or her needs change over time.

In the early 1950s, *Frederick Herzberg*, another psychologist, studied motivation by asking people to relate critical incidents about when they felt most satisfied and motivated on the job and when they felt most dissatisfied. Herzberg found that these questions received two different types of answers. Thus, the "two factor" theory was born. One factor Herzberg called *hygiene factors* which are things that make people unhappy when they are not taken care of but do not motivate them when they are provided. In other words, hygiene factors, or maintenance, prevent dissatisfaction but do not lead to motivation. Hygiene factors include a safe working environment, salary, and satisfactory working relationships with peers and superiors. The other factor, Herzberg called *motivators,* which are the things that, when present, cause motivation, but when absent, cause a lack of motivation (and not dissatisfaction). Motivators are such things as the work itself, autonomy, authority, and responsibility. As can be seen, Herzberg's motivators are equivalent to Maslow's "higher order needs" of self-esteem and self-actualization. Herzberg's hygiene factors are equivalent to Maslow's "lower order needs" of physical, security, and social.

Clayton Alderfer essentially modified Maslow's model by condensing the five levels of needs into three categories:

- E = Existence
- R = Relatedness
- G = Growth

Existence needs are equivalent to Maslow's physical and safety needs; relatedness equates to Maslow's social needs; growth refers to self-esteem and self-actualization. Managers and researchers can compare ERG theory to Herzberg's model of hygiene factors and motivators. Existence and relatedness equate to Herzberg's hygiene factors and growth relates to Herzberg's motivators. Alderfer sees needs as moving back and forth, not just upward in the hierarchy. Because of the recognition of forward movement, i.e., progression from lower needs (existence) to higher needs (growth), Alderfer's model is called a "need progression" theory. While Maslow's model generally portrays motivation as moving in one direction, which is upward, Alderfer feels that people move back and forth among these the three needs of existence, relatedness and growth as situations change. So, according to Alderfer, motivation is situation. As such, it is possible to regress from being motivated by growth needs to being motivated by "relatedness." This backward or downward movement means that Alderfer's theory is also a "frustration regression" theory.

David McClelland, another psychologist, looked at motivation from the perspective that people have either a high need for achievement, affiliation, or power and that this motivation would result in different behaviors in the workplace. Specifically, McClelland felt that high achievers only made up 10-15% of the population, but that these people were the real high producers in organizations. McClelland found that high achievers had the following characteristics:

- High achievers love moderate challenge.
- High achievers seek concrete feedback. They want to know how they are doing and they also want to know that the manager knows how they are doing.
- High achievers want to take personal responsibility for the work. They can be productive but they do not necessarily make good managers.

McClelland felt that high achievement was largely learned in childhood as people model themselves after high-achieving adults. McClelland also felt that managers could have influence over encouraging high achievement by urging people to have specific goals, face challenges, take risks, and enjoy taking personal responsibility.

Victor Vroom looked at the internal, cognitive processes that people go through in order to satisfy needs and thus become motivated. Vroom explains that the behavior workers decide to display depends upon what they expect to achieve from that behavior. According to the Expectancy Theory model, the individual effort one is motivated to exert depends on his or her judgment of how well s/he can perform (first level) and what s/he thinks that performance will earn (second level outcome). According to Victor Vroom and the Expectancy Theory:

- *Expectancy* is the probability that the level of effort workers put in will achieve the desired level of performance.
- *Instrumentality* is the probability that performance (first-level) will lead to the desired second level outcome or reward.
- *Valence*" is the value of the reward or how much workers want or do not want the second level outcome.

John Stacy Adams says that motivation comes and goes for the individual employee at least in part by his or her perception of equity in the workplace. Thus, the individual compares his or her inputs (skills, experience, time on job, seniority, etc.) and outputs (job title, benefits, salary, responsibility, for example) with the inputs and outputs of a "referent" person. Depending upon that comparison, the individual concludes that his or her own input/output ratio is equitable or inequitable. When inequity is perceived, the employee will feel ill at ease and probably try one of two things. First, s/he may reduce his or her own inputs. Secondly, s/he may increase his or her own outputs. Inequity may arise from faulty perception in which case the manager needs to correct the inaccuracy. If inequity exists, the manager needs to examine the situation carefully and find a remedy.

Reinforcement theory is based on concepts of how people learn. Most people remember hearing about Pavlov's dogs where dogs were taught to salivate at the ringing of a bell because they connected the bell with being fed. That type of "learning" is called classical conditioning as it is a trained stimulus-response reaction. The model that describes human behavior is known as "*operant conditioning.*" In this case, the expectation of a consequence determines a person's behavior. B.F. Skinner made the concept of "*behavior modification*" very popular in literature and in the work environment. Behavior modification depends upon various types of reinforcement techniques with the basic belief that you tend to get the behavior you reinforce. Literature discusses four basic reinforcement techniques as follows:

1. *Positive Reinforcement*: A technique used to increase the incidence of a desired behavior. Telling someone they are doing a good job or giving someone a raise are examples of positive reinforcement.

2. *Negative Reinforcement*. This designed to increase the incidence of a desired behavior. If someone walks into the class late and the teacher jokingly chide him or her by saying, "Good afternoon, Dean, nice that you could make it..." the student will likely be embarrassed into coming on time next time. On the other hand, the student may love the extra attention and continue to come late.

3. *Punishment*: Designed to decrease the incidence of an undesired behavior, punishment does not fit in well with today's values and may breed frustration and resentment. Examples of punishment include scolding someone in front of his or her peers or sending someone home from work. Naturally, there are some incidents which do deserve immediate punishment such as violence in the workplace.

4. *Extinction*: This strategy also serves to decrease the incidence of an undesired behavior. Extinction entails simply ignoring a given behavior and hoping it will disappear. It is often an appropriate response for a minor behavioral problem.

Process theories and satisfaction. These theories tend to identify "specific needs or values most conducive to job satisfaction" (Locke, 1976, p. 1302). According to Eccles (2003), process theorists "focus on how individuals' expectations and preferences for outcomes associated with their performance, actually influence performance" (p.32). These theorists are interested in how individual behavior is energized, directed, maintained, and stopped (Eccles, 2003; Ivancevich & Matteson, 1990). Process theories include Adam's equity theory, Vroom's expectancy theory, Skinner's reinforcement theory, Locke's goal setting theory, and they are central in understanding process theories (Eccles, 2003; Gibson et al., 1991; Rakich et al., 1992).

Content theories and satisfaction. These theories attempt to specify the particular needs that must be attained for an individual to be satisfied with his or her job (Locke, 1976, p. 1307). Two theories are most prominent in the study of content theories; Maslow's Need Hierarchy theory and Herzberg's Motivator-Hygiene theory (Locke, 1976). Maslow's Need Hierarchy theory is categorized in a defined order to include physiological needs, safety needs, belongingness and love needs, esteem needs, and self actualization needs (Maslow,

1943). Maslow's theory suggested that satisfied needs are not motivators. As lower level needs are satisfied, they no longer drive behavior, and, consequently, higher order needs take over as the motivating force (Maslow, 1943). Locke (1976) notes, "These needs are arranged in a hierarchy of "prepotency" or dominance, the order from most to least prepotent" (p. 1307). Unlike Maslow, Herzberg's Motivator-Hygiene theory argues that job satisfaction and dissatisfaction result from different causes and that satisfaction depends on "Motivators" while dissatisfaction is the result of "Hygiene factors" (Herzberg, 1968). Motivators deal with aspects of the work itself, which includes work, promotion, achievement, responsibility, and recognition (Locke, 1976). Hygiene factors reflected the "context in which the work itself was performed, to include working conditions, interpersonal relations, company policies and salary, and supervision" (Locke, 1976, p. 1310). Other theories that have also been proposed to further explain job satisfaction. These theories include social information processing model and social identity theory (SIT) (Yvonne & Rod, 2002).

Social information modeling. This theory states, "The social context and the employee's past behavior (in terms of actions and experiences) will determine the way the job is perceived and therefore will determine how satisfied the employee is with the job. The social information cues experienced are used to help construct and shape their realities" (Pollock, et al, 2000, p. 294). The effect of this model is contingent on the extent to which the employee takes notice of the available social information (Yvonne & Rod, 2002; Pollock et al., 2000).

Social identity theory. This theory presupposes that individuals categorize themselves into several social groups to include gender, age, socio-economic status, skills, and interests (Tajfel & Turner, 1987; Yvonne & Rod, 2002). These individuals may be part of more than one social group in their work place. Because of this, employees are not only members of their organization, but are members of other social groups within the organization. Tajfel & Turner (1987) notes that each individual derives either a positive or negative self-esteem from being a member of his or her organization or the sub group within the organization. When such individuals possess elevated levels of organizational identification, then they are likely to reflect elevated levels of organizational based self-esteem (Tajfel & Turner, 1987; Yvonne & Rod, 2002). Social identity theory allows members of these groups an avenue for systematically defining others. Because of this self-identification with a group, employees may experience a sense of purpose and belongings within the organization, hence increasing their level of satisfaction and commitment to the organization. Thus, the elimination of the likelihood that the employee will actually leave the organization voluntarily.

Generally, and regardless of the theory used in explaining job satisfaction, empirical evidence shows that job satisfaction is linked to turnover through intentions to quit, buttressed by perceived alternative employment opportunities. Nonetheless, these theories are important and informational to the readers and future researchers in this field. Job satisfaction is anteceded by the characteristics of the individual and job environment. More recently, these affective components have been categorized as individual characteristics, job/task related characteristics, and organizational characteristics (Zeffane, 1994).

Organizational Commitment

For many employers, the nature of employees' commitment attitude to their organization partly remains largely a mystery, which consequently warrants continued research and evaluation in order to determine which employee may leave or stay, and perhaps, predict an employee's potential departure (turnover) time from the organization. Because disruptive costs are associated with employees leaving an organization, many scholars have researched how commitment contributes to the overall turnover theory. It is well known that some employees stay in organizations because they believe in the goals of the organization, some stay because of benefits or financial reasons, and others stay because they have no alternative available to them.

Other more futuristic reasons also exist for studying commitment's linkage to turnover. Irrespective of the time and age, organizations will continue to exist. The question is not whether they will exist, but how will they exist. Robotics and advanced technologies inherent in the operations of modern organizations are unlikely to eliminate completely human intervention in organizations (Meyer & Allen 1997). Rather, organizations are getting smaller, and according to Meyer and Allen (1997), "jobs become more flexible and those who remain in the organization become more important" (p.5). This new reality is a marked departure from the organizational structure of the past. Jobs, which were once a collection of tasks and responsibilities, are experiencing expansions, shifting greater responsibilities to the line staff, while managerial hierarchy is flattened (Meyer & Allen, 1997). When this occurs, organizations will depend on the employee to do what is right in such a demanding environment—which is what commitment attempts to determine (Meyer & Allen, 1997). Furthermore, in this age of outsourcing, organizations want to be sure that their outsourced operations or functions achieve expected levels of performance—people drive and encourage performance, machines only aid. Finally, Meyer and Allen (1997) contend that commitment develops naturally because people need to be committed to something.

Many commitment studies attempt to distinguish commitment as either a behavior or attitude. However, contemporary researchers have now adopted an attitudinal perspective. Allen and Meyer (1996, p. 252) notes, "Although early work in the area was characterized by various, and often conflicting, one-dimensional views of the construct, organizational commitment is now widely recognized as a multidimensional work attitude" (Becker, 1992; Mathieu & Zajac, 1990; Meyer & Allen, 1984, 1991; Morrow, 1993; O'Reilly and Chatman, 1986). Allen & Meyer (1997) provided some clarity on the difference between attitudes and behaviors from notable researchers on behavioral and attitudinal commitment. They note:

> Attitudinal commitment focuses on the process by which people come to think about their relationship with the organization. In many ways it can be thought of as a mind set in which individuals consider the extent to which their own values and goals are congruent with those of the organization. Behavioral commitment on the other hand, relates to the process by which individuals become locked into a certain organization and how they deal with this problem. (Mowday et al., 1982)

Notwithstanding these distinctions, several researchers also have provided diverse conceptualizations concerning the definition of commitment. Researchers (such as Buchanan, 1974; Hunt, Chonko, & Wood, 1985; Porter, Crampton & Smith, 1976) have conceptualized commitment as an employee's internal feeling, belief, or set of intentions that enhances their desire to remain with an organization. Another definition, popularly known as "side-bet" theory, viewed commitment as a reflection of recognized, accumulated interests (e.g. pensions and seniority), binding one to a specific organization (Bhuian et al., 1996; Hrebiniak & Alutto, 1972; Meyer & Allen, 1984; Randall, 1993; Ritzer & Trice, 1969). Mowday, Steers, and Porter (1979) have defined organizational commitment based on attitudinal perspective as "a state in which an individual identifies with a particular organization and its goals and wishes to maintain membership in order to facilitate these goals" (p.225). Finally, Allen and Meyer (1991) conceptualized commitment as feelings of obligation to stay in the organization, and feelings resulting from the internalization of normative pressures exerted on an individual prior to entry into the organization.

Allen and Meyer's (1996) definition and conceptualization capture the essence of organizational commitment linkage to employee turnover in this study as in several other contemporary commitment-turnover studies. They defined organizational commitment as "a psychological link between the employee and his or her organization that makes it less likely that the employee will voluntarily leave the organization" (Allen & Meyer, 1996, p. 252). Meyer and Allen's (1997) construct of commitment appeared to be designed to link commitment to desirable work outcomes, such as lower absenteeism and turnover, higher productivity, and assessment of personal and situational characteristics leading to high commitment. They recognized the contributions made by other variables, such as job satisfaction and commitment in the study of actual turnover and turnover intention (Meyer & Allen, 1997). They note that "There is evidence that the contribution of organizational commitment to these variables (turnover and turnover intentions) is independent of that made by other work attitude constructs such as job satisfaction" (Meyer & Allen, 1997, p. 252). They both add that no definition is universally accepted but rather each definition is indicative of the researcher's investigative approach (Meyer & Allen, 1997). Each of the definitions, albeit their technical differences, reflects an affective orientation toward the organization, a recognition of costs associated with leaving the organization, and a moral obligation to remain with the organization (Meyer & Allen, 1997). These three distinctions, labeled by Allen and Meyer (1991), would later be known as affective, continuance, and normative commitment (Bhoiuan et al., 1996). It is preferable to consider these distinctions as components of commitment rather than types of commitment (Meyer & Allen, 1991, 1997). Meyer and Allen (1997) presented the following definitions:

- "*Affective commitment* refers to the employee's emotional attachment to, identification with, and involvement in the organization. Employees with a strong affective commitment continue employment with the organization because they *want* to do so.
- *Continuance commitment* refers to an awareness of the costs associated with leaving the organization. Employees whose primary link to the organization is based on continuance commitment remain because they *need* to do so.

- Finally, *normative commitment* reflects a feeling of obligation to continue employment. Employees with a high level of normative commitment feel that they *ought* to remain in the organization."

Intentions to Leave and Alternative Employment

Several studies have found that intentions to leave an organization as a reliable predictor of turnover (Michaels & Spector, 1882; Mobley, 1977; Fishbein & Azjen, 1975; Arnold & Feldman, 1982). In fact, Mobley et al. (1979) concluded, "the best predictor of turnover should be intention to quit" (p. 517). However, it has been estimated that it only explained six percent of the variance in employee turnover (Mowday, 1987). According to Vandenberg and Nelson (1999), "Turnover intention refers to individuals' own estimated probability that they are permanently leaving the organization at some point in the near future" (p. 1315). However, it must not be assumed that once an employee begins to express high tendencies of intent to leave that an actual termination or voluntary turnover will occur (Mobley, et al., 1982; Vandenberg & Nelson, 1999). This is so because the opportunity for employees to alter their work conditions may exist. When such an alteration occurs in favor of a positive outcome, it is assumed that the intent to leave will likely be reduced, and thus lower the probability of turnover (Vandenberg & Nelson, 1999).

In fact, Vandenberg and Nelson (1999) succinctly noted, "Thus it should not be assumed that high intention automatically results in voluntary turnover, and that once expressed, the intention cannot be lowered" (p. 1317). Vandenberg and Nelson (1999) further add that some individuals are unable to act on their high intentions to leave because of "perceived absence of alternative employment opportunities (p. 1315).

On the other hand, Mobley's (1977) intermediate linkage model also recognized alternative employment, in conjunction with intentions of leaving as playing a part in actual turnover. However, Mobley, et al. (1979) noted that, "It is not merely the visibility of alternatives but the attraction of alternatives that are most salient" (p. 519). March and Simon (1958) also recognized that ease of movement within and outside of the organization was linked to the availability of jobs in organizations and its visibility to the individual. Trevor (2001) noted that an individual's ease of movement (ability to acquire alternative employment) is important in voluntary turnover research. Bluedorn (1982) further added some thoughts on Mobley's (1977) intermediate linkage model by stating, "The behavioral space between job satisfaction and voluntary separations is a process composed of thoughts of quitting, evaluations of the utility of a job search, intentions to search, search, evaluation of alternatives, and intentions to quit or stay" (p. 85).

Trevor (2001) suggested that ease of movement was simultaneously determined by market level general job availability and the individual characteristic, which he termed, movement capital. This was possible due to economic factors; and March and Simon (1958), stated as, "Under nearly all conditions the most accurate single predictor of labor turnover is the state of the economy" (p. 10). Movement capital includes an individual's education, special experience, cognitive ability, and transferable skills (Trevor, 2001). Trevor (2001) further noted that the effect of general job availability, which is typically negative on turnover, depended on movement capital. Trevor (2001) states:

> I suggest that general job availability should be particularly important for those who are less able to rely upon their own movement capital to signal worth to external employers. Whereas those with impressive signals likely have other job opportunities under most market conditions, those without such signals likely are valued only in a friendlier job market where employers cannot be as discriminating among applicants (p. 626).

Research Theory

The general theory is that dissatisfied employees are far more likely to leave the organization and less likely to stay committed to that organization. Lambert (2001) notes that since job satisfaction and organizational commitment are the most widely studied variables related to voluntary turnover, that job satisfaction and organizational commitment should have negative but direct effects on turnover. The theory also suggests that perceptions of alternative employment outside of the organization by the employee may also induce them to quit. However, this premise remains weak, inconsistent, or nonexistent (Griffeth & Hom, 1998). The employee's age and tenure on the job also are expected to be related to their propensity to leave their organization. The higher their tenure on the job, the less likely the employee will leave the job, while the lower the individual's age, the more likely the employee will leave the job.

In addition, intention to quit has long been accepted to be a better predictor of turnover than the actual turnover data. This is perhaps so because actual turnover data consumes much time to collect, since the data is only available after the employee has left the organization. In contrast, intention to quit captures data on the leaving behavior within a specific frame of time, usually before the employee actually leaves the organization.
Bhuian and Al-Jabri (1996) conducted research in Saudi Arabia to determine the (1) nature of the relationship of expatriate employee turnover on expatriate worker job satisfaction (2) the extent of the relationship. They noted that cultural plurality was a dominant feature of the workforce in Saudi Arabia (Bhuian & Al-Jabri, 1996). Their research noted that age, a demographic variable was positively and significantly correlated to turnover (N = 504, r = 0.13, p<0.01). Intrinsic job satisfiers such as pay were found to be negatively and significantly correlated to turnover (N = 504, r = 0.13, p<0.001).

Instrumentation for Research

Turnover. Turnover data can be collected from the Human Resource Information System of the multinational corporation. Those officers who left can be coded as "1" and those who stayed can be coded as "0". Information on those who left can be collected few months after the administration of the surveys. Porter et al (1976) had suggested collecting data on attitudes from a sample of currently employed subjects and then waiting for a period of time before determining which of those individuals terminate.

Job satisfaction. This variable can be measured using the 20-item short form of the Minnesota Satisfaction Questionnaire (MSQ) (Weiss, Dawis, England, & Lofquist, 1967). The MSQ was selected because it embodies more specific factors that would otherwise not be available in other satisfaction instruments. These factors include; activity (I), independence (I), variety (I), social status (I), supervision (E), moral values (I), security (I), social service (I), authority (I), compensation (E), recognition (E), creativity (I), working conditions (E), company policies (E), achievement (I), and advancement (E). Note, intrinsic satisfiers are denoted with (I), while extrinsic satisfiers are denoted with (E). Peters et al (1981), while studying full and part- time employees using the 20-item MSQ, achieved a reliability of 0.92 at (N = 31 full time employees).

Organizational commitment. Meyer and Allen's (1993) revised three-item organizational commitment questionnaire, which measures three dimensions of organizational commitment—affective (ACS), continuance (CCS), and normative (NCS) commitment, can be used. The median reliabilities of these three dimensions of organizational commitment, using coefficient alpha, were reported to be 0.85, 0.79, and 0.73, respectively (Meyer and Allen, 1997).

Intention to quit. The research can use Colarelli's (1984) intentions to quit scale, with items noting, "If I have my own way, I will be working for my organization one year from now", "I frequently think of quitting my job", "I am planning to search for a new job during the next 12 months." Cronbach alpha for the overall scale of Colarelli (1984) intention to quit scale was reported at 0.76.

Perceived alternative employment. One can use Peters et al's (1981) scale called "expectation of finding alternative employment." The instrument was worded, "It is possible for me to find a better job than the one I have now", "Acceptable jobs can always be found", and "There is no doubt in my mind that I can find a job that is at least as good as the one I now have" (Peters, et al., 1981, p. 94). Its internal consistency was found to be 0.77.

Discussions

The issue of turnover has implications even if those implications are not initially obvious or evident. Mobley (1982) noted that there are cost, performance, social/communication, and morale issues tied to organizations that take turnover for granted.

Costs. In terms of costs, direct costs such as employee salaries, and indirect costs such as employee benefits come to mind very readily. However, other costs such as training, retention, and recruiting costs are easily incurred as a result of employee turnover. Because some of these costs are not very evident at the time the turnover phenomenon is occurring, management is apt to ignore the cumulative effect of employee turnover on the overall health of the organization. Multinational corporations have a greater stake in this thought because key employees who maybe responsible for operations in host nations may leave, thus disrupting the entire operations of the multinational firm in the host nation.

Performance. In line with the thought on costs, when a key employee of the multinational firm leaves, there is no guarantee that other employees will be keen or able to assume the previous duties of the leaving employee. Even when they do, there is no guarantee that the outcome of the replacing employee's performance will match the expectation of the organization. Thus, multinational corporations are forced to begin the process of searching and recruiting a replacement, hence, incurring recruiting costs. During the period such a search is being conducted, other staff, who may or may not be competent, may pick up the leaving employee's slack, which may affect their own performance as well.

Social/cohesiveness. Mobley (1982) noted, "formal and informal communication patterns are characteristic of any organization" (p. 20). In this regard it is employees who make communication within organizations possible. Given the nature of socialization within organizations, certain employees serve as bonds or binds between various social groups within the organization. These employees are enablers. They help to bridge the communication gap between groups. When such employees leave the organization, it appears a diminished sense of trust and communication break down immediately occurs between these groups, thus, potentially creating hostility and suspicion among and between members of these groups. The consequence of this phenomenon is a momentary gap in performance, or in a worst-case scenario, a cumulative and corresponding exit effect from the organization by other staff, thus leading the organization to incur recruiting costs much higher than anticipated replacing the leaving employees.

Morale. In line with social/communication cohesiveness, the principal leaving employee is likely to impact other leaving employees, thus, their motivation and morale to remain in the organization is diminished. In the case of morale, it either can be caused by voluntary or involuntary turnover.

Summary

Employee turnover is a very important human resource and management area that consistently requires attention within an organization. It is indeed a strategic management tool. While financial and operational concerns are likely to consume the resources of a multinational corporation, human concerns such as employee turnover, could just as easily lead to similar failures in organizations as would be expected from financial and operational concerns. Because both operational and financial issues in organizations exist because an employee of the firm is willing to accept and address financial and operational issues, one can argue that the human aspect of business maybe deemed more important than the two previous concerns.

Because multinational corporations function in host countries where so many unknowns are evident, to include cultural variations and etiquettes, it takes the skill of satisfied, experienced, and committed employees to get any meaningful results from host nations. Therefore, without further ado, the study of turnover, especially related to older and experienced workers, and its relationship to job satisfaction and organizational commitment cannot be over emphasized. Multinational firms must see to it that the best and most promising employees are recruited and retained regardless of age, since turnover obviously has costs associated with it.

CHAPTER 10

HIRING AND SOCIAL RESPONSIBILITY[3]

*D*oing business on a global scale has brought about many challenges including the expectations of fair business and the acceptance of "Corporate Social Responsibility" (CSR). Management not only needs to be concerned with managing the business, but also their profits and losses, and the impact that they will have doing business in other countries while maintaining fairness for all relevant parties.

With the continuous advancement of technology, businesses are growing at a more rapid rate, and on a global scale. The growth of business that has extended out on a global scale has created a business environment which requires businesses to be more socially responsible. In effect, management has found a need for their business to be accountable for "Corporate Social Responsibility" (CSR). However, is CSR driven by a business' profit statement? How does CSR affect global business operations and the way management produces profits? Companies from all across the globe are now forming committees to monitor their level of CSR. These companies want to make sure that business is being conducted in an ethical and responsible manner, no matter where they operate.

Understanding Social Responsibility

Corporate Social Responsibility is known as sustainable development, which involves the increased recognition by publicly held companies that they need to address and heed not only to shareholders, but all the multiple stakeholders impacted by the company's behavior. These include employees, customers, suppliers, governments, and non-governmental organizations. In the new paradigm of social responsibility, stakeholders also could include socially responsible investor organizations, consisting of investors who make investment decisions using various social and ethical screens" (Fraser, 2005). There are many different interpretations of the term CSR. According to Canada's Business and Consumer Site, CSR is "the private sector's way of integrating the economic, social, and environmental imperatives of their activities. Consequently, CSR closely resembles the business pursuit of sustainable development and the triple bottom line. In addition to

---

[3] - This material is based in part on the contributions of Mele Akuna, University of Phoenix, as well as the article by of Mujtaba, Cavico and Jones (2005).

integration into corporate structures and processes, CSR involves creating innovative and proactive solutions to societal and environmental challenges, as well as collaborating with both internal and external stakeholders to improve CSR performance" (Strategis, 2005). According to the Journal of World Business, "Business ethics and social responsibility pertains to the belief in the role businesses should play in a society to ensure that practices conducted are fair and with integrity" (Ang, 2000).

Due to the many interpretation of CSR, companies are working together to form a Universal/Global CSR. Countries are coming together in order to create a system which will help in leveling the playing field for all those who want to conduct business on a global scale. According to Hamann:

> The incentives for developing global norms and standards are apparent: a range of stakeholders are pushing for increased commitment by companies to widely recognized standards, and multi-national corporations are expected to apply the same standards in different parts of the world. Companies themselves are seeking to establish a level "playing field," especially in connection with international trade. For multinational corporations, there are strong pressures to be seen to be applying the same standards in different parts of the world. It is these growing pressures that motivated the ISO to consider the development of a standard for organizational social responsibility (Hamann, 2005).

Basically, what the South Africans are suggesting is that currently businesses that are doing business on a global scale have a different standard to follow than the South African businesses. What they would like to see happen with multinational corporations is a CSR that is universal for all companies to abide by and be held accountable for.

The way in which CSR currently works is that corporations need to pay close attention to the impact they have on society as a whole. Corporations are letting the public know that they are actively taking part in CSR by providing information in their annual reports. These companies that follow the CSR principles are separating themselves from those that are not, and they are pouring more money, time, and people into showing the public that they are a responsible company that cares. There are many multinational corporations in the United States of America that has been actively participating in adhering to the principles of CSR. Some of the companies commonly associated with socially responsible activities are:

- Ben and Jerry's
- Kraft
- Nestle
- Publix
- Lyons
- Lavazza
- AT& T
- Proctor & Gamble
- Ikea

- JP Morgan Chase

These companies are forming alliances with other companies that are following the principles of CSR in order cash in on the current consumer demand. Being a socially and ethically responsible corporation will attract consumers to the goods and services that they have to offer. This in turn, hopefully, will provide the profits their shareholders and stakeholders are looking for.

On the other hand, some companies are not "buying into" this CSR principle. "Across the globe, "corporate social responsibility" has become a mantra of multinationals accused of despoiling the planet and exploiting poverty or, at the least, being insensitive to the misery that coincides with their profitable operations" (Maass, 2005). These types of companies are reaping the profits no matter what kind of impact their business is having on the country, society, and the environment. Their main concern is to please their shareholders by presenting a profitable bottom line. The following is a list of some companies that have been or are recently being investigated for being irresponsible:

- Shell,
- Exxon,
- Enron,
- WorldCom, and
- Coca-Cola.

According to Welford (2004), the Shell case is about companies that participated in human rights violations against protesters in retaliation for their political opposition to companies' oil exploration activities in Nigeria. Welford continued to say that the case revolves around the murder of Nigerian activist Ken Saro-Wiwa in November of 1995, the torture and detention of his brother, and the shooting of a woman peacefully protesting Shell's planned pipeline in Nigeria. The Exxon case involves 11 villagers who were victims of human rights abuses by Exxon Mobil's security forces. The general theory of the case is that Exxon Mobil knowingly employed brutal troops to protect its operations, and the company aided and abetted the human rights violations through financial and other material support to the security forces. The case alleges that the security forces are either employees or agents of Exxon Mobil, and thus Exxon Mobil is liable for their actions (Welford, 2004).

Many companies that fail to comply with CSR have struggled to rise above the headlines and to make things right. They have been heavily penalized for the wrong-doings that have occurred that they were held liable for, and today's consumer is not very forgiving, nor forgetful. Companies extending their businesses globally need to heed the importance of CSR. As more businesses expand globally, the more society will get involved, the more investors will want to see how much the company invests in CSR, and of course one cannot forget the importance of the bottom line. With the advancement of technology, society is able to get information so quickly that technology has both a positive and negative impact on their business. The opponents of CSR question whether CSR is good for businesses. They think that it may just be a management fad. A fad that will affect their profits, which in turn will impact their future business plans. Currently, there is still opposition to the development and implementation of CSR with businesses. On a universal/global scale, the current CSR needs to be revised to address the concerns of the many countries involved. For society as a whole, CSR has had a positive impact, but not until all businesses comply will global business be good business for countries outside of the United States. As long as the intentions are good, and the principles are adhered to, society will welcome CSR with open arms.

Why Focus on Corporate Social Responsibility?

The traditional purpose of business has been viewed to make money for the shareholders, in a legal manner, of course. The key values were thus economic and legal ones. Business was not supposed to be concerned with moral and social values. Not too long ago, with the advent of business ethics courses in schools of business as well as pressure from consumer, labor, and environmental groups, as well as the media, business has been compelled to deal with the moral implications of its actions. Accordingly, the values of ethics and morality became part of business school education as well as business policy and planning. Very recently, yet a new value, social responsibility has emerged to challenge business leaders and business educators. Social responsibility had not heretofore been viewed as a concern, let alone an obligation, of business. Yet, today, business is being forced to concern itself in a practical way with the social dimensions of its activities and the welfare of society as a whole, including global society. In order to examine this emergent and important issue, one first must ascertain what social responsibility is, and plainly what it is not.

What is not "Social Responsibility"?

Social responsibility is not legality. Legality, of course, is based on the law – treaties, constitutions, statutes, administrative rules and regulations, and cases. The law may require the performance of good deeds, for example, by requiring a contractor who wants to do business with the government to adopt an affirmative action program, or by requiring a bank to make investments in certain communities. These good deeds are premised on the force of the law; and thus are not "pure" social responsibility actions, but legal ones.

Social responsibility is not morality. Morality is based on ethics, which is a branch of philosophy. There are many ethical theories, containing ethical principles and precepts, which one can use to reason to moral conclusions of right and wrong and duty and obligation. Thus, could it not be argued that there is an ethical duty on the part of business to engage in social responsibility efforts and contributions. The Ethical Principle of Last Resort answers this question. According to this traditional ethical precept, a person, including a corporate "person," has a moral obligation to rescue and to aid, but only if certain conditions are met. These conditions are: the presence of a dire need or peril; proximity in time and space to effectuate a rescue; the capability to do so; one's position as the "last resort" or last real chance to avoid the harm or peril; and finally the rescuing or aiding would not cause harm equal to or greater than the original peril. When these conditions are all present then one has a moral duty to rescue. The classic example is the case of a drowning victim when the five factors are present. The problem in employing the "last resort" principle to business, particularly regarding corporate social responsibility, on an international scale, emerges as the fourth and fifth factors. Who is truly the last resort for people who are unemployed and in need - business or government? Government leaders elected by and accountable to the people, and not business leaders, are charged with advancing the general welfare. Moreover, would a corporation "rescuing" such people harm the corporation, its shareholders, or other stakeholders? One example is the case of the U. S. Malden Mills Company in New England, whose very compassionate owner rebuilt the facility after a fire without terminating any employees. Yet due in part to the added financial strain of keeping those employees, forced his company to file for Chapter 11 bankruptcy protection in order to reorganize his finances, thereby resulting in a considerably, and permanently, diminished workforce (Cavico and Mujtaba, 2005). Business, therefore, based on the Ethical Principle of Last Resort, typically will not be morally obligated to perform any social responsibility actions; and consequently business cannot be condemned as immoral for not performing such good actions.

Social responsibility is not altruism. According to Cavico and Mujtaba (2005), altruism is taking the interests of others into account in such a manner that one's intentions and actions afford some real degree of preference to others. Altruism consequently requires a substantial cost in time, effort, expenditure, and/or discomfort; it implies a degree of effacement of self-interest, even sacrifice. For example, a member of a profession may be required to engage in altruistic behavior because the profession's code of ethics may demand such behavior. A person also may assume a particular role, such as a parent, that demands selfless devotion to the welfare of others. Business is neither required, nor expected, nor advised, to engage in altruistic behavior. Altruism is not social responsibility; and business is not expected by rational people to be altruistic.

Social responsibility is not heroism. A person is a hero if he or she performs an act or duty under circumstances in which almost all people would not perform the act or duty due to fear and the overwhelming interest in self preservation. Rescuing an assault victim from a knife-wielding bandit, or rescuing a distressed swimmer from shark-filled seas, would be examples of heroism. Heroism is not social responsibility; and no rational person can expect the business corporation to be heroic (Cavico and Mujtaba, 2005).

Social responsibility is not sainthood. Saint status (from a secular perspective for the purposes of this book) involves great sacrifice. A person is deemed to be a "saint" if he or she does an act or performs a duty under circumstances in which personal inclination, desire, or self-interest would lead almost all people not to do the act or perform the duty. An organ donation to a stranger is an example of a saintly action (Cavico and Mujtaba, 2005). Similarly, a physician who gives up a lucrative practice to devote himself or herself totally to the impoverished people of a "third world" country can be called a saint. Saint status is not social responsibility; and no rational person can expect the business corporation to be saintly.

What is "Social Responsibility"?

Now that one knows what social responsibility is not, what does this often used but admittedly ponderous term mean in a current global business context. Although business may not have a legal or moral responsibility to improve the quality of life in the community and society, business may be obligated by a standard of social responsibility to work for social as well as economic betterment. "*Social responsibility*," therefore, can be defined as taking an active part in the social, cultural, and charitable causes and civic life of one's organization, community, and society a whole (Cavico and Mujtaba, 2005).

Why should a company be socially responsible? The social responsibility "obligation" of business suggests that global or national society may demand that business consider the social implications of its actions, and concomitantly to act in certain socially responsible ways. Otherwise, perhaps, society will compel business by international or legal mandate or increased taxation to fulfill its perceived social obligations. Business, as illustrated by the Nike case, also gains an improved public image by being socially responsible. An enhanced public image will attract more customers and investors, and thus provide positive benefits to the firm and its shareholders. Academic studies generally are supportive of the proposition that there exists a positive relationship between socially responsible behavior and favorable financial performance. Employees also may possess a heightened social consciousness, and consequently will want to be associated with a firm that not only is concerned with making profits but also with the welfare of society. A corporation that acts more socially responsible not only secures public favor, but also avoids public disfavor. Sir John Brown, the CEO of British Petroleum, astutely comprehends that society wants and expects business to be socially responsible. Social responsibility, at least in some reasonable degree, is thus in the long-term self-interest of business. Furthermore, a corporation cannot long remain a viable economic entity in a society that is uneven, unstable, and deteriorating. It thus makes good business sense for a company to devote some of its resources to social betterment projects. To operate efficiently, business needs educated and skilled employees. Education and training, therefore, should be of paramount interest to business leaders, and a company can center its social responsibility efforts in these critical areas. Finally, in recent years, there has been a steady growth of organizations that rate corporate social responsibility and that supply these ratings to investors and consumers. It obviously is beneficial to a company to earn a favorable corporate social responsibility rating. The conception of social responsibility as envisioned in this article merely asks business to take a longer-term, more expansive, stakeholder view of its traditional profit-maximization role (Cavico and Mujtaba, 2005). Enlightened self-interest and rational egoism, therefore, provide the justification for the firm's social responsibility efforts and contributions.

How should a company be socially responsible? There are many ways that business can fulfill its social responsibility obligation. A corporation, for example, can be socially responsible by providing computers to community schools and by releasing employees on company time to provide the training. British Petroleum (BP), for example, markets itself as "Beyond Petroleum," and has been regarded as a very socially responsible firm for its global environmental and alternative fuel efforts. BP also is engaged in job training and building schools in the communities where it does business. Nike now offers small business loans to the family members of its employees. The pharmaceutical companies have been providing AIDS drugs at greatly reduced costs to African nations. Coca Cola has been using its extensive delivery system to transport the drugs to even the most remote African village. Pfizer loans a cadre of trained business and scientific professionals to aid groups in developing countries. Intel has computer clubhouses that provide Internet access and technology training to children in over 30 countries. General Electric is constructing hospitals in Ghana. Avon provides breast cancer programs and subsidizes mammograms in over 50 countries. Starbucks has built a health clinic in Guatemala. Home Depot is extensively involved with community efforts to develop and rehabilitate affordable housing. Office Depot has sponsored an international "best practices" conference on corporate giving. These are just a few of many examples of praiseworthy social responsibility contributions by business. Moreover, there is absolutely nothing wrong in a company's publicizing such social responsibility actions, and thereby receiving well-deserved acclaim.

To what degree should a company be socially responsible? Regardless of how meritorious a firm's social responsibility actions may be, a company nonetheless must be careful in the degree of its commitment to the societal welfare. As to the proper extent of a company's social responsibility efforts and contribution, Aristotle has provided the answer. According to his seminal principle, the Doctrine of the Mean, Aristotle counseled that the correct and virtuous choice is a rationally determined mean between two extremes of deficiency and excess, which if present in a moderate degree will be a virtue. The intelligent and virtuous person will choose the mean between the two extremes, which constitute the corresponding vices. Accordingly, regarding the degree to which a company should be socially responsible, Aristotle would advise the firm not to concentrate on profits only, and abjure good deeds, because such deficiency is a vice. Similarly, Aristotle would advise the firm not to subordinate profits to good deeds, since too much attention to good deeds at the expense of profits is also a vice. Rather, Aristotle would counsel a company to aim for the mean of social responsibility, that is, profits first and then prudent good deeds (Cavico and Mujtaba, 2005). So, for example, "Chainsaw" Al Dunlap would represent the one extreme, and thus vice of deficiency in social responsibility. Ben & Jerry's would represent the extreme and vice of excessive social responsibility. Such companies as Target, Hwelett-Packard, Proctor & Gamble, Johnson & Johnson, Coca Cola, Bank of America, and Microsoft would represent the virtuous means of moderate and prudent social responsibility. A corporation, of course, exists in a competitive global environment and thus is limited in its ability to solve the multitude of social problems. Business cannot and should not be expected to substitute for government or a "world government." If a corporation unilaterally or too generously engages in social betterment, it may place itself at a disadvantage when compared to other less socially responsible business entities. In a highly competitive market system, corporations that are too socially responsible may lessen their attractiveness to investors or simply may price themselves out of the market. The Ben and Jerry of Ben & Jerry's, as a matter of fact, were forced by shareholders to accept a buy-out offer from Unilever, the multinational conglomerate. Yet a corporation that disdains any social responsibility, especially in a supercilious manner, may find itself less attractive to consumers and employees who likely will prefer to do business with and work for a socially responsible firm that provides good value. The Nike case clearly underscores the practical importance of prudent social responsibility.

What Does it All Mean?

Differentiating among law and ethics, ethics and morality, doing business and social responsibility, as well as among ethical theories, emerges as a critical challenge for the international business person, especially managers. The moral assessment of a business situation is naturally made more difficult by the presence of different national, societal, and cultural perspectives as to what it means to be moral. Ethical relativism, of course, is an ethical theory that gives precedence to these cultural beliefs in determining moral conduct. Ultimately, however, the international business person morally may be required to act not only above and beyond the law, but also above and beyond relativism in ethics; and thus may be required to apply universal ethical principles and moral standards to employment practices wherever and whenever business is conducted.

World culture, national, and societal cultures encompass a variety of values, including legal prescriptions and proscriptions, ethical beliefs and moral norms, and cultural practices. Just as the law differs from one country to another country, so does the definition of moral behavior and the delineation of appropriate cultural norms. The law, of course, can be viewed as a foundational "value" prescribing one's behavior; yet ethical codes, moral rules, and cultural norms may impel one to exceed the "moral minimum" required by the law.

The United States possesses a highly developed legal system proscribing discrimination based on race, religion, national origin, gender, and age. Other nations, however, do not possess such comprehensive legal prohibitions. Many of these nations, as opposed to the multi-ethnic and multi-religious United States, are dominated by one ethnic group and/or religion. In some countries, moreover, the law actually may require discrimination in employment based on religion, ethnicity, or gender. In particular, if a nation does not differentiate between the state and a religion, such as in the case of Saudi Arabia and Iran, the law actually may require discrimination against "non-believers." Legal restrictions on women in the workplace also can be predicated on religion-based legal precepts. Consequently, the U.S. business person must be keenly aware of such laws when staffing foreign operations, and especially because the discriminatory laws are based on deeply rooted fervent cultural and religious beliefs. Violations of such laws thus can bring very adverse legal and practical sanctions from the host government.

When one is called upon to evaluate the propriety of an action, such as employment discrimination, one must consider not only the whole legal context, including U.S. employment discrimination law as well as the host country's law, but also the ethical, moral, and cultural context. Because the laws of the host country are frequently different from those encountered in the U.S., managers must review them carefully, not only for legalistic reasons, but also for the ethical attitudes the laws may reflect. A nation's laws historically have been shaped in part by its social traditions and conventions and beliefs, including its moral standards and mores.

As the preceding discussion of ethical relativism has emphasized, what is considered moral and appropriate behavior in one cultural setting, may not be so construed in another. Multinational business managers, therefore, often may be called upon to evaluate actions, such as employment discrimination, according to ethical codes, moral beliefs, and cultural norms that may not be commonly accepted in the host country within which they are operating. Cultural values and beliefs certainly can differ; and the possibility of cross-cultural misunderstandings and friction thereby is evident; and therefore the consideration of relativistic values, beliefs, and practices emerges as a paramount consideration for the international firm.

The increasing importance of global business and the internationalization of the world's economy should prompt the prudent manager of the multinational business firm to expect that U.S. standards, both legal and moral, will be further "exported" to other countries and societies, especially the legal principles and moral prescriptions against discrimination in employment and otherwise. As this book has illustrated, many of the legal and ethical dilemmas, confronting managers in the world of global business lack definitive answers. Consequently, business managers must strive to understand the complex environment of international business, particularly the multitude of at times conflicting laws and moral standards and values. The multinational business manager must not only understand this challenging environment, but also use good judgment to devise solutions that will serve the best interests of the firm and all its stakeholders and maximize value for all concerned constituent groups. The ethically egoistic firm will want to actively seek solutions to employment concerns, especially regarding discrimination, in its global economic operations.

Anxiety about the image of one's multi-national firm should be a significant motivating factor to the egoistic firm, particularly in an age of human rights compliance. A heightened public awareness and a concomitant increased concern with workers' rights violations should prompt the rational and ethically egoistic firm to abide by legal and ethical norms against discrimination in employment. Since the political systems of the world reflect their value-systems, the prudent multinational firm surely must recognize that a society's moral concerns readily can be legislated into legal prescripts, especially ones that may affect the multinational firm's ability to contract for labor as well as conduct employment relations. Ethical egoism, therefore, is one means for the multinational firm to use to help manage the risks as well as the rewards of doing business in a global and at times highly politicized world.

The doctrine of ethical egoism thus emerges as an efficacious method for business managers of multinational firms to recognize the legal and ethical as well as practical implications of their decisions, particularly in a cross cultural context, and to resolve business dilemmas in a mutually "valuable" way. For those multinational companies adept at managing a global workforce in a challenging legal and ethical environment, the practical rewards will be great. The firm's rational self-interest will motivate the wise firm to use prudence to help ensure success in its international business dealings.

An ethically egoistic approach to managing employee relations in a global context is important because it benefits the firm in a very practical way by ensuring adherence to the law and ethics, respecting all the firm's stakeholders, and by furthering commitment and cooperation on the part of the firm's employees. Ethical egoism thus is an exercise of right and practical reason that must be inculcated and acquired as a virtuous, moral, and pragmatic management trait for the manager of the multinational business firm.

Conclusion

It is certain that the globalization of business activities clearly presents opportunities, challenges, problems, and dangerous risks for multinational business firms. As the world economies apparently are beginning to blend into a truly global economy, both large and small firms are beginning to explore business opportunities outside of their country's borders. This globalization, though arguably beneficial in the long-term for global society and peoples as a whole, has produced nonetheless in the short term certain legal, ethical, and cultural clashes. This book has attempted to explain and illustrate one aspect of the complexity and uncertainty of doing business in an international business environment. Globalization has produced a variety of complex issues – legal, ethical, and practical – as well as values relating to business, especially regarding employment. One of the most significant and complex issues that arises in international business is the extraterritorial effect of U.S. employment laws. Determining which nation's laws will govern the activities and relationships between the U.S. firm and its overseas workers are a legal issue of paramount importance to the U.S. multinational business manager.

The ever-increasing integration of the world's economy in recent years has generated a growing demand for international business managers to assure that their firms are in compliance with the various nations' laws, especially employment laws, when business operations take place across borders. As more business firms enter the global marketplace in a material manner, these firms must consider when and to what extent the employment law of the U.S. applies to their overseas workforce. Business decisions now involve not only the analysis of U.S. law and its extraterritorial effect, but also the law of the host country. The result is that multiple levels of at times conflicting legal analyses must be performed.

One point is evident for U.S. employers: The U.S. civil rights laws that prohibit discrimination and harassment in the U.S. will apply overseas to protect U.S. citizens who are employed by a U.S. firm or a firm, including a foreign one controlled by a U.S. firm. The prudent U.S. multinational firm, therefore, will recognize the potential legal liability pursuant to anti-discrimination laws, and the concomitant negative impact on operations, profitability, and success. Accordingly, the egoistic U.S. multinational firm will be aware of U.S. employment law, its extraterritorial effect, as well as the employment law in the jurisdictions where it does business; and is well-advised to take proactive measures, such as adopting codes of ethics and conduct, to help ensure compliance with applicable employment laws. Any multinational business firm and its management, therefore, must be able to recognize the legal issues involved in doing business abroad and must communicate with specialized legal counsel so as to make legal business decisions in an environment of at times legal uncertainty and conflict.

The multinational business firm must first recognize that today it is a truly global business world. Thus, an astute multinational business firm, in tune with the law and universal ethical standards, must establish corporate governance policies on a global basis. The multinational business firm must be committed to the human rights of its employees, wherever located. The company must ensure an equitable workplace, respect its employees, and promulgate distinct and comprehensible anti-discrimination policies. Compliance audits regarding employment policies and practices should be conducted. Appropriate personnel policies must be developed. Potential litigation issues both at home offices and overseas must be identified. As there are a wide variety of laws, including some very particular employment laws, with both national and extraterritorial effect, a prudent firm should not hesitate to consult with specialized legal counsel. Concomitantly, professional human resource directors should be retained. Human resource practices at home and abroad must be coordinated. Training programs concerning discrimination and harassment should be conducted, both in the firm's home country, of course, but also in the firm's overseas divisions. The policies and programs and training must be predicated on the law, ethics, culture, societal as well as the culture of the firm and its overseas operations, and the values the firm possesses. The multinational business firm should know how to run its business globally – legally, ethically, in accord with cultural norms and personal values, and in a socially responsible manner.

The goal for all societies, legal systems, and companies must be the central element of equality in the sense of equal participation of all in all societal endeavors, commercial and otherwise. This objective of equality is premised on an equal concern for the dignity and respect of each unique and worthwhile individual. This emphasis on dignity and respect is, of course, essential in the area of age discrimination in employment. The removal of age obstacles – legal, ethically relativistic, societal, cultural, or individual – from employment, as well as in other important fields such as education and health care, means that people must be provided with a true range of employment choices as well as a genuine opportunity to choose; and that people must be afforded the unique consideration and unbiased judgment of their choices. Treating people with dignity and respect and as worthwhile human beings demands no less.

Summary

Can a global organization in the twenty first century environment afford not to be socially responsible? A short answer is "Not for long," as can be seen from Nike's case, since profiting from the international community must carry some obligations as well. Above and beyond the responsibility of business to act legally and morally is this very prevalent, undeniable, and practical issue of the social responsibility of business. The law determines legal accountability; philosophical ethics determines moral accountability; but ascertaining the definition, nature, and extent of social responsibility emerges as a serious challenge for today's business leaders, executives, and managers, especially in a global context. This task is certainly more than a mere "academic" one. Yet, if social responsibility is envisioned and accomplished in a right, proper, and moderate manner, as conceived in this paper, social responsibility is good business and thus "smart business"!

CHAPTER 11

CROSS-CULTURAL AGE AND GENERATION-BASED VALUE DIFFERENCES[4]

*T*his study explored whether there were cross-cultural, age, and generation-based value differences and similarities between 1,492 United States (US) and 209 Japanese respondents. The hypotheses were that there would be statistically significant cross-cultural age and generation-based differences in Terminal and Instrumental Values between the United States and Japan using the Rokeach Value Survey (RVS). The RVS was translated to Japanese from English and back translated to English by two Japanese language experts. The hypotheses were supported for cross-cultural (within) differences for 23 of 36 values, age (within) differences for 13 of 36 values, and then cross-cultural generation (across) differences for 24 of 36 values. The researchers explored both similarities and differences across the generations and explained the significance of these findings and made recommendations for further research.

Introduction to the Research and Study

As the world becomes a global marketplace, it is very important for managers, marketers, and senior organizational leaders to understand employee and customer cross-cultural, age and generation-based value differences and similarities because of their subsequent impact on attitudes and behavior. One of the most important indicators of employee attitudes and consumer purchase behavior is their value structures, since research has shown that values are the underlying structures that affect attitudes and subsequent purchase behavior (Ajzen, 1988; DeMooij, 1998; Kahle, 1984; Murphy and Anderson, 2003; Reynolds and Olson, 2001; Rokeach, 1979).

Studies have shown that there are cross-cultural differences, age differences and generation differences in value structures, but few studies have explored all three in research studies. For instance, Hofstede (1984 & 2001) explored cross-cultural value differences world-wide; Feather (1979) explored cross-cultural value differences between the US and Australia; Bond (1994, 1996) and Lau (1988, 1992) explored cross-cultural value

---

[4] - This chapter is writtn by Edward F. Murphy Jr., Embry Riddle Aeronautical University; John D. Gordon, NASA Ames Research Center; Thomas L. Anderson, Napa Flight Training Center; and Bahaudin G. Mujtaba, Nova Southeastern University.

differences between China and the US; Connor, Becker, Kakuyama and Moore (1993) explored value differences between the US, Japan and Canada, and numerous other researchers explored cross-cultural value, attitude and behavior differences. Further, Allport (1935, 1954, 1955), England (1967a, b; 1978), and Rokeach (1973, 1979, 1986) and other researchers have explored age and generation differences in the US, while Feather (1979, 1984) explored age and generation differences between Australia and New Zealand. Finally, Roscoe and Peterson (1989) and Murphy (2001) explored generation differences in the US; Ayguen (1999) and Ayguen and Imamoglu (2002) explored generation differences in Turkey; Chang, Wong, and Koh (2003) explored generation differences in Singapore, and Eskin (2003) explored cross-cultural and age differences between Sweden and Turkey. The basic problem is that few studies have explored the impact of cross-culture and age together within and across the generations. This study, originally presented at the Southern Academy of Management (Murphy, Gordon and Anderson, 2003), fills in the research gaps by exploring cross-culture, age and generation differences in the value structures of Japan and the United States, with working adult respondents in each country.

Workforce Generations in the United States

While each country and culture might have its own cycle in terms of workforce generations, this section briefly describes the diverse American workforce (Mujtaba, 2006). The four generations currently in the United States workforce are known as the traditionalists (or veterans), baby boomers, Gen X, and Gen Y individuals. The following sections provide certain general information about each generation of the US population.

- Traditionalists; born around 1900s-1945; about 75 million individuals that presumably value stability and security.
- Baby Boomers; born around 1946-1964; about 80 million individuals with a focus on teamwork and human rights.
- Generation X; born around 1965-1976; about 46 million individuals that supposedly value empowerment and social responsibility.
- Generation Y; born around 1977-1994; about 70 million individuals that use technology, and value personal growth in their careers.
- Cyberspace Gen.; born around 1995-Present; about 20 million individuals who are brought up with globalization and the cyberspace internet technology.

Members of each generation tend to share certain experiences, events, and history that help shape their "generational personality" during their socialization in the society. The characteristics discussed are generalities, and they do not necessarily all apply to each person, and some of the characteristics described for one generation may very well apply to individuals of other generations as well. However, the characteristics described are likely to apply more often to individuals of the specified generation. As such, managers must be cautious and not stereotype specific individuals when it comes to hiring and evaluation solely based on these categories since each person is unique and may not necessarily fit the mold for the specified generation based on his or her place or time of birth. Nonetheless, understanding the various generational personalities can help managers and leaders build bridges in the work environment to create collaborative teams in today's learning organizations. Furthermore, this understanding may assist managers and organizations to effectively recruit and retain diverse individuals by meeting the majority of their intrinsic needs in order to keep them loyal and committed to the organization. As one reads about the different generations, it is best to look for potential implications on one's own organizational systems and environments. As learning and wisdom increase, one can then appropriately use human systems (on an individual and organizational basis) to gain a true competitive advantage in the twenty first century work environment. Understanding the various generational personalities is essential in building bridges and creating new learning and development opportunities in the work environment.

Traditionalists (veterans) were born between the turn of the last century and the end of World War II (1900-1945). Traditionalists tend to be cautious, do not take much risk, speak only when spoken to, and have been obedient to societal rules. They expect career security of life-long employment and do not appreciate job-hopping or downsizing jobs. This generation prefers a learning environment that offers predictability, stability, and security.

Baby boomers, born between 1946-1964 years, grew up in suburbs, had educational opportunities above their parents, saw lots of consumer products "hit" the marketplace (calculators, appliances). The television had a significant impact on their views of the world regarding equal opportunity and other human rights. Many members of this generation served in the military throughout the United States and around the globe. They enjoy perks that allow them to have more free time like errand-running service, car washes, food service, etc. The preferred learning environment of the Boomers is interactive and team activities.

Generation X, making up about 46 million individuals in the United States, born from 1965 through 1976, transitioned into work environment during the 1990s. They have been able to demand that organizations adapt to their way of doing things. This generation has been raised in the fast lane with one or both parents working. They abominate micro-management in the work environment. Individuals from this generation, like many others, want constant "feedback" on how they are performing on the projects they complete. They are the "job-hopping" generation and are attracted to work projects instead of jobs. They expect firms to be socially responsible. For this group, freedom and autonomy are considered the ultimate rewards as this generation grew up being independent.

Generation Y individuals, mostly born between 1977-1994, are "techno-savvy," multi-tasking and have had access to cell phones, personal pagers, computers, and concern for personal safety most of their lives. It is predicted that this generation will be more loyal than the Gen Xers provided they are stimulated and have learning opportunities. Gen Y individuals will be more likely to deal with finding facts quickly and to find more of such data as they will have a short "shelf life." In terms of learning style, Generation Y, students expect education to be about application and doing of things that relate to their current interests. Also, they learn best when the learning process and facilitation involves them in a fun and humorous manner. This generation strongly resists the traditional style of lecturing by academicians and "know-it-all" experts since they prefer to be involved in the process.

Age and Generation-Based Value Differences between the U.S. and Japan

The research literature shows that hundreds of studies have explored cross-cultural differences in values, attitudes and behaviors. Further, numerous studies have explored age and generation differences, and some studies have explored cross-cultural age or generation differences in values, but few have explored cross-culture, age and generation-based differences in values in one research study. Even fewer have done so with the Rokeach Value Survey (RVS), which is one of the most used value instruments in the research literature.

For instance, in a review of Rokeach Value Survey studies from 1977 to the year 2003 (completed in May 15, 2003), there were 650 papers or articles. Of those 220 papers thirty-nine were cross-cultural studies, but only eight of those studies compared cross-cultural value differences between US and Japanese populations (Akiba and Klub, 1999; Connor et. al, 1993; Feather and Mckee, 1993; Hofstede and Bond, 1984; Howard, Shudo and Umeshima, 1983; Mayton and Furnham, 1994; Ng, 1993; Weinberg, 1986). Of these eight US and Japanese studies, five used college students (Akiba and Klug, 1999; Feather and Mckee, 1993; Hofstede and Bond, 1984; Mayton and Furnham, 1994; Ng et al. 1993) and three studies used business manager populations (Connor et al. 1993; Howard, Shudo and Umeshima, 1983; Weinberg, 1986).

For studies exploring cross-culture and age or generation differences in values, attitudes or behaviors, a review of the PsycINFO data base (completed on May 15, 2003) found 135 studies explored age and generation differences. While 35 of these studies explored cross-cultural age-based differences in values, 30 others explored cross-cultural value differences focusing on either age or generation differences, but none explored all three concepts together.

For instance, Allport (1935, 1954, 1955), England (1967a, b; 1978), and Rokeach (1973, 1979, 1986) explored age and generation differences in the US, finding that both age and generation were important indicators of the most and least important values. More recently, Roscoe and Peterson (1989) examined age and generation differences in the US between female adolescents, their mothers and grandmothers. Their findings showed that adolescent values were consistent with their parents, but that age and generation differences explained the majority of value differences. Fournet (1996) explored cross-cultural and generation differences in attitudes towards education between three generations (grand-parents, parents, and children) of African-Americans, Caucasian and Hispanic. The results showed that the Caucasians valued education more than the Hispanics or African-Americans; and those parents and grand-parents placed higher value on education for their children than the children did.

In studies of age and generation differences in the U.S., Eskilson and Wiley (1999) and McMichael (2000) found that the values of Generation X students were different than the adult population of the US. Murphy (2001) explored career value differences between

Matures (1925-1945), Baby Boomers (1946-1964), and Generation X (1965-1980), finding that only three of the career values varied significantly by generation, but the major differences came from occupational and sex differences.

In cross-cultural generation research Feather (1979, 1984) explored generation differences in Australia and New Zealand (1979, 1984) finding significant cross-cultural, age, and generation-based differences in values, attitudes and behaviors using the RVS and other attitudinal and behavioral instruments. Imamoglu and Ayguen (1999) and Ayguen and Imamoglu (2002) longitudinally explored generation differences between parents and students in Turkey using the Rokeach Value Survey and Schwartz Value Survey. The Rokeach instrument results showed that students' individualistic values increased in importance across the generations from the 1970s to the 1990s, while their values increased to more socio-cultural and normative conservative values during the same time period. Using the Schwartz instrument, they found that adults placed more importance on the traditional-religiosity, normative patterning, and benevolence domains.

Chang, Wong, and Koh (2003) conducted three studies using the Chinese Value Hierarchy instrument in Singapore to explore generation differences. Their study found that parents differed significantly from their children as parents valued the tradition factor while their children valued the modern factor. Finally, Eskin (2003) explored cross-cultural and age differences in self-reported assertiveness in adolescents and students in Sweden and Turkey, finding that the older students were more assertive than younger ones. The basic problem with these studies is that none fully explored cross-culture, age, and generation differences in value structures together, and none explored age and generation-based cross-cultural value differences between the United States and Japan. The review of the literature led to the development of the following problem statement.

Problem statement and Research Methodology

While some studies have explored cross-cultural value differences, some have explored cross-cultural age differences, and some have explored cross-cultural generation differences, very few studies have explored cross-culture, age and generation differences in value structures together in one study and even fewer have done so between Japan and the U.S. This problem statement led to this research study and the following methodology.

This study used a descriptive cross-sectional survey research design using stratified random sampling techniques to determine if cross-cultural age and generation differences existed in the Rokeach Value Survey (RVS) Terminal and Instrumental Values of adult populations between the ages of 18 and 50 in the U.S. and Japan. The researcher used the Rokeach Value Survey and an instrument that explored demographic variables (Murphy, 1994d; Murphy and Anderson, 2003).

Rokeach Value Survey

The Rokeach Value Survey was used in this research study to explore the cross-cultural, age and generation differences. The RVS is divided into two sets of 18 values each.

The first set consists of Terminal Values by Rokeach (1973, p. 5) were "end–state of existence" values, what Murphy and Anderson (2003) called "the most important goals each respondent sought in their lives" (p. 118). The second set were Instrumental Values by Rokeach (1973, p. 5) were "modes of conduct" values, what Murphy and Anderson (2003, p. 118) stated were "the behavioral techniques or methods respondents would use to obtain their terminal value goals." Respondents taking the Rokeach Value Survey (RVS) are told to rank order the values in order of importance "as guiding principles in your life" (Rokeach, 1973, p. 27). Rokeach (1979) reported test-retest reliability for each of the 18 Terminal Values considered separately, from three to seven weeks later, ranged from a low of .51 for A Sense Of Accomplishment, to a high of .88 for Salvation. Comparable test-retest reliability scores for Instrumental Values ranged from .45 for Responsible to .70 for Ambitious. Employing a 14-16 month test interval, median reliability was .69 for Terminal Values and .61 for Instrumental Values.

The RVS has been tested by numerous researchers in the US and in cross-cultural studies. While Feather (1999) and Rokeach and Ball-Rokeach (1989) and some other researchers claimed it was perfectly suited for cross-cultural research (Munson, 1980; Munson and McIntyre, 1980; Munson and Posner, 1980a, b; Lau and Wong, 1992). Some researchers claimed the instrument did not adequately pick up Chinese values (Bond, 1994; 1996; Lee, 1991). This research study does not statistically explore whether the instrument adequately picks up Japanese values, but the researchers interview respondents to explore whether they felt the RVS adequately explored their value structures.

Translation of Rokeach Value Survey

The Rokeach Value Survey (RVS) was translated to Japanese by a native Japanese speaker in the U.S. An independent confirmation of the translation was made by another native Japanese speaker who translated the instrument back to Japanese. Both then met to resolve any differences and to develop a consensus as to the proper translation. This consensus was necessary in order to have the Japanese translation as close as possible to the intent and content of the English language version. As a clarification, the English version was left in place beside the Japanese version.

Method of administering survey instruments

The first Japanese population consisted of 134 Japan Airlines pilots attending a two-year airline pilot training at a US Flight Crew Training Center (FCTC). The population consisted of male pilots ranging from 25 to 50 years of age. All were university graduates, with a very small percentage having completed a post-graduate degree. All had studied English throughout their school careers for an average of 11 years. Less than forty percent had been to the United States before, with 26 percent having lived in the United States for a short period of time (five days to five months). A small percentage of pilots were married, with an even smaller percentage having children. Of the 134 Japanese surveys sent out, a total of 120 were returned, for a 90 percent return rate. The second Japanese population consisted of a stratified random sample of an international population of 300 adults attending an aviation industry meeting in the Netherlands. One hundred fifty one respondents returned properly completed instruments for a fifty percent return rate. The respondents were eighty-nine Japanese and sixty-two non-Japanese. The final sample consisted of 209 Japanese.

The U.S. population consisted of a stratified random sample of 2,400 U.S. residents living in California. The final sample consisted of one thousand US pilots, while the remaining 1,283 were civilians, all living in California. The final sample for this research study consisted of 209 Japanese and 1,283 US respondents, for a total of 1,492 respondents.

In exploring the demographic variables, the researchers found that the sample as a whole consisted of 565 females and 1846 males; 452 had high school diplomas; 255 were working on their associate's degrees; 372 had associate's degrees; 300 had bachelor's degrees; 72 had master's degrees; 21 were working on their PhDs, and 20 had their PhDs. For work experience, 585 had 10 years or less work experience; 446 had 10-15 years of work experience; 135 had 16-20 years of work experience; 302 had 20-25 years of work experience, and 24 had 26 or more years of work experience. Finally, 677 were pilots and 734 were non-pilots, and 602 were civilians, and 890 were US government or military employees.

Results of hypothesis tests

The following are the hypothesis for this study:
1. H1: There are cross-cultural age differences in Rokeach Value Survey Terminal Values.
2. H2: There are cross-cultural age differences in Rokeach Value Survey Instrumental Values.
3. H3: There are cross-cultural generation differences in Rokeach Value Survey Terminal Values.
4. H2: There are cross-cultural generation differences in Rokeach Value Survey Instrumental Values.

The researchers evaluated the average group RVS means and medians in order to explore the hypotheses for statistically significant differences. The researchers evaluated each hypothesis using the SYSTAT for Windows statistical analysis software package with $p < .05$ set as the level of significance for hypothesis testing. The researchers first analyzed the data with Analysis of Variance (ANOVA) to explore cross-cultural and age differences in values for each nationality separately, by separating the data base into one containing the Japanese alone, and the other containing the U.S. alone. The ANOVAs showed that for the US sample, there were five statistically significant age differences for Terminal Values and twelve for Instrumental Values. For the Japanese sample, there were four statistically significant differences for Terminal Values and six for Instrumental Values. These results are not presented here for brevity purposes.

The researchers then used the combined data base to explore if there were cross-cultural differences and then age differences using Multiple Analysis of Variance (MANOVA). The MANOVA results showed that there were statistically significant cross-cultural value differences for fifteen Terminal and eleven Instrumental Values, and six Terminal and twelve Instrumental Values were different for age differences (Table 24). In order to analyze the generation differences, the researchers used an Analysis of Covariance (ANCOVA) to explore the impact of culture and age across the generations, finding statistically significant differences for thirteen of eighteen Terminal Values and ten of eighteen Instrumental Values (Table 25).

Analysis of Research Results

As shown in Table 24, the researchers explored hypothesis one and two with Multiple Analysis of Variance (MANOVA), finding that fifteen of eighteen Terminal Values (H1) were statistically significant for differences (A Comfortable Life, An Exciting Life, A Sense of Accomplishment, A World at Peace, A World of Beauty, Family Security, Freedom, Health/Happiness, Mature Love, National Security, Pleasure, Salvation, Social Recognition, True Friendship, Wisdom). For (H2) the researchers found fifteen of eighteen Instrumental Values (Ambitious, Broadminded, Capable, Clean, Courageous, Forgiving, Honest, Independent, Intellectual, Logical, Loyal, Obedient, Polite, Responsible, Self-Controlled) were statistically significant for cross-cultural and age differences.

The researchers then tested hypothesis three (H3) and four (H4) for cross-cultural generation differences across the samples with Multiple Analysis of Covariance with age as the covariate. As shown in Table 25, the research results for H3 found thirteen of eighteen Terminal Values (An Exciting Life, A Sense of Accomplishment, A World at Peace, A World of Beauty, Family Security, Freedom, Health/Happiness, National Security, Pleasure, Salvation, Social Recognition, True Friendship, Wisdom) and for H4 ten of eighteen Instrumental Values (Ambitious, Broadminded, Clean, Forgiving, Honest, Independent, Logical, Loving, Obedient, Self-Controlled) were statistically significant for generation differences. These research results allowed the researchers to accept hypotheses H1, H2, H3, and H4 and reject their null hypotheses. The next section discusses the results for cross-cultural age differences.

Table 24 - *Comparison of Cross-Cultural Age-Based Differences in Values—Statistical Test Results*

	MANOVA DF Effect	F	p < .05
Terminal Values			
A Comfortable Life	8, 1484	1.8303***	.0007
An Exciting Life	8, 1484	2.590**	.008
A Sense of Accomplishment	8, 1484	4.203***	.0001
A World at Peace	8, 1484	5.079***	.0001
A World of Beauty	8, 1484	4.482***	.0001
Equality	8, 1484	1.108	NS
Family Security	8, 1484	3.267**	.001
Freedom	8, 1484	3.457***	.0005
Health/Happiness	8, 1484	8.917***	.0001
Inner Harmony	8, 1484	1.434	NS
Mature Love	8, 1484	1.928**	.0002
National Security	8, 1484	10.746***	.0001
Pleasure	8, 1484	3.882***	.0001
Salvation	8, 1484	2.000***	.0001
Self-Respect	8, 1484	1.844	NS
Social Recognition	8, 1484	2.195*	.025
True Friendship	8, 1484	3.244*	.011
Wisdom	8, 1484	2.041*	.038
Instrumental Values			
Ambitious	8, 1484	5.213***	.0001
Broadminded	8, 1484	5.353***	.0001
Capable	8, 1484	1.799**	.002
Clean	8, 1484	2.201*	.024
Courageous	8, 1484	3.066***	.0001
Forgiving	8, 1484	3.348**	.0008
Helpful	8, 1484	1.405	NS
Honest	8, 1484	2.251*	.021
Imaginative	8, 1484	1.447	NS
Independent	8, 1484	4.865***	.0001
Intellectual	8, 1484	1.548**	.0122
Logical	8, 1484	4.108***	.0001
Loving	8, 1484	1.270	NS
Loyal	8, 1484	1.934**	.001
Obedient	8, 1484	6.517***	.0001
Polite	8, 1484	1.970**	.004
Responsible	8, 1484	1.850**	.0006
Self-Controlled	8, 1484	3.663**	.0002

* P < .05; ** p < .001; *** p < .001

Table 25 - *ANCOVA Nationality as Independent Variable, Dependent Variables Values, Covariate is Age*

	Mean sqr Effect	Mean sqr Error	F(df1,2) 8, 1484	p-level
COMFOR	43.414	25.5	1.70250	.092851
EXCITLIF	73.720	26.1	2.82702**	.004010
ACCOMP	90.683	21.4	4.24184***	.000045
WORLDPEA	146.250	29.5	4.95303***	.000004
WORLDBEA	90.762	19.7	4.61648***	.000013
EQUALITY	22.673	21.6	1.05202	.394298
FAMSEC	77.107	23.8	3.24317**	.001119
FREEDOM	77.713	21.5	3.62039***	.000340
HEALTH	170.808	18.4	9.25922***	.000000
INHARM	45.561	32.6	1.39703	.192567
MALOVE	38.567	22.4	1.72295	.088203
NASEC	251.171	23.1	10.87358***	.000000
PLEAS	88.088	23.7	3.72256***	.000245
SALV	159.499	38.7	4.12136***	.000067
SERESP	39.313	26.0	1.51435	.146823
SORECOG	44.240	20.1	2.19969*	.024820
TRUFRIE	60.746	19.7	3.07949**	.001859
WISD	43.627	21.4	2.04145*	.038326
AMBITIOU	147.290	26.6	5.54383***	.000001
BMINDED	122.117	23.5	5.20480***	.000002
CAPABLE	27.800	21.7	1.28147	.248401
CLEAN	50.321	25.2	1.99395*	.043559
COURAGE	6807.011	130128.8	.05231	.999932
FORGIVE	125.873	37.5	3.35509***	.000789
HELPFUL	32.754	24.2	1.35311	.212461
HONEST	60.134	25.2	2.39056*	.014477
IMAGINAT	33.444	23.9	1.39752	.192355
INDEPEN	120.955	26.2	4.62503***	.000013
INTELLEC	30.270	24.7	1.22521	.279786
LOGICAL	97.583	23.6	4.12983***	.000065
LOVING	93.548	28.7	3.25513**	.001078
LOYL	38.846	25.3	1.53291	.140504
OBEDIENT	153.707	23.8	6.44646***	.000000
POLITE	38.712	24.1	1.60946	.116854
RESPONS	31.432	22.3	1.40934	.187272
SELFCONT	91.787	25.4	3.61002***	.000352

* p < .05; ** p < .001; *** p < .0001

Cross-Cultural age differences

What do these results mean? In order to analyze the research results and their meaning, the research presents the results using cross-cultural age-cohorts. To explain the differences and similarities among the age cohorts the researchers compared the top five (most important, ranked one through five) and bottom five (least important, ranked fourteen to eighteen) values of importance for each cross-cultural age cohort, and then compared those results to the values that were simply important (ranked six through thirteen) for each age cohort. Rokeach (1973, 1979) said that the most important values to explore for differences and similarities were the top five and the bottom five of importance.

Respondents 18 – 25 year olds

The top five Terminal Values of importance for the Japanese respondents were Health/Happiness (1), Pleasure (2), Freedom (3), Family Security (4), and A Comfortable Life (5). The top five for US respondents were Health/Happiness, (1), Mature Love (2), True Friendship (3), An Exciting Life (4), and Family Security (5). Two of the top five Terminal Values of importance, Health/Happiness and Family Security, were identical for both groups, showing both similarities and differences among the cross-cultural age groups.

The top five Instrumental Values of importance for the Japanese were Honest (1), Responsible (2), Broadminded (3), Self-controlled (4), and Loving (5). The top five for US respondents were Honest (1), Intellectual (2), Loving (3), Responsible (4), and Independent (5). Three of the top five Instrumental Values of importance, Honest, Loving, and Responsible, were identical for both groups.

The researchers next compared the top five values of importance or most important values for each culture with the values of importance (six through thirteen) for the other culture. The results showed that there were even more similarities among the 18 to 25 year old respondents because each of the top five most important Terminal and Instrumental Values for the Japanese respondents was also ranked as important (six through thirteen) by the U.S. respondents. Also, each of the top five most important values for the US respondents was ranked as important by the Japanese. This meant that although there were cross-cultural differences between the Japanese and U.S. most important value rankings, their most important goals in life and techniques that would be used to obtain those goals were very similar, showing that they were part of the same age-cohort or generation. Other similarities were shown in the least important Terminal and Instrumental Values (ranked fourteen to eighteen).

When the researchers compared the Japanese least important or bottom five Terminal Values of importance they found four of the bottom five values of importance were identical for both groups (A World of Beauty, National Security, Salvation, and Social Recognition). There were more differences in instrumental values where only two value techniques were least important for both the Japanese and US respondents (Logical and Obedient).

In summary, the results showed that while the Japanese and U.S. respondents ranked certain values as more important than other values, only two terminal values and six instrumental values were considered important by one group but not important by the other group. For example, sixteen of eighteen Terminal Values were considered most important or important by both the Japanese and U.S. The major differences were for Equality, which was ranked an unimportant fourteen by U.S. respondents, and an important thirteen by the Japanese and Inner Harmony, which was ranked an unimportant sixteen by the Japanese and an important twelve by the U.S. respondents. Similarly, twelve of eighteen Instrumental Values were considered important by both the Japanese and U.S. The major differences were for the Instrumental Values Ambitious (ranked 6 by U.S. and 17 by Japanese); Clean (ranked 18 by US and 13 by Japanese); Helpful (ranked 12 by U.S. and 15 by Japanese); Independent (ranked 5 by U.S. and 16 by Japanese); Loyal (ranked 14 by U.S. and 8 by Japanese), and Polite (ranked 16 by U.S. and 7 by Japanese).

Respondents 26 to 30 year olds

The top five Terminal Values of importance for the 26 to 30 year old Japanese respondents were Health/Happiness (1), Family Security (2), True Friendship (3), A Sense of Accomplishment (4), and Pleasure (5). Their top five most important Instrumental Values were Honest (1), Responsible (2), Self-Controlled (3), Loving (4), and Broadminded (5). The top five most important Terminal Values for the US 26 to 30 year old respondents were Family Security (1), Health/Happiness (2), Freedom (3), Self-Respect (4), and A Comfortable Life (5). Their top five most important Instrumental Values were Honest (1), Responsible (2), Ambitious (3), Courageous (4), and Loyal (5).

For similarities, two of their most important Terminal Values (Family Security and Health/Happiness) were in the top five of importance for both groups, and two Instrumental Values (Honest and Responsible) were in the top five of importance for both groups. In addition, three of the bottom five or least important Terminal (A World of Beauty, National Security, and Social Recognition) and Instrumental (Clean, Logical, and Obedient) Values were identical for both. Finally, A Comfortable Life, An Exciting Life, A Sense of Accomplishment, A World at Peace, Family Security, Freedom, Health/Happiness Mature Love, Self-Respect, True Friendship, and Wisdom were either most important or important for the Japanese and US respondents. But, there were some differences noted.

For instance, the Terminal Value Equality was ranked an important eleven for the Japanese and unimportant fifteen for the U.S. respondents; Pleasure was ranked an important five for Japanese respondents and an unimportant sixteen for US respondents; Inner Harmony was ranked an important twelve for US respondents and an unimportant fourteen for Japanese respondents, and Salvation was ranked an important nine for US respondents and an unimportant seventeen for Japanese respondents. For Instrumental Values, the results were very similar with Ambitious ranked a most important three by US respondents and an unimportant seventeen for Japanese respondents; Imaginative was ranked an important eleven by the Japanese and seventeen by the US respondents; Forgiving was ranked an important twelve by the Japanese and an unimportant fifteen for US respondents, and Independent was ranked an important six by the US respondents and an unimportant fourteen by Japanese respondents.

Respondents 31 to 39 year olds

The five most important Terminal Values for the 31-39 year old Japanese respondents included Health/Happiness (1), Family Security (2), A Comfortable Life (3), A Sense of Accomplishment (4), and True Friendship, while the most important Terminal Values for the US respondents included Family Security (1), Health/Happiness (2), Freedom (3), Self-Respect (4), and Salvation (5). Three of the top five values of importance were in the top five for both groups, showing the similarities in their most important goals in life (A Comfortable Life, Family Security, and Health/Happiness).

The most important Instrumental Value techniques for the 31-39 year old Japanese respondents included Honest (1), Responsible (2), Loyal (3), Loving (4), and Polite (5), and the most important for the US respondents included Honest (1), Responsible (2), Ambitious Independent (3), Ambitious (4), and Loyal (5). Honest, Loyal and Responsible were in the top five of importance for both groups, showing the similarities in their behavioral techniques they would use to obtain their terminal value goals.

Once again, the similarities among the 31-39 year olds most important goals in life and in their behavior techniques are remarkable. Eleven of their eighteen Terminal Values and eleven of their eighteen Instrumental Values were most important or important for both the Japanese and US respondents. Further, three of their least important Terminal Values (A World of Beauty, National Security, and Social Recognition) and three of their least important Instrumental Values (Clean, Imaginative, and Obedient) were ranked in the bottom five of importance for both groups.

There were four major differences for Terminal Values (A World at Peace, Equality, Pleasure and Salvation) and four differences for Instrumental Values (Forgiving, Helpful, Logical and Polite). Japanese respondents ranked A World at Peace an important thirteen compared to the U.S. ranking of an unimportant fifteen, and Japanese respondents ranked Pleasure an important eleven compared to the U.S. unimportant sixteen. For behavioral technique differences, the Japanese respondents ranked Forgiving an important nine, and Polite a most important five, which the U.S. respondents ranked as an unimportant fifteen and fourteen respectively. The U.S. respondents ranked Equality an important thirteen and Salvation and important five, compared to the unimportant ranking of fourteen and fifteen for the Japanese. Similarly for behavioral techniques, the U.S. respondents ranked Helpful an important ten and Logical and important eleven compared to the Japanese rankings of unimportant fourteen and sixteen.

Respondents 40+ year olds

The top five values of importance for the Japanese 40+ year old respondents were Family Security (1), Health/Happiness (2), A Sense of Accomplishment (3), Self-Respect (4), and Wisdom (5), and their top five Instrumental Values were Honest (1), Responsible (2), Loving (3), Capable (4), and Self-Controlled (5). The top five values of importance for the US 40+ year old respondents were Family Security (1), Health/Happiness (2), Freedom

(3), Self-Respect (4), and A Comfortable Life (5), and their most important Instrumental Values were Responsible (1), Honest (2), Ambitious (3), Loving (4), and Capable (5).

The number of similarities in values was remarkable, as three Terminal Values and four Instrumental Values were in the top five for both groups. Both groups ranked as their most important terminal goals Family Security, Health/Happiness, and Self-Respect and their most important instrumental behavioral techniques of Capable, Honest, Loving, and Responsible. Similarly, three Terminal Values of least importance (A World of Beauty, National Security, and Social Recognition) and two Instrumental Values of least importance (Imaginative and Obedient) were identical for both groups. What do the results show for cross-cultural generation-based differences?

Cross-Cultural Generation Differences

For cross-cultural generation-based differences, the research results showed that there were not only cross-cultural generation-based differences in value structures, but also generation-based similarities among the generation-based cohorts. As shown in Tables 26 and 27 (at the end of this chapter), for generational similarities, the Terminal Values Family Security and Health/Happiness and Instrumental Values Honest and Responsible were in the top five of importance for all Japanese and U.S. generations. Further, sixteen of the eighteen Terminal Values and twelve of eighteen Instrumental Values for the 18 to 25 year olds were either most important (ranked one through five) or important (ranked six through thirteen) for all US and Japanese generations. Similarly, fourteen of eighteen Terminal and Instrumental Values of the 26 to 30 and 31-39 year olds were either important or most important for all U.S. and Japanese generations. Finally, sixteen of eighteen Terminal and thirteen of eighteen Instrumental Values were either important or most important for the 40+ year olds and all other U.S. and Japanese generations.

The results for generation based differences showed that there were an average of fifteen Terminal and fifteen Instrumental Values that were most important or important for each generation. This meant that an average of only three Terminal Value and five Instrumental Values were different among the generations as those values were important for one generation were not important for the other generation.

The authors next compared the bottom five or least important Terminal and Instrumental Values for the different generations (see Tables 28 and 29 at the end of this chapter). The results showed that three Terminal Values (Social Recognition, A World of Beauty, and National Security) and one Instrumental Value (Obedient) were in the bottom five of importance for reach generation. Further, the Terminal Value Salvation was not important for the U.S. 18 to 25 year olds and all Japanese age groups across the generations, and Equality was not important for the U.S. 18 to 25, 26 to 30, and 40+ year olds and Japanese 31 to 39 year olds. For Instrumental Values Logical was not important for the U.S. and Japanese 18 to 25 and 26 to 30 year olds, and Japanese 31 to 39 year olds. Finally, Clean was not important for the U.S. for all U.S. generations and the Japanese 26 to 30 and 31 to 39 year olds.

When the authors compared the most important and important values (one through thirteen) across the generations they found that nine Terminal Values (A Comfortable Life, An Exciting Life, A Sense of Accomplishment, Family Security, Health/Happiness, Mature Love, Self-Respect, True Friendship, and Wisdom) were important or most important for all generations and three values were unimportant for all generations (A World of Beauty, National Security and Social Recognition). This meant that twelve of the eighteen Terminal Values or most important goals in their lives were important, most important, or unimportant for all generations. On the other hand there were fewer similarities in the Instrumental Values or behavior techniques used to obtain the terminal value goals. For instance, only six were important or most important for all generations (Capable, Courageous, Honest, Loving, Responsible and Self-Controlled) and one was least important (Obedient). This meant that only seven of the eighteen behavioral techniques were important, most important or unimportant for all generations. In summary, a total of fifteen values were important across all generations and four were unimportant across all generations. This result meant that twenty of the thirty six values, or fifty-five percent of the values were identical across the generations, and only forty-five percent were different.

Research Conclusions and Discussion

The research results showed that cross-culture, age, and generation together impacted value structures as a combined group more than each variable separately. Further, the results showed the need to compare values within groups and across groups in order to bring out not only the differences, but also the similarities. These results showed that although there were cross-cultural differences and cross-cultural age differences, when the authors compared the results for generation differences, they found there were more similarities than differences among the cross-cultural generations. These are important findings for practitioners to understand because they would allow marketers to target the value similarities in each culture in their marketing campaigns in order to produce economy in advertising costs. For instance, Rose (1997) stated that "if similar segments of consumers can be identified, economies of scales in advertising production can be realized" (p. 397). Finally, global managers and marketers must understand the cross-cultural age and generation-based value differences and similarities found in this study in order to motivate their employees and market their products globally. How do these results compare to the results from other research studies on cross-cultural differences?

It is important for researchers to compare their results to other studies that have been conducted in order to allow future researchers to use their results for comparison purposes. The cross-cultural age and generation-based value difference and similarities found in this study confirm that the Japanese on the whole, are a collectivist culture where the group is more important than the individual, and confirm the individualistic nature of U.S. culture on the whole, where the individual is more important than the group. Yet, the results showed the need for breaking the cross-cultural differences down further into explorations of the impact of age and then generation on those values priorities.

Rokeach stated that the US culture is generally achievement-oriented. For instance, he stated that "the US achievement orientation was in the service of materialism instead of the service of personal competence" (Rokeach, 1973, p. 91). According to Rokeach (1973), western cultures like the US have an orientation toward materialism, competition and achievement that are shown in the higher importance they (US) place on A Comfortable Life, Social Recognition and being Ambitious and less on being Helpful, and more on being Ambitious than being Capable. The results of this study showed that U.S. respondents from each age category did value Ambitious more than Helpful and Capable and more than the Japanese respondents in each age category, confirming the U.S. individualistic culture. On the other hand, the US respondents placed high value importance on A Comfortable Life, but so did the Japanese, showing the Japanese had adopted an individualistic value. In fact, the 18 to 25 and 31 to 39 year old Japanese placed slightly higher importance on A Comfortable Life than the US respondents in the same age categories.

Another interesting finding was for the value Freedom which is normally ranked more important in individualistic cultures than in collectivist cultures. In this study Freedom was more important for the Japanese 18 to 25 year olds than the U.S. 18 to 25 year olds, but it was more important for the 26 to 30, 31 to 39 and 40+ year old U.S. respondents than the Japanese in the same age categories. This meant that the value Freedom has been adopted into the culture of the Japanese 18 to 25 year olds. Similarly, the value Independent was highly important for all U.S. generations. Further, the value Independent is normally not highly valued by collectivist cultures, but in this study the Japanese 31 to 39 year olds placed high importance on this value, showing they have adopted the value Independent into their culture. Another interesting finding was that both the Japanese and U.S. respondents felt Social Recognition was unimportant. Evidently this former U.S. individualistic value is now no longer important.

According to Rokeach, collectivist or group oriented cultures normally place higher importance on the value Capable than Ambitious, lower importance on Freedom and Independence, and higher importance on being Helpful, Clean, Polite, Obedient, and Self-Controlled. This study showed that the Japanese respondents placed much higher importance across the generations for the value Capable over the value Ambitious. In fact, Ambitious was ranked as unimportant by the Japanese 18 to 30 year olds. The Japanese 18 to 25 year old respondents placed higher importance on Freedom than the U.S. 18 to 25 year olds. Further, only the 40+ year old Japanese respondents ranked Freedom as unimportant (fourteen), showing that the Japanese 18 to 25, 26 to 30 and 31 to 39 year olds have adopted Freedom into their culture. The Japanese 26 to 30 year olds and 40+ year olds felt that Helpful was important, but the 18 to 25 and 31 to 39 year old Japanese ranked this value as unimportant, meaning they did not view it as an important collectivist value. Similarly, the Japanese 26 6o 30 and 31 to 39 year olds ranked Clean as unimportant, meaning they no longer viewed this collectivist value as part of their culture. Finally, Polite and Self-Controlled were important or most important for each Japanese age-cohort across the generations, confirming these collectivist values.

On the other hand, U.S. respondents ranked Helpful and Self-Controlled as important across the generations, showing they have adopted these two collectivist values as part of their culture. The results for the collectivist value Polite showed that it was only important for the US 26 to 30 and 40+ year olds, meaning these two groups have adopted this collectivist value as part of their culture. Finally, the collectivist value Obedient was not important for either culture or any of the age groups, showing that this value is no longer part of the Japanese collectivist culture.

Hofstede's, Feather's, and Ng's research studies have shown that world-wide travel, radio, television, global advertising, global distribution of products, and global trade have caused some values to converge globally as some individualistic values are adopted in the east and some collectivist values are adopted in the west (McQuarrie, 1989; Rokeach, 1977). For instance, the top five Terminal and Instrumental Values of importance for Egyptian, Arabian, American and African Executives (Elkhouly and Buda, 1997); US and Canadian managers (Connor et al. 1993); Australian adults (Feather, 1984); Turkish students (Cileli and Tezer, 1998); Chilean students (Ahmed and Rojas, 1998); US pilots (Murphy and Anderson, 2003) and US respondents in this research study. There were similarities and differences when comparing the most important Terminal and Instrumental Values found in this study with those in previous studies.

For instance, Australian (Feather, 1982), and French Canadian students (Ahmed and Rojas, 1998) placed high value importance on Self-Respect but not Family Security, while Japanese pilots (Murphy and Anderson, 2003), Japanese managers (Connor et al. 1993), the general population of the U.S. (Rokeach and Ball-Rokeach, 1989), and the U.S. in this research study placed high importance on Self-Respect and Family Security, but the Japanese in this research study highly valued Family Security but not Self-Respect.

Similarly, Health/Happiness was a Terminal Value that was in the top five of importance for Australian students (Feather, 1982) and adults (Feather, 1984); Japanese managers (Connor et al. 1993); Egyptian, Arabian, and American Executives (Elkhouly and Buda, 1997); Turkish students (Cileli and Tezer, 1998); French Canadian students (Ahmed and Rojas, 1998); U.S. and Japanese pilots (Murphy and Anderson, 2003), and the Japanese and US respondents in this research study.

The Instrumental Values Honest and Responsible were in the top five of importance for Australian students (Feather, 1982) and adults (Feather, 1984); US and Canadian managers (Connor et al. 1993); American, and African executives (Elkhouly and Buda, 1997); Chilean students (Ahmed and Rojas, 1998); the general population of the US (Rokeach and Ball-Rokeach, 1989); U.S. and Japanese pilots (Murphy and Anderson, 2003), and the Japanese and US respondents in this research study. A normally collectivist value, Broadminded, was most important for Australian students (Feather, 1982); African and Arabian executives (Elkhouly and Buda, 1997); Turkish students (Cileli and Tezer, 1998); French Canadian students (Ahmed and Rojas, 1998); the general population of the US (Rokeach and Ball-Rokeach, 1989); Japanese pilots (Murphy and Anderson, 2003), Japanese managers (Connor et al. 1993) and the Japanese population in this research study, but was not important for the US respondents in this study. Finally, a normally individualistic value, Ambitious, was most important for students from Mexico and Thailand (Munson and McIntyre, 1978); Canadian managers (Connor et al. 1993); Chilean and French Canadian students (Ahmed and Rojas, 1998); Egyptian, American and Arabian executives (Elkhouly and Buda, 1997); US pilots (Murphy and Anderson, 2003); and U.S. respondents in this research study, but was not important for the Japanese in this study. Finally, Self-Controlled was in the top five of importance for Japanese in this study and all Japanese respondents, including the Japanese managers (Connor et al. 1993) and Japanese pilots (Murphy and Anderson, 2003). It was in the top five of importance for the French Canadian students (Ahmed and Rojas, 1998), but was not in the top five of importance for any of the other cultures, including the US respondents in this study.

These research results are important for practitioners, managers, and marketers who are competing in the global economy to understand because the results showed that their customers or employees might not only have cross-cultural but also age and generation differences and similarities. For instance, when one compares the results to the top five values of importance for the Japanese and U.S. without regard to age, one finds that the most important Terminal Values for the US respondents as a group were Family Security, Health/Happiness, Self-Respect, Freedom and A Comfortable Life, while the most important for the Japanese respondents as a group were Health, True Friendship, A Sense of Accomplishment, Pleasure, and Family Security.

If a practitioner only uses the cross-cultural results for the Japanese as a group, they might develop an advertising campaign for a target market that is 31 years of age and older that emphasizes Pleasure or having an enjoyable and leisurely life. The marketing campaign might fail because Pleasure was a most important value for the Japanese as a group, but this research study of age-cohorts found that Pleasure was not a most important value for the Japanese 31 to 39 and 40+ year olds, who were their target market.

Further, managers must understand these research results because two of the top five Terminal Value goals or most important goals in the lives of the Japanese and US respondents in this study were taking care of their loved ones (Family Security) and maintaining a healthy and happy life style (Health/Happiness), and they would try to achieve these goals by being honest and responsible. This meant that employees would place their families and health before mission accomplishment; they would not do anything unethical, and they would take responsibility for their personal actions. If managers do not understand these value similarities and differences, they could be setting themselves up for failure or loss of a valuable employee by not knowing how to motivate the employee. Practitioners and researchers must understand that they can reach beneath the attitude and behavioral levels to explore the basic underlying assumptions or root causes of attitudes and behaviors, the value structures. Finally, practitioners and researchers must not only explore cross-culture, age and generation as separate constructs in their studies, but also together so they find the generation-based differences and similarities in their populations under study.

Recommendations for Further Research

The survey instrument used in this study was Rokeach's 1979 version. Minor changes were made in 1986 to reflect changes in societal values. For instance, the Terminal Value Happiness was changed to Health, because interviews with respondents stated they felt that health was much more important than happiness. Further cross-cultural research should use the newer survey instrument.

Within the first few administrations of the surveys, the researchers began getting feedback from the Japanese population about the translation of the survey into Japanese. The more fluent English speakers in the survey population expressed the view that some of the Japanese translations were not as accurate as they could be. For example, a few respondents felt that the Japanese translation of *A Comfortable Life* was actually closer to "*A Dull Life.*" Likewise, a few others felt that the translation of *Broadminded* contained an element of *Broadmindedness*, but also included a touch of *Forgiving*. Some felt that *Freedom* was actually translated as *Independent*. In addition, some felt that the Japanese translation of *Pleasure* contained some sexual connotations. The majority of the Japanese respondents were from two basic areas in Japan, Tokyo and Osaka, the two most populated areas, with a smaller minority from outlying areas such as Sapporo in the north, to Miyazaki in the South. Another translation of the instrument should be completed so that the proper terminology could be converted from English to Japanese to ensure that the Japanese translation could be understood equally well by a survey population throughout Japan.

Further, recent research by Hofstede and Bond (1988) developed the Chinese Value Survey instrument which has been used alongside the Rokeach Value Survey in China and Taiwan to measure the Eastern or Asian culture. This instrument found that Confucian Dynamism was a new value dimension that must be explored in Eastern cultures. This new value dimension explores the time orientation and Confucian values. The researchers recommend further studies of Japanese and American adult populations with the Chinese Value Survey and Rokeach Value Survey together.

In addition, many of the research studies reviewed in this literature review did not report standardized results that could be used by future researchers in their studies. For instance, Meglino (1998) told the values research community that this was a problem in the 1990s. That problem still continues today as many researchers using the Rokeach Value Survey do not report the Terminal and Instrumental value means and rankings, and top and bottom five values of importance. The researchers recommend that future research studies take into consideration the needs of future researchers and report the RVS means, rankings, and top five and bottom five values of importance for their populations under study.

Table 26- *Top Five Most Important Terminal Values Japanese Respondents*

US 18-25 Year Olds	JA 18-25 Year Olds	US 26-30 Year Olds	JA 26-30 Year Olds	US 31-39 Year Olds	JA 31-39 Year Olds	US 40+ Year Olds	JA 40+ Year Olds
Health/Happiness	Health/Happiness	Family Security	Health/Happiness	Family Security	Health/Happiness	Family Security	Family Security
Mature Love	Pleasure	Health/Happiness	Family Security	Health/Happiness	Family Security	Health/Happiness	Health/Happiness
True Friendship	Freedom	Freedom	True Friendship	Freedom	Comfortable Life	Freedom	Accomplishment
An Exciting Life	Family Security	Self-Respect	Accomplishment	Self-Respect	Accomplishment	Self-Respect	Self-Respect
Family Security	A Comfortable Life	Comfortable Life	Pleasure	Comfortable Life	True Friendship	Comfortable Life	Wisdom

Table 27- *Top Five Most Important Instrumental Values Japanese Respondents*

US 18-25 Year Olds	JA 18-25 Year Olds	US 26-30 Year Olds	JA 26-30 Year Olds	US 31-39 Year Olds	JA 31-39 Year Olds	US 40+ Year Olds	JA 40+ Year Olds
Honest	Honest	Honest	Honest	Honest	Honest	Responsible	Honest
Intellectual	Responsible	Responsible	Responsible	Responsible	Responsible	Honest	Responsible
Loving	Broadminded	Ambitious	Self-Controlled	Independent	Loyal	Ambitious	Loving
Responsible	Self-Controlled	Loving	Independent	Loyal	Loving	Loving	Capable
Independent	Loving	Loyal	Loyal	Ambitious	Polite	Capable	Self-Controlled

Table 28 - *Bottom Five Least Important Terminal Values US and Japanese Respondents*

US 18-25 Year Olds	JA 18-25 Year Olds	US 26-30 Year Olds	JA 26-30 Year Olds	US 31-39 Year Olds	JA 31-39 Year Olds	US 40+ Year Olds	JA 40+ Year Olds
Equality	Social Recognition	National Security	Social Recognition	National Security	Equality	Equality	Freedom
Social Recognition	A World of Beauty	Inner Harmony	A World of Beauty	A World at Peace	Salvation	National Security	Salvation
A World of Beauty	Inner Harmony	Pleasure	Pleasure	Salvation	A World of Beauty	A World at Peace	A World of Beauty
Salvation	Salvation	Social Recognition	Salvation	Social Recognition	Social Recognition	A World of Beauty	National Security
National Security	National Security	A World of Beauty	National Security	A World of Beauty	National Security	Social Recognition	Social Recognition

Table 29 - Bottom Five Least Instrumental Values US and Japanese Respondents

US 18-25 Year Olds	JA 18-25 Year Olds	US 26-30 Year Olds	JA 26-30 Year Olds	US 31-39 Year Olds	JA 31-39 Year Olds	US 40+ Year Olds	JA 40+ Year Olds
Loyal	Logical	Logical	Independent	Polite	Helpful	Forgiving	Obedient
Logical	Helpful	Forgiving	Logical	Forgiving	Clean	Intellectual	Polite
Polite	Independent	Clean	Clean	Imaginative	Logical	Obedient	Imaginative
Obedient	Ambitious	Imaginative	Ambitious	Obedient	Imaginative	Imaginative	Independent
Clean	Obedient	Obedient	Obedient	Clean	Obedient	Clean	Broadminded

Table 30 - Other Cross Cultural Studies Terminal Values

Munson & McIntyre Thai Students 1978	Munson & McIntyre Mexican Students 1978	Munson & McIntyre US Students 1978	Feather Australian Students 1982	Feather Australian Adults 1984	Cileli and Tezer Turkish Students 1998	Ahmed and Rojas Students Chile 1998	Ahmed and Rojas Students French Canada 1998	Rokeach and Ball-Rokeach 1989 Civilians US
Social Recognition	Salvation	Salvation	Inner Harmony	Family Security	Family Security	Freedom	Exciting Life	Family Security
Comfortable Life	National Security	Social Recognition	True Friendship	Happiness/Health	Inner Harmony	Self-Respect	Accomplishment	World Peace
Exciting Life	Social Recognition	World Beauty	Happiness/Health	Self-Respect	Health	Accomplishment	Self-Respect	Freedom
World Beauty	World Beauty	National Security	Mature Love	Wisdom	Self-Respect	Family Security	True Friendship	Social Recognition
Pleasure	Comfortable Life	Equality	Self-Respect	Freedom	True Friendship	True Friendship	Happiness/Health	Wisdom

Table 31 - *Other Cross Cultural Studies Instrumental Values*

Munson & McIntyre Thai Students 1978	Munson & McIntyre Mexican Students 1978	Munson & McIntyre US Students 1978	Feather Australian Students 1982	Feather Australian Adults 1984	Cileli and Tezer Turkish Students 1998	Ahmed and Rojas Students Chile 1998	Ahmed and Rojas Students French Canada 1998	Rokeach and Ball-Rokeach 1989 Civilians US
Imaginative	Obedient	Obedient	Loving	Honest	Independent	Capable	Honest	Honest
Obedient	Logical	Clean	Honest	Responsible	Honest	Honest	Ambitious	Ambitious
Ambitious	Polite	Helpful	Responsible	Loving	Courageous	Ambitious	Capable	Responsible
Loyal	Forgiving	Loyal	Broadminded	Courageous	Forgiving	Responsible	Broadminded	Social Recognition
Forgiving	Ambitious	Polite	Helpful	Capable	Broadminded	Intellectual	Self-Controlled	Broadminded

CHAPTER 12

THE PHILOSOPHY AND SCIENCE OF AGING[5]

*T*wenty first century human beings are living in a society where youth and youthfulness are highly prized. Today's modern technological society desires youthfulness more than anything as we are driven by the bright lights of Hollywood and the idea that success is predicated on staying young as long as is possible. The advances in cosmetic medicine and surgery have acted as balancing evidence to this highly desirable culture of youthfulness in which nip tucks, Bo tux, face lifts, etc., and other cosmetically devised jargons have become part of the daily language of life. Furthermore, there are famous worshipful icons that have perpetuated the interest in an anti-aging revolution through a combination of knives and drugs. Such individuals have altered the effects of time and defied our ideas and concepts of age and aging as they seem to grow younger with time's passing. However, knowing that society is baffled by mundane surface reality, one should consider aging from a biological viewpoint, and then it becomes clear that aging is a highly internal process despite the illusionary aspects of outward or external appearances which will inevitably vanish to give way to time's indelible prints, wrinkles, and old age!

Definitions and Concepts of Age and Aging

Aging from a medical point of view is the process of growing old or maturing, and also describes the gradual changes in the structure of a mature organism that occur normally over time and increase the probability of death. The fear of aging is the fear of death which typifies the process across all cultures and societies. "Man" is ever searching for ways to escape his mortality and aging gives no comfort to him, for as one ages naturally, provided no other defects lead to death, then aging eventually leads to death as the definition above communicates.

Aging from a biological viewpoint refers to the cumulative changes in an organism, organ, tissue, or cell leading to a decrease in functional capacity. This is one valid reason why age and aging are stigmatized as weakness, that is, physical weakness. When most young people think of the elderly fro example, they think of weakness and the associated degenerative aspects which the process brings along to human body and functionality. In

[5] - This material is written by *Donovan A. McFarlane, City College- Fort Lauderdale,* and *Bahaudin G. Mujtaba, Nova Southeastern University.*

humans, aging is associated with degenerative changes in the skin, bones, heart, blood vessels, lungs, nerves, and other organs and tissues. These degenerative changes increase the likelihood of death and diseases and thus it is valid to associate age and aging with certain diseases and functional weaknesses. In fact, there are diseases and functional imbalances in human beings and other creatures which are age-specific.

According to Hayflick (1994), biologists have proposed a variety of theories to explain aging, but most of them agree that this process is largely determined by genes. Aging is a very highly studied phenomenon and the branch of medicine that deals with the disorders associated with aging in humans is called Geriatrics. Gerontology on the other hand is the discipline which studies aging in all its scope. It can be called the "Philosophy of Aging" since it takes on numerous avenues and perspectives across cultures, academics, and other fields. The human species has long been fascinated or more concerned rather with the aging process which seems to eventually culminate with death.

The so-called anti-aging revolution has been long in its battle to conquer the "aging gene" in man. This battle is still ongoing and the results of delayed aging have only been successful in laboratories, and in non-human creatures. According to Hayflick (1994), scientists have learned how to double the lifespans of such laboratory organisms as roundworms and fruit flies through genetic manipulation, and mutant genes in mice have also been observed to have a comparable effect in postponing aging. However, there is still much research and knowledge to be obtained on aging in the human body as far as causes and "prevention" are concerned. The human body is complex, more so than any laboratory animal and the process of aging seems to be cumulative on both the mental-psychological and physical.

Aging is a process deeply embedded in human genetics, and as such takes place at the cellular level. According to Hayflick (1994), lifespans of cells in the human body are determined by strings of DNA (genetic material) called telomeres, which are located at the ends of the chromosomes. Each time a cell divides, the telomere becomes shorter; the senescence and death of the cell is triggered when the telomere is reduced to a certain critical length. Telomerase, an enzyme that can intervene in this process, is being closely studied in relation to cancer as well as aging (Answers.com™, 2005). Aging is a biological process, and thus phrases such as one's "biological clock ticking" do have validity. Man's life is a race against time and biology in essence; aging, the result of both simultaneously acting in unison.

Chronological and Mental Aging

Human beings age mentally as well as chronologically or physically. Mental aging reflects itself in our abilities to remember, understand, and perform mental functions and operations with increased or decreased dexterity. Mental aging is both a negative and positive process, as it can reflect itself in the decrease capacity of the brain or mind to perform regular mental functions such as memory tasks and logical operations. Old age mental diseases such as Alzheimer, Parkinson and others are dysfunctional processes closely associated with aging; they can be uniquely called aging disorders. The quest of an individual therefore, should be to age healthily in both mind and body. Another aspect to mental aging is intelligence quotient or component; one's mental age usually reflects increased acuity in mental functioning, abilities and operations regardless of their unequivocal physical or chronological age. For example, a twelve year old child with high social, psychological, and other aspects of intelligence would have a mental age which is far above that of an average twelve years old. In this case, mental aging has a positive side.

Chronological or physical age is our true age reflective of time and the degenerative physical breakdown of body and bodily organs, tissues, etc as a result of the aging process; that is, the medical or biological aging process which eventually expresses itself in the form of external wrinkles and postural imbalances or changes. It is a natural process that every living creature experiences overtime and can only be affected minimally given our knowledge of the aging process and the interaction of nature and nurture in effectuating this process.

Nature and Nurture in the Aging Process

Aging is affected by both natural biological and environmental factors. While people are still studying the biological processes and functions responsible for aging, environmental factors have been observed to affect aging as well. Accordingly, scientists have discovered that they can significantly delay aging in mice by providing them with very low-calorie diets (Hayflick, 1994). In addition recent studies of rhesus monkeys on low-calorie diets appear to be having the same results, and it is believed that these diets slow the aging process by lowering the rate at which tissue-damaging substances called free radicals are produced in the body (Answers.com™, 2005). With these successful studies scientist aim to develop antioxidant drugs that could slow the aging process in humans by protecting against free radicals. If this becomes an achievement however, the environmental factors which affect aging in humans will need forms of studies and control as well. Scientists need to study the pattern and rates of aging across different terrains, cultures and people in order to uniquely understand how significantly physical environmental factors, as well as social lifestyles affect the aging process.

Aging in a human being is a combination of environmental, natural, biological, and social factors interacting with each other to produce the effects and signs of his progress and transition through time. Age and aging shape the contexts in which we live our lives as we become more and more aware of our mortality approaching old age. Man fears aging because he fears mortality and age more than any other natural process typifies human mortality as an intelligent species. Therefore, the quest of man to arrest the aging process or eliminate its causes is a natural inclination towards perpetuating this life. The views one holds on aging will affect this inclination greatly, and thus a mark difference in the attitudes of individuals, nations and cultures regarding the phenomena of age and aging have greatly impacted the anti-aging revolution and the fields of geriatrics and gerontology. Gerontology is the study of the physiological and pathological phenomena associated with aging, while geriatrics is the medical study of the physiology and pathology of age. Geriatric medicine has much to do before we can even consider arresting the aging process. The biomedical knowledge required to modify the processes of aging that lead to age-associated pathologies confronted by geriatricians does not currently exist. They argue that until we better understand the aging processes and discover how to manipulate them, these intrinsic and currently immutable forces will continue to lead to increasing losses in physiological capacity and death even if age-associated diseases could be totally eliminated (Olshansky, Hayflick and Cranes, 2004; Hayflick, 1994; Medina, 1996; Gosden, 1996; Bailey, 2001; Bailey, Sims, Ebbesen, Mansell, Thomsen, and Moskilde, 1999; Wick, Jansen-Durr, Berger, Blasko, Grubeck-Loebenstein, 2000).

Though the anti-aging revolution has made progress, most of the progress has been relegated to lifestyle practices designed for healthy living rather than a direct elimination of the aging process. According to Olshanksy, Hayflick, and Carnes (2004), optimum lifestyles, including exercise and a balanced diet along with other proven methods for maintaining good health, contribute to increases in life expectancy by delaying or preventing the occurrence of age-related diseases. They further argue that there is no scientific evidence, however, to support the claim that these practices increase longevity by modifying the processes of aging. This is quite true, since scientist have yet to arrive at the direct causes of aging in humans, much less to provide an aging antidote to arrest the process.

Aging: Cultural and Religious Factors

Western cultures are more preoccupied than any other with age and the aging process. Old age has a decisively negative view in western societies where the elderly or being old is associated with weaknesses, diseases, waste, the "once a man twice a child philosophy," and other negative conceptions, views, and jargons. In western societies such as the United States, being old or being referred to as "old" is extremely abominable. Most persons would rather be called elderly than old. In some smaller traditional nations where the extended family is the norm and traditional practices have remained intact; nations such as Afghanistan, Turkey, Jamaica, and some other small Caribbean nations, being called "old" is not taken as disrespectful, but taken with reverence and pride, since it is considered a privileged blessing to live to see old age. In such smaller traditional nations with a more collectivist social culture, the old or elderly is an integral part of the society and the family and are regarded as wise, noble, virtuous, and right. In American society, this is uniquely the opposite and thus explains the attitudes of young people towards age and the elderly. In fact, Donovan McFarlane recently had a conversation with a nurse in her 50's after 35 years of practice in the field. She lamented on the attitude of young people towards age in America and seems to express a concern that the young generation, teenagers in particular seem to think of any one above 30 years of age as "old." This was quite a fascinating and interesting consideration given the trend in society to posit things and self towards the young and non-conforming. American and European societies are far too conscious of age distinction in shaping social attitudes, relationships and climates.

Eastern cultures have rigid lines between the young and old. However, the old are seen in a noble light and regarded with great reverence and respect. For example, in Chinese and Japanese, as well as Indian cultures, the old persons or elderly is the sage who is well-enlightened and knows the seasons, the past, present, and future. The old persons or elderly is treated as the head of the family; a grand matriarch or grand patriarch who never loses that post regardless of functional capacity or physical debilitation. This fact may stem from the phenomenon known as "ancestral homage or worship" that prevails in some eastern cultures. Regardless, the differences in attitudes towards age, aging, and the old are markedly different. Not all western cultures treat age, aging and the elderly with negative regards. The attitude towards age and aging will depend on a combination of factors, mainly on the particular culture and social make-up of that society, though it can be predicted that the more collectivist nations or cultures would have greater reverence and more positive views concerning age and aging.

Religion and religious beliefs and practices also have impacted the attitudes towards age and aging. A religion that holds old age in high esteem will influence a society to be more mindful of the elderly and less concerned with age as a distinctive factor separating people. Throughout the Bible and Quran for example, many of the leaders or patriarchs were aged people and this seems to have influenced a tradition of the elderly or the old being succinctly privileged in positions of religious leaderships or authorities on matters concerning life. For example, the papacy has been a great reflection of this, as well as the hierarchy of spiritual leadership. Age is seen from a religious point of view as part of God's plan for man in his current life; people grow old and die with the possibility of being reborn into a new light.

Old Age versus Young Age: The Age and Aging Hierarchy

The distinction between young and old is highly emphasized in all societies and cultures, especially through our social expressions, values and social practices and lifestyles. This distinction has resulted in what can uniquely be called age discrimination or an "age divide" which is more pronounced in American society than any other. The age divide represents a battle of viewpoints and attitudes between young and old which affects their interactions and the opportunities available to each in numerous settings and institutions. One area in which the age divide becomes very evident is the job market, and this usually reflects itself in the disparity of experiences between young and old when it comes to job requirements and pay. Decisively, age acts as a discriminating factor in the job market as well as in various institutional settings and social environments. For example, there are positions and ranks in various institutions and society which through tradition or law has age barrier requirements, a unique example of this is the presidency of the United States; another is the office of the pope. Other examples can be drawn from corporate American companies in which the CEOs or Board of Directors of companies seem to be from only within a specific age group. Age divide becomes an issue only when it deprives individuals of positive growth opportunities and advantages that would be open to them otherwise.

Age is normally divided according to lifespan, and as such, over a human being's lifespan he or she passes through different age stages: infancy, toddler, childhood, adolescence, young adult, adulthood, middle age and finally, old age, which culminates in death. Life span is defined as the observed age at death of an individual; maximum lifespan is the highest documented age at death for a species (Olshansky, Hayflick and Carnes, 2004). In most countries, including the United States, adulthood legally begins at the age of eighteen or nineteen, and old age is considered to begin at age sixty-five. (Note: This age category should not be confused with the definition of "older worker" which begins at the age of forty.) However, this view has been changing over the years, as countries like New Zealand seem to have a lower chronological base age for the declaration of adulthood. This is also typical of many African nations, as well as subcultures as influenced by their social, cultural and religious practices. The division of the aging stages of man has long been around and Shakespeare's "*As You Like It*" demonstrated it as follows:

All the world's a stage,
And all the men and women merely players,
They have their exits and entrances,
And one man in his time plays many parts,
His acts being seven ages.

According to Shakespeare, these are infancy, childhood, lover, soldier, adult, old age, and senility and death. Over the past the aging of man has been grouped according to decades and this seems to confirm the idea of "old age" beginning much earlier in the minds of those not in the decade divisions of age. Age division according to decade is shown in Table 32.

Table 32 – Aging Division for Older Workers
Quadragenarian: someone between 40 and 49 years of age
Quinquagenarian: someone between 50 and 59 years of age
Sexagenarian: someone between 60 and 69 years of age
Septuagenarian: someone between 70 and 79 years of age
Octogenarian: someone between 80 and 89 years of age
Nonagenarian: someone between 90 and 99 years of age
Centenarian: someone between 100 and 109 years of age
Supercentenarian: someone over 110 years of age

Aging is simply the process of getting older and all human beings must pass through this process. In modern societies, especially in American society there is considerable social pressure to hide signs of aging, especially among women. This has been one central factor fueling the anti-aging revolution and booming the market for anti-aging products. One of the consequences of the pressure to hide signs of aging has also been the shift in relationship patterns and dynamics among the aging and elderly, as most people within specific age groups tend to gravitate towards having younger partners, and even unhealthy social relationships. This often shows itself in the form of many older persons taking up with much younger ones, breaking a kind of age-relationship norm which society reacts to, and sometimes very harshly.

The aging process begins as early as birth and inevitably ends in death. Therefore, aging is a part of the growth and maturation processes of all creatures. As one grows and matures old age will naturally set in, and eventually death arrests the processes of growth and maturation. The concept of old age and aging spells the mortality of man, and this sets man racing against time to accomplish his goals and dreams. Old age and death have become synonymous in languages and cultures, and man understands that aging and old age in particular increase the probability of dying. Aging is a natural gravitation towards death, and as such slowing the process of aging should have the same result on death, slowing one's inevitable demise. See Figure 15.

Figure 15: The Aging Process

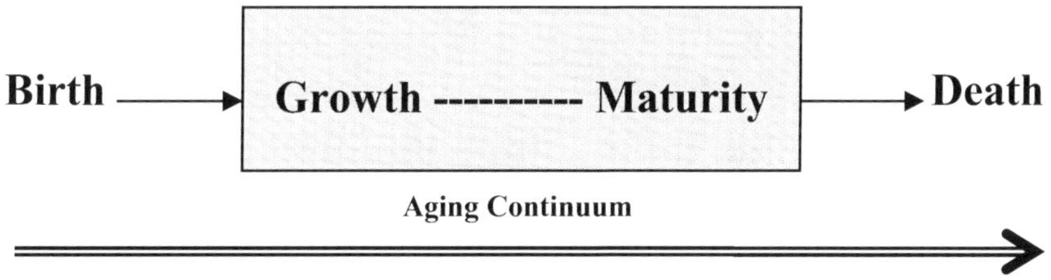

Age and Privileges

There is no doubt that age and privileges are closely tied together. This was illustrated in the earlier chapters with the discussion of "unearned advantages and privileges" that tend to come with the natural progression of aging at various times depending on the cultures' views regarding age. Sometimes these unearned privileges are provided for younger workers and at other times, they are given to older workers depending on the culture or sub-culture. In today's society there are many institutions and situations in which one's age will act as a barrier towards some form of social or other physical activities. For example, persons under the age of 21 years are deprived of the ability to purchase alcoholic beverages in some places, and are also prohibited from entering certain entertainment establishments such as adult entertainment centers and night clubs. On the other hand, there are also exclusive social clubs based on age group requirements. This includes clubs which are designed for the purpose of entertaining teenagers only or senior citizens clubs. Age has become an issue which reflects the gender divide in corporate America as described by McFarlane and Mujtaba (2005). According to these authors, the differences between the genders are fundamentally at the heart of the gender debate, since each gender possesses unique qualities and attributes serving as foundation for distinction. This also becomes quite true when it comes to the young and the old; the differences between young and old will naturally perpetuate any existing barriers of opportunities and privileges exclusive to either group.

Certain institutions in society have come to exemplify the privilege distinctions and barriers associated with age and aging. The most notable among these are political and religious institutions in which the old will naturally hold positions of authority and leadership above the young. There seems to be a tendency for presidents of the United States as well as senators to be decisively quinquagenarians or sexagenarians. In fact these particular age divisions based on decade factoring seem to be the most popular groups from which positions of authority and leadership naturally derive in the beginning in our institutional settings. This seems to be more of tradition than an age divide. However, it still results in discrimination since it deprives younger persons of the opportunities to hold such offices and posts based on age contingent factor. Whatever the case, the young and the old both have certain privileges and opportunities which naturally seem to derive from age rather than abilities and other factors.

Aging and Business: Age Distribution Effects

Within the field of marketing researchers have seen how age and age characteristics have been used as instruments for marketers in reaching and meeting consumer needs and wants. Business and economics have made great use of age by dividing consumers into various cohorts. The area of marketing known as marketing segmentation refers to a demographic segmenting type which focuses on age and other integrally related people characteristics.

Age classifications become central to businesses and marketing companies in attempting to capture the support of consumers. One of the most valuable business and marketing cohorts is that age group known as young adults because of their spending stemming from possession of an income and few other responsibilities demanding their income. Children and teenagers are also valuable cohorts and their abilities to influence the spending patterns of their parents make them even significant to marketers and economists. The young are the central target of marketers (Answers.com™, 2005). Furthermore, it is stated that there is a popular belief that the middle aged and the old are less likely to buy things and are traditionally viewed as being set in their buying habits and not nearly as open to marketing. Older people tend to be much wealthier and to save a much higher percentage of their income.

Global aging trends hold significance for marketers, businesses, economists and governmental planning agencies. Age distribution affects the availability and use of resources and provision of services. Increase in the number of elderly, for example, means that a society or business will have to devote more effort, resources and time in providing for a larger senior population. According to Shackman, Liu and Wang (2003), there have been small changes in age distribution between 1990 and 2000. Accordingly, the percent of population that is older increased slightly between 1990 and 2000 from 9% to almost 10% and this growth trend is expected to continue. Shackman, Liu and Wang (2003) believe that this increase was larger within more developed countries, from 17.7% to 19.4%. The percent of population that is older is almost three times as high in more developed countries (19.4%) as it is in less developed countries (7.7%).

There are numerous factors operating to effect the above changes in age distribution, and foremost among these factors is the HIV/AIDS epidemic, especially on the continent of Africa where in some areas there is no longer a typical population-age-pyramid as the young adults and parents have been decreased rapidly in numbers leaving children and older folks behind. McGeary (2001) supports this viewpoint by stating:

> AIDS in Africa bears little resemblance to the American epidemic, limited to specific high-risk groups and brought under control through intensive education, vigorous political action and expensive drug therapy. Here the disease has bred a Darwinian perversion. Society's fittest, not its frailest, are the ones who die — adults spirited away, leaving the old and the children behind.

This trend seems to be proliferating on the African continent as the HIV/AIDS epidemic becomes more serious. According to reports from UNAIDS, as of 2003 there were 3.2 million new infections, 2.3 million deaths and 26.6 million victims to the epidemic. These figures have had tremendous effects on age distribution across Africa, as there are now thousands of children without parents, and families now comprise grandparents and children in many regions. The effects on the age distribution of African population can be uniquely grasped from this grotesque description by Johanna McGeary (2001):

> As the HIV virus sweeps mercilessly through these lands — the fiercest trial Africa has yet endured — a few try to address the terrible depredation. The rest of society looks away. Flesh and muscle melt from the bones of the sick in packed hospital wards and lonely bush kraals. Corpses stack up in morgues until those on top crush the identity from the faces underneath. Raw earth mounds scar the landscape, grave after grave without name or number. Bereft children grieve for parents lost in their prime, for siblings scattered to the winds.

Unfortunately, life expectancy in most African nations currently stand at 47 years (UNAIDS), and without the epidemic around 67 years. According to Olshansky, Hayflick and Carnes (2004), life expectancy in humans is the average number of years of life remaining for people of a given age, assuming that everyone will experience, for the remainder of their lives, the risk of death based on a current life table. For newborns in the U.S. today, life expectancy is about 77 years. According to these authors, this high expectancy which the U.S and many other developed nations not being ravaged by epidemics experiences stems from the rapid declines in infant, child, maternal and late-life mortality during the 20th century that led to an unprecedented 30-year increase in human life expectancy at birth from the 47 years that it was in developed countries in 1900.

The Ideological Dichotomies of Aging: Theoretical Conceptions

There seems to be two extreme dichotomies when it comes to society's perspectives on age and aging; aging as progressive and aging as dysfunctional (See Figure 16).

Figure 16 – Progress and Dysfunctional Perspectives of Aging

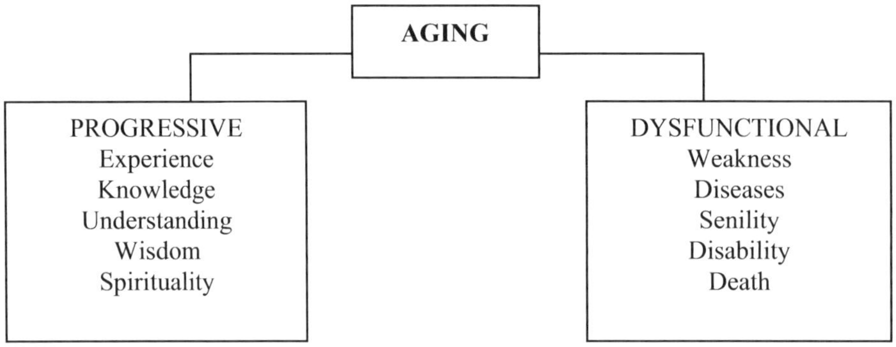

```
                        ┌─────────────────────┐
                        │       AGING         │
                        └─────────────────────┘
          ┌──────────────────────┐        ┌──────────────────────┐
          │     PROGRESSIVE      │        │     DYSFUNCTIONAL     │
          │      Experience      │        │       Weakness       │
          │      Knowledge       │        │       Diseases       │
          │     Understanding    │        │       Senility       │
          │        Wisdom        │        │      Disability      │
          │     Spirituality     │        │        Death         │
          └──────────────────────┘        └──────────────────────┘
```

The progressive view of aging can mostly be ascribed to eastern cultures and societies that are typically collectivist and highly traditional, while the dysfunctional view of aging is very reflective of western societies where youthfulness and non-conformist ideologies are more rampant.

The dysfunctional view of aging views aging with a stigma of negativity and thus age and aging, particularly old age, are equated with developmental and progressive weaknesses, decrease in mental and physical capacities, illnesses, diseases, lack of mobility, and all the "down-sides" of degeneration that occurs naturally in the aging process. These defects of aging and the aged are well-emphasized in American society where youthfulness is equivalent to fortune and beauty, especially where the entertainment industry weighs in heavily on the American mind. The dysfunctional view of aging mainly focuses on the idea of aging as it culminates in death as a degenerative physical and biological mental process affecting human species. The old then is regarded and treated by the young with a conscious awareness of death impending. The dysfunctional view of aging is highly operative in American society where the elderly is associated with nursing homes, social security, disability, age-specific diseases such as Alzheimer, and loneliness. The dysfunctional view of aging is logical despite its negativity. After all, aging is a degenerative process in which organs, tissues, limbs, and bodily and mental processes are affected adversely with increased age. The process seems to be varied however across cultures and individuals and this needs specific attention if scientists and those preoccupied with aging are to make any significant discoveries in the anti-aging revolution.

The progressive view of aging is a highly adaptive perspective for the human specie. With our inevitable mortality we must come to view aging as part of our natural transcendence. We must come to understand that aging eventually leads to death, and such a death is not the end of conscious spiritual development. This is a less popular view because it entails deep metaphysical and religious convictions which our scientific and technological societies have not fully grasped. Though the advent and ideology of life after death are part of most religious theologies, the idea has not become fully entrenched in our daily lives, and this causes us to have the fear we do of death and our mortality. Therefore, the dysfunctional view of aging prevails stemming from the fear of death which is synonymous with old age.

The progressive view of death is highly entrenched in traditional practices, thoughts, legends, cultures, and ideals. The old or aging is seen as the birth and possession of wisdom, wide and far-reaching knowledge, superior understanding, indispensable experiences, virtues and compassion; and in fact to grow old is a blessing since one could naturally die young. Many Eastern and Caribbean cultures have this progressive view of aging, and this explains the differences in treatment of old age and the elderly when it comes to reverence and respect from the younger generations within society. In Japan and China, for example, the elderly or old folks are treated with utter reverence and their opinions and experiences, knowledge and wisdom are highly prized and look upon as guidance throughout all areas of life. These two cultures are predicated on the idea of the "sage becoming" through old age and years of knowledge and experience developed through decades of life and learning. This ideology is typical of many Asian, Middle Eastern, African, and Caribbean cultures and relegated to many societies in which tradition and ceremonies prevail with a close tie to nature and the past. In the United States such practices have been replaced by the non-conforming ideas of young generations detached from the past; from the old and wise.

The dysfunctional and progressive views of aging represent more of an interaction than an opposition, since both are valid within their constructs and assumptions regarding the aging process. In aging we degenerate towards weakness and death, illnesses and diseases, and simultaneously grow in wisdom and understanding, experience and knowledge, spirituality and love. Therefore, the balance is an eclectic view of the aging process, its pros and its cons all relevant part of the transcending process of human conscious spiritual growth, yet demonstrative of limitations and time.

Creative Techniques for Managers and Older Workers

The August issue of Business Week (August 1, 2005) included a special report on the "*Creativity Economy.*" Business Week mentioned the "Top 20 Innovative Companies in the World" from a 2005 study conducted by the Boston Consulting Group (BCG). Design strategy (and customer-centric innovation) seems to be the next big things according to the article and "increasing top-line revenue through innovation has become essential to success in their industries" as cited by the 940 senior executives studied in the same BCG study. So, implementing innovative strategies and unleashing the unlimited power of an organization's human resources asset can be a powerful tool in resolving age-related challenges facing older workers in this new economy.

In order to tackle the "ugly faces" of stereotypes regarding older workers today's workforce along with their managers and organizational leaders can begin brainstorming on innovative strategies to have a productive and healthy work environment for all workers. Fred Koury, in his 2005 article entitled *"Creating a winning culture: How to become and stay innovative in a competitive marketplace,"* states that "the key to surviving in a competitive marketplace is innovation." Koury further states that there are many core principles of innovation that companies can benefit from in the twenty first century's work environment. The manager's challenge is to carefully balance the cost of innovation with its prospective gains. For innovation to occur, a rewarding organizational culture must be created. With the creation of a rewarding organizational culture, innovation can naturally occur from various avenues. Koury (2005) offers four core principles that will help organizations become and stay innovative in the twenty first century environment and they are:

- Effective leadership is key to innovation. It doesn't matter the size of a company; what matters is who is leading it. The right leadership is essential for the success of any company. Once the CEO has embraced innovation, it allows for the culture of the company to naturally fall into place.
- Encourage new ideas, even if they don't work out. Employees need to feel free to experiment. Don't punish failures, but rather celebrate the attempt at innovation. Encourage managers and employees to speak their minds. Too often, people feel they need to be politically correct or are afraid they will show up a manager. You need to know everything that is on their minds. The best ideas don't always come from the top.
- Calculate the risk vs. the investment. With risk comes reward. Some of the most successful companies today are the ones that allocate the most dollars and resources for research and development. It doesn't matter the size of the company, there needs to be a certain percentage of revenue, profit or other number you feel comfortable working off of reinvested back into the company for innovation purposes. If you don't have the dollars to do so, you probably haven't been innovative. With no investment made for innovation, innovation and profits will probably be lacking.
- Be patient. The farmer plants the seeds and waits patiently for the rain to fall. He is not in control of this element. We must do the same with innovation. Once we have done our best, our customers will determine if our calculated risk was in the right place (Koury, 2005).

Koury (2005) goes on to say that creativity and innovation are not easy. Managers have to invest the time and money to make it happen at all levels of their organization in order to establish an innovative culture. Then, managers and employees can start reaping the benefits of being part of an innovative culture where all employees, regardless of their age, are fairly rewarded for their work.

In another article, entitled *"Selling the vision: motivate your managers with more than just money,"* Fred Koury encouraged leaders and managers to recognize, realize and reward the true value of your senior workers and team members in the organization. Some of these senior workers are also managers and valuable formal or informal team leaders.

Koury (2005) explains that these senior employees are the organization's inner circle of advisers who help guide the company through many difficult decisions. To get the most out of these individuals, leaders must create a motivational work environment for them. Koury states that engaging senior employees and getting them to take an ownership role can be a difficult but a rewarding task. He explains that the initial steps are the easiest. Monetary rewards and compensation should be tied to the growth goals of the company, and you should also make sure these senior employees get the recognition they deserve. Give them the responsibility that comes with the authority of their positions and levels of expertise. If they are given appropriate levels of freedom to be independent thinkers without them having to worry about obtaining approval for each action, then these senior employees will take more of an ownership role, and, in turn, will empower and develop others around them.

So, as good coaches, give senior employees the flexibility to try new things, measure them by performance, not hours worked, and offer steady encouragement. The most important key to motivating senior workers is laying out the vision for the company and having them understand what their role in it is. They need to believe in that vision so they can help the team move the organization forward.

According to experts, the best way to sell employees on the vision is to involve them in its creation. It is a leader's responsibility and obligation tell employees what the final destination is and let them help in mapping out how to get there. Koury (2005) states that "As part of the vision-making team, each person will intimately know what their responsibilities are and what they committed to. Each one will want to uphold his or her portion of the plan so the team as a whole succeeds." Koury further states that leaders can be surprised at what happens when employees are truly involved. These senior employees might stretch the leader's vision of where the company can go. So, motivate employees, especially senior or older workers, by involving them to be part of the vision creation, implementation, and execution processes.

In the article, entitled *The Fuel of Business*, Robert Preziosi (2005) discusses eight ways to light the fires of creativity and innovation in an organization. Preziosi said "It is widely known that innovation is the fuel of American business. Innovation, of course, is built upon the creativity of individuals and groups within organizations." Furthermore, Preziosi added that innovation and creativity are important elements of success in process improvement and other change efforts within an organization. It is the responsibility of managers and organizational leader to find effective ways to spark the creative and innovative power within their employees. Preziosi offers the following eight ways to light the fires of creativity and innovation in one's organization. The following are the eight suggestions Preziosi, 2005):

1. Be receptive to your own ideas and those of others. Listening to all suggestions and avoid dismissing ideas that people come up.
2. Expose yourself to other people's creative products.
3. Avoid accepting your first "right" idea.
4. Take calculated risks. Stretch the limits of your willingness to take risks.

5. Look for new ways to combine ideas, approaches, products or services. Many great products have been the result of combining two or more things that no one had thought of before.
6. See yourself as successful with your creative endeavor.
7. Use part of your day stretching your creativity muscles. Some ways to enhance your creativity can include spending time with creative people and reading magazines that you don't normally read.
8. Remember that flexibility keeps the options developing. Avoid rigidity.

Robert Preziosi pointed out that "professionals and executives have the knowledge and skills to be creative and innovative." However, if that is not the case, then it is very possible to enhance their knowledge and/or skills through formal techniques while considering the eight suggestions mentioned above.

Spiritual Affirmations for Aging Healthfully and Harmoniously

The aging process is a very beautiful one and brings experiences and knowledge despite the associated degenerative aspects. A child yearns to grow and become an adult, a teenager yearns to become an adult for the freedom and experiences which adulthood brings. Aging is a process of growth, maturity and change which brings us closer to our human, individual, spiritual purposes, and destiny. One ages to become better individuals as one grows wiser and more beautiful in being. One must recognize aging as part of metaphysical spiritual growth and cherish every stage of the process. One must strive to age healthfully and harmoniously while going through this reality. The aging process must guide one's ways and values while striving to accomplish goals and living happily. Below are some metaphysical spiritual affirmations for growing healthfully and harmoniously:

*   I believe that to grow old is to grow wise and beautiful, fulfilling my destiny and the Creator's will.
*   I will age healthily and harmoniously, growing in love, wisdom, knowledge, and understanding.
*   I know that old age is a divine gift from the Creator, and he or she who grows to be old is blessed.
*   I acknowledge that aging is a natural process that attunes one to the flow and rhythm of life and nature.
*   I will age in happiness and prosperity, appreciating each and every day with joy.
*   I will grow beautiful with each day's passing and shine bright with each rising sun.
*   I value the belief that to age is to become love, truth and virtue.
*   I will age with strength, vigor and vitality, knowing only laughter and gladness.
*   I age not towards death, but towards eternal life and eternal youth.
*   I will age without sorrow and grow old without sickness.

Insightful spiritual affirmations can help one develop a positive and progressive view of aging. He or she will come to recognize aging as part of the Creator's plan for humanity, as a natural process which brings wisdom and understanding, and brings along the path towards our purpose and destiny. One should look forward to aging and aging beautifully and happily. Aging is a human reality, yet in good will and love, this is what the authors wish each man, woman, and living creature.

CHAPTER 13

CONCLUSIONS, QUESTIONS, AND CASES

Conclusions

*A*ge discrimination, in the preface and throughout the various chapters, has many causes, and one of them seems to be cultural conditioning based on stereotyping of older workers. The word stereotype comes from two Greek words: *stereo* meaning "solid," and *typos* meaning "a model." When applied to people, it symbolizes rigid, repetitive, and formalized behavior. Schneider (2004) states that "Stereotypes have been accused of being bad because they are created or at least supported by cultures that are prejudiced and discriminatory." When using stereotypes, people allow their cultures to do their thinking for them instead of using factual information to be their guide. Schneider (2004) asks the question of whether stereotypes regarding age and other such characteristics are cultural products. The answer is yes. Schneider (2004) states that, "cultures provide many "accurate generalizations and some really faulty ones as well." Stereotypes become bad, ugly, and ineffective when people use them to discriminate against a person or groups of individuals without considering the current facts or evidence. The word discrimination takes its root from the Latin word *discrimino*, which means "to divide or separate" into a division or category. While discrimination has it positive meanings, in most cases it is used to refer to making judgment about an individual's or people's behaviors solely based on their unique characteristics based on stereotypes or generalizations. Such is the case about age discrimination, which negatively impacts many "older workers" in the twenty first century's work environment.

Through personal observations and conscious thinking about employment practices, one can tell that it is not unusual to quickly find several headlines each week about employment discrimination cases through various genres and media outlets. There are many discrimination cases currently that are keeping lawyers, law firms, and the court system busy as they attempt to bring about fair employment practices. Gregory (2001) states that, "Discrimination against middle-aged and older workers has long been a common practice of American business firms. Nearly all middle-aged and older workers, at some time during their work careers, will suffer the consequences of an age-biased employment-related action." Gregory (2001) continues to state that while the law prohibits age discrimination in the American workplace, workers over the age of 40 are "nevertheless subjected to adverse employment decisions motivated by false, stereotypical notions concerning the physical and mental abilities of older workers." As such, older workers in the American workplace are often encouraged into premature retirements, denied developmental opportunities that can lead to promotions, denied deserved transfers or job promotions, terminated for causes that have little to nothing with their performance, and are excluded from long-term decision-making due to biases and assumptions. Gregory (2001) pointed out that "I can still state, without fear of contradiction, that age discrimination continues to be a common practice in the American business firms."

Age discrimination in employment, therefore, is a multi-faceted subject matter that emerges as a most important challenge to the modern-day global executive, manager, and entrepreneur. Stereotyping and perceptions, "Machiavellian" mind-sets, clashing societal norms, cultural conditioning, and conflicts in legal systems present the international business person with a major test; that is, how to attract, retain, and develop an increasingly aging as well as diverse workforce in a legal, ethical, and socially responsible manner that maximizes the value of not only the organization but also all of its stakeholders.

This book has attempted to address certain aspects of age discrimination in employment in a comparative academic approach, focusing on five countries, that the authors hope will be enlightening intellectually and also efficacious in a realistic business sense. Accordingly, the authors commenced their work with a discussion of the difficult areas of stereotyping and cultural conditioning regarding age discrimination, of course, but also the related and even more problematic area of appearance discrimination. The growing global nature of the increasingly older and more diverse workforce will mean that companies and organizations should intensify diversity and sensitivity training efforts in order to secure employees and also to ensure they are treated with dignity and respect.

The legal "world" in which the global manager exists surely is a perplexing one, as some legal systems, such as the United States, have an extensive corpus of anti-discrimination law, including age discrimination; yet many countries, surprisingly, do not yet have any explicit legal norms or enforceable legal precepts regarding age discrimination in employment. Thus, the global business person who decides to do business in the United States is well-advised to be keenly aware of all the U.S. laws that prohibit and punish discrimination in employment, including age discrimination, of course. Yet, the U.S. business person doing business in a foreign country should not feel secure legally even if the host country lacks anti-discrimination law concerning age or otherwise, as there exists the distinct possibility that the law of the business person's home country, that is, the United States, will have extraterritorial effect. The authors consequently have attempted to delineate the key aspects of U.S. anti-discrimination law, together with a discussion of the extra-territorial application of the law. The authors also pointed out the absence of such age anti-discrimination law generally and in the countries examined, aside from the U.S., of course, although the European Community now is making some strides to further develop its body of anti-discrimination law by addressing age. Thus, ascertaining the legal norms regarding age and the workforce is an important task for the business executive, manager, and entrepreneur; however, determining the law, or the absence thereof, is just the first step.

The prudent business person also must address the moral nature of the subject matter of age discrimination in employment. The serious problem that immediately confronts such a moral examination, as the authors have underscored, is the doctrine of ethical relativism, which treats morality as societal-based, and thus which may allow certain types of discrimination if such practices are the prevailing moral norms of a particular society. The authors presented the research results secured by a professional colleague of the authors which displayed clearly the differing value perceptions in an age and generational study of U.S. and Japanese participants. Nonetheless, despite the varying values and moral norms, the authors have sought to supersede such "relativistic" thinking by emphasizing the intrinsic dignity and worth of human beings that demands that people be treated with fairness and respect, regardless of an absence of laws or the presence of any countervailing societal-based moral norms. Similarly, the authors developed the "ethics" of the Italian political scientist and philosopher, Niccolo Machiavelli, in an effort to warn the readers of "Machiavellian" practices in business generally and specifically regarding the disparate treatment of employees. Treating employees in a dignified and equable manner, the authors underscored, is not only the moral and socially responsible thing to do, but the smart thing too in an egoistic and strategic business sense.

It is a fact that there are many firms that are in search of wisdom, more specifically, the type of wisdom that comes with age and experience which make companies and organizations successful. It is projected that about 43% of the civilian labor force will be eligible for retirement within the next ten years. Therefore, there will be a shortage of talented and skilled professionals that accompany top leadership. So, companies will have to implement effective strategies for attracting, hiring, developing, and retaining an experienced workforce. In order to accentuate the practical managerial aspect of the book, the authors presented extensive useful material on accommodating workers, enhancing their skills, recruiting and retaining older workers, as well as motivating and satisfying employees. In the twenty-first century work environment, the social responsibility obligation of managers and corporations goes beyond ensuring that people are not discriminated against in the job application process, hiring, discharge, promotion, as well as training opportunities. Social responsibility obligations and reasonable accommodations are about providing resources, if necessary, and training all employees on how to appropriately treat and interact with colleagues of all ages and capabilities. An organization that creates an inclusive environment for individuals of all ages, genders, races, body sizes, disabilities, and ethnicities will benefit in many ways from having diverse employees and diverse customers. There are many excellent practices in attracting and hiring a diverse population of older workers, and the process can start with the elimination of behaviors stemming from one of the most common barriers which are traditional biases and stereotypes toward older workers. The authors also provided several actual business examples from firms such as Wal-Mart, Target, Publix Super Markets, and McDonalds, as well as discussion thereof, to illustrate the benefits of such proactive efforts. The authors, moreover, in an attempt to afford the reader a comprehensive examination, discussed the topic of aging from biological, psychological, and spiritual perspectives.

A very interesting, thought-provoking, and indeed provocative component of the book was the presentation and discussion of the research results obtained by the authors from their four country-based survey of employees in Afghanistan, Turkey, Jamaica, and the United States. The most prominent research result was the response of the U.S. respondents regarding age discrimination, to wit, the prevalence of such discrimination in the workplace, and this occurrence despite the presence of an extensive body of anti-age discrimination law as well as prevailing societal and personal norms condemning such discrimination as immoral. Based on the comments from the U.S. respondents, the authors concluded that one reason for such illegal and immoral discrimination against older workers may be a perception that older workers lack the necessary technological knowledge and skills and will not readily adapt, change, and learn. Thus, in addition to promulgating more laws, emphasizing the universal moral norm of dignity and respect, and providing workers with diversity and sensitivity training, an employer is well advised to increase the technological education and training of its employees, especially older ones, and the workers, most particularly the older workers, are strongly counseled to take advantage of any knowledge and skill building education and training, above all in the technological field. Applied knowledge truly is power, for the older worker, and for all of us.

In 2001, Gregory wrote that "isolated instance of enlightened thinking on the subject of age discrimination might very well be a harbinger of fairer days for older workers in the future. The hope is that "America will be an even better country once age discrimination in the workplace is eliminated" (Gregory, 2001). We also hope that the elimination of age discrimination in the workplace comes faster; and, of course, managers can be a critical factor in this process by doing their part to become aware of such biases and not letting inaccurate stereotypes and myths about older workers negatively impact their hiring practices. Eliminating biased thinking and stereotypical practices can best be achieved through the acquisition and application of factual knowledge as well as through conscious decision-making habits that are based on facts, instead of preconceived assumptions.

Besides the application of factual knowledge, managers and leaders should take the time to think about their lives, their attitudes toward others and, most importantly, to determine how they want to live their lives, and how they want to be remembered by their family members, friends, and colleagues. In other words, take the time to determine your life's purpose which is really the secret to the "fountain of youth," and that can be the beginning of your journey to living purposefully. According to Sophia Loren, the actress, "There is a fountain of youth: it is your mind, your talents, the creativity you bring to your life and the lives of the people you love. When you learn to tap this source, you will have truly defeated age."

Stay "Forever Young" – by Rod Stewart

Written by Kevin Stuart, James Savigar, James Cregan, Rod Stewart, and Bob Dylan.

May the Good Lord be with ya down every road you roam
And may sunshine and happiness surround you when you're far from home
And may you grow to be proud, dignified, and true
And do unto others as you would have done to you

Be courageous and be brave
And in my heart you'll always stay
Forever young (forever young)
Forever young (forever young)

May good fortune be with you, may your guiding light be strong
Build a stairway to heaven with a prince or vagabond

And may you never love in vain
And in my heart you will remain
Forever young (forever young)
Forever young (forever young)

For ever young
For ever young
Yeah!

And when you fin'lly fly away I'll be hopin' that I served ya well
For all the wisdom of a lifetime no one can ever tell

But whatever road ya choose
I'm right behind you, win or lose
Forever young (forever young)
Forever young (forever young)

For ever young
For ever young
For! For! Ever young
For ever young!

Questions for Discussion

Group One:
1. What is discrimination? Discuss its definition and practical examples of what you have seen in various cultures.
2. What is age discrimination?
3. Discuss the legal forms of discrimination both in employment practices as well as in the society in general?
4. What is culture and how can it drive one's behavior?
5. Is age discrimination culturally based? Discuss and provide examples.

Group Two:
6. Is there age discrimination in employment practices today in the United States or other countries throughout the World? Explain and mention specific examples of overcoming such forms of discrimination.
7. In what ways are cultures "the collective programming of the mind that distinguish one human group from another" as stated by Gert Hofstede?
8. How are cultures conditioning people when it comes to "time orientations"?
9. How are cultures conditioning people when it comes to "age discrimination"?
10. Is there a tendency to view "older workers" differently in individualistic cultures versus collectivitistic societies? Discuss.

Group Three:
11. What are some forms of discrimination that workers experience today?
12. Is there are relationship between culture and age discrimination?
13. What is the difference between monochronic and polychronic cultures?
14. How is unearned privilege related to aging?
15. Is there developing a global culture that condemns age discrimination? Discuss.

Group Four:
16. Despite the fact that the United States of America has specific laws and policies about age discrimination, many respondents report that they periodically see age discrimination in corporate America. Does this mean that people are not paying attention to the laws and policies of circumventing laws and policies? What is the cause of such discrimination? Discuss your thoughts and facts.
17. Afghanistan and Turkey are countries where the least amount of age discrimination is being reported toward older workers, even though employers don't do much diversity training or education. What are some of the reasons for such differences when compared to the United States?
18. Despite the fact that USA respondents report that they personally in their society regard age discrimination as morally wrong, nonetheless they report material evidence of age discrimination. Why?

19. Is there age discrimination in Japan? Why or why not? Discuss.
20. How are the values of people in Japan different from the values of Americans? How are the values of Japanese different or similar to people in Jamaica, Turkey, and Afghanistan?

Group Five:

21. How would a "machiavellian" manager deal with the situation of older workers in the workforce? Discuss and provide examples from your society and others if appropriate.
22. Why should American firms be concerned with the retention of their older workers?
23. Discuss the trends toward aging and retirement impact of "baby boomers" in the United States.
24. Why and how should global organizations pay attention to their older workers?
25. What is the benefit of recruiting, developing, and retaining older workers in large multinational organizations?

Case 1: Age Discrimination – Young Employees

Today, it is no longer older workers who are complaining about discrimination based on their age. In this tepid economy, some workers in their 20s and 30s contend that their age is being unfairly used against them; and consequently, new legal developments mean more reverse age discrimination claims may soon be ending up in court.

Some of these reverse age discrimination complaints can be attributed to the "jobless recovery." As jobs dwindle, younger employees now are competing against older hires for work. The unemployment rate for workers age 25 to 34 was 6.3% in September of 2003, eclipsing the 3.9% rate for employees 55 and older, according to the Department of Labor.

This age discrimination issue now is getting much more attention due to a case before the U.S. Supreme Court. The case, brought by employees against a division of General Dynamics Land Systems, will determine whether workers can sue when special pay or benefit packages are offered only to older employees. While the workers suing were ages 40 to 49, the case nonetheless could lead to protections for employees who are far younger. If the Supreme Court rules in favor of the workers, other similar claims from employees who are younger than 40 could follow. These legal claims, moreover, could pressure political leaders to expand the key federal law – the 1967 federal Age Discrimination in Employment Act – that protects worker ages 40 and older from job discrimination. And if the states become more willing to accept discrimination claims by younger workers, Congress may expand the scope of the federal law.

In the case before the Court, before 1997, workers at the General Dynamics division could retire with full health benefits if they had 30 years of service. Yet, under a new union agreement, the company had to provide those benefits only if the retirees were at least 50 years old on July 1, 1997. About 200 workers ages 40 to 49 as of the July 1 date sued for age discrimination. The 6th Circuit U.S. Court of Appeals agreed with the employees, and the Supreme Court is expected to hear the case in late 2003.

In the past, older workers have always been the focus of age discrimination lawsuits, but this case represents a contrary approach. Business groups, including the U.S. Chamber of Commerce, as well as some employment lawyers, fear that this new reverse age discrimination will threaten the long-accepted corporate practice of offering early retirement and special severance packages to employees based on age.

The case clearly could pave the way for more lawsuits from people in their 20s and 30s who may contend that they have been discriminated against in employment because of their age.

There are several key factors that are now making reverse age discrimination a legal issue. First is the current weak economy. Younger workers were more adversely affected by the 2001 recession and the slow recovery. Second, delayed retirements have younger workers feeling stuck. That is, they are experiencing career stalemate as graying "baby-boomers" appear reluctant to retire. Lastly, there is a feeling by some younger workers that they are viewed by some as slackers who tend to be less loyal to the company than older workers. Of course, some studies do show that younger workers are more likely to "job hop" and often tend to put family as a top priority. Employers fear that younger workers will leave more readily, and that the employer will be burdened with the costs of hiring other workers to replace them as well as retraining costs.

It is important to note hat although the federal law offers legal protection only to workers 40 and older, a number of states, including Alaska, Florida, Maine, Maryland, and Mississippi, have their own employment discrimination laws that specify no age limits. Other states have a cut-off of 18. Moreover, the NJ Supreme Court ruled in 1999 that an employee could sue under state law for age discrimination even though the employee was only 25.

Source: USA Today. October 8, 2003.

Questions:
Should the protections under federal age discrimination law be broadened to encompass young employees? Why or why not? What is the moral course of action pursuant to Utilitarian ethics? Discuss.

Case 2: Eminent Domain and the Elderly – U.S. Supreme Court (2005)

A divided U.S. Supreme Court, in a significant property rights decision, ruled 5-4 in June of 2005 that local governments can take private property by the Constitutional power of eminent domain and turn the property over to private developers for economic development, thereby increasing the tax base and/or creating jobs.

The case considerably expanded the scope of the Fifth Amendment, which grants government the power through eminent domain to seize property for "public use." The decision, though predicated on a Connecticut municipal seizure, has nationwide implications. Specifically, the Fifth Amendment states that private property shall not be taken for *public use* without just compensation.

The case is significant because historically used the power of eminent domain for projects that were clearly "public," such as roads, schools, and airports. All state constitutions also have a "public use" requirement for eminent domain. The public use requirement had been thought to restrict eminent domain to the government taking private property only to create things directly owned or primarily used by the general public, such as bridges, parks, and public buildings. Presently, however, many state and local governments have been using the eminent domain power to take property that was "blighted" or in a blighted area that local government wanted to redevelop. The decision is especially important for areas in which there is little vacant land and where local governments are seeking to redevelop urban areas.

In the specific case, Kelo v. City of New London, Conn., Susette Kelo and several other homeowners in a working class, but not blighted, neighborhood of New London, decided to fight eviction from their homes, filed suit after city officials announced plans to raze their homes for a river front hotel, condominiums, health club, and offices, as well as a pedestrian riverwalk, to be developed by a private entity, called the New London Development Corporation. City officials contended that the private developer's plans served a public purpose by increasing economic development, and that the economic growth outweighed the homeowners' private property rights, even though the area to be condemned was not a slum.

Between 1998 and 2002, according to the Institute for Justice in Washington, D.C., which argued the case on behalf of the property owners, there were more than 10,000 instances of government using or threatening to use the power of eminent domain, called the "takings clause," to transfer property from one private owner to another. The Court's decision surely lifts a "cloud" that was hanging over those private-public development efforts. As a matter of fact, one attorney for the Institute of Justice declared that the decision was an "open invitation" for local government and private developers to use the eminent domain power.

Justice John Paul Stevens, writing for the Court's majority, said promoting economic develop is a traditional and long-accepted function of government, and also that local officials know best in deciding whether a particular development will benefit the community. He said, in addition, that promoting economic growth is at times achieved more efficiently by the private sector than the public sector. His opinion underscored the benefits to the community of the city's "carefully formulated" and detailed development plan, including the expectation of new jobs and increased tax revenue. The decision thus clearly reinforces local government's broad power to define "public" purpose. Now, the word "public" certainly does not modify the government's eminent domain power as it once did.

Justice Sandra Day O'Connor, in a written dissent, stated that the decision gives "disproportionate influence and power" to the wealthy. She stated: "Under the banner of economic development, all private property is now vulnerable to being taken and transferred to another private so long as it might be upgraded. She also stated: "Nothing is to prevent the state from replacing any Motel 6 with a Ritz-Carlton, any home with a shopping mall, or any farm with a factory. Furthermore, she said that it would be "likely" that the beneficiaries of the decision will be people with "disproportionate influence and power in the political process, including large corporations and development firms. Justice Antonin Scalia, during oral arguments, stated in essence that the city of New London's claim was that "you can take from A and give to B if B pays more taxes." Justice Clarence Thomas, also dissenting, stated that a court should not defer to what the majority considered to be the "considered judgment" of the city regarding what constitutes seizing property for public use. Moreover, he stated that such a decision by a local government might be a "self-interested" one. Furthermore, he stated that a "vague promise" of new jobs and enhanced tax revenues is insufficient to qualify as a public purpose.

The Court emphasized that the states, either judges or legislatures, can provide as much protection to property owners as they choose, and thus put tighter restrictions on politicians who seek to transfer private property from one owner to another. For example, the Michigan Supreme Court recently decided that economic development is not a valid reason to take property from owners who do not want to sell.

The NAACP, AARP, and the late Martin Luther King's Southern Christian Leadership Conference filed a supporting brief on behalf of the homeowners, stating in part that eminent domain often has been used against politically weak communities with high concentrations of minorities and the elderly.

Another problem is to ascertain what "just compensation" is pursuant to eminent domain. Just compensation may be quite different from the standard formulation of "fair market value," considering the sentimental value many people attach to their homes. Also, there is a fear that developers will not "low-ball" their bids to property owners, knowing that they can freely threaten to get government to invoke the eminent domain power. The possibility of condemnation by means of eminent domain certainly could motivate "holdout" owners to sell.

One point is clear, and that is that the decision now will further embolden local governments and private developers to take property for economic development.

Sources:
Hiaasen, Scott, and Viglucci, Andres, "U.S. Supreme Court: Ruling on land is vital locally,"
      Herald, June 24, 2005, pp. 1B,10B; O'Boyle, Shannon, Perez, Luis, and Wallman,
      Britany, "Court extends property seizures," *Sun Sentinel*, June 24, 2005, pp. 1A, 15
      A; Will, George, "Profit can rule the day," *Sun Sentinel*, June 26, 2005, p. 5H;

Bravin, Jess, "Court Upholds Eminent Domain," *Wall Street Journal*, June 24, 2005, pp. A3, A10; Review and Outlook, *Wall Street Journal*, June 24, 2005, p. A12.

Questions:
1. Is the Court's decision moral on Utilitarian ethical grounds? Why or why not?
2. Is the Court's decision moral on Kantian ethical grounds? Why or why not?
3. Do you agree with the U.S. Supreme Court or the Michigan Supreme Court regarding economic development by a private developer as a rationale for a "taking" of private property? Why or why not?
4. Do you agree with Justice Stevens in that, in essence, local government "knows best" when it comes to local development? Why or why not?
5. Do you agree with the NAACP and others that minorities and the elderly will be groups disproportionately harmed by the decision? Why or why not?

Case 3: Age Discrimination – U.S. Supreme Court (2005)

In March of 2005, the U.S. Supreme Court enunciated a major decision regarding age discrimination in employment in the case of *Smith v. City of Jackson.* The decision significantly expands the protection afforded older workers pursuant to the Age Discrimination and Employment Act (ADEA). The decision allows protected workers, over the age of 40, institute age discrimination lawsuits even evidence is lacking that their employers never purposefully intended to discriminate against the workers on the basis of age.

The decision substantially lessens the legal burden for the approximately 75 million employees covered by the statute by allowing aggrieved employees to contend in court that a presumably neutral employment practice nonetheless had an adverse or disparate or disproportionately harmful impact on them.

However, the Court allowed the employer to defend such an age discrimination case, by interposing that the employer had a legitimate, reasonable, and job-related reason for the employment policy.

The case was brought by older police officers in Jackson, Mississippi, who argued that a pay-for-performance plan instituted by the city granted substantially larger raises to employees with five or fewer years of tenure, which the officers contended favored their younger colleagues. The lower courts had dismissed the lawsuit, ruling that these types of claims were barred by the statute. The U.S. Supreme Court, however, in a 5-3 decision, ruled that the officers were entitled to pursue the lawsuit against the city.

Justice John Paul Stevens, writing for the majority, stated that the Age Discrimination in Employment Act of 1967 was meant to allow the same type of "disparate impact" legal challenges for older workers that minorities and women can assert pursuant to the Civil Rights Act. Yet Justice Stevens also noted in the decision that the same law does allow employers the legal right to at times treat older workers differently. It is important to note that pursuant to the Civil Rights Act, employers can successfully defend a disparate impact case only by showing the "business necessity" for a neutral but harmful employment policy, which is a much more difficult test to meet than the "reasonable" explanation standard of the ADEA.

Justice Sandra Day O'Connor, writing for the minority, disagreed, stating that the age discrimination statute bars such impact claims. She also noted that Congress never intended that such lawsuits should occur because employers should have the flexibility to make business decisions that might unintentionally harm older workers. She also stated that there is a "correlation" between a person's age and his or her ability to perform a job. She also said that it is to be "expected" that physical ability declines with age, and in some cases, she said, mental capacity too.

The Court's decision emerges as a significant victory for older workers who now do not have to have direct or "smoking gun" evidence of intentional age discrimination in order to file a lawsuit, merely evidence of disproportionate harmful impact stemming from a neutral age employment policy.

Employers, of course, now must be much more conscious of the consequences of their employment policies on older workers, particularly regarding the criteria used to determine hiring and termination, especially layoffs, as well as pay scales and retirement plan changes. Employers also must be prepared to provide and explain the "reasonable" factors other than age that would justify the employment policy causing the disparate harmful impact on older protected workers.

Sources:
Herald, March 31, 2005, pp. 1C, 4C; *Sun-Sentinel,* March 31, 2005, pp. 1A, 6A; *Wall Street Journal*, March 31, 2005, pp. B1, B3.

Questions:
1. Is the Supreme Court's decision a moral one pursuant to Utilitarian and Kantian ethics? Discuss.
2. What proactive measures can an ethically egoistic company take in order to avoid age discrimination lawsuits? Discuss.
3. What would be an example of a neutral employment policy that would have a disparate or adverse impact on age protected workers? Why?
4. What would be an example of a legitimate and reasonable business justification that the employer could arguably assert to defend a neutral employment policy that adversely affects older workers? Why?

REFERENCES & BIBLIOGRAPHY

Adams, S. M. (1999). Settling cross-cultural disagreements begins with "where" not "how." *Academy of management executive, vol.13*.

Adamec, Ludwig. (2003). *Historical Dictionary of Afghanistan*. Maryland: Rowman & Littlefield.

Administration on Aging (2001). Department of Health and Human Services. [Online]. Retrieved November 13, 2003 from: http://www.aoa.dhhs.gov/

Advantages & Opportunities in Hiring Disabled Workers. (June, 2003). *HR Focus*. Institute of Management and Administration.

Age Discrimination in Employment Act, 2005. Thompson West. Sections 621-634.

Aging with Technology . . .A Way to Stay Independent. *TechConnect*. Retrieved February 3, 2004, from http://www.iltech.org/agingtechnote.htm

Aging. Retrieved July 23, 2005, from http://www.answers.com/topic/ageing

Ajzen, I. (1988). *Attitudes, personality and behavior*. Chicago, IL: The Dorsey Press.

Ahmed, M. M., Chung, K. Y., & Eichenseher, J. W. (2003, March). Business students' perception of ethics and moral judgment: A cross-cultural study. *Journal of Business Ethics*, 43(1/2), 89.

Ahmed, S. A., and Rojas, J. (1998). *A comparative study of job values of North and South American business students*. Unpublished manuscript. Downloaded from the web on November 1, 2002, from: http://www.sbaer.uca.edu/Research/1998/98sri230.txt.

Akiba, D., and Klub, W. (1999). The different and the same: Reexamining east and west in a cross-cultural analysis of values. *Journal of Social Behavior and Personality*, 27-5, 67-473.

Allen, N. J. & Meyer J. P. (1996). Affective, continuance, and normative commitment to the organization: An examination of construct validity. *Journal of Vocational Behavior, 49,* 252-276.

Allport, G. W. (1935). Attitudes. In C. Murchinson (Ed.), *Handbook of Social Psychology*. Worchester, MA: Clark University Press.

Allport, G. W. (1954). *The nature of prejudice*. Garden City, NY: Doubleday.

Allport, G. W. (1955). *Becoming: Basic considerations for a psychology of personality* (pp. 1-35). New Haven: Yale University Press.

Ang, SW. (2000). The power of money: a cross-cultural analysis of business-related beliefs. *Journal of World Business,* 35 (1), 42. Retrieved March 1, 2005, from the EBSCO Host database.

Anonymous (2005). Diversity at McDonald's: A way of life. *Nation's Restaurants News*, 92, 3.

Arnold, H. J. & Feldman, D. C. (1982). A multivariate analysis of the determinants of job turnover. *Journal of Applied Psychology, 67,* 350-360.

ALPA v. TACA, 748 F.2d 965, 971-72 (5th Cir. 1984), cert. denied, 417 U.S. 1100 (1985).

American Association of Retired People. Retrieved February 12, 2004, from http://www.aarp.org

American Banana Company v. United Fruit Company, 213 U.S. 349 (1909).

Anderson, C., Glassman, M., & Pinelli, T. (1997). A comparison of communication practices among Indian and US scientists and engineers. Working paper, Old Dominion Univeristy.

ASA American Society on Aging Online. Retrieved February 2, 2004, from http://www.asaging.org/

Avila, A. C.; Edward, A.; Fitzpatrick, T; Williams, C.; and Wohl, J. (2004). *Wal-Mart's Twenty First Century Management Practices.* Graduate team research project presented on March 13th at the Huizenga School of Nova Southeastern University.

Ayguen, A. K., and Imamoglu, E. O. (2002). Value domains of Turkish adults and university students. *Journal of Social Psychology*, 142(3), 333-351.

Badaracco, Jr., Joseph L. Defining Moments: When Managers Must Choose Between Right and Right. Boston, Massachusetts: *Harvard Business School Press*, 1997.

Bailey, A.J. (2001). Molecular mechanisms of ageing in connective tissues. *Mech Ageing Dev.* 122:735-755

Bailey A.J, Sims, T.J, Ebbesen, E.N., Mansell, J.P., Thomsen, J.S., Moskilde, L. (1999). *Age-related changes in the biochemical and biomechanical properties of human cancellous bone collagen: Relationship to bone strength.* Calcif Tis Res.;65:203-210.

Barnett, John H; Weathersby, Rita; Aram, John. (Winter-Spring 1995). American Cultural Values: Shedding Cowboys Ways for Global Thinking. *Business Forum. Vol. 20*, (n1-2), 9. Retrieved Feb. 8, 2005 from ProQuest database.

Bay v. Times Mirror Magazines, Inc., 936 F.2d 112 (2nd Cir. 1991).

Beard, Marty. "Web's less than senior friendly." *New Media.* Retrieved February 5, 2004, from http://www.medialifemagazine.com/news2002/apr02 /apr15/4_thurs/news5thursday.html

Beauchamp, Tom L. Philosophical Ethics. New York: McGraw-Hill Book Company, 1982.

Becker, K, PhD. (2000). *Culture and International Business.* Binghamton: International Business Press.

Becker, T. E. (1992). Foci and bases of commitment: Are they distinctions worth making? *Academy of Management Journal, 35,* 284-297.

Bennett-Alexander, D. (1998). Employment Law for Business, 2nd ed. Blacklick, OH: Irwin/McGraw-Hill. As cited in Regulation of Discrimination in Employment, p. 326.

Bernbach, M. J., (1996). *Job Discrimination: How to Fight, How to Win.* Crown Trade Paperbacks / New York.

Bhuian, S. N., Al-Shammari, E. S., & Jefri, O. A. (1996). An extension and evaluation of job characteristics, organizational commitment and job satisfaction in an expatriate, guest worker, sales setting. *International Journal of Commerce and Management, 57,* 57-80.

Biesada, A. (2004). Wal-Mart Stores, Inc. Hoover's On-Line. Retrieved January 18, 2004 from http://www.hoovers.com/wal-mart/--ID_11600--/free-co-factsheet.html.

Black, S., Morrison, A. & Gregersen, H. (1999). *Global Explorers.* New York & London: Routledge . Pages 6-8

Bloom, D. E., Mahal, A., King, D., Henry-Lee, A. & Castillo, P. Globalization, liberalization and sustainable human development: Progress and challenges in Jamaica. UNCTAD/ UNDP Kingston, February 21, 2001.

Bluedorn, A.C. (1982). A unified model of turnover from organizations. *Human Relations, 35,* 135-153.

Bluedorn, A.C. (1982). The theories of turnover: Causes, effects, and meaning. *Research in the Sociology of Organizations, 1,* 75-128.

Bond, M. H. (1994). Finding universal dimensions of individual variation in multicultural studies of values: The Rokeach and Chinese value surveys. In Bill Apuka (Ed). 1994. *New research on moral development: Moral development a compendium,* Vol 5. (pp. 385-391). New York, NY: Garland Publishing, Inc.

Bond, M. H. (1996). Chinese values. In Michael Bond (Ed) (1996). *The handbook of Chinese psychology* (pp. 208-226). New York, NY: Oxford University Press.

Bonner, B. (2004, Jan 4). Inner Grove Heights;Minn., Wal-Mart to open despite intense local opposition. *Knight Ridder Tribune Business News.* Retrieved April 8, 2004 from http://www.proquest.umi.com.novacat.nova.edu/

Bravin, J. (March 31, 2005). Court Expands Age Bias Claims for Work Force, *Wall Street Journal*, pp. B1, B3.

Brinton, Crane (1990). *A History of Western Morals.* New York: Paragon House.

Bronowski, J. and Mazlish, Bruce (1962). *The Western Intellectual Tradition.* New York: Harper and Row.

Brunetto, Y., & Wharton, R. (2002). Using social identity theory to explain the job satisfaction of public sector employees. *International Journal of Public Sector Management, 15,* 534-552.

Bucher, Richard D. (2000). *Diversity consciousness: opening our minds to people, cultures and opportunities.* Upper Saddle River, NJ: Prentice-Hall.

Bureau of Labor Statistics, 2002. *Occupational Outlook Handbook.* 2002-2003 edition. Washington DC: U.S. Department of Labor.

Business Wire. New York. (Feb 3, 2005). *ACLJ Encouraged by President Bush's Remarks on Values Issues in State of Union Address.* 1. Retrieved Feb. 8, 2005 from ProQuest database.

Cabrillo College (2001). *Older Workers in the Labor Market: A Report from the Congressional Research Service.* [Online]. Available: http://www.cabrillo.cc.ca.us/

Cant, A.G. (Sep 2004). Internationalizing the Business Curriculum: Developing Intercultural Competence. *Journal of American Academy of Business. Vol.5*, (iss1/2), 177. Retrieved Feb. 6, 2005 from ProQuest database.

Cavalier, Robert J. (ed.), Govinlock, James (ed.), and Sterba, James P. (ed.), (1989). *Ethics in the History of Western Philosophy.* New York, St. Martin's Press.

Cavico, F. and Mujtaba, B. (2004). *Machiavellian Values "The Prince": Bullying, Begulling, Backstabbing, and Bargaining in the Twenty First Century Management.* The Association on Employment Practices and Principles (AEPP) Proceedings. 12th Annual International Conference.

Cavico, F. & Mujtaba, B., (2004). *Business Ethics: Transcending Requirements through Moral Leadership.* Pearson Custom Publications.

Chang, C. M. (1997). A three generation assessment of strengths and needs of African-American, Caucasian, Hispanic and Chinese grand-parents. *Dissertation Abstracts-International Section-A: Humanities and Social Sciences,* 1997, 57(7-A): 2862.

Chang, W. C., Wong, W. K., and Koh, J. B. K. (2003). Chinese values in Singapore: Traditional and modern. *Asian Journal of Social Psychology*, 6(1), 5-29. Cileli, M., and Tezer, E. (1998). Life and value orientations of Turkish university students. *Adolescence*, 33(129), 219-228.

Chappell, Tom. The Soul of a Business: Managing for Profit and the Common Good. New York: Bantam Books, 1993.

Cheng, K. (March/April 2003). Silent Minority: Reaching Employees and Consumers with Mental-Health Concerns. *Diversity Inc.* New Jersey. Diversity Inc. Media,LLC.

Civil Rights Act of 1991. Thomson West, 2005. Section 2000.

Clark, K., (2003). *Judgment Day.* Money & Business. U.S.News.com. Retrieved on January 13, 2003 from URL: http://www.usnews.com/usnews/biztech/articles/030113/13performancehtm

Colias, Mike (2005). McDonald's plans to continue healthy focus. *The Associated Press/Chicago*, 1-2.

Complaints, (2004). Number of complaints suggest Wal-Mart disrespects worker's, laws. (January 17). *St. Louis Post.* Retrieved April 1, 2004 from Nova Southeastern's ProQuest database.

Comtex (2003). *McDonalds Targets Older Workers.* Retrieved October 30, 2003, from Infotrac.

Connor, P. E., Becker, B. W., Kakuyama, Y. (1993). A cross-national comparative study of managerial values: United States, Canada and Japan. *Advances in International Comparative Studies*, 8, 3-11.

Connor, P. E., Becker, R. W., Kakuyama, T. and Moore, L. F. (1993). A cross-national comparative study of managerial values: United States, Canada and Japan. In S.

B. Prasad and R. B. Peterson (1993) *Advances in international comparative management*, Volume 8. Greenwich, CO: Jai Press, Inc.

Cook, C. (2005). Wall Street Project on Social Responsibility. *Wall Street Journal,* 1-2.

Cornell Law School (2001). *Age Discrimination in Employment.* As cited in United States Code; Title 29-Labor: Chapter 14. [Online]. Available: http://www.law.cornell.edu/.

Colarelli, S. M. (1984). Methods of communication and mediating processes in realistic job previews. *Journal of Applied Psychology, 69,* 633-642.

Cook, J. D., Hepworth, S. J., Wall, T. D., & Warr, P. B. (1981). The experience of work. California: Academic Press, Inc.

Critchley, R. K. (2002). Rewired, Rehired, or Retired? A Global Guide for the Experienced Worker. San Francisco: Jossey-Bass/Pfeiffer.

Dalton, M., Ernest, C., Deal, J., & Leslie, J. (2002). *Success for the New Global Manager: What You Need to Know to Work Across Distances, Countries, and Cultures.* San Francisco: Jossey-Bass, A Wiley Company.

Dastoor, B.; Roofe, E.; and Mujtaba, B., (March 2005). Value Orientation of Jamaicans Compared to Students in the United States of America. *International Business and Economics Research Journal,* Volume 4, Number 3. Pages 43-52.

David, P. (2003). National Jeweler; Vol. 97 Issue 7, p30, 2/3p. Retrieved February 14, 2005 from the Business Source Premier database.

DeGrazia, Sebastian. Machiavelli in Hell. Princeton, New Jersey: Princeton University Press, 1989.

Demby, E. R. (2004). *Two stores refuse to join the race to the bottom for benefits and wages. Workforce Management.* (February 2004). Pages 57-59.

DeMooij, M. 1998). *Global marketing and advertising: Understanding cultural paradoxes.* Thousand Oaks, CA: Sage Publications.

Denty v. SmithKline Beecham, 109 F.3d 147 (E.D. Pa. 1997).

D'Innocenzio, A. (2003, September 21). *Wal-Mart suppliers flocking to Arkansas. The State and wire service sources.* Retrieved February 20, 2004 from http://retailindustry.

DiDomenico, N. & Mujtaba, B. (October 2004). *Tempered Radicals: The Leadership Style for Making Changes Quietly.* The Association on Employment Practices and Principles. Published in the AEPP Proceedings, Pages 86-91.

Disability Discrimination. (2002). EEOC. http://www.eeoc.gov/types/ada/html

Di-ve.com (2005). *Run for Fun: The McDonald's Olympic Day Run 2005. www.di-ve.com*, 1-2.

Dorfman, P. W., Howell, J. P. (1998). Dimensions of national culture and effective leadership patterns: Hofstede revisited. In R.N. Farmer & E.C. McGoun (Eds.), Advances in International Comparative Management, 3, 127-150.

Dougherty, L. (2004). Immigration to America. Retrieved November 23, 2004, from Northwest High School Library Media Center Web Site: http://www.kn.pacbell.com/wired/fil/pages/ listimmigratli.html.

Dowling, D. (1996). From the Social Charter to the Social Action Program 1995-1997: European Employment Law Comes Alive, *Cornell International Law Journal, 29*(43), p. 60f.

Downes, A (2003). Productivity and competitiveness in the Jamaican economy. Prepared for the Inter American Development Bank, Washington DC, USA.

Downes, M., Thomas, A. S., & Singley, R. B. (2002). Predicting expatriate job satisfaction: The role of firm internationalization. *Career Development International, 7,* 24-36.

Dworkin, G. Paternalism. The Stanford Encyclopedia of Philosophy, Winter 2002 ed., Edward N. Zalta (ed.). Retrieved on November 11, 2003 from http://plato.stanford. Edu/archives/win2002/entries/paternalism/ perspective. Journal of Economic Issues, 34, (2) 393-401.

Eccles, S. (2003). *The relationship between job satisfaction and organizational commitment as perceived by irrigation workers in a quasi irrigation company in Jamaica.* Michigan: Proquest Information and Learning Company. (UMI No. 3096346).

EEOC v. Arabian American Oil Company, 499 U.S. 244 (1991).

EEOC Compliance Manual (October 20, 1993). *EEOC Enforcement Guidance on Application of Title VII to Conduct Overseas and to Foreign Employers Discriminating in the U.S.*, Notice 915.002, p. 2169.

Elashmawi, F. & Harris, P. R. (1993). *Multicultural Management.* Houston: Gulf Publishing.

"Elderly get a taste of the net" *BBCNews.* Retrieved February 5, 2004, from http://news.bbc.co.uk/2/hi/technology/3020719.stm

Elkhouly, S. M. E., and Buda, R. (1997). A cross-cultural comparison of value systems of Egyptians, Americans, Africans and Arab executives. *International Journal of Commerce and Management*, 7, 102-199.

England, G. W. (1967a). Personal value system of American managers. *Academy of Management Journal*, 10, 53-68.

England, G. W. (1967b). Organizational goals and expected behavior of American managers. *Academy of Management Journal*, 10, 101-117.

England, G. W. (1978). Managers and their value systems: A five country comparative study. *Columbia Journal of World Business*, 13, 35-44.

Eskilson, A., and Wiley, M. (1999). Solving for the X: Aspirations and expectations of college students. *Journal of Youth and Adolescence*, 28-1; 51-70.

Eskin, M. (2003). Self-reported assertiveness in Swedish and Turkish adolescents: A cross-cultural comparison. *Scandinavian Journal of Psychology*, 44(1), 7-12.

Ethics and Excellence: Cooperation and Integrity in Business. New York: Oxford University Press, 1992.

Farber, M. L. (1955). English and Americans: Values in the socialization process. In D. C. McClelland (Ed.), *Studies in motivation* (pp. 323-330). New York, NY: Appleton-Century-Crofts

Feather, N. T. (1970). Educational choice and student attitudes in relation to terminal and Instrumental Values. *Australian Journal of Psychology*, 22-2, 127-143.

Feather, N. T. (1975). Value systems and delinquency: Parental and generational discrepancies in value systems and delinquent and non-delinquent boys. *British Journal of Social and Clinical Psychology*, 14-2, 117-129.

Feather, N. T. (1979). Human values and the work situation: Two studies. *Australian Psychologist*, 14-2, 131-141.

Feather, N. T. (1982). Reasons for entering medical school in relation to value priorities and sex of student. *Journal of Occupational Psychology*, 55, 119-128.

Feather, N. T. (1984). Protestant ethic, conservatism and values. *Journal of Personality and Social Psychology*, 46-5, 1132-1141.

Feather, N. T. (1986). Value systems across cultures: Australia and China. *International Journal of Psychology*, 21, 697-715.

Feather, N. T. (1988). Value systems across cultures: Australia and China. *International Journal of Psychology*, 21-6, 697-715.

Feather, N. T. (1999). *Values, achievement and justice: Studies in the psychology of deservingness*. New York, NY: Kluwer Academic/Plenum Publishers.

Feather, N. T. and Mckee, L. R. (1993). Global Self-esteem and attitudes toward high achievers for Australian and Japanese students. *Social Psychology Quarterly*, 56-1, 65-76.

Federal Laws Prohibiting Job Discrimination Questions and Answers. The U.S. Equal Employment Opportunity Commission. Retreived on October 04, 2003 from: http://www.eeoc.gov/facts/qanda.html

Finn, Jeffrey. "Aging and Information Technology: The Promise and the Challenge." *ASA: Generations Journal*. Retrieved February 3, 2004, from http://www.gener ationsjournal.org/index.cfm?page=gen-21-3/gen-21-3-toc.html

Firoz, N. M. & Ramin, T. (2004). Understanding cultural variables is critical to success in International Business. *International Journal of Management, 21,* 307-324.

Fishman, C. (2003). The Wal-Mart you don't know. *Fast Company,* (77). Retrieved March 30, 2004 from http://fastcompany.com/magazine/77/walmart.html.

Foley Bros. Inc. v. Filardo, 336 U.S. 281, 285 (1949).

Fordahl, Matthew. "Elderly Reach for the Digital Age" *Associated Press.* Retrieved February 2, 2004, from http://www.globalaging.org/elderrights/us/digitalage.htm

Forever Young. (2005). Retrieved July 25, 2005, from http://www.leoslyrics.com/listlyrics.php?hid=Wxj%2BxWLcwrg%3D

Formal Interest Group. Technology & Aging. *Gerontological Society of America(GSA).* Retrieved February 3, 2004, from http://www.gsa-tag.org/1999 /mainsymposium.html

Fournet, L. M. (1996). A three generation assessment of strengths and needs of Africa American, Caucasian and Hispanic grandparents. *Abstracts-International Section-A: Humanities and Social Sciences,* 1996, 57(5-B): 3421.

Fowler – Hermes, J., (2001). Appearance-based Discrimination Claims Under EEO Laws. *The Florida Bar Journal*, April, Page 32F.

Frankena, William K. Ethics (2nd ed.). Englewood Cliffs, New Jersey: Prentice-Hall, 1973.

Fraser, B. (2005). Corporate social responsibility. *Internal Auditor*, 62 (1), 42-47. Retrieved March 1, 2005, from the EBSCO Host database.

Friedman, M. (1970). "The social responsibility of business is to increase its profits". In Hoffman W. and Moore J. (1990), *"Business ethics, readings and cases in corporate morality*: 153-157. NY: McGraw-Hill.

Furnham, A., and Albhai, N. (1985). Value differences in foreign students. *International Journal of Intercultural Relations*, 9, 365-375.

Fyock, C. D. & Dorton, A. M. (1994). UnRetirement: A Career Guide for the Retired…the Soon-to-be-Retired…the Never-Want-to-be-Retired. New York: Amacom.

Gale Group (1999, Oct). Associates keystone to structure (Wal-Mart). Retrieved March 19, 2004 from http://www.findarticles.com/cf_dls/m3092/1999_Oct/ 57578936/print.html

Garver, Eugene. Machiavelli and the History of Prudence. Madison, Wisconsin: The University of Wisconsin Press, 1987.

General Dynamics Land Systems, Inc. v. Cline, 540 U.S. 581, 592 (2004).

Gender interests divide silver surfers" *BBCNews*. Retrieved February 4, 2004, from http://news.bbc.co.uk/2/hi/technology/2205941.stm.

Ghobar, M.G.M. (1967). Afghanistan dar Masir-e Tarikh, Volume I. Kabul, Afghanistan.

Gibson, J., Ivancevich, J. & Donnelly, J. (1991). *Organizations: Behavior, structures, processes.* Homewood, Il: Irwin.

Girlando, A., P. (1998) A study of the influence of national culture on Russian students in the US.

Gosden, R. (1996). *Cheating Time: Science, Sex, and Aging.* W.H. Freeman & Co.: New York

Green, Ronald M. The Ethical Manager: A New Method for Business Ethics. New York: Macmillan Publishing Company, 1993.

Gregorian, Vartan. (1969). The Emergence of Modern Afghanistan. California: Stanford University Press.

Gregory, F. R., (2001). *Age Discrimination in the American Workplace: Old at a Young Age.* Rutgers University Press. New Jersey.

Griest, G. (2004, Jan). *Kmart Posts $250 Million Profit, 13.5 Percent Drop in Sales.* Retrieved March 29, 2004, from http://0-proquest.umi.com.novacat.nova.edu/ pqweb?index+13&sis= 1&srchmode=1&vins.

Guy, V., & Mattock, J. (1995). *The International Business Book: All the Tools, Tactics, and Tips you need for doing Business across Cultures.* Lincolnwood: NTC Business Books.

Hale, R. L. (1995). *Systat: Statistical applications*. Cambridge, MA: Course Technology.

Hall, E. T. and Hall, M. R., (1987). *Understanding Cultural Differences*. Intercultural Press, Inc. USA.

Hamann, R., Agbazue, T., Kapelus, P., Hein, A. (2005). *Universalizing corporate social responsibility? south african challenges to the international organization for standardization's new social responsibility standard.* Retrieved March 1, 2005 from the EBSCO Host database.

Hambrick, D. C., Canney D. S., Snell, S. A. & Snow, C, C., (1998). When groups consist of multiple nationalities: towards a new understanding of the implications. Organizational studies, 19, 181-205

Hamlyn, D.W. A History of Western Philosophy. London: Penguin Books, 1988.

Hampshire, Stuart. *Morality and Conflict.* Cambridge, Massachusetts: Harvard University Press.

Harvard Business Review (2001). *HBR on Managing Diversity.* Harvard Business School Publications.

Harvey, Carol P. and Allard, M. June (2002). *Understanding and Managing Diversity: Readings Cases and Exercises.* Second ed., Prentice Hall.

Harris, P. R., Moran, R. T., & Moran, S. V. (2004). *Managing Cultural Differences: Global Leadership Strategies for the 21st Century* (6th ed.). Burlington: Elsevier Butterworth-Heinemann

Hayflick, L. *How and Why We Age* (1994). Ballantine Books: New York.

Henke, H. (1999). Jamaica's decision to pursue a Neoliberal development strategy: realignment in the state-business – class triangle. Latin American Perspectives 108, (26) 7-33.

Heller, Agnes. Renaissance Man. New York: Schocken Books, 1981.

Henderson, Verne E. What's Ethical in Business. New York: McGraw-Hill, 1992.

Herzberg, F. (1968). One more time: How do you Motivate employees? In S. J. Ott (ed.), *Classical readings in organizational behavior.* 2nd Edition. Orlando, Florida: Harcourt Brace & Company.

Hoecklin, L (1995). Managing cultural differences: strategies for competitive advantages. New York: Addison – Wesley Publishing.

Hoffman, J., J. (1998). Evaluating international ethical climates: A goal-programming model. *Journal of Business ethics*, 17, 1861-1869.

Hofstede, G. (2003). Geert Hofstede Cultural Dimensions downloaded on September 9, 2003 from ITIM website http:// geert-hofstede.com/ ofstede_united_states.shtml

Hofstede, G. (1997). *Cultures and organization: Software of the mind.* London: McGraw Hill.

Hofstede, G. (1993). Cultural constraints in management theories. *Academy of Management Executive,* 7 (1) 81-90

Hofstede, G., Neuijen, B., Ohayv, D.D, & Sander, G. (1990). Measuring organizational cultures: a qualitative and quantitative study across 20 cases. *Administrative Science Quarterly*, 35, 286-316.

Hofstede, G. (1980). *Culture's consequences: International differences in work-related values.* Beverly Hills, CA: Sage Publications.

Hofstede, G. (1983). National cultures in four dimensions a research-based theory of cultural differences among nations. *International Studies of Management and Organization*, 13, 46-74.

Hofstede, G. (1984). *Culture's consequences: International differences in work-related values* (Abridged Edition). Newbury Park, CA: Sage.

Hofstede, G. (2001). *Culture's consequences: Comparing values, behaviors, institutions and organizations across nations* (2nd ed). Thousand Oaks, CA: Sage Publications.

Hofstede, G., and Bond, M. (1984). Hofstede's culture dimensions: An independent validation using Rokeach's Value Survey. *Journal of Cross-cultural Psychology*, 15(4): 417-433.

Hodgetts, R. M., & Luthans, F. (2002). *International Management: Culture, Strategy, and Behavior* (5th ed.). New York: McGraw-Hill/Irwin.

Holt, D. H., Ralston, D. & Terpstra, R., H., (1994). Constraints on capitalism in Russia: The managerial psyche. California Management Review, 124-141.

Hosseini, Khaled (2003). *The Kite Runner*. Riverhead Books, New York. ISBN: 1-59448-000-1.

Howard, L. (2005). Global Balanced Lifestyles. *Associated Press and NewsCom*, 1-2.

Howard, A., Shudo, K., and Umeshima, M. (1983). Motivation and values among Japanese and American managers. *Personnel Psychology*, 36(4): 883-898.

Hsu, J. C. (2002). *Does organizational commitment affect turnover in China's internet industry* Michigan: ProQuest Information and Learning Company. (UMI No. 3042263).

Hulliung, Mark (1983). *Citizen Machiavelli*. Princeton, New Jersey: Princeton University Press.

Hunt, S. D., Chonko, L. B., & Wood, V. R. Organizational commitment and marketing. *Journal of Marketing, 49,* 112-126.

Imamoglu, E. O., and Ayguen, Z. K. (1999). Value preferences from the 1970s to 1990s: Cohort, generation and gender differences at a Turkish university. *Turk-Psikoloji-Dergisi*, 14(44), 1-22.

Introduction to the Americans with Disabilities Act. (2003). Available at: http://www.usdoj.gov/crt/ada/adaintro/htm

Ivancevich, J. & Matterson, M. (1990). *Organizational behavior and management.* Homewood, IL: Irwin.

Jackall, Robert. Moral Mazes: The World of Corporate Managers. New York: Oxford University Press, 1988.

Jacobs, J. (2005). Global Balanced Lifestyles. *Associated Press and NewsCom,* 1-2.

Jamaican Handbook, 2001. *The Jamaican Handbook for the Elderly*. A Blue Cross of Jamaica Sponsored Publication.LMH Publishing Limited. ISBN: 976-8184-26-4.

Jamrog, J. and McCAnn, J. (2003). *Blindsided: Working through the Coming Knowledge Crisis* (Working Paper). Tampa, FL. Human Resource Institute, The University of Tampa.

Job Applicants and the Americans with Disabilities Act. (2003). EEOC.gov/facts/jobapplicant.html

Johnson, A. (June/July 2003). Americans with Disabilities Act: Is Your Company Compliant? *Diversity Inc*. New Jersey. Diversity Inc. Media, LLC.

Johnson, A. (Oct/Nov. 2003). They had No Idea What to Say to Me. *Diversity Inc*. New Jersey. Diversity Inc. Media, LLC.

Johnson, T. (February 9, 2005). Taking care of older parents is law of the land. *The Herald,* p.17A.

Johnson, Bill & Weinstein, Art (2004). *Superior Customer Value in the New Economy: Concepts and Cases.* Boca Raton, FL; CRC Press LLC.

Jones, G. & George, J. (2003). *Contemporary Management.* Third ed. New York: McGraw-Hill.

Kahle, L. R. (1984). Attitudes and social adaptation: A person-situation interaction approach. *International Series in Experimental Social Psychology*, Volume 8, Pergamon Press.

Kaiser, E. (2004, Jan 27). *U.S. retailers give Wal-Mart a head start on RFID. USA TODAY.* Retrieved April 1, 2004 from http://www.usatoday.com/tech/news/techinnovations/2004-01-27-walmart-pioneers-rfid_x.htm.

Kanfer, R. and Ackerman, P. L. (2004). *Aging, Adult Development, and Work Motivation.* Academy of Management Review. Vol. 29, No. 3, pp. 440-458.

Kelly, E. P., (2003). Ethical Perspectives on Layoffs of Highly Compensated Workers and Age Discrimination in Employment. *The Journal of Applied Management and Entrepreneurship.* Val. 8, No. 3. Pages 84-97.

Kern v. Dynalectron Corporation, 577 F. Supp. 1196 (N. Tex. 1983), *affirmed* 746 F.2d 810 (5th Cir. 1984).

Kalakota and Robinson (2003, Aug). From e-Business to Services: Why and Why Now? Retrieved April5, 2004 from http://www.informit.com/isapi/product .

Khan, S.Y. (2003). *Desperately seeking older employees.* Retrieved October 1, 2003, from Infotrac.

Kluckhohn, C. (1951). The study of values. In D. N. Barrett (Ed.), *Values in transition* (pp. 17-45). Notre Dame, IN: University of Notre Dame Press.

Kluckhohn, C. M. (1962). Values and value-orientations in the Theory of Action. In T. Parsons and E. A. Shils (Eds.), *Toward a general theory of action* (pp. 388-433). New York: Harper and Row.

Kmart Corporation (2004). Hoover's Company Information. Retrieved March 19, 2004 from http://cobrands.hoovers.com/global/cobrands/proquest/factsheet. xhtml?COID= 10830.

Kmart Corporation (2004). About Kmart. Retrieved April 3, 2004 from http://www.kmartcorp.com/corp/.

Konovsky, M., & Haynie, B.G. (2001). *Performance criteria in RIF and their impact on age discrimination lawsuits.* Employee Rights Quarterly. Autumn. Retrieved October 1, 2003 from Infotrac.

Koury, F., (July 2005). *Selling the vision: motivate your managers with more than just money. SmartBusiness*, Retrieved on July 26, 2005 from: http://broward.sbnonline.com/marticle.asp?periodicalKey=23&particleKey=9821

Koury, F. (January 2005). *Creating a winning culture: How to become and stay innovative in a competitive marketplace.* SmartBusiness,. Retrieved July 26, 2005 from: http://broward.sbnonline.com/marticle.asp?periodicalKey=23&particleKey=9135.

Lambert, E. G. (2001). To stay or quit: A review of the literature on correctional officer turnover. *American Journal of Criminal Justice, 26,* 61-76.

Lambert , E., Hogan, N. L., & Barton, S. M. (2002). Satisfied correctional staff: A review of the literature on the correlates of correctional staff job satisfaction. *Criminal Justice and Behavior, 29,* 115-143.

Lau, S. (1988). The value orientations of Chinese university students in Hong Kong. *International Journal of Psychology*, 23(5): 583-596.

Lau, S. (1992). Collectivism's individualism: Value preference, personal control, and the desire for freedom among Chinese in Mainland China, Hong Kong, and Singapore. *Personality and Individual Differences*, 13(3): 361-366.

Lau, S., and Wong, A. (1992). Value and sex-role orientation of Chinese adolescents. *International Journal of Psychology*, 27(1): 3-17.

Laukaran VH, Winikoff B, Myers D. (1986). The impact of health services on breastfeeding: common themes from developed and developing worlds. In: Jeliffe A, Jeliffe E, eds. *Advances in International Maternal and Child Health.* 121-128.

Leininger M. (1985). Transcultural care diversity and universality: a theory of nursing. *Nurse and Health Care.* 6:209-212.

Leonard, Dorothy (2005). *Knowledge Management: How To Salvage Your Company's Deep Smarts.* Retrieved August 3, 2005 from: harvardbusinessonline.hbsp.harvard.edu.

Lee, K. (1991). The problem of appropriateness of the Rokeach Value Survey in Korea. *International Journal of Psychology*, 26(3): 299-310.

Locke, E. A. (1976). The nature and consequences of job satisfaction. In M. D. Dunnette (Ed.), *Handbook of industrial and organizational psychology.* Chicago: Rand-Mcnally.

Lomax, A. (2005). McDonald's Fun Fast Food. *The Motley Fool.com,* 1-2.

Maass, P. (2005). Niger delta dispatch road to hell. *The New Republic*, 232 (3), 15. Retrieved from the EBSCO Host database.

Machiavelli, Niccolo. The Prince (translated and edited by Adams, Robert M.). New York: W.W. Norton Company, 1977.

Machiavelli, Niccolo. The Prince (2nd ed.) (translated and edited by Mansfield, Harvey C.). Chicago: The University of Chicago Press, 1998.

MacIntyre, Alasdair. A Short History of Ethics. New York: Macmillan Publishing Company, 1966.

Mackie, J.L. Ethics: Inventing Right and Wrong. New York: Penguin Books, 1990.

Macoby. (Jan/Feb 2005). Creating Moral Organizations. *Research Technology Management. Vol.48*, (iss.1), 59. Retrieved Feb. 6, 2005 from ProQuest database.

Mahoney v. RFE/RL, Inc., 47 F.3rd 447 (D.C. Cir. 1995).

Mansfield, E. D. (1995). *A comparison of more and less generative adults according to psychological variables, demographic characteristics, and generativity types.* Dissertation Abstracts International, Section A, Humanities and Social Sciences, 56(3-A): 0870.

Mansfield, Harvey C. (1995). *Machiavelli's Virtue.* Chicago: University of Chicago Press.

March, J. G., & Simon, H. A. (1958). *Organizations.* New York: Wiley.

Marquardt, M. & Berger, N. (2000). *Global Leaders for the 21st Century.* Albany, New York: State University of New York Press. Pages 1-32 & 175-189

Maslow, A. H. (1943). A theory of human motivation. In S. J. Ott (ed.), *Classical readings in organizational behavior.* 2nd Edition. Orlando, Florida: Harcourt Brace & Company.

Mathieu, J. E., & Zajac, D. (1990). A review and meta-analysis of the antecedents , correlates, and consequences of organizational commitment. *Psychological Bulletin, 108,* 171-194.

Mayton, D., and Furnham, A. (1994). Value underpinnings of antinuclear political activism: A cross-national study. *Journal of Social Issues*, 50(4): 117-128.

McFarlane, D.A., and Mujtaba, B. (2005). Gender Issues in the Corporate World. In Mujtaba, B. (2005). *The Art of Mentoring Diverse Professionals: Employee development and retention practices for entrepreneurs and multinational corporations.* Aglob Publishing Inc.

McGeary, J. (2001). Death Stalks a Continent. *Time Magazine.* Retrieved July 25, 2005, from http://www.time.com/time/2001/aidsinafrica/cover.html

McMichael, S. H. (2000). *The X factor in air traffic control training at Travis Air Force Base.* Graduate Research Project Master's Thesis, Embry Riddle Aeronautical University, Travis Academic Center, California.

McQuarrie, E. (1989). The impact of a discontinuous innovation: Outcomes experienced by owners of home computers. *Computers in Human Behavior*, 5(4): 227-240.

McShane, M., Williams F., & McClaine, K. (1991). Early exits: Examining employee turnover. *Corrections Today, 53,* 220-225.

Mattingly, Garrret. "Machiavelli." *Renaissance Profiles.* Plumb, J.H. (ed.). New York: Harper and Row, 1965.

Maurer, T.J., & Rafuse, N.E. (2001). *Learning, not Litigating: Managing employee development and avoiding claims of age discrimination.* Academy Management Executive. Retrieved September 12, 2003, from AgeLine.

Medina, J. (1996). Th*e Clock of Ages. Why We Age – How We Age – Winding Back the Clock.* Cambridge University Press.

Meglino, B. M. (1998). Individual values in organizations: Concepts, controversies and research. *Journal of Management*, May-June 1998. Downloaded from www.findarticles.com.

Melbin, M. (1961). Organization practice and individual behavior: absenteeism among psychiatric aides. *American Sociological Review, 26,* 14-23.

Meyer, J. P. & Allen, N. J. (1984). Testing the "side-bet theory" of organizational commitment: Some methodological considerations. *Journal of Applied Psychology, 69,* 372-378.

Meyer, J. P. & Allen, N. J. (1997). *Commitment in the workplace: Theory, research, and application.* California: Sage Publications.

Mendenhall, M., Kuhlmann, T. & Stahl, G. (2001). *Developing Global Business Leaders: Policies, Processes, and Innovations.* Pages 2-16, 54-55, & 75-80.

Microsoft Encarta (1993-2000). *Age Discrimination* [Computer Software]. Microsoft Encarta Encyclopedia 2000: Microsoft Corporation.

Michaels, C. E. & Spector, P. E. (1982). Causes of employee turnover: A test of the Mobley, Griffeth, Hand, and Meglino model. *Journal of Applied Psychology, 67,* 53-59.

Mitchell, O., Mackenzie, D. L., Styve G. J., & Gover, A. R. (2000). The impact of individual, organizational, and environmental attributes on voluntary turnover among juvenile correctional staff members. *Justice Quarterly. 17,* 333-357.

Mobley, W. H. (1977). Intermediate linkages in the relationship between job satisfaction and employee turnover. *Journal of Applied Psychology, 62*, 237-240.

Mobley, W. H., Griffeth, R. W., Hand, H. H., & Meglino, B. M. (1979). Review and conceptual analysis of the employee turnover process. *Psychological Bulletin, 86,* 493-522.

Mobley, W. H. (1982). *Employee turnover: Causes, consequences, and control.* Philippines: Addison-Wesley Publishing Company, Inc.

Mojo, J. (2004). Convenience is Good Business. *Brandweek,* 45, 16.

Moncur, Michael. (1994-2004). The Quotations Page. Retrieved Feb 6, 2005, from www.thequotationspage.com.

Moore, S. (2004, Feb 18). Beaumont, California approves Wal-Mart; Critics say small businesses will suffer. *Knight Ridder Tribune Business news.* Retrieved April 11, 2004 from Nova Southeastern's ProQuest database http://0-proquest.umi.com.

Morelli v. Cedel, 141 F.3d 39, 42-43 (2nd Cir. 1998).

Morris, Tom. If Aristotle Ran General Motors: The New Soul of Business. New York: Henry Holt and Company, 1997.

Morrow, P. C. (1993). *The theory and measurement of work commitment.* Greenwich: JAI Press.

Mowday, R. T., Porter, L. W., & Steers, R. M. (1982). *Employee-organization linkages: The psychology of commitment, abseentism, and turnover.* New York: Academic Press.

Mujtaba, Bahaudin G. (2006). *The Art of Mentoring Diverse Professionals: Employee development and retention practices for entrepreneurs and multinational corporations.* ISBN: 1-59427-052-X. Aglob Publishing Inc. Hollandale, Florida.

Mujtaba, B. G.; Cavico, F.; Edwards, R. M.; and Oskal, C. (January 2006). Age Discrimination in the Workplace: Cultural Paradigms Associated with Age in

Afghanistan, Jamaica, Turkey, and the United States. *Journal of Applied Management and Entrepreneurship,* Volume 11, Num. 1.

_____ and Cavico, F., (2006). *Age Discrimination in Employment: Cross Cultural Comparison and Management Strategies.* Textbook publication in progress.

_____ and Rhodes, J., (2006). The Aging Workface: Best Practices in Recruiting and Retaining Older Workers at Publix. *The 2006 Pfeiffer Annual: Human Resource Management.* Edited by Robert C. Preziosi. Pages 87-95. ISBN: 0-7879-7824-8.

_____ (2006). *AFGHANISTAN: Realities of War and Rebuilding.* Aglob Publishing Inc. Hollandale, Florida USA.

_____ (2005). *The Ethics of Management and Situational Leadership in Afghanistan.* AGLOB Publishing Inc. ISBN: 1-59427-047-3. Fort Lauderdale, Florida USA. Website: www.aglobpublishing.com. Phone: (954)465-1476.

_____ & Hinds, R. M., (2004). *Quality assurance through effective faculty training and development practices in distance education: The survey of Jamaican graduates.* THE CARIBBEAN AREA NETWORK FOR QUALITY ASSURANCE IN TERTIARY EDUCATION (CANQATE). Conference on November 3-4. Ocho Rios, Jamaica.

_____; Richardson, W.; and Blount, P. (2003). Age Discrimination and Means of Avoiding It in the Workplace! Presented & published in SAM International Conference Proceedings on *"Trust, responsibility, and business."* April. Orlando, Florida.

Mullman, J. (2005). Ronald McDonald houses, charity unite. Crain's Chicago Business, 28(10), 18.

Munson, M. J. (1980). Concurrent validity of a modified Rokeach Value Survey in discriminating more successful from less successful students. *Educational and Psychological Measurement,* 40-2, 479-485.

Munson, M. J., and McIntyre, S. H. (1980). Developing practical procedures for the measurement of personal values in cross-cultural marketing. *Journal of Marketing Research,* 16-1, 48-52.

Munson, M. J. and Posner, B. Z. (1980a). The factorial validity of a modified Rokeach Value Survey for four diverse samples. *Educational and Psychological Measurement,* 40-4, 1073-1079.

Munson, M. J. and Posner, B. Z. (1980b). Concurrent validation of two value inventories in predicting job classification and success for organizational personnel. *Journal of Applied Psychology,* 65-5, 536-542.

Murphy, E. F. Jr.; Gordon, J.D.; and Anderson, T.L., (2003). *An examination of cross-cultural age and generation-based value differences between the United States and Japan.* Proceeding of the Southern Academy of Management 2003 Conference.

Murphy, E. F. Jr. (1994) *Military organizational culture: An investigation of sex and gender differences in the values, sex role stereotype attitudes, and situational leadership II behaviors of Air Force middle-level managers.* (Doctoral

Dissertation, Nova Southeastern University, 1994). University Microfilms International UMI No. 9525247.

Murphy, E. F. Jr., and Anderson, T. (2003). A longitudinal study exploring value changes during the cultural assimilation of Japanese student pilot sojourners in the United States. *International Journal of Value Based Management*, May 2003, 16(2), 111-129.

Murphy, E. F., Jr., Eckstat, A., and Parker, T. (1995). Sex and gender differences in leadership. *The Journal of Leadership Studies, 2,* 116-131.

Murphy, E. F., Jr., Snow, W. A., Carson, P. P., and Zigarmi, D. (1997). Values, sex differences and psychological androgyny. *International Journal of Value-Based* Management, 10, 69-99.

Murphy, S. A. (2001). A study of career values by generation and gender. *Dissertation Abstracts-International Section-A: Humanities and Social Sciences,* 2001, 61(9-A): 3781.

Nail, T. & Scharringer, D. (2002). Guidelines on Interview and Employment Application Questions. *HR Magazine.* Virginia. HR Press

Nash, Laura L. (1990). *Good Intentions Aside: A Manager's Guide to Resolving Ethical Problems.* Boston: Harvard Business School Press.

Ng, A. H. (1993). Exploring country values and information technology adoption in business schools. *Proceedings of the Academy of Management, Poster Sessions* (p. 418). Atlanta, GA.

Nicholson, J.D., Stephina, L.P., & Hochwarter, W. (1990). Psychological aspects of expatriate training and effectiveness. In G. Ferris & K. Rowland (Eds.), Research in personnel and human resource management (Suppl. 2, 127-145). Greenwich, CT: JAI Press.

Nobile, R.J. (1998). *Essential Facts: Employment* (Age Discrimination). Warren, Gorham & Lamont: Boston, Massachusetts, Section 6.4, pp6-12 – 6-13.

Noelle, Christine (1997). *State and Tribe in Nineteenth-Century Afghanistan.* Britain: Curzon Press.

Norman, Richard (1991). *The Moral Philosophers: An Introduction to Ethics.* Oxford: Clarendon Press.

Nunally, J. C. (1978). *Psychometric theory.* New York: McGraw-Hill.

Nuttall, Jon (19932). *Moral Questions: An Introduction to Ethics.* Cambridge: Polity Press.

O'Reilly, C. A., & Chatman J. (1986). Organizational commitment and psychological attachment: The effects of compliance, identification, and internalization on prosocial behavior. *Journal of Applied Psychology, 71,* 492-499.

Offermann, L. R. & Hellmann, P. S. (1997). Culture's consequences for leadership behavior: National values in action. Journal of Cross-Cultural Psychology, 342-351.

Olson, W. (1999). *Kansas Journal of Law and Public Policy (West), 8*(32), p. 7.

Olshansky, S.J., Hayflick, L., and Carnes, B.A. (2004). *Position Statement on Human Aging.* Retrieved July 25, 2005, from http://www.quackwatch.org/01QuackeryRelatedTopics/antiagingpp.html

Orzel v. City of Wauwatosa Fire Department, 697 F.2d 743 (7th Cir. 1983).

Quirk, J. (1993). A Brief Overview of the Age Discrimination in Employment Act A (ADEA). Reviewed June 1999. Available online: http://my.shrm.org/whitepapers/documents~agediscrimination.

Patten R. (2004, September/October). From implicit to explicit: Putting corporate values and personal accountability front and centre. *Ivey Business Journal Online, p. H1.*

Peters, L. H., Jackofsky, E. F., & Salter, J. R. (1981). Predicting turnover: a comparison of part-time and full-time employees. *Journal of Occupational Behavior, 2,* 89-98.

Pohlman, R. & Gardiner, G. (2000). *Value Driven Management: How to Create and Maximize Value Over Time for Organizational Success.* New York: AMACOM.

Pollock, T., Whitbred, R., & Contractor, N. (2000). Social information processing and job characteristics: a simultaneous test of two theories with implications for job satisfaction. *Human Communication Research, 26,* 292-330.

Porter, L. W., Steers, R. M., Mowday, R. T. & Boulian, P. V. (1974). Organizational commitment, job satisfaction, and turnover among psychiatric technicians. *Journal of Applied Psychology, 59,* 603-609.

Porter, L. W., Crampon, W. J., & Smith, F. J. (1976). Organizational commitment and managerial turnover: A longitudinal study. *Organizational Behavior and Human Performance, 15,* 87-98.

Preziosi, R. (August 2005). *The fuel of business: 8 ways to light the fires of creativity and innovation.* Smart Business, Vol. 1, Number 12. Retrieved on August 30, 2005 from: http://broward.sbnonline.com/marticle.asp?periodicalKey=23&particleKey=9910.

Preziosi, C. & Gooden, D. (2003). *Machiavelli Revisited: MBA Students' Perspectives.* International Business and Economics Conference Proceedings, Las Vegas, Nevada. October, 2003.

Publix Careers, 2004. Retrieved on August 18th from: http://www.publix.com/about/careers/Careers.do

Publix, 2004. Publix News Release. Retrieved on August 20th from: http://www.publix.com/about/newsroom/NewsReleaseItem.do

Publix Awards, 2005. Retrieved on August 20th 2005 from: http://www.publix.com/

Rachels, James (1986). *The Elements of Moral Philosophy.* New York: McGraw-Hill.

Rakich, J., Longest, B., & Darr, K. (1992). *Managing Health Service Organizations.* Baltimore, MD: Health Professional Press.

Ralston, D. A., Gustafson, D. J., Cheung, F. M. & Terpstra, R. H. (1993). Differences in managerial values: A study of U. S., Hong Kong and PRC managers. *Journal of International Business Studies*, 24 (2) 249-275.

Ramlall, S. (2004). A review of employee motivation theories and their implications for employee retention within organizations. *Journal of American Academy of Business, 5,* 52-63.

Randall, D. M. (1993). Cross-cultural research on on organizational commitment: A review and application of Hofstede's value survey module. *Journal of Business Research, 26,* 91-110.

Recruiting Seniors, 2004. Why Hire Seniors and Retirees? Retrieved on August 19th from: http://www.recruitersnetwork.com/articles/seniors.htm

Redding, S.G., Norman, A, & Schlander, A. (1994). *The nature of individual attachment to theory: A review of East Asian variations.* In H.C. Triandis, M.D. Dunnett, and L.M. Hough (Eds.), Handbook of industrial and organizational psychology, 4, 674-688. Palo Alto, CA: Consulting Psychology Press.

Reidenbach, R.E. and Robin D.P. (1989). *Ethics and profits.* NY: Prentice-Hall.

Reyes-Ganoan v. North Carolina Growers Associatio,n 250 F.3d 861, 866-67 (4th Cir. 2001), cert. denied, 122 S.Ct. 463 (2001).

Reynolds, T. J., and Olson, J. C. (Eds) (2001). *Understanding consumer decision making: The means-end approach to marketing and advertising strategy.* Mahwah, NJ: Lawrence Erlbaum Associates.

Ricks, D. A., Toyne, B. & Martinez, Z. (1990). Recent developments in international management research. *Journal of Management*, 16, 219-252.

Rice, A. K., Hill, J. M., & Trist, E. L. (1950). The representation of labor turnover as a social process. *Human Relation,, 3,* 349-372.

Rioux, M. (2003, Mar). Lessons Learned from Kmart. *IDEA Article.* Retrieved April 9, 2004 from http://www.naedtechnolgyinformer.com/feature_archive_4-04-03-2.html

RMHC (2005). Ronald McDonald House Charities. *Ronald McDonald House Charities, Inc.* 1-3.

Robertson, C. J., and Hoffman, J. J. (2000). How different are we? An investigation of Confucian values in the United States. *Journal of Managerial Issues*, 12(1), 34-48.

Roscoe, B. and Peterson, K. (1989). Age-appropriate behaviors: A comparison across three generations of females. *Adolescence*, 24(93), 167-178.

Rokeach, M. (1973). *The nature of human values.* New York: Free Press.

Rokeach, M. (1977). Can computers change human values? *Revista Latinoamericana de Psicologia*, 9-3, 449-458.

Rokeach, M. (1979). *Understanding human values: Individual and societal.* New York: Free Press.

Rokeach, M. (1986). *Beliefs, attitudes and values: A theory of organization and change.* San Francisco, CA: Jossey-Bass Publishers.

Rokeach, M., and Ball-Rokeach, S. J. (1989). Stability and change in American value priorities. *American Psychologist*, 44, 775-784.

Rokeach, M. and Regan, J. F. (1980). The role of values in the counseling situation. *Personnel and Guidance Journal*, May 1980, pp. 576-588.

Rose, G. M. 1997). Cross-cultural values research: Implications for international advertising. In L. R. Kahle and L. Chiagouris (Eds). *Values, lifestyles and psychograhics*. New Jersey, Lawrence Erlbaum.

Russell, Bertrand (1972). A History of Western Philosophy. New York: Simon and Schuster.

Schwartz, S.A. (1999). A theory of cultural values and some implications for work. *Applied Psychology: An International Review, 48(1), 23-47.*

Sadat, Mir Hekmatullah, (2004). *Afghan History: kite flying, kite running and kite banning.* June. Retrieved on June 2, 2004 from: http://www.afghanmagazine.com/2004_06/articles/hsadat.shtml

Salter, Chuck (2001). Attention, Class! 16 Ways to Be a Smarter Teacher. Fast Company. Retrieved on 3/5/04 from: http://www.fastcompany.com/magazine/53/teaching.html

Sargeant, M. (June 2004). Age As An Equality Issue: Legal and Policy Perspectives. [Book review], *Industrial L.J. 33*(208).

Saunderson, R. (2004). Survey findings of the effectiveness of employee recognition in the public sector. *Public Personnel Management. 33,* 255-275.

Schramm, Jennifer (2005). The Future of Retirement. *Visions*, No. 2-2005. Society of Human Resource Managers.

Schneider, J. D., (2004). *The Psychology of Stereotyping.* The Guilford Press, NY.

Scrivano, K. (2004).Global Balanced Lifestyles. *Associated Press and NewsCom,* 1-2.

Segrave, Kerry (2001). *Age Discrimination by Employers.* McFarland & Company, Inc., Publishers. Jefferson, North Caroline, and London.

Senior Journal, 2004. *Website Helping Seniors Find Jobs Adds 12 New Employers.* Retreived on August 8, 2004 from: http://www.seniorjournal.com/NEWS/WebsWeLike/4-02-09Jobs.htm

Shackman, G, Liu, Y., and Wang, G. X. (2003). *Global Social Change reports.* Retrieved July 24, 2005, from http://gsociology.icaap.org/reports.html

Shapiro, Phil, (2004). Computer Use and the Elderly. *Washing Apple Pi Journal.* Retrieved February 1, 2004, from http://www.his.com/~pshapiro/computers.and elderly.html

SHRM, 2002. *School-to-Work Program Survey.* Alexandria, VA: Society of Human Resource Management.

Sikula, A, Sr., and Costa, Adelmiro, D. (1994). Are age and ethics related? *The Journal of Psychology*, 6(128), 659-689.

Silver surfers are taking to the net" *BBCNews.* Retrieved February 5, 2004, from http://news.bbc.co.uk/2/hi/science/nature/1899354.stm

"Silver Surfers Day." *Silver Surfers.* Retrieved February 4, 2004, from http://www.silversurfersday.org/

"Silver surfers do well at Westminster" *BBCNews.* Retrieved February 4, 2004, from http://news.bbc.co.uk/2/hi/technology/2581103.stm

Simon, S., (2005). *Phyllis Diller: Still Out for a Laugh.* Rretrieved on July 25, 2005 from: http://www.npr.org/templates/story/story.php?storyId=4764906.

Singhapakdi, Marta, Rawwas, & Ahmed (1999). A cross-cultural study of consumer perceptions about marketing ethics. *Journal of Consumer Marketing, 16(3), p. 257.*

Singhapakdi, M. & Vitell, S. J.(1993b). Personal and professional values underlying the ethical judgments of marketers. *Journal of Business Ethics, 12, p. 528.*

Smith v. City of Jackson, Mississippi, 125 S. Ct. 1536 (2005).

Soeters, J. L. & Recht, R. (2001). Convergence or divergence in the multinational classroom? Experience from the military. International Journal of Intercultural Relations.

Solomon, Robert C. (1993). Ethics: A Short Introduction. Dubuque, Iowa: Brown and Benchmark.

Sonnenberg. (2002). Mental Disabilities in the Workplace. *Workforce.* ACC Communications Inc.

Spector, P. E. (1997). *Job satisfaction: Application, assessment, causes, and consequences.* California: Sage Publications.

Stamberg, Susan (2005). Miss Lilly Keeps Them Talking in Paris. Morning Edition of NPR. July 26, 2005. Retrieved from: http://www.npr.org/templates/story/story.php?storyId=4770776

Steinhauser, S. (1998). Age Bias: Is Your Corporate Culture in Need of an Overhaul? Available online: http://my.shrm.org/hrmagazine/articles/default.asp~htm.

Strategis. (2005). *Corporate social responsibility.* Retrieved March 1, 2005, from http://strategis.ic.gc.ca/epic/internet/incsr-rse.nsf/en/Home

Stoddard, S., Jans, L., Ripple, J. and Kraus, L. (1998) Chartbook on Work and Disability in the United   States, 1998. *An InfoUse Report.* Washington, D.C.: U.S. National Institute on Disability and Rehabilitation Research

Strauss, Leo, (1958). Thoughts on Machiavelli. Chicago: University of Chicago Press.

Sunstein, C. (2002). Switching the Default Rule. *N.Y.U. L. Rev. 77,* pp. 106-107.

Tajfel, S. & Turner, S. (1987). The social identity theory of intergroup behavior. In Worchel, S. & Austin, W. (eds.), *Psychology of intergroup relations.* 2nd Edition. Chicago, Illinois: Nelson Hall.

The ADA: Your Responsibilities as an Employer. (2003). EEOC. Retrieved on June 23, 2005. http://wwww.eeoc.gov/facts/ada17/html

The Family & Medical Leave Act Compliance Guide. (2003). *Business & Legal Reports, Inc.* www.hr.blr.com/article.ctm/nav/1.0.0.0.28997#6

The Sunday Gleaner (March 6, 2005), Kingston, Jamaica, p. 16.

Thompson, R.W. (January 2000). Tight Labor Market Seen as boon for Older Execs. HR Magazine. P.10.

Thomson West. (2005a). Age Discrimination in Employment Act, *United States Code Annotated, 29,* sections 621-634.

Thomson West, (2005b). Civil Rights Act, *United States Code Annotated, 42,* sections 2000e, 12101b.

Thomas, G., Mujtaba, B., (2004). *Effective Global Leadership in the Twenty First Century and Preventing Disasters from Occurring in Developing Nations.* The

Association on Employment Practices and Principles. Proceedings of Twelfth
 Annual AEPP International

Tinkler, H. (2004, November 16). Ethics in business – the heart of the matter.

Triandis, H.C. (1982). Review of cultural consequences. International differences in
 work related values. Human Organization, 41, 86-90.

Twin, A. (2003, Dec). 2003's Biggest Losers. *CNN Money*. Retrieved March 30, 2004
 from http://money.cnn.com/2003/12/12/markets/yir_biglosers03/.

Trevor, C. O. (2001). Interactions among actual ease-of-movement determinants and job
 satisfaction in the prediction of voluntary turnover. *Academy of Management
 Journal, 44,* 621-638.

Uchitelle, L. (2003). *As jobs shrink, older workers thrive.* International Herald Tribune,
 September10. Retrieved October 1, 2003, from Infotrac.

UNAIDS. (2003). *HIV and Aids in Africa.* Retrieved July 25, 2005, from
 http://www.aidsandafrica.com/

United Nations, 1948. *Universal Declaration of Human Rights*, December 10, 1948,
 Article 2.

Upbin, Bruce (2004). *"Wall to Wall Wal-Mart: The Retailer Conquered America and
 Made it Look Easy. The Rest of the World is a Tougher Battleground."* Forbes:
 The World's 2000 Leading Companies. April 12, 2004 issue.

U.S. Bureau of the Census, 2002. Population : Older Americans 2000 : Key Indicators of
 Wll-Being. Retreived 4/3/2003 from :
 http://www.agingstats.gov/chartbook2002/population.htmal

U.S. Bureau of the Census, 1996. Current Population Reports, P25-1130, "Population
 Projections of the United States, by Age, Sex, and Hispanic Origin: 1995 to
 2050," February 1996; and "U.S. Population Estimates, by Age, Sex, Race, and
 Hispanic Origin: 1990 to 1994."

Vandenberg, R. J. & Lance, C. E. (1992). Examining the causal order of job satisfaction
 and organizational commitment. *Journal of Management, 18*, 153-167.

Vandenberg, R. J. & Nelson, J. B. (1999). Disaggregating the motives underlying
 turnover intentions: When do intentions predict turnover behavior? *Human
 Relations, 52,* 1313-1336.

Verschoor, Curtis C. (Dec 2004). Strategic Finance. *Montvale. Vol. 86,* (iss.6), 15

VSA Partners (2004). McDonald's Worldwide. McDonald's Corporation, 1-83.

Wal-Mart Corporation (2004). Hoover's Company Information. Retrieved April 10,
 2004 from http://cobrands.hoovers.com/global/cobrands/proquest/ops. xhtml?

Wal-Mart Corporation (2003, October 29). Wal-Mart Named America's Largest
 Corporate Cash Giver. *Wal-Mart News*. Retrieved March 30, 2004 from
 http://www.walmartstores.com/ wmstore/wmstores.

Wal-Mart Stores (2004). Home page. Retrieved April 9, 2004 from
 http://www.walmartstores.com/wmstore/wmstores/HomePage.jsp.

Walsh, L. (2003). *Older, wiser and still enjoying the rat race.* Europe Intelligence Wire.
 July 5. Retrieved October 1, 2003, from Infotrac.

Walton, S. and Huey, J. (1992). Made in America. New York: Doubleday.

Watson, Charles E. Managing with Integrity. New York: Praeger, 1991.

Weinberg, S. J. (1986). Decision making style of Japanese and American managers.*Asian American Psychological Association Journal*, pp. 62-64.

Weinstein, J. (Spring 2002). A Survey in Changes in United States Litigation. *St. John's L. Rev. 76*, p. 379.

Welford, R. (2004). *Unocal decision impacts shell, coca-cola, exxon, and gap.* CSR Asia. (18 September 2004). Retrieved March 1, 2004, from http://www.csr-asia.com/index.php/archives/2004/09/18/unocal-decision-impacts-shell-coca-cola-exxon-and-gap/

Wick, G., Jansen-Durr, P., Berger, P., Blasko I, Grubeck-Loebenstein, B., (2000). Diseases of aging. *Vaccine.* 2000; 18:1567-1583.

Williams, R. M., Jr. (1979). Change and stability in values and value systems: A sociological perspective. In M. Rokeach (Ed.), *Understanding human values: Individual and societal.* New York: Free Press.

Wilson Web (2005). Social Responsibility: An ongoing mission for a good corporate citizen. *Nations Restaur News*, 39, 15.

Yeatts, D.E., Folts, W., & Knapp, J. (2000). *Older workers' adaptation to a changing workplace: Employment issues for the 21st century.* Retrieved October 1, 2003, from Biomedical Reference Collection: Comprehensive.

Zeffane, R. M. (1994). Understanding employee turnover: The need for a contingency approach. *International Journal of Manpower, 15,* 22-38.

Appendices

Age and Cultural Values Questionnaire – Demographics

This study is primarily concerned with the view of age from the perspective of individuals socialized in different cultures. You are not required to record your name and the information you provide will be totally confidential. Please check/circle the appropriate sections; and your cooperation deserves heart-felt thanks and gratitude.

A. *What is your gender?*   1.____Male   2._____Female

B. *What is your age?*
    1.____16 – 25   2.____26 – 39   3.____40 -49
    4.____50 – 59   5.____60 or above

    - *How would you describe yourself?*
    1____White,   2____Black,   3____Hispanic
    4____Asian/Pacific Islander
    5____American Indian/Alaskan Native
    6____Other (please specify) _____

D. *Which country have you lived in most of your life?*
    1.____USA   2.____Jamaica   3.____Turkey
    4.____Afghanistan   5.____Other (*specify*): _____.

E. *How many years have you lived in the United States of America?*
    1.____Never lived in the USA   2.____1 - 5 years
    3.____6 – 10 years   4.____11 – 19 years
    5.____20 or more years

F. *What is the highest academic schooling you have acquired until the present time?*
    1.____Less than twelve years
    2.____High School Diploma or Equivalent.
    3.____Bachelors Degree – *Specify discipline*: _____.
    4.____Masters Degree – *Specify discipline*: _____.
    5.____Doctorate Degree – *Specify discipline*: _____.
    6.____Other (please specify)_____

G. *Which country do you currently reside in?*
    1.____USA   2.____Jamaica   3.____Turkey
    4.____Afghanistan   5.____Other (*specify*): _____.

H. *How long have you worked with your current employer?*
    1.____Less than one year   2.____1 – 5 years   3.____6 – 15 years
    4.____16 -29 yrs.   5.____30 or more years

I.   ***What industry do you work for currently?***
1.___Educatation
2.___Government
3.___Private sector
4.___Retail
5.___Health
6.___Other (please specify)_____

L.   ***Have you ever any had diversity training (workshop) with your past or current employers?***
1.___Yes   2.___No

Age and Cultural Values Questionnaire – Perceptions of Age

Please answer based on the perspective of the country where you have lived most of your life. For example, if you have lived in Jamaica, Turkey, or Afghanistan most of your life, but are currently living in the USA, then answer these questions from the perspective of Jamaica, Turkey, or Afghanistan. Please keep in mind that for the purpose of research in the USA, "older workers" are those individuals who are 40 years of age or older.

1. ***Do "older workers" get more respect than "younger workers" in your country?***
   a. Yes_____.
   b. No _____.

2. ***Do "older workers" get more respect than "younger workers" from managers and employers in your country?***
   a. Yes_____.
   b. No _____.

3. ***Do you prefer to work with:***
   a. "Older workers" (those who are 40 years of age or above) _____.
   b. Younger workers (those who are less 40 years of age) _____.
   c. All workers – I have no preference on age _____.

4. ***Do most managers in your culture prefer to work with:***
   a. "Older workers" (those who are 40 years of age or above) _____.
   b. Younger workers (those who are less 40 years of age) _____.
   c. All workers – They have no preference on age _____.

5. ***Based on your observations, do most managers in your country believe:***
   a. "Older workers" are more productive than younger workers _____.
   b. Younger workers are more productive than "older workers" _____.
   c. All workers are equally productive _____.

6. ***Is it more difficult for "older workers" to find jobs in your country?***
   a. Yes_____.
   b. No _____.

7. *Is it more difficult for "younger workers" to find jobs in your country?*
   - **a.** Yes_____.
   - **b.** No _____.

8. *Have you ever seen evidence of age discrimination toward "older workers" by managers in your country?*
   - **a.** Yes_____.
   - **b.** No _____.

9. *Have you ever seen evidence of age discrimination toward "younger workers" by managers in your country?*
   - **a.** Yes_____.
   - **b.** No _____.

10. *Is age discrimination against "older workers" legally wrong in your country?*
    - a. Yes_____.
    - b. No_____.
    - c. Do not know_____.

11. *Is age discrimination against "younger workers" legally wrong in your country?*
    - a. Yes_____.
    - b. No_____.
    - c. Do not know_____.

12. *Is age discrimination against "older workers" regarded as morally or ethically wrong in your country?*
    - a. Yes_____.
    - b. No_____.
    - c. Do not know_____.

13. *Is age discrimination against "younger workers" regarded as morally or ethically wrong in your country?*
    - a. Yes_____.
    - b. No_____.
    - c. Do not know_____.

14. *Is age discrimination against "older workers" regarded by you personally as morally or ethically wrong?*
    - a. Yes_____.
    - b. No_____.

15. *Is age discrimination against "younger workers" regarded by you personally as morally or ethically wrong?*
    - a. Yes_____.
    - b. No_____.

16. *Do you have any comments on age issues, discrimination, and older workers that you would like to share?*

The Man in the Glass- by Dale Wimbrow

When you get what you want in your struggle for self
      And the world makes you king for a day,
Just go to a mirror and look at yourself
      And see what THAT man has to say.

For it isn't your father or mother or wife
      Whose judgment upon you must pass;
The fellow whose verdict counts most in your life
      Is the one staring back from the glass.

Some people may think you a straight-shootin' chum
      And call you a wonderful guy,
But the man in the glass says you're only a bum
      If you can't look him straight in the eye.

He's the fellow to please, never mind all the rest,
      For he's with you clear up to the end.
And you've passed your most dangerous, difficult test
      If the man in the glass is your friend.

You may fool the whole world down the pathway of life
      And get pats on your back as you pass,
But your final reward will be heartaches and tears
      If you've cheated the man in the glass.

Index Table

Biographies of the Authors

Dr. Bahaudin Mujtaba

- ***Dr. Bahaudin Mujtaba*** is an Assistant Professor of Human Resources and International Management at Nova Southeastern University. He also has been the Director of Undergraduate Business Programs and the Director of Institutional Relations, Planning, and Accreditation for NSU at the H. Wayne Huizenga School of Business and Entrepreneurship in Fort Lauderdale, Florida. He currently serves on the editorial review boards for the Society for Advancement of Management (SAM) Journal, Journal of Applied Management and Entrepreneurship (JAME), and others. Bahaudin has worked with various firms in the areas of management, cross-cultural communication, customer value/service, mentoring, and diversity management. He was born and raised in Logar of Afghanistan and attended Allowdin Elementary School and Habibia High School in Kabul. Bahaudin's undergraduate degree is from the University of Central Florida. His masters and doctorate degrees are from NSU. Bahaudin has lectured and taught management and leadership topics both nationally and internationally (including Hawaii, Puerto Rico, Bahamas, Jamaica, Brazil, and Afghanistan). Besides being a certified management, leadership, diversity, and cultural competency trainer, Bahaudin is the author and co-author of six books and over 100 academic articles. Bahaudin can be contacted at mujtaba@nova.edu or by calling (954) 262-5000 at NSU.

Dr. Frank J. Cavico

- ***Dr. Frank Cavico*** is a professor of ethics and law at the H. Wayne Huizenga Graduate School of Business and Entrepreneurship of Nova Southeastern University. In 2000, he was awarded the Excellence in Teaching Award by the Huizenga School. His fine record is manifested by numerous research endeavors, principally law review articles, in the broad sectors of business law and ethics. Professor Cavico holds a J.D. degree from St. Mary's University School of Law and a B.A. from Gettysburg College. He also possesses a Master of Laws degree from the University of San Diego School of Law and a Master's degree in Political Science from Drew University. Professor Cavico is licensed to practice law in the states of Florida and Texas. He has worked as a federal government regulatory attorney and as counsel for a labor union; and has practiced general civil law and immigration law in South Florida. Professor Cavico is married; and he and his wife, Nancy, a Registered Nurse and adjunct nursing professor, reside in Lauderdale-by-the Sea, Florida. They not long ago co-authored a law review article on nursing malpractice law.

Made in the USA